BOOKS BY RICHARD O'CONNOR

Fiction

GUNS OF CHICKAMAUGA

COMPANY Q

OFFICERS AND LADIES

THE VANDAL

Nonfiction

THOMAS: ROCK OF CHICKAMAUGA

HOOD: CAVALIER GENERAL

SHERIDAN THE INEVITABLE

HIGH JINKS ON THE KLONDIKE

BAT MASTERSON

JOHNSTOWN: THE DAY THE DAM BROKE

HELL'S KITCHEN

WILD BILL HICKOK

PAT GARRETT

BLACK JACK PERSHING

GOULD'S MILLIONS

THE SCANDALOUS MR. BENNETT

COURTROOM WARRIOR: THE COMBATIVE CAREER
OF WILLIAM TRAVERS JEROME

JACK LONDON: A BIOGRAPHY

BRET HARTE: A BIOGRAPHY

AMBROSE BIERCE: A BIOGRAPHY

THE GERMAN-AMERICANS

THE GERMAN-AMERICANS

THE GERMAN-AMERICANS

An Informal History

by Richard O'Connor

LITTLE, BROWN AND COMPANY   BOSTON • TORONTO

LIBRARY OF CONGRESS CATALOG CARD NO. 68–21880

00179   10   SL

Fourth Printing

The author wishes to thank Professor Donald A. Erickson for permission to quote
from an article on the Amish published in the *Saturday Review*, November 19, 1966;
and The Bruce Publishing Company for permission to quote from *The Life of
James Cardinal Gibbons* by Msgr. John Tracy Ellis, published in 1952 by The Bruce
Publishing Company.

All photographs courtesy of Brown Brothers.

*Published simultaneously in Canada
by Little, Brown & Company (Canada) Limited*
PRINTED IN THE UNITED STATES OF AMERICA

✛

To my Hessian great-grandfather

✛

CONTENTS

ix

CONTENTS

ILLUSTRATIONS

xi

1

SETTLERS AND CITIZENS

1. A NATION OF MIGRANTS

In August of 1914, shortly after France and most of Europe went to war, the French government was astounded by the fact that eight thousand German and Austrian residents of the country immediately offered to serve in the French army or the Foreign Legion against their homelands. So many volunteered that they were formed into special marching regiments of the Legion and brigaded with cadres of *anciens* from the colonies just to make sure their enlistment was not some Teutonic version of the wooden horse. The safeguards, though quite understandable, were not necessary. As Count Albert de Mun, a leading member of the Chamber of Deputies, exclaimed, "*La France a des volontaires étranges, l'Allemagne, elle, a des deserteurs!*" — France has foreign volunteers, Germany has deserters.

Perhaps deserters is too harsh a word, but it is paradoxically true that Germany, one of the most nationalistic of modern nations, produces a strikingly large minority of anti-Volkish strays and sports who turn up later to bedevil the Fatherland. The most vigorous anti-Germanism has always been generated by Germans themselves, and the historic drive of the nation, often aimed southward toward the warmer sun, has frequently seemed a massive armed attempt to break the bounds of the gray skies and cold Baltic winds of its homeland.

Not the menacing Prussian eagle but the *Wandervogel* is the

3

German national bird. The German is a migratory creature. His ancestors, the hairy ferocious Teutonic tribesmen, were the most restless of all who lived under the Pax Romana. Teutonic legions formed the bulk of the army with which the Roman general Aetius defeated Attila and his Huns at Orléans. After that Germanic tribes were fragmented by their almost explosive instinct to part company with each other. Many of the Visigoths stayed on in Gaul, settling what is now northern France; the Angles and Saxons crossed the channel to Celtic Britain; the Vandals, coming from the coldest and most northern regions of Germany, went the farthest south in search of warmth and colonized North Africa; the Burgundians moved to the Vosges Mountains and the plains of the Jura. One Germanic tribe, the Franks, migrated across the Rhine en masse and provided a strong Teutonic infusion, so that modern France, a union of Roman Gaul and Frankish Gaul, is distinctly Frankish, or Germanic, in culture and temperament north of the Loire, particularly between the Rhine and the Somme. The first great French general was the Frank whose name is Clovis to the French, Chlodwig to the Germans; and naturally enough the great victory with which his name is associated was over the German tribe known as the Alemanni. German blood, the mystique of which has been formulated so often by kaisers and fuehrers and their tame philosophers, has frequently been shed in Germans fighting Germans. And that blood, instead of being concentrated in *Ein Volk* as its false leaders have recommended, is one of the most diffused in all the world. Large colonies of Germans settled themselves in the Ukraine. Others were scattered through South America, Asia and Africa. The blond, blue-eyed prototype of the Gothic warrior, who often came with a sword but was quick enough to take up the plow once he was guaranteed a plot of ground under a kindlier sun, manifests itself today throughout northern Italy, parts of Spain and North Africa, as well as the semi-Teutonic nation of Great Britain. All the nations of western Europe west of the Vistula have their considerable fraction of German blood, though events of the past century have made them understandably reluctant to boast of it.

Nowhere, however, has the migratory instinct of the German nation had a greater effect than on North America. From colonial times until the First World War there was a constant stream of German immigrants heading for the American shore. It has recently been estimated that thirty-five million Americans — one-sixth of the nation — have some fraction of German ancestry. The German-Americans are the largest minority in the United States. They are also the least noticeable.

Their history on this continent, as in most places colonized by Germans, is a study in the process of assimilation. There has been no demonstrable reluctance on their part to mingle their Aryan blood, which various prophets and geopoliticians advised was so precious in its purity, with that of other nations and races. Hessian mercenaries brought over by the British during the American Revolution fled into the New Jersey hills and married Negro bond servants, escaped slaves and freed Negroes. Many German pioneers married Indian women in the early West. Exceedingly few German-American families which migrated as long ago as the 1840's, and have been in this country for five or six generations, have not intermarried with other nationalities. The stream of "pure" German blood, on reaching this shore, disappeared as though it had coursed onto a bed of sand. The typical German-American is often part English, Irish, French, Scandinavian, Polish or Italian, with perhaps a Cherokee great-grandmother. No other minority has so vigorously spanned the ethnic rainbow.

The purpose of this book is to attempt a discovery of what social and historical impact the German-American has made on the United States — admittedly not as a scholarly exercise, because the author leaves that task to the academic historians and social scientists, but as an informal inquiry into the subject. There is more to the process than the German-American's gradual self-grafting onto what has been called the "great white whale" than a simple exchange of Mittel Europa for Middle America. Did a sea-change come over him which converted him from a subject of authoritarian Germany to a citizen of democratic America — or did he, bringing some of his attitudes with him, influence the development of the United States in ways which only the future will make apparent? Was the prevailing isolationism of the Middle West, the German-American heartland, one of the symptoms of his inherent attitudes? Is America's current and immensely significant about-face

5

from intimate concern over Europe (always the fixation of the Anglo-Saxon majority but distasteful in varying degrees to German-Americans) to involvement and intervention in eastern Asia, a reflection of those attitudes? Middle Western isolationism has always been directed against the Atlantic, not the Pacific nations.

German-Americanism is a wildly various, unpredictable and contradictory quantity. It has produced such phenomena as the late Senator Joseph McCarthy of Wisconsin, who was partly German; a spectacular array of anarchists, socialists and utopians; the two commanders of the American Expeditionary Forces against Germany in the two World Wars; impeccably and fearlessly liberal statesmen such as Carl Schurz and John Peter Altgeld; ruthless masters of exploitation such as John Jacob Astor and John D. Rockefeller, Sr.; and such totems of the popular imagination as Babe Ruth, Lou Gehrig, Clark Gable (Pennsylvania Dutch), Grace Kelly (whose mother is of German descent), Doris Day, Dutch Schultz, H. L. Mencken, Walter Reuther, Johnny Weissmuller, Bix Beiderbecke, Senator Everett Dirksen, and others too numerous to mention. Obviously, even from this sampling, it would be difficult to define, except in the loosest and most general fashion, the composite German-American. It is easier to sketch in the negative aspects. On the whole the German-American has not distinguished himself in politics, as the Irish have; nor in the arts, as the Russian-Jews have; nor in the daring advancement of the democratic ideal as the Anglo-Saxons have; nor in cultural aspects as the French and other smaller minorities have — at least not in proportion to his weight in numbers.

In many ways, however, the influence of the German-Americans in shaping the American destiny has been of decisive importance. The West could hardly have been conquered and developed so quickly without German blood, sweat and muscle. And German brains, with their obvious aptitude for science, education and technology, have contributed more than their share to America's unchallenged industrial establishment. More than any other nationality, they have been responsible for settling, clearing and developing the black earth of the Middle Western states until they have become the agricultural wonder

6

of the world. This section is already feeding millions of people outside the United States and undoubtedly will be of the utmost importance in the future when the survival of overpopulated nations will depend upon the productivity and ingenuity of the great-grandsons of the thousands of Germans who came over more than a century ago and hardly paused at the entry ports before heading for the free land of the frontier.

They came in the knowledge that they were among the most welcome of migrants, benefited from a certain amount of prejudice on the part of the Anglo-Saxons for newcomers from the northwestern part of Europe. Their reputation for hard work, orderliness, ingrained respect for authority, relative sobriety and political docility placed them in the most-favored category; even with the handicap of speaking a different language, they fitted in better with their neighbors in the new land and made them part of the sturdy yeomanry which filled out the open spaces west of the Alleghenies.

Yet the German portion of this judicious mixture was not always a model of tractability. There were times when the assertively Teutonic strain found itself in conflict with the prevailing opinion of the majority. Early in the nineteenth century German influence in the United States had reached the point at which a bumptious quality manifested itself. In Texas, Missouri and Wisconsin there were aggressive movements afoot aimed at the establishment of German republics based on the Prussian social system, with sharply defined layers of authority and responsibility. Several years later German-American groups petitioned Congress for permission to colonize sections of the Northwest which would be recognized as independent German states. The movement was quickly discouraged, but German communal societies of a highly eccentric pattern, as they seemed to other Americans, were allowed to flourish as they pleased. In any case the separatist urge died down quickly enough.

Hyphenated Americanism, however, became the great Germanic sin against the will of the majority. It was also responsible, during World War I, for the signally traumatic exception to the otherwise tranquil record of the German in America. The German-Americans, in sizable numbers, sought both openly and deviously to prevent the United

7

States from joining the Allies in the war against Germany and the Central Powers; an enterprise, incidentally, in which they were joined by the anti-English Irish-Americans, whose migration to America generally paralleled their own. This divisive effort rose to crescendo as the United States made its decision and the American majority suddenly, and in an atmosphere of patriotic hysteria, fixed upon the German-American element as seditious and possibly treacherous. Incredulously the German-American found himself a detested outsider in American life.

Many people of German descent were, of course, against the war because they were repelled by the necessity of killing Germans. But there were many others, inheritors of the pacifist-socialist tradition that ran through German-American life as a strong and idealistic current, who were against any and all wars. The immensely talented journalist Ernest L. Meyer, then a student at the University of Wisconsin, was one of those conscientious objectors and would write: "In the year of the whirlwind, what should the dissenter's own attitude and conduct be? My friends, warm friends, marched away to war. We had many sorrowful partings. It would have been so good, so easy to join them . . . Ah, what conceit to set yourself up against all these good and honest people; is it possible that you are only stubborn, an egoist and a pro-German? That is what a professor of philosophy, whom I revered, told me . . . and never spoke to me again . . . But I knew that no matter what might come there was no turning back. No friendship or force in the world could lead me to the battlefield to take life and consecrate error in human blood."

But there were so many others who reacted out of different motives, expressed in violence and conspiracy against the war effort, that anyone with a German-sounding name was regarded as a potential traitor and saboteur. Two of the most daring fliers in the fledgling United States air force were a pair of German-Americans, Frank Luke and his wingman, Joe Wehner, both of whom were killed in action partly because of their bitter determination to prove they were loyal Americans, and that the suspicions of intelligence agents who kept them under constant surveillance were unwarranted.

8

The open wound in the relations of the German-descended with those of other nationalities slowly cicatrized. German-Americans, in their tens of thousands, proved in the trenches as Luke and Wehner had in the skies over the Western front that they were as pro-American and pro-Allied as any other element of the American Expeditionary Force.

A score of years later, when another World War broke out with virtually the same adversaries confronting each other in Europe, there was a less accusatory questioning of German-American loyalty. This time suspicion was centered briefly around the activities of the German-American Bund, principally in the eastern cities and among first-generation German-Americans. The mass of German-Americans, however, exhibited little sympathy with the aspirations, even less with the methods, of Hitler and the Nazis. Hyphenated Americanism was a dead issue.

The monstrous aberrations of the German nation during World War II did raise the question of whether the chances for a peace-loving and democratic national life for Germany had not been destroyed by what might be called the spiritual drain, the selective migration of so many of its more dissident people all through history. The Nazi assumption of power might not have been possible if so many of the "good" Germans had not fled in revolt against Prussian authoritarianism, against the militarism and nationalism which began rising in Germany during the middle of the nineteenth century. It is a question which will remain in suspension as Germany continues to struggle with her destiny.

"THOSE DAMNED DUTCH"

One indication that German-Americans are secure in their belief that the process of assimilation has been completed is the absence of any protective organizations to defend them against slurs. Germanic villains crop up in motion pictures, television and popular fiction without a single public outcry that people of German descent are being vilified. They have no protective association such as the Ancient Order

9

of Hibernians, the Anti-Defamation League or similar organizations formed by Italians and Poles to protect themselves when they feel that their people are being insulted. The German-American's attitude is merely a bland "Who? Me?"

It was not always so. In their earliest appearances on the American continent the Germans were often referred to as "those damned Dutch," not so much for their knavishness as for their obsession with hard work and their tough-minded independence.

They were among those hapless followers of Captain John Smith who settled the colony at Jamestown in 1607, with men named Unger, Keffer and Volday in the German contingent Smith had recruited as a leavening for the listless and work-dodging Englishmen, who imagined the New World would be an Eden with breadfruit dropping from branches to their open mouths. In writing to the Crown authorities back home, Captain Smith himself, like the other Englishmen in his colony, often characterized the Germans and Poles as "damned Dutch," collectively, because of their sturdy sense of independence and their refusal to wait hand and foot on the "gentlemen" of the colony. When it was proposed that reinforcements be sent to Jamestown, however, he beseeched the authorities to send him "thirty carpenters, husbandmen, gardiners, fisher men, blacksmiths, masons, and diggers up of trees' roots" from Germany and Poland rather than a thousand Englishmen of the type he had been burdened with. In contrast to the sober-minded and industrious Germans and Poles, Captain Smith wrote in his history of the colonization of Jamestown, the English with him were "Adventurers that never did know what a day's work was" as well as "poore Gentlemen, Tradesmen, Serving-men, libertines, and such like" who were "ten times more fit to spoyle a Commonwealth than either to begin one or but help to maintaine one."[1]

The Germans became "damnable" in Captain Smith's eyes when they objected to doing all the work for the gentlemen drones and even more so when they flung down the white man's burden and sided with the Indians. Three Germans were assigned to build a house for King Powhatan, the purpose of which, as they revealed to the Indian chief, was to get him into Captain Smith's power. Powhatan and some of his followers immediately seceded from the colony, and were accompanied by a number of Germans. The English were so outraged that they bestirred themselves for once and launched a pursuit of the defectors into the interior. One luckless German was captured and, as Captain Smith laconically described it, "went by the heels."

The fabulous continent of America had inflamed German imaginations long before Smith colonized Jamestown. According to the Norse sagas, one member of Leif Ericson's expedition to the northern coasts of the continent was a German named Tyrker. The legend says he wandered away from his comrades one day and found vines and grapes, thus causing Leif to name the New World Wineland the Good.[2] Subsequently German interest in the New World was stimulated by the cosmographers and cartographers who speculated on its existence and location. One was Martin Behaim, born in Nuremberg, who was employed as a cosmographer by the King of Portugal and was one of the inventors of the astrolabe. Another was Mercator, whose name was Latinized from Gerhard Kremer and who developed the Mercator system of projection which took the curvature of the earth into account in map making and thereby eased the problems of navigation. Still another was Martin Waldseemüller, born in Freiburg, who published his *Cosmographiae Introductio* in 1507, and suggested that the new continent "be named after Americus, its discoverer, a man of sagacious mind, Amerige, that is the land of Americus, or America, since both Europe and Asia derived their names from women."

However, the German role in discovering and exploring the new continent was more theoretical and speculative than active and physical. During the period of discovery, the German states, with the Hanseatic League a vanished glory, had only a narrow strip of seacoast to the north and were no longer a maritime power able to compete with the English, French, Spanish, Dutch and Portuguese. In the competition which developed among those nations, the Germans were only bemused supernumeraries, who were occasionally allowed to carry a spear but gave no orders; none distinguished themselves in exploration as had such members of the Latin nations as Cortez, De Soto, Pizarro, Marquette, Champlain and La Salle. It was said that in the struggle for possession of the American continent France, Spain and Portugal sent officers without an army, the Germans an army without officers, and the English, with a thoroughness that eventually won them the prize, both an army and officers. Only the British realized that to hold the continent they would have to colonize it. Since Britain's own population did not have a sufficient surplus to accomplish that task, it invited the woebegone and impoverished people of the disunited German states, so often ravaged by wars with their more powerful neighbors, to join in the work of colonization.

The first German of prominence in the New World was a Rhinelander named Peter Minuit (Minnewit in German), who was engaged by the Dutch government as director of the colony of New Netherland. He arrived in New Amsterdam in 1626 with almost dictatorial powers. One of his first actions on arriving on the site of the future New York City was negotiating the greatest real estate coup in history, when he bought the island of Manhattan from the Indians for sixty guilders (twenty-four dollars in gold). His second move was to build a stone fort at what is now called the Battery, on the tip of the island, to remind the Indians that they no longer owned Manhattan and encourage increased settlement on the island. Under his supervision the fur trade was expanded and the colony's shipbuilders constructed a thirty-gun warship named the New Netherlands to protect their interests against the fur traders of the New England colonies to the north. Minuit was recalled in 1632 when protests arose over the land-grabbing maneuvers of the patroons, who had established a semifeudal system on their manors up the Hudson. Subsequently Minuit joined the colonial service of Sweden and settled a shipload of its citizens on the banks of the Delaware near the present city of Wilmington, governed the colony himself and built Fort Christina, where he was buried in 1641.

The first German-born martyr to policital liberty was also associated with the early history of New York City. He was Jacob Leisler, who was born in Frankfort-on-the-Main in 1660 and came to the New World as a soldier in the Dutch West India Company. When his term of enlistment was over, he prospered as a trader and shipowner, and when he was captured by Tunisian pirates in 1678 he was able to pay a ransom of

12

five hundred pounds. His fortunes were assisted by an aristocratic marriage — one of his great-great-grandsons was Gouverneur Morris — and he was soon able to afford a political career of notable rectitude and independence. By the time the English had united the colonies of New York, New England and New Jersey, Leisler was regarded as the leader of the resentful Dutch population.

The Dutch rebelled against the dictates of King James II in 1689 and formed a Committee of Public Safety, which named Leisler as lieutenant governor and commander in chief of the colony. A few months later he was confronted by the possibility of an invasion of French and Indians by way of the Mohawk Valley, Albany and the Hudson. He organized a militia to protect the colony and summoned a council of the governors of Massachusetts, Plymouth, East and West Jersey, Pennsylvania, and Maryland, which was convened in New York City. The council decided to launch an expedition against Quebec, which turned out to be a disastrous failure; more importantly, though, it served as a pattern for the first Continental Congress.

By the end of 1690 the English managed to reassert their control over the rebellious colony of New York and sent out a new governor, Colonel Henry Sloughter, with instructions to deal severely with the insurgents. Leisler and his son-in-law, Milborne, along with other members of the dissident council which had been ruling New York during the lapse in English authority, were arrested. Leisler and his son-in-law were charged with high treason and quickly condemned to death.[3]

On May 19, 1691, the two men were brought to a scaffold at the corner of Pearl and Centre streets, where the Tombs now stands, in the presence of a crowd muttering threats that if they were hanged there would be another uprising in the city. Leisler, however, addressed the crowd pressing against the ring of English infantry and asked them to maintain peace and order, not to avenge his death, and requested that his ashes be scattered to "destroy all vestiges of discord and dissension." Something finer than vengeance was accorded Jacob Leisler — the judgment of history that he was the first American to stand as a leader of the people, as a democrat, against the aristocracy, the Tory element — and five years later his family was successful in petitioning the

English Parliament for justice to his name and restoration of the family's property and civil rights.[4]

Another commanding figure in the cause of American liberty, especially the freedom of the press, was John Peter Zenger. Zenger migrated as an apprentice, technically a bond servant, from the Palatinate. In 1711 the English governor of New York obtained a grant of ten thousand pounds from his government for the importation of between three and four thousand able-bodied Germans who had been impoverished by French invasion and occupation of the Palatine districts. Zenger and his fellow migrants signed contracts by which they had to work for American employers until their passage was repaid. For six years Zenger was apprenticed to William Bradford, the royal printer for the colony of New York. Later he worked as a journeyman in Maryland, then returned to New York to open his own printing establishment, one of his early volumes being the first arithmetic textbook published in the colonies.

In December, 1733, he began publication of the New York *Weekly Journal* and immediately launched a running battle against the colonial government as corrupt and dishonest. Less than a year later the British authorities arrested him on charges of seditious libel. His trial, beginning August 4, 1735, was a signal fire in American legal history. Under English common law, any statement which brings scandal or disrepute on an individual or an institution — whether true or false — is criminally libelous. The laws under which Zenger was tried made it an open and shut case. He had seditiously libeled the governor of the colony. His only possible defense — that the statements were true — was beside the point. That a libelous statement was true only compounded the felony under the English law.

A Philadelphia lawyer, Andrew Hamilton, maneuvered his way around the point. He maintained that Zenger had the right to publish his attacks on the governor because they were true, and that the jury of colonists was invested with the right of deciding the issue of law as well as the truthfulness of Zenger's charges. And the jury, disregarding the rulings of the trial justices, agreed with Hamilton and acquitted Zenger.

The verdict established truth as the criterion in American libel suits

Numb. II.

THE
New-York Weekly JOURNAL

Containing the freſheſt Advices, Foreign, and Domeſtick.

MUNDAY November 12, 1733.

Mr. *Zenger.*

INcert the following in your next, and you'll oblige your Friend,
CATO.

Mira temporum felicitas ubi ſentiri quæ velis, & quæ ſentias dicere licit.
Tacit.

THE Liberty of the Preſs is a Subject of the greateſt Importance, and in which every Individual is as much concern'd as he is in any other Part of Liberty : therefore it will not be improper to communicate to the Publick the Sentiments of a late excellent Writer upon this Point, ſuch is the Elegance and Perſpicuity of his Writings, ſuch the inimitable Force of his Reaſoning, that it will be difficult to ſay any Thing new that he has not ſaid, or not to ſay that much worſe which he has ſaid.

There are two Sorts of Monarchies, an abſolute and a limited one. In the firſt, the Liberty of the Preſs can never be maintained, it is inconſiſtent with it ; for what abſolute Monarch would ſuffer any Subject. to animadvert on his Actions, when it is in his Power to declare the Crime, and to nominate the Puniſhment ? This would make it very dangerous to exerciſe ſuch a Liberty. Beſides the Object againſt which thoſe Pens muſt be directed, is

their Sovereign, the ſole ſupream Magiſtrate ; for there being no Law in thoſe Monarchies, but the Will of the Prince, it makes it neceſſary for his Miniſters to conſult his Pleaſure, before any Thing can be undertaken : He is therefore properly chargeable with the Grievances of his Subjects, and what the Miniſter there acts being in Obedience to the Prince, he ought not to incur the Hatred of the People ; for it would be hard to impute that to him for a Crime, which is the Fruit of his Allegiance, and for refuſing which he might incur the Penalties of Treaſon. Beſides, in an abſolute Monarchy, the Will of the Prince being the Law, a Liberty of the Preſs to complain of Grievances would be complaining againſt the Law, and the Conſtitution, to which they have ſubmitted, or have been obliged to ſubmit; and therefore, in one Senſe, may be ſaid to deſerve Puniſhment, So that under an abſolute Monarchy, I ſay, ſuch a Liberty is inconſiſtent with the Conſtitution, having no proper Subject in Politics, on which it might be exercis'd, and if exercis'd would incur a certain Penalty.

But in a limited Monarchy, as *England* is, our Laws are known, fixed, and eſtabliſhed. They are the ſtreight Rule and ſure Guide to direct the King, the Miniſters, and other his Subjects : And therefore an Offence againſt the Laws is ſuch an Offence againſt the Conſtitution as ought to receive a pro per adequate Puniſhment ; the ſevera Conſtil

John Peter Zenger's defiant page one

and widened the limits, sometimes intolerably, of the press's freedom to comment. Partly as a reward for his libertarian zeal, Zenger was appointed public printer for the colonies of New York and New Jersey and continued publishing the *Weekly Journal* until his death in 1746.

A GOODLY LIFE IN THE WILDERNESS

Earnestness is both the German vice and the German virtue. With all the solid worth of the early German migrants to the colonies, they brought little in the way of venturesome humor, gaiety or intellectual curiosity. Their eyes were uplifted to the Christian heaven but they always kept their hands on the plow and their feet possessively planted in their own soil. The first sizable German settlement, in fact, was carried out by the Pietist sects, the Quakers, the Mennonites and the Schwenkfelders, all of them existing outside the German laws which recognized the Catholic and Lutheran religions but held all others to be atheistic.

Their migration was encouraged by the American Quaker, William Penn, who made two visits to Germany to whip up interest among his coreligionists and those Pietistic sects which resembled the Quaker faith in a large-scale movement to America. Penn had acquired a huge grant of land, subsequently Pennsylvania, from the English government in exchange for sixteen thousand pounds which it owed his admiral-father for his services.

The man who organized the migration in Germany was a thirty-two-year-old lawyer, scholar and linguist named Franz Pastorius, who was a member of the Pietist circle in Frankfort-on-the-Main. He arranged for the sailing of the English vessel *Concord*, which became known as the "German Mayflower," with thirteen families of Mennonites from the Rhineland town of Crefeld aboard. For five pounds apiece the Rhinelanders were transported from Gravesend to Philadelphia, where they arrived on October 6, 1683. That date has since been celebrated by Germans as the beginning of their history as settlers in this country.

Pastorius, who had sailed from England six weeks earlier, was on the dock to greet them and impart to them his solemn purpose in establishing a German colony in the New World, "a desire in my soul," as he put it, "to continue in their society and with them to lead a quiet, godly, and honest life in a howling wilderness." He had already experienced a warm welcome from Governor Penn and his friends. "The governor often summons me to dine with him," he recorded. "As I was recently absent from home a week, he came himself to visit me and bade me dine with him twice every week, and declared to his counsellors that he loved me and the High Germans very much and wished them to do so likewise."[5]

The German colonists were established on a 43,000-acre tract soon to be called Germantown. They were joined by other settlers from South Germany, and began raising flax and making linen, as well as cultivating the rich soil. Unlike Captain Smith's unfortunates at Jamestown, they were mostly artisans, craftsmen and farmers, with no exalted idea of becoming lily-handed gentry in the new land. Wilhelm Ruttinghausen (Anglicized to Rittenhouse) built the first paper mill in Pennsylvania on a creek running into the Wissahickon River. Within a few years the Germantown area was bustling and prosperous, the silence of the virgin forest broken by the shuttles of the linen weavers, the whirring of mill wheels, the shouts of towheaded children. In the settlement itself each dwelling had a vegetable and flower garden of three acres, and surrounding the village were cultivated fields, vineyards, orchards, beehives and market gardens.

The town was incorporated in 1689 with Pastorius as its first burgomaster. He not only served as a civic exemplar — complaining as he did to Governor Penn that his people were so lacking in public spirit that it was necessary to levy a three-pound fine on any citizen who refused to serve in a public office to which he had been elected — but worked industriously at tilling his own land. He also kept a journal and scrapbook called "The Beehive," in which he ruefully said of his training as a classical scholar in the old country that it was a poor preparation for pioneering in a wilderness. He was one of the breed of educated men later to be called, with scant respect, a "Latin farmer." The scorn, he thought, was merited, because "never have metaphysics and Aristotelian logic made of a savage a Christian, far less earned a loaf of bread." He was summoned to more congenial labors in 1698 at the Quaker School in Philadelphia, and several years later was appointed head of the first school in Germantown. One innovation, testifying to Pastorius's talents as an educator and his fellow citizens' thirst for learning, was a night school attended by adults who had to work during the day and younger people who had advanced beyond the studies in the day school.

The colony at Germantown generally was more orderly, law-abiding and industrious than similar settlements elsewhere in North America. Among the few offenses against the peace and order brought before the magistrate were, the records show, a charge against Caspar Karsten that he called a policeman a rogue and against a man named Muller for having wagered that he could smoke one hundred pipes of tobacco in a day. Beer was being brewed and more potent spirits distilled almost as soon as the colony was established, and evidently few of its members had lost their thirst on leaving the old country. The elders of German-town, at any rate, felt it necessary to adopt an ordinance forbidding any person from buying, during one day, more than two quarts of beer or half a pint of rum. That allowance would hardly have wet the whistle of the yeomen in Massachusetts Bay Colony.[6]

So Arcadian was the spirit of Germantown that at the end of at least one of its early years, 1697, the town fathers declared in their minutes, "All crimes that have been committed previous to this date are to be forgiven . . ."[7]

In only one instance did the Germans find themselves at odds with the English in Philadelphia a half-dozen miles away. Several years after they colonized Germantown they awakened to the fact that the English Quakers condoned or were indifferent to the practice of Negro slavery. (There was also literally, though not so unremittingly, the practice of white slavery. Many whites came to the colonies as indentured servants, completely in the possession of their masters until they were released from bondage.) The German Quakers were unable to understand how the English reconciled slavery with their avowed belief in a common and equal humanity. On April 18, 1688, was recorded the first known

18

protest against slavery in North America. A mass meeting in German-town resolved to draw up a document of formal protest, which was executed in Franz Pastorius's handwriting and forwarded to the Quakers of Philadelphia. When the latter held their next meeting, they took note of a message "protesting against the buying and keeping of slaves, received from several German Friends," but decided to delay acting on it. At quarterly meetings thereafter the matter was brought up each time and tabled without discussion; it wasn't until seventeen years later, in fact, that the Philadelphia Quakers finally got around to passing a resolution against the slave trade.

Within the Germantown colony itself there was a lesser division of opinion on the question of how a man must prepare himself for the afterlife. A sect sprang up which called itself the Mystics. They believed that the world was soon coming to an end — a doctrine which, through history, has oddly appealed to German sectarians, many of them more fanatical than the Mystics — and that the true believer when he died would be transported in the flesh to a happier realm.

In accordance with their beliefs the Mystics of Germantown, led by Johann Kelpius, broke away from the settlement in 1694 and removed themselves to a high ridge overlooking the Wissahickon where they could meditate undisturbed. It was the first of a number of essays in religious communal living — some of which took odd forms indeed, in seeming variance with what other nationalities considered the stolid, pragmatic, unimaginative German character — which distinguished German-American life for almost two centuries. The Kelpius colony established itself in a cave, which was enlarged and made habitable, and proceeded to build a community. Circumstances did not permit them to give all their time to Mystical contemplation; Kelpius himself taught the colony's children, another member busied himself with bookbinding, others tilled the soil, and still others functioned as astrologers. The farmers around Germantown, though scorning their other beliefs, made regular trips up to the ridge occupied by the Mystics to have their horoscopes cast and to seek advice on the laying of cornerstones and the planting of crops. Kelpius's followers also performed with their divining rods at locating wells and hidden springs for the farmers around

Germantown. Kelpius himself was often consulted by nonbelievers who, nevertheless, believed that he had healing powers; such powers were of no avail, however, when Kelpius fell ill from tuberculosis and died in 1708. His sect later established itself in a stone church near the site of the tabernacle in the forest where Kelpius had presided over rites his ancestors, worshiping at Druidic temples in a Rhenish grove, might not have found too strange.

The Mystics provided the seedbed, if such were needed, for a fascination with the occult that has endured for almost three centuries among the Germans in Pennsylvania — the Pennsylvania Dutch, as they were called — and that may be traced today in the "hex" signs on barns in the back country.

<h2 style="text-align:center">"CORRUPTED LIKE CATTLE"</h2>

When word reached the German states of the success of the emigrant colonies in Pennsylvania and elsewhere, thousands began migrating to North America, particularly after the turn of the eighteenth century. Of all the countries in Europe, Germany had the greatest surplus of population to be drained off, the greatest number of people eager to start a new life almost anywhere they had a fighting chance for survival. Conditions in Germany, both political and economic, were desperate, particularly in the south, and more particularly in the Palatinate, Württemberg and Baden. The causes were a succession of devastating invasions, religious persecution, and the tyranny of the princes of the German states.

A symptom of that desperation was noted in 1709 following the devastation caused by the War of the Spanish Succession, when the rumor spread that Queen Anne of England would provide free transportation for all Germans willing to migrate to America. Thirteen thousand ragged and penniless Germans somehow made their way to England and lived in the streets of London and Liverpool until they could be disposed of, some sent to Ireland, many more to America.

It is astonishing that the German appetite for war was not permanently satisfied by the events which preceded the migrations to colonial America. The Thirty Years' War from 1618 to 1648 had all but extinguished civilization in Germany; 75 percent of the population was killed off in many states, and the Rhenish provinces were overrun time after time by the French, the Swedish, the Spanish and the Bavarians. The Palatinate, one of the most fertile sections of Germany, was left a desert of ruined farms and burned houses. Later in the century Louis XIV of France sent his troops in again to apply the scorched earth policy to the Palatinate so that it could never again serve as a granary for his enemies; the whole city of Mannheim was leveled, along with Speyer and Worms. The Thirty Years' War, the War of the Palatinate, the War of the Spanish Succession and the War of the Austrian Succession — all of them bickerings among European kings in which the South German people had no political interest — simply used the German provinces along the Rhine as an arena and then abandoned it to a homeless people ravaged by disease.

As if they had not borne enough, the people of those states and principalities were then subjected to persecution for their religion. Protestants were driven from Catholic districts and vice versa. Even more severe proscriptions were placed on those who were neither, the "heretics" known as Mennonites, Quakers, Dunkards, Moravians and Schwenkfelders who were entirely outside the law.

Enthroned on top of all this misery were the multitude of princelings who modeled their behavior upon that of Louis XIV. Germany was not then a nation but an amorphous collection of hundreds of tiny states, duchies and principalities, almost all of them misruled by petty tyrants who levied merciless taxes and spent them immediately on hunting, feasting and reveling. Their subjects were thumbscrewed for their last sack of grain or until they were reduced to serfdom or vagrancy.[8]

Miserable and degraded as they were, there was still profit to be wrung from the displaced and starving people of the Rhineland. Shipowners and emigration companies seized the opportunity to transport those people to America. Their emigration agents, known as "newlanders," promised an easy and abundant life in America for anyone healthy enough to walk on board a ship. But how would the prospective migrant pay for his passage when all he had was his rags? It was simple enough, he was told by the shipowner's agent; all he had to do was sign a contract by which he would work for three to seven years as an indentured servant; it was called the redemption system. As one pamphlet published to encourage emigration promised, after a few pleasant years of working off their passage to America "the maid had become a lady, the peasant a nobleman, the artisan a baron; the officers of the government held their places by the will of the people."

Reality struck them the moment their ship docked in an American port. A prominent German citizen of Philadelphia described the scene as one immigrant vessel arrived there in 1728: "Before the ship is allowed to cast anchor in the harbor, the immigrants are all examined, as to whether any contagious disease be among them. The next step is to bring all the new arrivals in a procession before the city hall and there compel them to take the oath of allegiance to the king of Great Britain. After that they are brought back to the ship. Those that have paid their passage are released, the others are advertised in the newspapers for sale.

"The ship becomes a market. The buyers make their choice and bargain with the immigrants for a certain number of years and days, depending upon the price demanded by the ship captain or other 'merchant' who made the outlay for transportation, etc. Colonial governments recognize the written contract, which is then made binding for the redemptioner. The young unmarried people of both sexes are very quickly sold, and their fortunes are either good or bad, according to the character of the buyer. Old married people, widows, and the feeble, are a drug on the market, but if they have sound children, then their transportation charges are added to those of the children, and the latter must serve the longer. This does not save families from being separated in the various towns or even provinces. Again, the healthiest are taken first, and the sick are frequently detained beyond the period of recovery, when a release would have saved them!"[9]

The redemptioners could also be peddled on the open market, as advertisements in the Pennsylvania *Gazette* indicated, until they had served out their indenture: "To be sold — a likely Servant Woman having three and a half years to serve. She is a good Spinner . . . To be sold — an apprentice who has five years and three months to serve; he has been brought up in the tailor's business."

Even though some of the redemptioners fell into the hands of cruel, lecherous or abusive employers, they were the lucky ones. The less fortunate were those who died on the voyage from Europe or were lost in the frequent shipwrecks. Many died of starvation or disease on the way over. One historian of the migrations of the middle 1700's, Gottlieb Mittelberger, who migrated himself in 1750, wrote in his *Journey to Pennsylvania* that many emigrant vessels were lost at sea and the shipwrecks went unreported out of fear that they might discourage other immigrants from Germany. Others often took months to make the stormy crossing in winter. "In the year 1752 a ship arrived at Philadelphia, which was fully six months at sea from Holland to Philadelphia. The ship had weathered many storms throughout the winter, and could not reach the land; finally another ship came to the assistance of the half-wrecked and starved vessel. Of about 340 souls this ship brought 21 persons to Philadelphia, who stated that they had not only spent fully six months at sea, and had been driven to the coast of Ireland, but that most of the passengers had died of starvation, that they had lost their masts and sails, captain and mates, and that the rest would never have reached the land if God had not sent them another ship to their aid, which brought them to land."[10]

The immigrants were packed into the vessels almost as tightly as African slaves. "Children from one to seven years," Mittelberger wrote, "rarely survive the voyage; and many a time parents are compelled to see their children die of hunger, thirst, or sickness, and then see them cast into the water. Few women in confinement escape with their lives; many a woman is cast into the water with her child."[11]

When word got around that migrating to America wasn't necessarily the end to all earthly problems, the shipping companies' agents and other promoters stepped up their recruiting by sending caravans of brightly colored wagons and plumed horses, with trumpets blowing and drums beating, and free schnapps poured for all comers, through the villages of South Germany. They were lured on to Bremen or some other port, much as the Pied Piper of Hamelin made off with the children in the old fairy tale, and suddenly were acquainted with reality. The moment they stepped on board their ship they were required to sign a document, with an "X" if necessary, promising that if any died at sea the remaining redemptioners would have to serve out the bondage of those who died as well as their own. Many arrived in America to learn that, instead of being indentured for a half-dozen years, they would have to spend the rest of their lives in bondage.

The system worked so well for those who profited by it that even governments joined in exploiting it. In 1709, England shipped several hundred German redemptioners and gave them land at what is now Newburgh, New York, in return for their labor in manufacturing naval stores. At times the system worked rather freakishly, as when the Lutheran congregation in Frederick, Maryland, passed the plate and bought themselves a young theological student who was installed as their pastor. The German traveler D. von Bulow, writing from New York in 1791, noted that occasionally "an unsaleable article creeps in which remains a long time on the shelf. The worst of these are military officers and scholars . . . I have seen a Russian officer for more than a week on board of a vessel, heavy as ballast . . . He was, in fact, unsaleable."

Conditions in the emigrant traffic improved a little after influential Germans managed to propel a law through the Pennsylvania legislature providing that an immigrant could sue a ship captain who treated him unjustly or inhumanely. A little later, in 1819, the American Congress passed a law limiting the number of passengers to two for every five tons of the ship's weight, and that was almost the end of the redemption system, since profits could be made only if the steerage was packed like the hold of a slave ship. The cost of a passage rose to seventeen gold *louis d'or* (about eighty-five dollars), which often had to be worked off for a seven-year period of indenture. That made the "wage" of a redemptioner, who often had to work in the fields from dawn to dark, about twelve dollars a year.

Even at that rate, according to one reverend but unsympathetic observer, many of the migrants who came over in the mid-eighteenth century were a bad bargain. In a letter written in 1750, Peter Brunnholz, a Lutheran pastor in Philadelphia, related that twenty-five ships loaded with immigrants had landed there the previous autumn with slightly more than a thousand survivors of the crossings. Many were educated, but ill-fitted for the rigors of settling a new land, and they "would have better remained where they were." The state was becoming so crowded with importunate landsmen that the Reverend Brunnholz's Christian charity was wearing thin.

"In this month," he explained, "ships again frequently arrive with Germans, so that about ten have already come. The province is crowded full of people, and living continually becomes more expensive. Those who come in free — who had something in the old country, but consumed that which they had on an expensive voyage — and see that it is otherwise than was represented to them, whine and cry. Woe on the emigrants, who induced them to this! One of those in Germantown had wished to shoot himself recently from desperation. The Newlanders, as they are here called, are such as do not work and still wish to become rich speedily, and for this reason they go out into Württemberg and vicinity, and persuade people to come into this country, alleging that everything was here that they could wish for, that such a country like this there was none in the world, and that everyone could become as rich as noblemen, etc.

"These deceivers have this profit in it, that they with their merchandise are brought in free, and in addition, for every head they bring to Amsterdam or to Rotterdam, they receive a certain sum from the merchants. The owners of these vessels derive much money herefrom in freightage. They pack them into the ships as if they were herring, and when they arrive, there are so many sick and dying among them that it is pitiful to behold them.

"These, however, who have nothing, and are in debt also for their passage, are taken into small huts, where they lie upon straw, and are corrupted like cattle, and in part half deprived of their reason, so that they can scarcely perceive anything of the parson's consolations. The government and assembly have meanwhile made some ordinance and institutions, but whether the difficulty will be remedied thereby time will show. It would be just and right if a regular report of such things were put into the German newspapers here and there in Europe. Still what good would it do? The farmers don't get to read the papers, and

25

many indeed would not believe it, as they moreover have a mind to come."[12]

An English traveler, William Eddis, in his *Letters from America*, reported that it was "fallacious" for anyone to believe that redemptioners would be "treated with tenderness and humanity," as they were promised. Their American employers, he wrote, considered that "the difference is merely nominal between the indented servant and the convicted felon." The result was that decent, often educated and wellborn people found themselves in "a servile situation in a remote appendage to the British Empire."[13]

The redemptioner did not realize the wretchedness of his situation, Eddis noted, until he was bartered like an animal on the docks of Philadelphia and other colonial ports. Then, "stung with disappointment and vexation," he would "meet with horror the moment which dooms him, under an appearance of equity, to a limited term of slavery."

Eddis believed that bond servants in colonial America were treated far worse than servants in Britain. "You have heard of convicts who rather chose to undergo the severest penalties of the law, than endure the hardships which are annexed to their situation, during a state of servitude on this side of the Atlantic. Indolence, accompanied with a train of vicious habits, has, doubtless, great influence on the determination of such unhappy wretches; but it is surely to be lamented that men whose characters are unblemished, whose views are founded on honest and industrious principles, should fall a sacrifice to avarice and delusion, and indiscriminately be blended with the most profligate and abandoned of mankind."

All this was nonsense to that most talented of publicists for the American colonies, J. Hector St. John de Crèvecoeur, the publication of whose *Letters from an American Farmer* both in England and on the Continent created much interest in migration.* The few years of a

* Many believed that de Crèvecoeur painted such an alluring picture that it would lead to overexpectations on the part of immigrants. To rub some of the gloss off his book, Samuel Ayscough in the following year published the cautionary *Remarks on the Letters from an American Farmer*, London, 1783.

young man's life paid in return for his passage to America were nothing compared to the rewards which awaited him if he was willing to work and save. "What an epoch in this man's life!" enthused de Crèvecoeur. "He becomes a freeholder, from perhaps a German boor — he is now an American, a Pennsylvanian, an English subject. . . . Instead of being a vagrant he has a place of residence; he is called the inhabitant of such a country, or of such a district, and for the first time in his life counts for something; for hitherto he has been a cypher. I only repeat what I have heard many say, and no wonder their hearts should glow . . . From nothing to start into being; from a servant to the rank of master . . ."

Almost from the moment of arrival the European "boor," de Crève-coeur noted, found his scale of values adjusted sharply upward, and while "two hundred miles formerly appeared a very great distance, it is now but a trifle; he no sooner breathes our air than he forms schemes, and embarks in designs he would never have thought of in his own country. There the plenitude of society confines many useful ideas, and often extinguishes the most laudable schemes which here ripen into maturity. Thus the Europeans become Americans."

Of all his fellow Pennsylvanians, de Crèvecoeur considered the Germans the most adaptable to the task of pioneering the virgin forest-covered lands. He observed that of every twelve German families nine would succeed in their struggle against the wilderness; the Scottish rate was seven and the Irish four. "How much wiser, in general, the honest Germans than almost all other Europeans; they hire themselves to some of their wealthy landsmen, and in that apprenticeship learn everything that is necessary . . . Their astonishment at their first arrival from Germany is very great — it is to them a dream; the contrast must be powerful indeed; they observe their countrymen flourishing in every place; they travel through whole counties where not a word of English is spoken; and in the names and the language of the people, they retrace Germany. . . . The recollection of their former poverty and slavery never quits them as long as they live."

By contrast, the Scots and the Irish, though they may have come from almost as impoverished circumstances, had enjoyed a greater measure of civil liberty and "the effects of their new situation do not strike them so forcibly, nor has it so lasting an effect . . . The Scotch are frugal and laborious, but their wives cannot work so hard as the German women, who, on the contrary, vie with their husbands, and often share with them the most severe toils of the field, which they understand better." The Irish did neither as well as the Scottish nor the Germans, he said, because "they love to drink and to quarrel; they are litigious, and soon take to the gun, which is the ruin of everything . . ."[14]

A stately old home called the White Chimneys, near Lancaster, stands as testimony to the diligence and determination with which the Germans established themselves in Pennsylvania. The family which has owned and occupied it through the generations is the Slaymakers. Originally the name was Schleiermacher. The founder of that modest but continually prospering dynasty was Mathias Schleiermacher, who came to the Colonies long before the Revolution and was given a land grant by William Penn. His son Henry would have been classified "upwardly mobile" by today's sociologists. Henry, with his name Anglicized to Slaymaker, married the granddaughter of the local squire, a prosperous Welshman named Samuel Jones. Henry Slaymaker educated himself, read for the law, cultivated the local politicians, became a judge and bought up the old Jones homestead and land. His son Amos, who fought through the Revolution from Brandywine to Monmouth Courthouse, increased the family's holdings by speculating in land on which the first east-west toll road was built, and in 1779 was rich enough to afford his own indentured servants, including one William Smith.* There were, evidently, few bad apples in the Slaymaker barrel; like so many German-Americans they have held on to what their ancestors acquired, added on to it, and flourished. White Chimneys has survived and been lovingly preserved — thanks partly to a family enterprise, the Slaymaker Lock Corporation, founded late in the last century — and is still the homeplace of the Slaymakers.[15]

Another case of the success of a German immigrant to Pennsylvania

---

* Under the contract of indenture, the hapless William Smith "shall not commit Fornication, nor contract Matrimony; at Cards, Dice or any other unlawful games he shall not play . . . nor haunt Ale Houses, Taverns, nor Playhouses."

was one Frederick Pfoerschin, whose name (after being Anglicized) was made one of the most honored in American military history. Pfoerschin started on his great adventure with less than many of his migrating countrymen. An Alsatian of the Lutheran faith, speaking both French and German, he left his native province in the summer of 1749, came over on the sailing ship *Jacob* and landed in Philadelphia on October 2, 1749. Like most of his fellow passengers he was a redemptioner. Five years of hard work as a bond servant and he was a free man. He moved to Westmoreland County, cleared his own farm and married Mari Elizabeth Weygandt. His own life was otherwise undistinguished except for work and Lutheran piety. That of his descendants was fairly typical of that time and place; part of the family stayed in the neighborhood of the family farm, part joined in the westward migration.[16]

"Each generation," wrote his famous great-grandson, "furnished pioneers as the frontier moved westward. They were found in the columns that settled the Western Reserve; in the trains that carried civilization to Indiana, Illinois, Missouri and the Middle West, and were represented among the early settlers of Oregon and California. Their log cabins have dotted every state from Pennsylvania to the Pacific."

One of Frederick Pfoerschin's sons, Conrad, a Lutheran pastor, accompanied the punitive expedition against the Indians around Fort Liggonier in 1792 as its chaplain. He insisted on leading the militia company in prayer just as the Indians were located, and prayed so loudly that the Indians took alarm and fled. On reading an account of the Reverend Conrad's untimely dedication to his calling, his famous descendant scrawled on the margin: "Hardly a military proceeding."[17]

One of Frederick Pfoerschin's grandsons migrated to Missouri by working his way down the Ohio on the flatboats. He married a Missouri girl, went to work as a section boss on the railroad and settled down in Laclede. By then the family name had been changed from Pfoerschin to Pershing. The railroad worker's son, born in what had been a section house, was John J. Pershing, General of the Armies, commander of the first A.E.F. and chief of staff of the United States army.

For all their early tribulations on American soil, most of the redemptioners, like Frederick Pfoerschin, managed to survive and flourish in colonial America.

FROM MAINE TO GEORGIA

Generally the German immigrants made a favorable impression on the English, Scotch and Irish who had preceded them to America by a generation or two. They had a marked tendency to keep to themselves, mind their own business and settle their disputes — not in the courtroom or on the dueling ground as so many of the Irish preferred — through their ministers, priests or more educated fellow Germans. This self-containment was observed wherever the Germans settled, from the Canadian border to the swamps of the Florida peninsula. Neighborliness, as Americans understood the term, was not ingrained in them as with emigrants from the British Isles; the concept was foreign to a people who had learned through the repeated occupations and devastations in their native land that each family must be responsible for itself and could not look to its neighbors for assistance. As a whole, however, they were remarkable for a desire to live in peace even on the frontiers where a good fistfight in a tavern yard, followed by handshakes once broken teeth were spat out, was accounted a form of manly endeavor.

One of the few recorded instances in which the German settlers exhibited a tendency toward riotous behavior was in Winchester, the seat of Frederick County in the Shenandoah Valley of Virginia. There they had the heady experience of trying to coexist with an Irish colony of almost equal size. None in either national group had experienced the problems of living with people speaking a different tongue; the fact that both the Irish and Germans were mostly Catholic did not alleviate the stresses between them, and the chosen occasions for letting off international steam, oddly enough, were their respective saints' days.

"It was customary for the Dutch [that is, the Germans] on St. Patrick's Day," wrote Samuel Kercheval, the historian of the Shenandoah Valley settlements, "to exhibit the effigy of the saint, with a string of Irish potatoes around his neck, and his wife Sheeley, with her apron loaded also with potatoes. This was always followed by a riot. The Irish resented the indignity offered to their saint and his holy spouse, and a battle followed. On St. Michael's Day the Irish would retort, and exhibit the saint with a rope of sauerkraut about the throat. Then the Dutch, like the Yankee, 'felt chock full of fight,' and at it they went, pell-mell, and many a black eye, bloody nose, and broken head was the result."

The Anglo-Saxon magistrates of Frederick County naturally looked upon both the Irish and the Germans as drunken barbarians. The custom of rioting on saints' days, Kercheval related, "was finally put down by the rigor with which the courts of justice punished the rioters." The longer the Irish and Germans lived together and learned they had common interests, Kercheval added, the more "they began to appreciate one another and frequently intermarried."[18]

Like the English, the Scotch and the Irish, the early German settlers in America rarely clung to the coastal cities on arrival but immediately pushed inland in search of good land. The later the arrival, the farther one had to go into the wilderness. Thus the Germans found themselves clearing land and building rude forts at the outer limits of civilization on the continent.

In New York State they pushed a line of settlements up the Hudson and along the Mohawk and Schoharie. Generally the policy of the Germans in New York was to live on peaceful terms with the Indians. Some German fathers adopted the custom of sending their sons to live with the Mohawks for several years to learn their language and ways of living and thinking. The Germans, in fact, exhibited so much sympathy for the Mohawks that the English colonial governor became suspicious and ordered an investigation.

Most of the Germans' difficulties were with the Dutch who had preceded them. Although they were racial cousins, there was considerable friction over the large tracts of land the Hollanders had staked out for themselves. (The Germans called themselves the "High Dutch" and the Hollanders the "Low Dutch," not giving themselves any the worst of it, semantically.) An instance of the ill-feeling between "High" and "Low" Dutch occurred when a young Hollander named Adam Vrooman appeared in the German settlement of Weiserdorf, near

Schenectady, and claimed his patrimony of fourteen hundred acres, a tract which prevented the Germans from spreading westward beyond the Schoharie Valley. Young Vrooman complained to the colonial administration that the Germans drove their horses over his fields, tore down his buildings and "told the Indians all sorts of lies."[19]

The northern counties of New Jersey were also thickly settled by German immigrants, who first arrived on Jersey soil in 1707. One of them was Johann Peter Rockefeller, who migrated from Germany in 1733 and worked a farm near Flemington in Hunterdon County until his death fifty years later. One of his descendants was John D. Rockefeller, Sr. Hundreds of Germans also settled in Maryland, built the first brewery in Baltimore and formed a large part of that city's population in its earliest years. A more interesting group were the Labadists, who came over from the Rhineland in 1684 and established a colony on the Bohemian River. They were Christian communists, followers of Jean de Labadie, who refused to observe the Sabbath (on the grounds that life is a perpetual Sabbath) and denied the concept of original sin. Christian communism did not thrive in the American air, and the colony had dwindled to eight families by 1698. A few years later it broke up completely, and its leader, Peter Sluyter, became a wealthy tobacco planter and slave trader.

In Virginia the earliest German settlement was at Germanna in what is now Orange County where twelve families of ironworkers migrated to set up a foundry at the invitation of the colonial governor in 1714. Subsequently a migration of eighty families from Württemberg colonized Madison County. One of the few instances of German condonation of slavery in Virginia was credited against the account of the colony's spiritual leader, a Reverend Klug, who was pastor of the Hopeful Evangelic Lutheran Church, which was built at the forks of the Robinson River and White Oak Run. Surplus funds which remained after the church was built were devoted to buying a seven-hundred-acre farm for Klug, who promptly insisted on buying a number of slaves to work them. He was no severe, plain-living pastor of the usual Lutheran type. He was "given to the evil habits of his time, particularly to drinking," according to one eminent German-American historian, "for which, no doubt, he found plenty of examples among his well-to-do friends, the colonial gentry, with whom he consorted. He was not accustomed to plain living as an incentive to high thinking, and confessed generously to one of the Moravian missionaries that he was no Pietist, gratuitous information in the face of stories current about the minister's tipsy rides homeward from functions not ministerial."[20]

The historical town of Harpers Ferry was established by a German immigrant named Robert Harper, and hundreds of German families poured into the Shenandoah Valley as soon as reports circulated of its great fertility. The only part of Virginia which the Germans avoided was the Tidewater country, where they objected to the practice of letting Negro slaves do all the work while their masters gazed vacantly from their verandas; they insisted on working their own land, which was taken by the Anglo-Saxon gentry of the Tidewater as an indication of their stubborn peasant-mindedness.

In both the Carolinas the Germans appeared in force from 1710 onward, many of them settling in the coastal towns at first and then pushing inland for more and better land. A sizable colony of silkworkers established themselves at Purysburg, in Beaufort County, South Carolina, under the leadership of John Peter Pury, a migrant from Neufchatel. They were assigned a tract of forty thousand acres on which to raise the white mulberry trees and grapevines to cultivate silkworms. The silk itself was manufactured in the town under an arrangement with the colonial authorities who paid Pury four hundred pounds sterling for every worker he persuaded to settle in Purysburg and its surrounding silkworm plantations. Other German settlements sprang up along the South Carolina frontier in Orangeburg and Lexington counties. The northern counties of North Carolina, on the other hand, received their German immigrants as an overflow from Pennsylvania, where the more attractive farmlands had already been taken up.

In the colonization of Georgia, King George II of England authorized twenty-one gentlemen to find the most suitable and industrious people available, with the most favorable status being given to Scottish Highlanders and German Salzburgers — both mountaineering breeds, oddly enough — for settlement of the swampy lowlands of the new colony. About that time, 1732, Count Leopold of Firmian expelled from his realm all who were not Catholics, and among those religiously

33

displaced persons were the first Salzburg families to migrate to Georgia. Their leader, Baron von Reck, and several of his advisers were allowed to select their own site for settlement, a tract about twenty-five miles from Savannah. On landing there the Germans "after singing a psalm set up a rock which they found upon the spot, and in the spirit of the pious Samuel named the place Ebenezer [the stone of help]." Ebenezer, for all the piety attending its founding, proved to be a poor choice for settlement because its soil was thin, and the Germans were soon permitted to move eight miles away to a place they doggedly named New Ebenezer. This too was an unhappy location because it was surrounded on three sides by malarial swamps, but they stuck it out and engaged in the silkworm industry like their countrymen in neighboring South Carolina.

By 1751 the colony of New Ebenezer was able to ship a thousand pounds of cocoons and seventy-four pounds of raw silk to England. Their only later difficulty was with the large Anglo-Saxon landowners of the district, who hotly resented the Salzburgers' plainspoken views on Negro slavery. The Germans held that America was supposed to be a refuge, not a trap, for the oppressed. A more practical motive, less loudly expressed, was that the Spanish in neighboring Florida might stir up the slaves to rebel against the whites. The pressure from their fellow Georgians was so intense, finally, that the settlement of New Ebenezer withdrew its objections to the use of slave labor on being informed by their pastor — the Lutheran dominie was often the practical as well as the spiritual leader of his flock — that "If you take slaves in faith, and with the intent of conducting them to Christ, the action will not be sin, but it may prove to be a 'benediction.'" There was a certain nicety of expression about putting benediction in quotation marks.

In the New England colonies, the principal German settlement was Waldoborough in the Broad Bay district of Maine. It was named for Samuel Waldo, a Pomeranian soldier who migrated to Boston and became involved in land speculation in Maine, which was then part of the Massachusetts Bay Colony. For his services in obtaining a royal patent to lands along the Muscongus River for a land company, Waldo was awarded the tract on both sides of the Medomak River. Two years later, in 1738, Colonel Waldo returned to his native Germany to recruit forty families from Saxony and Brunswick to settle on his land. More German families soon followed. A hard winter and various diseases almost wiped them out, but they clung to their foothold in the vast forests and in 1745 a number of the men in the colony joined the punitive expedition against the French fort of Louisburg on Cape Breton Island, Nova Scotia. In the spring of 1746 the Waldoborough settlement was attacked by Indians, most of its inhabitants were killed and all they had built was destroyed. The survivors crept back from their hiding places in the forest and with thirty families of German immigrants from Philadelphia reinforcing them they rebuilt the settlement. After that a number of German villages sprang up in the Broad Bay region and along the Kennebec.

By the time of the Revolution, almost a quarter of a million Germans were living in the American colonies from the northernmost German settlement at Waldoborough, Maine, to the southernmost at New Ebenezer, Georgia. They formed part of a sturdy yeoman stock, otherwise mostly of English, Scottish and Irish blood, which possessed the hardihood and determination to last out the brutal winters, survive the endemic diseases, fight the Indians if necessary, fend off the French in their incursions from Canada, and slowly, without quite being conscious of it, build a new nation in the forest lands of eastern North America. At the time the colonies revolted it was estimated that there were 1,500 Germans in New England, 25,000 in New York, 110,000 in Pennsylvania, 15,000 in New Jersey, 20,500 in Maryland and Delaware, 25,000 in Virginia, 8,000 in North Carolina, 15,000 in South Carolina and 5,000 in Georgia.[21]

Silkworm growers and ironworkers, Saxon barons and Palatine redemptioners alike were united in one determination: not to be ruled by kings or princelings from across the sea. More than any of the other nationalities in the wilderness of the New World they had cut themselves loose from ties that might have bound them to the Europe from which they had escaped at risks no actuary would have recommended to them.

2. REDCOATS, BLUECOATS AND

TURNCOATS

Disunion and disaffection were the most striking features of the American political atmosphere at the beginning of the Colonies' struggle for independence. There was a cleavage between Loyalist and Rebel more dangerous to the cause than any amount of military force the British could apply. A quarter of a century after independence had been achieved President John Adams estimated that about one-third of the Colonies' population was opposed to fighting for secession from the British Empire. The estimate was given in an exchange of letters with Thomas McKean, chief justice of Pennsylvania, who added the opinion that not only were a third of all Americans against the Revolution but "more than one third of influential characters were against it."

Very few of the pro-English faction were German. The Germans, not so much because they were anti-English but because they were anti-royalist, lined up solidly behind the movement for independence. One indication of their feeling was the forty-page pamphlet issued by the vestries of the German Lutheran and Reformed churches of Philadelphia and circularized among their coreligionists in New York and South Carolina, in which it was noted that the Germans in Pennsylvania were forming militia companies and urged that this example be followed elsewhere. Hundreds of Germans also joined the armed groups which called themselves the "Associators" and sprang up throughout the Colonies to help form the basis of a revolutionary army.

The Associators, armed to the teeth and operating much like the vigilance committees of a later period in the West, performed their self-appointed duties with an occasional excess of enthusiasm. Woe to the English traveler who fell into their hands, as one innocent Briton learned in 1775 when he was journeying through Maryland on private business. Many of the Associators in that colony were German. The traveler, whose name was Smyth, fell under their suspicion when he appeared in Fredericktown. He was invited to present himself before the Revolutionary Committee of the local Associators to explain what he was doing there and prove that he wasn't acting as an agent of the Crown.

Smyth had no taste for being arraigned before a tribunal of colonial ruffians and decided not to keep the appointment. Instead he took to his heels, fleeing through Middletown and Funktown with the Associators in close pursuit. The vigilantes caught up with him in Hagerstown. He was confronted by musketeers speaking in a barbaric dialect which he attempted to reproduce in his book (*A Tour of the United States*) published in London nine years later. One of the partisans, he related, seized him by the throat and roared:

"Got tamn you, how darsht you make an exshkape from this honorable committish?"

Mr. Smyth finally satisfied his inquisitors that he was not plotting their extermination and was allowed to go on his way, but not without gaining the impression that the German settlers in the Colonies were an unmannerly horde of Visigoths determined, as one of them told him, to "make Shorsh know how to behave himself." The Associator was referring to George III, whose own accent was almost as execrably Hanoverian as that of his American detractor.[1]

THE REVEREND BRIGADIER

When the people of Pennsylvania were invited to nominate a representative citizen whose statue would stand in the Capitol, their choice was John Peter Gabriel Muhlenberg. In his youth, as a remarkably lively and urbane pastor, he was the Reverend Muhlenberg. Later he was Brigadier General Muhlenberg, one of Washington's most trusted officers. To the Hessians whom he fought at Brandywine he was "that devil Pete."

Hardly a "representative" citizen of Pennsylvania, the reverend brigadier was a member of one of the first American political dynasties, one of his brothers becoming speaker of the House of Representatives, one of his nephews also a congressman.

The patriarch of the family was Henry Melchior Muhlenberg, who migrated from Germany in 1742 and became the leader of the Lutheran clergy in Pennsylvania. As pastor of the famous Zion Church of Philadelphia — the future site of Henry Lee's eulogy of Washington, "First in war, first in peace, first in the hearts of his countrymen" — he was also a powerful political and social influence in the state. The Reverend Muhlenberg exerted much of that influence on behalf of the Revolutionary cause. His greatest contribution, however, was his eldest son. Like his father, Peter Muhlenberg, whose mother was the daughter of Conrad Weiser, the venturesome leader of the Palatine Germans who settled the Mohawk Valley of New York, was born with a taste for both spiritual and temporal power. He was eloquent in the pulpit when he followed his father's wishes and became a Lutheran pastor, but even more inspiring and effective as the commander of a brigade of Virginia light infantry which performed with distinction at Charleston, Brandywine, Germantown, Monmouth, Stony Point and Yorktown.

Born in 1746, Peter Muhlenberg was sent to study theology at his father's alma mater, the University of Halle, when he reached the age of twenty-one. The discipline of a German university, both personal and scholastic, did not appeal to a young man who had breathed the freer air of the American Colonies. Before finishing his first year at Halle, he was requested by the school authorities to take up his education elsewhere.

Instead, to the great disappointment of his father, he returned to America and announced he was ready to begin preaching. His first pastorate was in Philadelphia, where his father could keep an eye on him. Tall, dark-haired, eloquent, rather sophisticated for a Lutheran clergyman, young Muhlenberg became noted for his fiery sermons, which often devoted as much passion to political matters as those of the spirit. In 1772 he was summoned to the Lutheran church in Woodstock, Virginia, where his lusty personality soon commended him not only to his parishioners but the hearty, fox-hunting Anglo-Saxon squires of the Blue Ridge valleys. Within a year he was discussing plans for a colonial uprising with Patrick Henry and hunting bucks with Colonel George Washington.[2]

"In the Valley of the Blue Ridge," as George Bancroft would remark, "the German congregations, quickened by the preaching of Muhlenberg, were eager to take up arms."[3] Within two years of taking up his pastorate at Woodstock, the Reverend Peter Muhlenberg succeeded in raising more sentiment against George III than against the works of Satan himself. He was the moderator of a meeting in Woodstock on June 16, 1774, which adopted resolutions with more than a whiff of treason. Muhlenberg and his followers resolved that "it is the inherent right of British subjects to be governed and taxed by representatives chosen by themselves only, and that every act of the British Parliament respecting the internal policy of America is a dangerous and unconstitutional invasion of our rights and privileges." The meeting went on to declare that "we will most heartily and unanimously concur with our suffering brethren in Boston and every other part of North America, who are the immediate victims of tyranny, in promoting all proper measures to avert such dreadful calamities, to procure redress of our grievances, and to secure our common liberties." The meeting then appointed the Reverend Muhlenberg the chairmen of the county's Committee of Safety and Correspondence, about half of whose members were Anglo-Saxons, the others German. As Dunmore County's representative at the Virginia convention in March, 1775, he eloquently supported Patrick Henry's declarations and seconded his friend's motion that the province of Virginia begin raising militia regiments to defend its aspirations against the Crown.

Without a moment's hesitation over the propriety of a professional man of God taking up the sword, as well as promoting a cause which was regarded as treasonous by many, Muhlenberg then accepted the mission of raising the Eighth Virginia Regiment and assuming its command.

On a Sunday in January of 1776, he calculatingly and characteristically made the gesture which won him a place in any schoolchildren's history of the American Revolution. Before his congregation in Woodstock he delivered a blazing sermon on the people's duty to revolt against oppression, ending it with the eloquent sentence: "There is a time for preaching and praying, but there is also a time for battle, and that time has now arrived!"

With that, he cast off his ministerial robes and revealed himself in the silver and blue uniform of a colonel in the Continental army. After pronouncing the benediction, he gave a signal for his drum corps posted outside the church doors and slowly descended from the pulpit. With the drums beating as a background, he stationed himself at the door, fastened every able-bodied man with his commanding glare, and enlisted his parishioners as members of the Eighth Virginia before they could escape to second thoughts about the danger of rebelling against imperial Britain. Three hundred men were mustered in that day, another hundred the following day.

The Muhlenberg charisma was so evident on and off the battlefield that General Washington accounted the "fighting parson" one of his ablest commanders and promoted him to brigadier less than a year after hostilities with the British began. It was also evident to the enemy. At the Battle of Brandywine the reverend brigadier's troops were thrown against a force of Hessian mercenaries. The Hessians paid him a highly unclerical compliment. Recognizing him at the head of the Virginia brigade, the Hessians, according to legend, cried out, *"Heir Kommt Tuefel Pete!"* — Here comes Devil Pete. It was the nickname he had earned as an unruly student at the University of Halle.

REVOLUTION WITH A GERMAN ACCENT

Whatever the depth of their patriotic impulses, the German-born and German-descended in America possessed a considerable stake in the success of the Revolution. By the time the Colonies revolted, it had been noted, the German migrants had settled on much of the best farming lands in the Colonies. They had cleared and cultivated the fertile limestone belt stretching from the Northeast to the Southwest, middle Pennsylvania largely settled by Germans became the granary of the Revolution, and some of the finest farms in the Mohawk and Shenandoah valleys were in their possession as well as the best agricultural areas in the Carolinas. Thus a Hessian officer estimated that less than one-sixth of the German population of the Colonies was Tory-minded, compared to one-third of the other Americans.

Furthermore the German settlers had acquired considerable military experience during the French and Indian War. The Pennsylvania frontier was defended by German militia along with the Scotch and Irish. In New York State the Mohawk Valley, largely occupied by Germans, thrust the deepest into the territory of the Six Nations and had to be constantly defended against the incursions of the French and their Indian allies. In 1757 a French-led force of Indians attacked the settlement of German Flats, killed forty men, women and children and took a hundred prisoners; the next year they descended upon the place again, and this time were driven off by settlers under the command of Captain Nicholas Herkimer (formerly Herckheimer), who later became a Continental general and one of the heroes of the Revolution.

George Washington himself gradually formed a high opinion of the sticking power shown by the German immigrants. His first glimpse of the incoming Germans occurred when, as a sixteen-year-old surveyor, he made a trip over the Blue Ridges in 1748 and came across a group of them pushing westward in search of land. They struck him as "ignorante," he wrote in his journal. So unprepossessing were those first Germans he met that he decided "they would never speak English but, when spoken to, they speak all Dutch." By Dutch, of course, he meant German. On closer acquaintance, particularly with the German companies which formed part of the division of Virginia troops he commanded in the French and Indian War, he decided the Germans would make good soldiers and citizens.

German regiments were organized almost immediately as a matter of

41

Revolutionary necessity. One of the first levied on orders of the Continental Congress on May 22, 1776, consisted of four companies of Pennsylvanians and another four of Marylanders. Regarding this levy, General Washington wrote Congress on June 30: "The battalion [sic] of Germans which Congress has ordered to be raised will be a corps of much service, and I am hopeful that such persons will be appointed officers as will complete their enlistment with all possible expedition."[4] Washington showed even greater faith in the loyalty of the German-Americans when his first "bodyguard," or headquarters company, was disbanded on reports that it contained a number of Tories. On his adjutant's advice it was replaced by the Independent Troop of Horse, consisting of fourteen officers and fifty-three enlisted men, almost all of them German and recruited in Bucks and Lancaster counties, Pennsylvania, under the command of a Prussian who served as a cavalry lieutenant under Frederick the Great during the Seven Years' War. It rode with and protected the commander in chief during all of his campaigns.

Thousands of Germans served not only in their own regiments but in formations which included men of other national origins. Along with the Irish, they were often the staunchest troops in the line when the stand-up fighting against the British and their involuntary Hessian allies began.

Both the humble and exalted served Washington well. In the former class, by choice, was Christopher Ludwig, a veteran of Frederick the Great's army. When money was being collected for arms and ammunition to supply the Continental army, Ludwig, a Philadelphia baker, told a meeting of General Washington's supporters, "I am of course only a poor gingerbread baker, but write me down for two hundred pounds." A few months later, though fifty-five years old, he enlisted as a private in the Pennsylvania militia. General Washington appointed him the chief baker for the Continental army, upon which Ludwig was informed that he was expected to produce one hundred pounds of bread for each one hundred pounds of flour he requisitioned. "No," replied the honest baker, "Christopher Ludwig does not wish to become rich by the war. He has enough. Out of one hundred pounds of flour one gets one hundred and thirty-five pounds of bread, and so many I will give." Washington, with justice, called him "my honest friend." He lost heavily, as was to be expected, when the British occupied Philadelphia, but recouped after the war and left a sizable estate on his death at the age of eighty-nine. The celebrated author-physician Benjamin Rush considered him so notable a character that he wrote the unassuming baker's biography (*Life of Ludwick*, published in 1801).

Another Ludwig, equally humble by birth but not by disposition, was the tough little vivandière known to Revolutionary legend as Molly Pitcher. ("Here comes Molly with her pitcher," as the troops shouted when she appeared on a battlefield with water and food.) Her maiden name was Maria Ludwig, and she had been a maidservant in the home of a Carlisle, Pennsylvania, physician until her marriage to William Hayes. When Hayes marched off to war with an artillery company, his young German wife decided the life of a camp follower was preferable to sitting at home and waiting for William. She apparently had not been indoctrinated in the German code for females: kitchen, church and children. Her opportunity came when Hayes was wounded in an early engagement. Molly went to care for him, and Revolutionary discipline being what it was, stayed on with him and his comrades for seven years of fighting, marching and bivouacking.

Molly was accepted as one of the boys, helped serve the battery's fieldpieces, smoked a pipe, chewed tobacco and swore with all the expertise of an artilleryman. She helped care for the wounded, acted as a stretcher-bearer and filled in as the battery's cook and commissary sergeant. Her husband was wounded again at Monmouth, and on that occasion, according to the legend, she took his place at one of the guns and persuaded his comrades to make a stand when they were about to abandon their position.

Private Joseph Plumb Martin of the Eighth Connecticut saw her in action during a skirmish in New Jersey, and in his narrative (*Private Yankee Doodle Dandy*) offered reproof to sobersided historians who tended to view "Molly Pitcher" as more a myth than a legend. Martin saw her at her husband's side during the engagement, swabbing, loading and firing a fieldpiece. Counter-battery fire from the British guns did not alarm her in the least, Private Martin observed. "While in the act of reaching for a cartridge and having one of her feet as far before the other as she could step, a cannon shot from the enemy passed directly between her legs without doing any other damage than carrying away all the lower part of her petticoat. Looking at it with apparent unconcern she observed that it was lucky it did not pass a little higher, for in that case it might have carried away something else, and continued her occupation . . ."[5]

Molly, as well as her husband, survived British shot and shell. Even as a grandmother her disposition remained that of a Continental artilleryman. One of her grandchildren was quoted as saying she had acquired masculine manners, swore "like a trooper," and had a temper to match her red hair and blazing blue eyes.[6] Along with the more sedate Betsey Ross, she became one of the durable and indispensable legends of the Revolution.

Less humble Germans than the two Ludwigs also came to offer their services to the Continental army. One of these was Frederick William Augustus Henry Ferdinand, Baron von Steuben, who became the drillmaster of the Continental army and one of the two chief totems of the German-Americans ever since. There was also, it appears, a strain of the Baron Munchausen in the jovial Steuben; as with so many distinguished foreign officers who offered their services to the American armies in both the Revolution and the Civil War, he promoted himself in rank and honors as soon as he crossed the Atlantic. Steuben came bearing a letter from Benjamin Franklin stating that he had been a lieutenant general "in the king of Prussia's service," that is, Frederick the Great, the "model general of the world."

Actually Steuben was a penniless captain who had been dropped from the great Frederick's service fourteen years before and since had been employed as chamberlain at a minor European court. On coming to America with Benjamin Franklin's blessings he had simply promoted himself from captain to lieutenant general, and let it be known that he had spent most of his adult life soaking up military knowledge beside the Prussian genius. Nevertheless, aside from his false pretensions, Steuben was a well-trained soldier and had been instructed in general-

The Reverend Brigadier Muhlenberg,
or "Devil Pete"

Johann de Kalb, not a baron, but
a hero

Nicholas Herkimer, heroic amateur

Baron von Steuben, genial drillmaster

staff duties. It must also be said that he was quite sincere in his professions of devotion to the American cause.

Some of that sincerity shone through his letter to Washington offering his services in any capacity the Americans saw fit, and adding that "the object of my greatest ambition is to render your country all the services in my power and to deserve the title of a citizen of America by fighting for the cause of liberty. If the distinguished ranks in which I have served in Europe should be an obstacle, I had rather serve under your Excellency as a volunteer than to be the subject of discontent to such deserving officers as have already distinguished themselves amongst you."[7]

Steuben's modest proposal coming from a Prussian "lieutenant general," struck Washington so favorably that he sent for Steuben immediately. He had just been harassed endlessly by the claims of a French officer named Philippe Charles Tronson du Coudray, who had been insisting that he be elevated to major general in command of all the army's artillery and engineers until he drowned when his horse bolted off the ferry across the Schuykill. It was also warming to Washington that such a distinguished foreigner should be volunteering his services in the middle of the Continental army's desperate winter at Valley Forge, with his soldiers half-starved and living in flimsy huts.

One February day in 1778 Baron Steuben and his retinue proceeded up the Lancaster Road toward Valley Forge. The Baron, traveling in style and, presumably, on credit, was accompanied by his translator (the Baron spoke no English), a young Frenchman named Pierre Duponceau; two aides-de-camp and a German manservant. A huge Italian greyhound trotted at his heels. The Baron, a stout, bald, red-faced and big-nosed man with a bluff hearty manner, was resplendent in a new blue uniform with the glittering, saucer-sized, bejeweled Star of the Order of Fidelity of Baden blazing away on his chest.

General Washington received him immediately at his headquarters in the midst of the stricken winter camp, and spent hours talking to him that afternoon. Four days later Washington wrote a friend that Steuben "appears to be much of a gentleman and, as far as I have had an

46

opportunity of judging, a man of military knowledge and acquainted with the world."[8]

As soon as possible, considering the delicate feelings of his other officers, Steuben was appointed inspector general of the Continental army and assigned to retraining it to fight more effectively against disciplined redcoats. The Baron quickly demonstrated his capacity as a drillmaster; he was a disciplinarian but not a martinet. His worldliness, as perceived by Washington, made him realize that American soldiers could not be drilled like Prussian grenadiers. "In the first place," as Steuben soon was writing a friend in Germany, "the genius of this nation is not in the least to be compared with that of the Prussians, Austrians, or French. You say to your soldier, 'Do this,' and he doeth it, but I am obliged to say, 'This is the reason why you ought to do that,' and then he does it."

Desertion and disease had winnowed the Continental army from seventeen thousand to five thousand gaunt survivors, but Steuben took them in hand and soon had them drilling from six in the morning to six at night. All day his guttural voice was heard above the shuffling of hundreds of feet. At night he composed the first manual of field regulations for the American army, writing them in French, which young Duponceau translated into English, and in his spare moments the Baron set about learning enough English to make himself understood on the drill field. At first he selected a model company of one hundred men to be trained in the maneuvers of infantry warfare as it was practiced in Europe, with modifications suitable to the American temperament. This company was drilled in marching, in the manual of arms, in deploying into columns, in loading and firing precisely on command; then it was used as a cadre for the instruction of the others, a process by which Steuben created a corps of sergeants which the army had grievously lacked. He also reorganized the force into fourteen brigades of more or less equal size.

To help supervise the training activities, which now filled the whole muddy plain of Valley Forge, Steuben selected a group of young officers whom he called "my sans-culottes," among them a New Yorker named Benjamin Walker, who wrote that the Baron often lost his temper on

47

the drill field, amidst an endless vista of awkward squads, but his "fits of passion were comical and rather amused than offended the soldiers." When the company he was drilling failed to execute the proper maneuver, Captain Walker observed, the Baron "began to swear in German, then in French, and then in both languages together. When he had exhausted his artillery of foreign oaths, he would call to his aides, 'My dear Walker and my dear Duponceau, come and swear for me in English. These fellows won't do what I bid them.' A good-natured smile then went through the ranks and at last the maneuver or the movement was properly performed."

Long before the snow vanished from Valley Forge's slopes, Steuben was able to boast that he now had the Continentals marching in step and "I also made maneuvers with ten and twelve battalions with as much precision as the evolution of a single company."

What the Americans particularly admired about Steuben was his willingness to break with the English tradition, also deeply imbedded in the Rebel army, that to lead the drilling of troops was beneath the dignity of an officer and a gentleman. As Colonel Alexander Seammell wrote: "To see a gentleman dignified with a lieutenant general's [sic] commission from the great Prussian monarch condescend with a grace peculiar to himself to take under his direction a squad or ten or twelve men in the capacity of a drill sergeant, commands the admiration of both officers and men."

Inculcating his own system of infantry tactics — largely Prussian with modifications taking into account the Yankee temperament — was not always acceptable to his fellow officers, particularly those on Washington's staff who had been seconded from the French army or who had received their military education from the English, as Steuben quickly learned. With Washington's backing, with the troops' goodwill, and by exercising his own unpolished brand of diplomacy, he was able to prevail. An army was hammered into shape on the cold wet plain of Valley Forge. The men learned that the bayonet was a weapon, not a cooking tool. The Baron taught them that each man was responsible for his musket; until Steuben became Inspector General the army lost from five to eight thousand a year, but twelve months after he took over that number was reduced to an incredible three. Furthermore when *Steu-*

ben's *Regulations*, popularly known as "the Blue Book," was published, each Continental officer knew exactly what his duties were in camp, on the march and in battle.

Regarding his difficulties with those on Washington's staff who persisted in remaining under the influence of the English or French military systems, Baron Steuben wrote a friend in his native Prussia that he had to bull his way over their objections. The French, predictably, were touchy about falling in with a Prussian's concepts. "My good republicans," the Baron wrote in regard to the Yankees under his brisk tutelage, "wanted everything in the English style; our great and good allies [the French] wanted everything in the French mode, and when I presented a plate of sauerkraut dressed in the Prussian style, they all wanted to throw it out the window. Nevertheless, by the force of proving by *Goddams* that my cookery was the best, I overcame the prejudices of the former; but the second liked me as little in the forests of America as they did on the plains of Rossbach [a Franco-Prussian battlefield on which Steuben had served]. Do not, therefore, be astonished if I am not painted in very bright colors in Parisian circles."[9]

The Baron's "plate of sauerkraut" was so much appreciated by the time the Continental army left its winter quarters that the Congress, on Washington's recommendation, commissioned him a major general and confirmed his appointment as Inspector General. His value to the Revolutionary cause has been inflated by German-American historians, and overestimated by his biographer (John M. Palmer in *General von Steuben*), but it is doubtless true that the American army came out of Valley Forge with a strength in morale and discipline, as well as tactical virtuosity, that it had never possessed before. That spring Washington was able to get his columns moving within fifteen minutes after issuing the order. At Monmouth the army was able to conduct that most difficult of maneuvers, an orderly retreat, under heavy pressure from the enemy.

Thereafter Washington relied on Steuben constantly as an advisor as well as a watchdog over his brigades' training and discipline. Later he was sent south to whip the Virginia militia regiments into shape when their "plundering activities" became a national scandal, and was General Nathanael Green's right-hand man when that valiant officer took

49

over the southern army after the disaster at Camden, where they had been deserted by their commander. At Yorktown, finally, he was the only member of Washington's staff with personal experience of conducting siege operations.

The passion for drill and maneuver so permeated the American forces that for a time they seemed in danger of becoming an overseas branch of the Prussian army. Even Steuben saw that the American commanders were overdoing it. During the heat of the summer of 1780, Private Joseph Plumb Martin of the Eighth Connecticut has recounted, his regiment was kept at its field exercises until the men were stumbling with exhaustion. Then General von Steuben came by on an inspection tour. "When he found out our situation, he ordered us off immediately. 'You may as well knock these men on the head,' said he, 'as keep them there; they will die if kept there much longer, and they can do no more if you knock their brains out.' He had more sense than our officers, but they did not feel the hardships which we had to undergo, and of course cared but little, if anything at all, about us."

History leaves some unfortunate gaps. It would be interesting to know if Washington, later held up to the nation as an eternal symbol of veracity, ever found out that his "Prussian lieutenant general" was actually a retired captain. If so, it wasn't held against Steuben. The ingratitude of republics was not visited upon the doughty Baron. After the war he formulated plans for a permanent military academy, and was awarded a twenty-five-hundred-dollar annual pension by Congress as well as a grant of sixteen thousand acres by the State of New York. For several generations *Steuben's Regulations* was the handbook of the American army, and the survival of that "plate of sauerkraut" would undoubtedly have pleased him as much as any of the honors posterity bestowed on the man who provided the ramrod for the Continental army's spine.

Another German officer who misrepresented his background in the old country, and who also made up for it by valiant service as a soldier, was the one who styled himself the Baron Johann de Kalb. Actually he was born plain Johann Kalb, the son of a Franconian peasant. He had bestowed the title upon himself after marrying the daughter of a Dutch millionaire. Guilty of social pretensions, he was nevertheless a seasoned soldier, a veteran of the Seven Years' War, with the sort of technical training — as a topographical engineer — which the American army lacked to an alarming degree. Kalb came over with Lafayette and immediately offered his services to General Washington, who recommended that he be commissioned a major general. The self-styled baron served under Washington in the New Jersey and Maryland campaigns with distinction, and was accounted the "most experienced, calculating and cautious" of all the foreign officers serving with the Continental army.

In 1780 General Kalb was sent south with his Maryland Division to form part of the ragtag army under General Horatio Gates, which was supposed to fend off the well-equipped British forces in the Carolinas. The two armies collided at Camden, with disastrous consequences for the Americans. General Gates had placed his untried Virginia militia regiments opposite the veteran formations of Lord Cornwallis. When the British attacked, the Virginia militiamen dropped their muskets and fled for the rear, carrying General Gates and most of the other American commanders with them. Gates, as George Bancroft detailed the action in his magisterial history of the Revolution, "outdistanced the most terrified of the militia and was altogether ignorant of the fate of his army."

Only Kalb and his Marylanders, with an attached regiment from Delaware, tried to hold their ground. "The division which Kalb commanded," as Bancroft related, "continued long in action, and never did troops show greater courage than those men of Maryland and Delaware. The horse of Kalb had been killed under him and he had been badly wounded; yet he continued to fight on foot. At last, in the hope of victory, he led a charge, drove the division under Rawdon, took fifty prisoners, and would not believe that he was not about to gain the day, when Cornwallis poured against him a party of dragoons and infantry. Even then he did not yield until disabled by many wounds. The victory cost the British about five hundred of their best troops; 'their great loss,' wrote Marion, 'is equal to a defeat.' "

Kalb, his gigantic figure looming over the field, sacrificed himself to the lost battle. He was carried away, finally, with blood dripping from eleven bayonet and musket-ball wounds; his gold-braided uniform and even his bloody shirt had been stripped off him by English looters. He died three days later.

Other professional soldiers from Germany also served the Revolution with considerable distinction. There was Baron von Weissenfels, who had long served in the British army and participated in Wolfe's capture of Quebec but who joined the Continental army as soon as the Revolution began. He led his regiment at White Plains, Trenton, Princeton, Monmouth and Saratoga; later was second-in-command of General Sullivan's division. Another German who brought his Prussian army training to the service of the Revolution was Heinrich Emanuel Lutterloh, who had commanded the guard of the Duke of Brunswick. Major Lutterloh was attached to General Washington's staff and in 1780 was made quartermaster general of the Continental armies.

"MY WOUNDS STINK . . ."

The man of German blood who best served his adopted country at what Washington himself said was one of its most crucial hours was a plainspoken, middle-aged upstate New York farmer named Nicholas Herkimer. A German immigrant who had prospered in the new land, Herkimer had raised militia to fight on the British side in the French and Indian War, had become the leading citizen of the Mohawk Valley and built himself a brick mansion which was the wonder of the countryside. Herkimer, however, refused to clothe himself with the lordly manner of a patroon and remained a homespun, blunt-speaking, pipe-smoking citizen-soldier, who regarded it as his duty to protect his community of German, Irish, Dutch and English settlers against the dangers which threatened them from the day they first started clearing the wilderness.

Built like a beer barrel, with black hair and vivid blue eyes, he insisted that his neighbors must prepare for the day when the American

Colonies revolted and the English would lead the Indian tribes against them again.

As leader of the Committee of Safety in Tryon County, he organized four battalions of infantry, composed mostly of Germans, in the summer of 1775. All men in the valley between the ages of sixteen and sixty were ordered to join their ranks.

The eight hundred men of his battalions, experienced in Indian-style fighting, with no nonsense about forming squares or deploying into columns, thus were ready to march and fight when the British made their decisive move in the summer of 1777. Gentleman Johnny Burgoyne launched a drive down New York State on a line from the Canadian border along the shores of Lake Champlain, down the Hudson to New York. If successful, this campaign would have cut off New England from the rest of the colonies. One prong of his advance was Colonel Barry St. Leger's forces of fourteen hundred English and Hessian soldiers and their Iroquois allies, which was ordered to collect the rich harvest of the Mohawk Valley, kill everything that moved, and then march on to join Burgoyne in Albany.

Only the American militia stood in his way, principally General Herkimer's four battalions.

Colonel St. Leger's force first appeared on the narrow plateau forming the watershed between the St. Lawrence and the Hudson, where a New York regiment was posted behind the walls of the star-shaped Fort Schuyler (now the site of Rome, New York).

Herkimer and his battalions immediately marched to the relief of Fort Schuyler, and on the night of August 5, 1777, reached Oriskany Creek a few miles from the beleaguered fort. He sent runners to the fort to arrange the firing of three signal guns, upon which the garrison would make a sortie while the battalions from the Mohawk Valley attacked the British force from the rear.

On August 6, still waiting for the signal guns from Fort Schuyler, the officers commanding Herkimer's battalions became near-mutinous in their demands that an attack be launched at once. Some charged Herkimer with being a coward, others that he was secretly a Tory like his brother (who was serving with Colonel St. Leger's forces).

53

Herkimer merely puffed on his pipe and calmly told his raging subordinates, "I am placed over you as a father and guardian, and I will not lead you into difficulties from which I may not be able to extricate you."

The rebellious battalion commanders went back to their men and obtained their support for an immediate attack. Then they presented "Old Honikol," as Herkimer was called, with the majority decision. Herkimer was forced to yield, though he believed that an incautious advance, unsupported by an attack from Fort Schuyler's garrison, might be disastrous. "If you will have it so, the blood will be upon your heads," Herkimer told his subordinates.[10]

Blood aplenty flowed as a result of the military decision taken along the lines of democratic procedure. Herkimer felt in his aging bones that a precipitous advance, unsupported by the forces inside the fort, would give Colonel St. Leger the opportunity to throw his main strength against the battalions from the Mohawk Valley. At ten o'clock on the morning of August 6 he led his column along a corduroy supply road leading toward the fort. About six miles east of Fort Schuyler the road dipped into a marshy-bottomed ravine. On the heights St. Leger, warned by his scouts of Herkimer's advance, had posted all his available forces — about four hundred Indians and a detachment of Tories.

At 11:00 A.M. most of Herkimer's column had reached the western end of the ravine while the rear guard and the baggage train were just descending the eastern slope. Herkimer hadn't had time to scout the territory through which he had to approach the fort, and his whole column was taken by surprise.

Musket balls and arrows rained down on the Americans from the high ground occupied by St. Leger and his allies. The rear guard, composed of the battalion commanded by Colonel Fischer, who had been one of the loudest in denouncing Herkimer as a coward and possible Tory, panicked and fled from the ravine, abandoning the baggage train and all the column's supplies.[11]

St. Leger's Indians broke out of the heavy brush which had served them as cover in their first assault on the American column, and attacked the Americans hand to hand. Inside that first hour of the ambush almost two hundred of Herkimer's men were killed and many of them scalped (St. Leger had posted an eight-dollar bounty on every American scalp presented to him.)

The three battalions directly under Herkimer's command did not, however, follow the example of the fleeing rear guard. Herkimer calmly ordered his men to form a circle on a knob west of the ravine, to which they retreated in good order, fighting a running battle with the Indians along the way with their long knives and musket butts. The Americans established themselves on the knob and began taking a heavy toll of the attackers. Herkimer then ordered a counterattack by Colonel Belleville's battalion which drove the Indians from the high ground overlooking the ravine.

About noontime, while riding along the ragged line established by his troops, General Herkimer was wounded by a musket ball which smashed his knee. He was carried up to the knob and placed under a beech tree. Though blood was gushing from his shattered knee, Herkimer insisted on having his saddle brought up. He sat in the saddle, lit his pipe and announced that he would continue to exercise command. During the early afternoon hours, under Herkimer's direction, every attack on their positions was repulsed. In midafternoon fighting was suspended for an hour while a heavy rainstorm beat down on the ravine. In the meantime the garrison of Fort Schuyler, having heard of the ambush of Herkimer's column, made a successful sortie from the fort and attacked the headquarters of the British force, captured five flags and seized much of its supplies. Among the booty was a large assortment of "presents" for the Indian chiefs who were fighting with the English, the loss of which later decided the Indians against continuing the campaign.

Herkimer used the interval afforded him by the rainstorm to regroup his battalions and change their tactics of defense. Despite the intense pain of his wound, he had observed that the Indians invariably watched the tree from which a shot was fired against them, then leaped forward to attack the rifleman with their tomahawks before he could reload. Herkimer ordered that two men be posted behind each tree, one to protect the other while his musket was being reloaded. When the fighting was resumed in the dripping forest, the Indians began suffering heavy casualties because of Herkimer's change of tactics. The Indians were discouraged by their losses and the fire went out of their attacks. By nightfall the Indians were so disheartened they withdrew, berated their British leaders and plundered the English officers' baggage. The battle of Oriskany was over. It was a disaster for American arms, in a sense, but the punishment they inflicted on the Indians ruined St. Leger's campaign and blunted that prong of the British advance toward Albany.[12]

"Old Honikol" was borne away on a litter when the battle ended, carried all the thirty miles back to Fort Dayton, from which his column had set out. From there he was taken to his brick mansion. A surgeon was summoned to amputate his leg above the knee.

A fellow officer called on him shortly after that crude operation was performed, and found the general sitting up in bed, smoking his pipe as usual, with his family gathered around him. It was nine days after the battle of Oriskany and Herkimer was eager for news of the campaigning. General Benedict Arnold, he was told, was hurrying toward the valley with reinforcements, and other American forces were in the field to halt Burgoyne's drive to cut the Colonies in two.

Later that day there was a hemorrhage from the incompetent surgery which had been performed on his leg, and by nightfall the news sped through the valley that "Old Honikol" was dying.

His family still grouped around him in one of those bedside tableaus which accompanied every respectable death of the time, General Herkimer called for the family Bible, and began reading aloud from the Thirty-eighth Psalm. He evidently held himself responsible for the deaths of almost half his men in battle, blaming himself for not following his own intuition and attacking before the signal guns sounded from Fort Schuyler.

"My wounds stink and are corrupt because of my foolishness . . ." he quoted the Psalmist.

Then he wearily shut the Bible, closed his eyes and sank into unconsciousness and death.

General Washington did not agree that Herkimer had failed at Oriskany, because as subsequent events showed, his stubborn stand on that sultry August day took the heart out of St. Leger's offensive, prevented a joining up of the British columns at Albany and was a principal factor in Burgoyne's surrender at Saratoga. "It was Herkimer who first reversed the gloomy scene" of the war in New York State, Washington said. "He served from love of country, not for reward. He did not want a Continental command or money."

THE HESSIANS ARE COMING!

One of the few popular successes in fictional or dramatic form dealing with the American Revolution was produced thirty-odd years ago by the Theater Guild. It was Lawrence Langner's play *The Pursuit of Happiness* and dealt with a Hessian soldier who deserted his regiment, took refuge with an American family and learned the colonial custom of "bundling" with the daughter of the household and other delights of a free country.

And that was exactly what many Hessians, as all the German soldiers involuntarily serving under the British colors were called, did the moment they found an opportunity. Hessian almost became a synonym for deserter. The muster rolls of the Hessian regiments showed that 29,875 were sold into British service in the Colonies and only 17,313 eventually returned to their various German states. Of the remaining 12,562 many lost their lives fighting under the Union Jack, but thousands, probably much more than half, simply took to their heels and settled down as peaceful citizens of the Colonies they had been sent to subdue.

One of those thousands of deserters was a man named Küster, who quickly shed his scarlet uniform and settled down to working a small farm in Pennsylvania. His descendants changed their name to Custer and moved on to more plentiful land in Michigan. One of the great-grandsons of Private Küster was Major General George Armstrong Custer, who unfortunately proved to be less light-footed than his ancestor at the battle of the Little Big Horn.

The Hessians indeed were among the unhappiest and most demoralized soldiers ever pressed into service. They had literally been sold to the

57

British government by the corrupt and spendthrift princelings who ruled their native lands. The Hessian contingents in the English expeditionary force came from six German principalities or states — 5,723 from Brunswick, 16,992 from Hesse-Kassel, 2,422 from Hesse-Hanau, 2,353 from Anspach, 1,225 from Waldeck and 1,160 from Anhalt-Zerbst. In return, as blood money, the rulers of those German provinces were estimated to have received seven million pounds sterling.[13]

Frederick the Great, as king of Prussia, was one of the few German rulers who not only refused to sell his soldiers to be used as British mercenaries but openly opposed the practice. "If that [the English] crown would give me all the millions possible," he said, "I would not furnish it two small files of my troops to serve against the Colonies." Frederick, in fact, encouraged France in its efforts to aid the American Colonies, and instructed his minister to Paris to inform the colonial commissioners: "The king desires that your generous efforts may be crowned with complete success. He will not hesitate to recognize your independence, when France, which is more directly interested in the event of this contest, shall have given the example."

Other German princes were in needier circumstances than the Prussian king, however, and paid no heed to his strictures. The Duke of Waldeck, in describing his human merchandise to the Earl of Suffolk, wrote that his regiment of six hundred was "composed of officers and soldiers who . . . did not wish for anything better than to find an occasion of sacrificing themselves for his British Majesty." The Duke, of course, did not intend to place himself anywhere near the sacrificial firing line but claimed to be speaking for his subjects. Actually, many of the Hessians who served against the Continental army were kidnaped by their rulers. Press gangs searched the streets for able-bodied recruits. If the parents of a young man pressed into service protested, the father would be sent to work in the iron mines, the mother to jail. Whatever the later enthusiasm of Germans for goose-stepping regimentation, those of the eighteenth century abhorred military service. The handbook issued to recruiting agents was an indication of how Germans struggled to evade serving in the various armies. Recruiters were instructed that the men they enlisted must be searched and disarmed, lodged in hotels with rooms specially outfitted with bars, locks and bolts, and when marched off to the nearest caserne the buttons on a recruit's trousers and his suspenders must be cut so that he would have to hold up his britches with both hands and couldn't take to his heels. If he attempted to escape, he was to be put in irons or have the thumbscrews applied. If, on being mustered in, he deserted from his training battalion, he must be forced to run the gauntlet twelve times a day, two days in succession.[14]

The Margrave of Anspach, who managed to round up 2,353 of his unfortunate subjects and sell them to the British, was a fair sample of the brutish creatures who lorded it over the minor German courts. One day he and his mistress were gazing out the window of his castle, Bruckberg, while a chimney sweep was clambering up a roof across the way. She suggested it might be fun to watch a man tumble off such a steep roof. The Margrave agreed, summoning a servant to shoot the chimney sweep off the roof. His Grace paid the widow five guldens as compensation. The Margrave was so determined that his involuntary mercenaries would reach their port of embarkation and he would be paid on the spot for every warm body delivered, that he marched his column down the roads to the seaport himself flourishing his whip like a cattle drover; up the gangplank of their ship; into the hold, where he personally assigned each man to a bunk, calling them his "children" until it was time to settle up with the British officers who had brought his sacks of gold coin.

Once their ships had disgorged the Hessians onto American soil, the German troops were a trial both to their officers and to the people living in the vicinity in which they were quartered. They were eminent chicken thieves, even worse than their English comrades — not much better off than the Germans, but at least they were fighting under their own flag — when it came to looting. Those who served under competent officers fought bravely on occasion, but for the most part the Hessians were a highly unreliable element in the British expeditionary force. First into the chow line, last into the battle line seemed to be their motto.

The Hessians seemed to regard it as their duty to disgrace their unloved uniform. They were a whole corps of Good Soldier Schweiks. One example of the Hessian nimbleness at evading duty and bilking their British masters was provided by Private Joseph Plumb Martin in his journal. Martin and his regiment momentarily occupied a British fortification at Billingsport, New Jersey, and found a drunken Hessian who had lagged behind when his comrades fled. He hardly seemed worth taking prisoner, so the Continentals left him behind when they evacuated the fort. "The British," he recounted, "took him to Philadelphia where, not being known by them, he engaged again in their service, received two or three guineas' bounty, drew a British uniform, and came back to us again at Valley Forge."[15]

Fortunately for the Hessians, the Americans as a whole understood their plight and sympathized with it. Private Martin of the Eighth Connecticut, no sentimentalist, expressed the Yankee attitude when he described an old battlefield near White Plains, on which his regiment came across "Hessian skulls as thick as bombshells. Poor fellows! They were left unburied in a foreign land. They had, perhaps, as near and dear friends to lament their sad destiny as the Americans who lay buried near them. But they should have kept at home; we should then never have gone after them to kill them in their own country. But, the reader will say, they were forced to come and be killed here, forced by their rulers who have absolute power of life and death over their subjects. Well then, reader, bless a kind Providence that has made such a distinction between your condition and theirs. And be careful, too, that you do not allow yourself ever to be brought to such an abject, servile and debased condition."

It became the policy of the Americans, approved by the Congress and by General Washington, to lure the Hessians away from service with the British forces. As Christopher Ludwig, the "honest baker" of Washington's army, expressed that policy, "Bring the captives to Philadelphia, show them our beautiful German churches, let them taste our roast beef and homes, then send them away again to their people and you will see how many will come over to us."[16]

The Continental Congress thereupon ordered General Washington not to exchange the Hessians he had captured during the Battle of Trenton. Instead wagons and provisions were provided Ludwig to take

Molly Pitcher, Our Lady of Artillery

Hessians packed off to American service

them to Bucks, Lancaster and Lebanon counties in Pennsylvania. After that guided tour of the rich Pennsylvania farmlands, many of the Hessians volunteered on the spot to serve in the American army. Many German-Americans urged Washington to form a regiment of Hessian deserters. He refused. They had won more than one battle for him, as with their mass wassail on the eve of the Battle of Trenton, and the American commander in chief did not care to risk having them perform a similar favor, under his auspices, for the British. Most of the Hessian defectors were settled with German farming families in Pennsylvania, New Jersey and Maryland, and never went back to Germany. In Frederick, Maryland, the salute signaling the end of the war for independence was fired by Hessian gunners under a former Bayreuth artillery captain. The captain also supervised the fireworks display, and former Hessian regimental musicians played for the victory ball that evening.

Among the German officers serving with the British forces there were a number of professional soldiers who performed with bravery and competence. Many of them were of the nobility and treated as equals by the British commanders; their circumstances were naturally more comfortable than those of the press-ganged men serving under them. General Wilhelm von Knyphausen led a Hessian brigade in the capture of Fort Washington early in the war and was accounted one of the more reliable German officers in British uniform (Old ties were still strong enough with Knyphausen, however, for him to order his troops not to fire upon Baron von Steuben, an old comrade of his in the Seven Years' War, if they sighted him in the enemy lines.) Another German officer highly regarded by the British was General Burgoyne's second-in-command, the stocky, aggressive Baron Friedrich Adolph von Riedesel, who commanded a force of three thousand, levied in Brunswick, during Burgoyne's ill-fated New York campaign. The Baron brought over his beautiful, high-spirited wife, their three young children and two maids to follow his brigade through the American wilderness in a comfortably appointed calash, a low-wheeled and covered carriage.

To the journal kept by the lively Baroness Riedesel, history is indebted for a feminine view of Gentleman Johnny's style of campaigning and a graphic account of the suffering caused by his blunders. General Burgoyne, she observed, did not share in that suffering. "It is very true," she wrote, "that General Burgoyne liked to make himself easy and that he spent half his nights in singing and drinking and diverting himself with his mistress . . . who was as fond of champagne as himself." The Baroness's blithe personality, along with Gentleman Johnny's champagne, evidently aided considerably in alleviating the gloom of British headquarters as it was afflicted by constant reverses. During the retreat toward Saratoga, she wrote: "The greatest misery and the utmost disorder prevailed in the army. The commissaries had forgotten to distribute provisions . . . More than thirty officers came to me who could endure hunger no longer. I had coffee and tea made . . . and divided among them all the provisions with which my carriage was constantly filled, for we had a cook who, although an arrant knave, was fruitful in all expedients, and often in the night crossed small rivers to steal from the country people sheep, poultry, and pigs. He would then charge us a high price for them . . ." During the death rattle of Burgoyne's army, the Baroness, her children and other women and children attached to Burgoyne's headquarters had to take refuge in a cellar. "Eleven cannonballs went through the house and we could plainly hear them rolling overhead . . . Many persons, who had no right to come in, threw themselves against the cellar door. My children were already under the cellar steps and we would all have been crushed if God had not given me strength to place myself before the door and with extended arms prevent all from coming in . . ."[17]

There was a fairly happy ending for the Baroness and her family. They surrendered themselves to the hospitality of the American Revolution and were made comfortable by Thomas Jefferson, among their other hosts, whom they delighted with chamber music produced by a string quartet of retired German warriors.

THE FINISH AT YORKTOWN

In the later phases of the Revolution, both Peter Muhlenberg and Baron von Steuben, separately and together, added considerably to the

63

credit balance of German-Americans as citizens and soldiers. The two great German-American heroes of the Revolution served together in the Tidewater campaign of 1781, with Steuben as a divisional commander charged with the advance on the fortified city of Portsmouth and Muhlenberg commanding the troops of the Virginia Line under him.

General Washington invested that campaign with his highest hopes — not so much because of the strategic value of Portsmouth but because the arch-traitor, General Benedict Arnold, was now commanding the British forces defending that city. It was hoped that Arnold could be captured alive and, as Washington directed in a rare display of passion, executed "in the most summary way."

The plan designed to bring about Revolutionary vengeance upon Benedict Arnold was drawn up by Steuben, who made his headquarters in Richmond, and was to be executed by Brigadier General Muhlenberg with two infantry regiments and a legion of cavalry. The problem that confronted them was the fact that Muhlenberg's attacking forces were far weaker than General Arnold's defenders, though they should have been much stronger. To equalize the situation, it was proposed that a French fleet under Admiral de Tilley attack the fortifications of Portsmouth from the water side.

The naval attack was essential to the success of Steuben's plan, but Admiral de Tilley had his own ideas of how he should operate in the treacherous waters of the Elizabeth River, which flows between the cities of Norfolk and Portsmouth. On his first sortie up the river, the French admiral managed to capture a British frigate and was so pleased with himself that he withdrew. On the second attack, timed with Muhlenberg's advance against the land fortifications, Admiral de Tilley withdrew just as Muhlenberg's advance began, complaining that the water was too shallow for his ships to maneuver. Benedict Arnold was thus allowed to survive the Revolution and sail off to England afterwards as a guest of his benefactors.

Both Muhlenberg and Steuben were prominent in the siege of Yorktown, where Germans fought in the three armies involved in that climactic event of the Revolution. Hessians in British uniform, other Germans among the American divisions, and hundreds of German auxiliaries in the French Count de Rochambeau's corps. German oaths and battle cries filled the air on both sides of the fortifications behind which Cornwallis sheltered himself at Yorktown.

Brigadier Muhlenberg led one of the storming parties which reduced the British redoubts one by one until Cornwallis was left with his back to the York River.

Steuben and his division were flanked by French forces which contended with him for the honor of finally subduing the British defenders. While he was sapping and storming his way through the inner defenses of the British position, the Count Deux Ponts offered to support his attack. Steuben rejected the offer, and in the presence of General Anthony Wayne somewhat exaggerated the strength of his troops. After the French general left his headquarters, Wayne asked Steuben why he had done so.

"If I was guilty of a certain amount of gasconade," replied Steuben, "it was for the honor of your country."

General Wayne turned to his own officers and said, "Now, gentlemen, it is our duty to make good the exaggeration of Baron Steuben and to support him just as if he had double the number of troops that he has."

When Cornwallis surrendered on October 19, 1781, Steuben himself planted one of his regimental standards on the rampart of the British fort opposite his position. Two hours later he and Brigadier Muhlenberg were prominent among Washington's generals as they witnessed the ceremony of surrender. Both were well rewarded, Steuben with his spreading acres, Muhlenberg with two terms as senator from Pennsylvania in the First and Third Congresses, later with the posts of superintendent of the Internal Revenue and collector of the port of Philadelphia. A further reward, perhaps, was the knowledge that their accomplishments as soldiers speeded the process of acceptance for all Germans coming to America.

In the triumphant aftermath of the American Revolution Peter Muhlenberg was to perform another, though more oblique, service to the new republic. Contrary to pious legend, General Washington was not averse to having his Presidency garnished with a certain amount of transatlantic pomp and ceremony. He rejected the idea of a kingly crown being pressed upon his republican brow, but encouraged talk of a resounding title to be added to those of General and President. Even John Adams believed that "chamberlains, aides-de-camp, secretaries, masters of ceremony, etc.," would be necessary to impress of the people with the dignity of the Presidency, and Chief Justice McKean of the United States Supreme Court solemnly proposed at a New York dinner table, shortly before the opening of Congress in 1789, that Washington should be addressed as "His Serene Highness the President of the United States."

Washington himself decided that it might be appropriate to be styled "High Mightiness," the title used by the Stadtholder of Holland.

That idea was ruined by Peter Muhlenberg one evening when he dined with Washington and spoke with the jesting familiarity of an old fox-hunting companion. "Among the guests," it was recorded, "was Mr. Wynkoop of Pennsylvania, who was noticeable for his large and commanding figure. The resolutions before the two houses being referred to, the President, in his usual dignified manner, said, 'Well, General Muhlenberg, what do you think of the title of High Mightiness?"

Muhlenberg laughed and replied, "Why, General, if we were certain that the office would always be held by men as large as yourself or my friend Wynkoop, it would be appropriate enough, but if by chance a president as small as my opposite neighbor should be elected, it would become ridiculous."[18]

Washington and all of his successors, thanks to Peter Muhlenberg, have had to be content with the title "Mr. President."

3. DREAMS OF A GERMANIA-IN-AMERICA

The Germans live scattered and apart, as a spring, a hill or a wood entices them.

— TACITUS, *Germania*

THE URGE FOR SEPARATISM

With the end of the wars of liberation from the Napoleonic system, German migration to the United States began increasing from the comparative trickle of the eighteenth century — a quarter of a million up to the American Revolution — to the floodtide of the nineteenth. And with that came the first wispy elements of a dream: the concept of a transplanted Germany. Why shouldn't there be a Germania in North America? There had been such successful colonizations as those bearing the proud titles of a New Spain, a New England, a New Netherlands, a New Sweden and a Nova Scotia in the new world.

Until the nineteenth century, Germany was "only a geographical expression," like Italy, and its disunited states did not possess the resources or the political energy to join the race for colonies. The war against Napoleon had provided the Germans with a new national consciousness, particularly among the students and educated people, the type which on migrating became known to their scornful landsmen already on the scene as "Latin farmers," men who could quote from the Latin but couldn't plow a straight furrow.

They formed part of a second wave of migration, the first having been composed mostly of dispossessed peasants and other uneducated people who had to sell themselves into bondage to obtain their passage to America. They were drawn, rather than driven to, America by a romantic hope, an illusion of America as a New Eden more compelling than that which beset any other country. By 1830 James Fenimore Cooper's *Leatherstocking Tales* had been translated, published and widely read in Germany. It was the beginning of a love affair with an idealized and romanticized America which never existed — with all its Noble Savages and unending bounty of field and forest — but which long endured in the German conscience; somewhat later it would produce the enormously successful "western" novels of Karl May and his heroic Old Shatterhand, who fought side by side with the Indians. Those who were enchanted by Cooper's version of life in a country open and free — appealing as it was to those living in an overpopulated region so regimented socially that no man could hope to rise above the station to which he was born — turned to more factual writers for confirmation, and they found it. There was no disillusionment for those fascinated by Natty Bumpo in the reportage of Gottfried Duden, who went over to investigate the wonders of the New World, lived on a Missouri farm for three years, and returned to Germany in 1829 to write of his experiences first in the periodicals, then in a volume of his collected reminiscences.

Duden wrote glowingly of his everyday experiences on the Middle Western farm. One article would relate the hard but rewarding labor of clearing a patch of forest — that there was virgin soil, not that which had been worked for centuries, was enthralling in itself to Germans — and another would tell of bringing in the bountiful harvest. Others dwelled almost poetically on the forests which enclosed every farm, appealing strongly to the atavistic tree worship of his countrymen, and on the rivers flowing through the wilderness, the majesty of western sunsets and the overwhelming effulgence of moonlight, but little mention of hard winters or spring floods or steaming summers. He also remarked frequently on the absence of overbearing princes and clergymen, strutting soldiers and ruthless tax collectors (a farm large enough to keep eight horses was taxed only twelve dollars annually), but passed over the crudity of frontier manners and the frequent brutality of the frontiersmen.

The message conveyed by Duden in his enormously popular volume was passed along by the reading clubs which had sprung up in most German villages. They were usually sponsored by the local pastor and met in the village inn or a schoolroom. At each meeting parts of a book or a magazine were read, then freely discussed. The readings were usually from a book or magazine article about conditions in America and the problems of getting there. America, for most of the early decades of the nineteenth century, was a fever in the German blood.

Villagers and farmers who were lucky to have meat on the table once a week listened with watering mouths to Duden's descriptions of bountiful America.

"As long as the settler does not have sufficient meat from the domestic animals," he wrote in his book about farming in Missouri, "the hunting grounds keep him in provisions. Flesh of the domestic animals is, to be sure, not dear here; a pound of ox flesh costs only 1½ cents, and pork, 2 cents. But there are so many deer, stag, turkeys, hens, pigeons, pheasants, snipes and other game that a good hunter without much exertion provides for the needs of a large family. Throughout the whole United States, hunting and fishing are entirely free, and in the unenclosed spaces anyone can hunt when and how he pleases, small as well as large game, with dogs, slings, nets and rifles.

"There are two varieties of deer here in Missouri, and they are for the most part very fat. The meat is savory, but the hunter rarely takes the whole animal with him. He is satisfied with the hind quarters and the skin, and hangs the rest of the animal on a tree so that someone else can take home a roast if he pleases. Wild turkeys are found in droves of twenty to fifty. They are especially fat toward Christmas. I have my neighbor deliver some to me every week for soups, for I am not a good hunter. These turkeys must weigh at least 15 pounds or the hunter would not even take them home with him . . ."

In addition, the "best European garden vegetables" could be grown with little effort, and brandy could be made from peaches or apples, or bought from a neighbor. "I have bought old corn brandy" — presumably Duden was referring to a distillation later known as bourbon — "at 30 cents a gallon, which came up to the best French brandy." Once the migrant farmer had cleared his farm and built his house, Duden said, "the whole family lives carefree and happily without a single piece of ready money . . . For taxes alone is ready money needed." Soon enough, the farmer could become a planter, an aristocrat, through the purchase of Negro slaves. "If the planter has two slaves, he can confine himself entirely to duties of inspection without laying his own hand to anything; and the housewife will have just as little to complain of in the work of the household."[1]

Not surprisingly, Duden's *Hericht über eine Reise nach den westlichen Staaten Nordamerikas und einen mehrjährigen Aufenthalt am Missouri* was reprinted three times and its message reached the remotest corners of Germany. His work made America the "political Utopia of young Germany," as T. S. Baker has written. "It was Duden who, in a time of universal discontent and uncertainty, directed the attention of the German masses to the Western parts of the American Union." The pastoral beauty and bounty of America, as he described it, made the New World "all the more attractive to the minds of his readers," Baker remarked, "and when it is remembered that Duden was supposed to be a thoroughly trustworthy man — a man who had enjoyed a university education, had served creditably in the army, and had occupied important positions in the Prussian civil service — the attention which his utterances attracted does not seem strange."[2]

Nor did it seem strange that migrants who found to their dismay that Duden had not also described the hardships of pioneering were soon calling him "Duden der Lügenhund."

Aside from the material benefits which Germans expected to find in America, many were motivated by a desire to live in an atmosphere of intellectual and political freedom. By 1830 the young German intel-

lectuals and libertarians saw that their hopes for constitutional government were not likely to be met. Although hounded by the Prussian
secret police, they founded the Giessen Society as part of the *Burschenschaften* movement. If the promise of democracy would not be
met in Germany itself, its seeds could be transplanted to America. But
the leaders of the Giessen Society also wanted to make sure that such
seeds would be nurtured in a German atmosphere, if on American soil.
Educated Germans did not want to see their people totally assimilated
by the Anglo-Saxons.

German liberalism, it is evident, was darkly tinged by nationalism.
Gustav Koerner, a young German intellectual who migrated to Illinois
and became lieutenant governor of the state, did not join the Giessen
Society but for a time he approved of its objectives. "It is well known
that recently, in Germany," he wrote in 1834, "a number of gallant men
conceived the idea of emigrating in a body to a certain point in the
United States, and of there founding a new state, in which preferably
German customs, and laws corresponding to these customs, should be
established and protected."[3]

It was also evident that the illiterate German peasants who scraped
together their last pfennigs to transport themselves and their families
were more willing to Americanize themselves than the educated Germans. All the lowborn Germans asked was a chance to make a living,
eventually to own their own land. They did not partake of that
Teutonic intellectual arrogance, so certain that its concept of how a
Germanic democracy should function on free soil was superior to any
system formed by and fought for by native Americans, which insisted
upon its right to be transferred intact to the American hinterland. Nor
would they have been inclined to follow the dictates of one of the
Giessen Society's leaders, when he proclaimed, with a lack of humility
ill-suited to any migrant, that "we ought not to depart from here [Ger-
many] without first giving expression to a national idea. The foundations of a new and free Germany in the great North American republic
can be laid by us, so we must take as many as possible of the most
worthy of our countrymen, and at the same time make the necessary
arrangements to ensure that each year a considerable group shall follow

71

us. Thus we may, in at least one of the American territories, create a state that is German from its foundations up, in which all those to whom in the future the situation here at home may seem, as it does to us now, intolerable, can find refuge, and which we may develop to be the model state for the whole commonwealth of man."

The man who so confidently proposed to establish a model German state in the midst of the United States of America was Paul Follen, who with his brother Carl and Friedrich Muench were founders of the Giessen Society. Of the three only Muench seemed to have sustained his vision of a Teutonic America. Paul Follen died of a fever in Missouri a dozen years after migrating, and his brother Carl took up a more congenial occupation as professor of German literature at Harvard.

Not all of Germany's rebellious intellectuals were committed to the idea of a separate German state in the New World. The credentials of Francis Lieber, a Prussian, were as impeccable as any of those in the Giessen Society. His career as a rebel was almost incredibly precocious: at fifteen he served in the Prussian army against Napoleon, a year later he was imprisoned in Berlin for writing songs hymning the universal longings for political liberty. At twenty-one, with something more than a Byronic gesture, he threw himself into Greece's fight for independence from Ottoman Turkey. Two years later he was again imprisoned by the Berlin police for advocating libertarian ideas. By 1827 he was convinced that one man could do little to bring about democracy in Germany, and took himself to America, eventually becoming an illustrious member of the Columbia University faculty. To Lieber all schemes for German separatism on American soil were dangerous nonsense. They would end in failure, and worse yet would alienate Germans from their fellow Americans. Even if Germans outnumbered the Anglo-Saxon majority eventually, as the Giessen Society apparently hoped to bring about, they had no business implanting any special Germanic influence on this soil.

Undoubtedly he and others who saw no moral or practical benefits in resisting assimilation were particularly alarmed when the "New Germany" propaganda, largely an issuance of the Giessen Society, began infecting considerable numbers of German-Americans who should have known better, many of them second- or third-generation Americans.

A nation less airily tolerant of dissent, or one less conditioned by the diversity of peoples who came to its shores, might have considered some of their utterances as bordering on sedition. At a meeting of the new German Society of Philadelphia in 1836 the members were told that by arranging a "partial isolation" for themselves they could "enjoy both the advantages of America and the pleasures of the Fatherland." One member got up and proclaimed that they must work toward creating a "New Germany" in the United States, which would provide "a secure refuge for ourselves, our children and our descendants" and in which "our families may pursue their social existence more quietly and more independently than we here have been accustomed to do." The president of the society then rose to declare that the "exalted task" of his group must be to organize "A union of the Germans in North America, and as a result the foundation of a New German Fatherland."[4]

None of the stout, bearded gentlemen addressed themselves to the problem of what their fellow Americans would think of such a movement. Undoubtedly they were counting on the notorious political lethargy of the Anglo-Saxon majority. America was so vast and unoccupied that other nationalities couldn't reasonably object to the chipping off a few Teutonic bits and pieces.

Nor did the German-Americans influenced by the idea of a "New Germany" ask themselves just what they found so distasteful about America. They didn't have to, they'd been grumbling about it in unison for years. First of all, they objected to the English language. Even so sainted a figure as Pastor Muhlenberg, with all the political honors which had accrued to his family, confessed that he resisted as long as possible and with all his energy the idea of conducting any church services in English. But they had other, less easily defined complaints. Principally there was a feeling among urban and educated German-Americans that they possessed a superior culture, that their grave appreciation of music and philosophical discussion was shared in only the slightest degree by their non-German neighbors. They regarded themselves as guardians of a cultural heritage which might be destroyed in the raw inclemency of the New World. The only way they could preserve their *Kultur*, as they saw it, was to remove it to a "partial

73

isolation" from American preoccupation with material pursuits. And they would live not only in geographical separation from the mainstream, but would, if they could, have it hedged by political guarantees.

Even among the less *Kultur*-conscious German working and farming classes, though they were not bedazzled by visions of a separate life, there was dissatisfaction with one facet of American ways: the dominance of the Puritan ethic. The Germans were straightlaced about many things, particularly sexual morality, but they resented the imposition of the Puritan observance of the Sabbath. Germans believed that the day of rest should be taken literally, and that they should be allowed to drink their beer, congregate in beer and wine gardens with their families, and enjoy their one day of leisure in unbuttoned if not unlimited joviality. In this they made common cause with the Irish, whose Catholic view of Sunday was very similar. Eventually they were successful in wearing down the strict observance of Sunday, and in New York City, as elsewhere, were largely responsible for turning out reform administrations intent on enforcing the blue laws. "To the influence of the German immigrants in particular," as John F. Kennedy wrote in his *A Nation of Immigrants*, "we owe the mellowing of the austere Puritan imprint on our daily lives. The Germans clung to their concept of the 'Continental Sunday' as a day . . . of relaxation, of picnics, of visiting, of quiet drinking in beer gardens while listening to the music of a band."

The ideologues of German separatism, however, had something more serious and potentially hazardous in mind than the public consumption of beer, wurst and brass-band music on Sunday. In 1835, enthused by their proclamations, various German groups began organizing to unite all of their nationality to formulate plans for a separate commonwealth and for preserving German cultural ideals. A "German convention" was held in Pittsburgh on October 18, 1837, at which delegates were urged to find ways to "maintain the German language, to sustain the German press, to establish a central normal school for the education of German teachers, and to protest and counteract the efforts of nativistic American societies." Similar conventions were held annually for the next five years, despite a protest before one of the conclaves by Gustav Koerner, who had now grown very cool to the separatist movement and who held that, "no number of persons emigrated from foreign soil should form a separate commonwealth among people already settled and not inferior in culture . . . such an attempt on the part of the German immigrants would, just on account of their numbers, be injurious to the welfare and the permanence of this free country, which alone among all other states, offers by its liberal institutions a consolidation to every right-thinking man."

Koerner was not generally heeded, however, and the effort to establish German states within the United States was vigorously promoted. So alarming did this tendency become that a dozen years later, at the convention to revise the state constitution of Kentucky, a congressman named Garrett Davis delivered a long speech demanding greater restrictions on immigration, particularly from Germany. "Look at the myriads who are perpetually pouring into the northwestern states from the German hives — making large and exclusive settlements for themselves, which in a few years will number their thousands and tens of thousands, living in isolation; speaking a strange language, having alien manners, habits, opinions, and religious faiths, and a total ignorance of our political institutions; all handed down with German phlegm and inflexibility to their children through generations. In less than fifty years, northern Illinois, parts of Ohio, and Michigan, Wisconsin, Iowa and Minnesota will be literally possessed by them; they will number millions and millions, and they will be essentially a distinct people, a nation within a nation, a new Germany . . .

"We can't keep these people wholly out, and ought not if we could; but we are getting more than our share of them. I wish they would turn their direction to South America, quite as good a portion of the world as our share of the hemisphere. They could there aid in bringing up the slothful and degenerate Spanish race; here their deplorable office is to pull us down. . . . In a few years, as a distinctive race, the Anglo-Americans will be as much lost to the world and its future history as the lost tribes of Israel . . . Let us withdraw from the newcomers the premium of political sovereignty. These strangers have neither the right nor the competency to govern the native-born people, nor ought they to be allowed the power to misgovern them. . . .

"This truly foreign power nestled in the bosom of our country may, in its arch and crooked policy, occasionally act with one or another of the parties that spring up inherent in this republic. But it has its own paramount ends to circumvent; and when it seems to ally itself to any party, it is only a ruse; and the true motive is the belief that it helps on to the consummation of these ends . . ."[5]

The Kentuckian's concern over the political power being exercised by Germans, often in "bloc" voting, probably arose from their general opposition to the Whig party. The Whigs contained most of the "nativist" politicians — many of them later to become Know-Nothings — who deplored the influx of German and Irish immigrants. Naturally enough, the Germans as well as the Irish voted Democratic. It was estimated by Gustav Koerner that three-quarters of the German-American population usually gave their votes to the Democrats, up to the middle 1850's and the formation of the Republican party.[6] They were especially enthusiastic about Andrew Jackson and his crusade against the "money power," and Whig politicians were alarmed by the sight of German youths, formed into military companies, marching on the streets of New York, Baltimore, Philadelphia, Pittsburgh and Cincinnati and carrying the banners of the Democratic party. Around 1840 the Whigs made a determined appeal to the German-American vote and largely by the attraction of Henry Clay succeeded in winning many of them over temporarily. But Whiggery again lost much of its appeal when Clay tactlessly remarked, "The only thing I do not like about the Germans is their politics," by which he presumably meant their habit of voting as a bloc and thereby increasing their influence out of proportion to their numbers. The Democrats, on the other hand, from Jackson on down, curried favor with the Germans and credited them with Democratic victories in state and national elections.

With such encouragement from one of the two major political parties, the "New Germany" advocates were quite bold in pressing their claims for a certain amount of autonomy within the American system. Dr. Ernest Ludwig Brauns, in a book published in 1829 which urged the extension of German-speaking in America, declared as "praiseworthy" the Pennsylvania custom of translating all the legislation passed in that state into German every year at the end of a legislative session. He was quite belligerent, as became a professional holy man, in reciting the fact that German had been spoken in America for almost a century and "we shall probably never see it disappear and give way to English, though many a pseudo-German minister and many a rich Anglo-maniac ardently wishes this to happen." He especially deplored the fact that "some Germans who had become rich thought that they were superior to their less wealthy associates, and their children began to be ashamed of the German language, and to regard it as the language of the rabble."

Dr. Brauns was outraged by the activities of Germans who had intermarried with the Irish and thus became enemies of the German language. "And as for the Irish-Germans, who dislike everything German and who wish to attend an English church service, why do they not visit one of the numerous places where church services are held in English — places which are only too common in America in the cities and country districts? The answer is easily found. They want to take the churches which are richly endowed from the Germans who built them and they wish to reap the harvest which the Germans have sown." Efforts at compromise by having alternate services in English were, Dr. Brauns charged, "presumptuous and Jesuitical as well as unfair. By such insidious means the Irish-Germans try to smuggle the English language into the German churches. But beware if once it gets a foothold!"[7]

German exclusiveness was also advocated in a widely read book published by Franz Lohrer, who insisted that "Germans can remain German in America; they will mingle and intermarry with non-Germans, but they can still remain essentially German. They can plant the vine on the hills and drink its wine with happy song and dance, they can have German schools and universities, German literature and art, German science and philosophy, German courts and assemblies — in short, they can form a German state in which the German language is as much the popular and official language as the English is now, and in which the German spirit rules."[8]

The flaw in all such German theorizing was a characteristic first noted centuries before by Tacitus, the Roman historian, when he remarked on the tendency of the German barbarians to "live scattered and apart." Friedrich Muench, one of the Giessen Society founders, lamented in 1870 that the Germans' failure to concentrate in one or two states of the Union had cost them the opportunity to establish a separate German republic or two in the years before the United States consolidated their hold on the West and Southwest. If the Germans had not failed to concentrate, Muench wrote, "the future predominance of German characteristics would be assured . . ."

Francis Lieber, who arrived in America as a political refugee with little but his honorable wounds from the Napoleonic war and his honorable police record in Berlin, also remarked on the German tendency to scatter, to isolate themselves from other Germans as well as other human beings. "The German, as I said, pushes on; if he has not the means to proceed immediately to the west, and must take his temporary abode in a large place, it is only to save, as soon as he possibly can, the requisite sum to carry him and his family to those parts of the Union where the land is cheap and fertile," he wrote in his memoir. Lieber was convinced that they would "mingle with the Anglo-American race" and ignore the nationalistic appeals of the false prophets. The idea of a "whole German state in our west," Lieber declared in 1835, was ridiculous. " 'Ossification,' as the Germans call it, would be the unavoidable consequence . . . everything would remain stationary at the point where it was when they brought it [German culture] over from the mother country, and within less than fifty years our colony would degenerate into an antiquated, ill-adapted element of our great national system, with which, sooner of later, it must assimilate . . ."

German-Americans would be valuable to the United States "only if they mix," Lieber declared, adding the warning that "twisting of facts, and stating or being silent according to convenience, is an unmanly thing — unworthy of a lover of his species . . . It is painful indeed for a German that his descendants in this country . . . have not only done less for the common education of their offspring than their neighbors, but have often frustrated the endeavors of the government to establish a system of general education. How a scion of a people who have done more for education than any other on earth comes thus to neglect one of the most sacred duties would be inexplicable, were it not for the fact . . . that it is difficult for a community, severed from the mother country, and severed from a surrounding population by the barrier of a different language, to prevent mental stagnation."

The calm, reasoning voices of men like Francis Lieber and Gustav Koerner were, in the long run, more influential than the clamor of the "New Germany" prophets. Amalgamation was the one inexorable principle of the American system; it would tolerate almost anything except secession, whether by national groups or political movements, and it would prevail even against the strongest impulses of German yearnings for exclusivity. The tragicomedy of German separatism, however, had its brief run on the historical stage.

THE LATIN FARMERS

Few of the physical traces of the German enclaves remain intact after the leveling, building and rebuilding processes which characterize the American landscape. There is still visible the determined quaintness of the Pennsylvania Dutch, but little is left of the German attempts at colonizing sections of the Middle West. Time has wiped out, for the most part, the distinctive features of the German migration to the Missouri Valley and large sections of north and central Missouri and southern Illinois.

One enduring reminder, however, is the small neat city of Belleville, Illinois, across the river from St. Louis. Well into this century it was called "Little Germany." Its streets are lined with small brick houses, built close to the sidewalks without porches or lawns in the old German fashion, much resembling the row houses of Baltimore and Philadelphia. A Teutonic sense of order, of neatness and precision, still prevails, even under the blanket of smog from the industrial environs of St. Louis.

The eminent English social historian, Professor John A. Hawgood, whose penetrating study *The Tragedy of German America* is a landmark in its field, enhanced but never superseded by the work of others, was fascinated by the Belleville area, which he visited in 1929. By then

German influence had all but disappeared from the region. "The German stock of Belleville was said to have no further connections with German culture, and immigrants from Germany arriving in recent years had little or nothing in common with them and did not appear to fit into the community." Less than a century earlier Belleville had been almost completely a Germanic city, with a German mayor and a majority on the city council and three of its five newspapers published in German. So pervasive was the Teutonic influence that even many of the local Negroes spoke German. This influence lingered to the end of the century, by which time "no German was spoken in the homes of the descendants of German immigrants any longer, nor was the growing generation even learning German," as Hawgood learned.

For contrast, there was the still robustly German community of Hermann across the river in Gasconade County, Missouri, where in 1929 the "older inhabitants of the town," Hawgood noted, "naturally spoke German together." Much of the energy of the residents was focused on defying the Prohibition laws, which German-Americans particularly resented as a surviving testimonial to the Puritan influence on their fellow Americans. "The vineyards had disappeared," Hawgood said, "though their site was still kept clear for 'better days.' The local distillery had developed in its cellars a mushroom-forcing industry of impressive proportions, the *Hermanner Pilz* being in great demand and being unequivocally said to possess a flavour 'all its own.'" The special flavor of Hermann's mushrooms, it seemed, owed much to the secret brewing, winemaking and whiskey-distilling operations being carried on by the residents. "True to their traditions, the stalwart Germans of Hermann continued to show their opinion of Prohibition by leading the visitor to the toolshed or cellar directly introductions had been made, for a strictly private and illegal *Wein-*, *Schnapps-*, or *Bier-probe*, in some cases all three!"

Both Belleville, Illinois, and Hermann, Missouri, had been settled largely by migrants who had been members of the Giessen Society or other German students' political fraternities (the *Burschenschaften*). With Muench and the Follen brothers as their leaders, they landed in New Orleans and took the riverboats up to St. Louis, from which they fanned out through the Missouri Valley in search of farmlands. Some followed Muench and Follen to Warren County, where the inspiration for their colonization, Gottfried Duden, had lived. Among them were counts and barons, scholars, preachers, former army officers, gentlemen with no aptitude except for gentle living. Only a few were practical farmers. Those who prospered quickly were among the latter, and they were smart enough to settle on the good land, such as that around the township of Hermann. By 1855, Franz Loher, the literary advocate of the "New Germany," made a tour of inspection which included Hermann, where the purity of German life in that Missouri enclave aroused his enthusiasm. Hermann, he wrote, was "a collection of lovely little houses and gardens, of vine-clad hills and neat farms . . . Here is to be found a most inviting countryside, in which exists more German sociability than perhaps anywhere else in America." He took pride in the fact that "their Anglo-American neighbors are being bought out, thanks to the Germans, who give them dollars for their improved land, and they then proceed deeper into the backwoods to clear new ground."[9]

Obviously the community of Hermann might have served as a pilot-model for the "New Germany" which Loher and other intellectuals hoped would spring up in the parts of Missouri settled by the Giessen Society and others of the same persuasion. The trouble was, few of them had the capability for pioneer farming showed by the more or less uneducated people who settled around Hermann. One historian of the Giessen migration, most of whose members had been carefully selected by Follen and Muench for their idealism and intellect but not their practical knowledge of farming, believed that their hopes of succeeding as colonists — not to mention their high-flown theories of founding a "New Germany" — were doomed from the start. He wrote:

"They had wielded the pen, but had never handled the hoe; they had stood in the pulpit but never behind a plow; they had lectured from the catnedra and pleaded in court, but had never driven an ox-team. They were but little prepared for the hardships that were in store for them."[10]

The "New Germany" plan for northern Missouri and southern Illinois foundered on ironic circumstance: those who were most enthusiastic about it failed as pioneers, while those who simply came along for the ride, and cared little about cultish vaporings, went to work and prospered. Follen himself clung vainly to his ideals until his early death, but Muench quietly abandoned them, fell in with the individualistic ways of his Anglo-American neighbors and by 1848, he wrote, "we and our families had taken deep root in the life of the new world."

Other "Latin farmers" simply bogged down in their frustration. They had come to America in pursuit of an ideal, the vain hope for a "new Fatherland," and could not reconcile themselves to making a new life minus the dreams they had nurtured in students' beer halls in the old country. "The plain farmers," Albert B. Faust recorded, "prospered almost without exception, but the others constantly went backward. When they had completely exhausted their means of support, they would go to ruin utterly, or begin life anew with the determination to labor and succeed." In tracing the later careers of the educated migrants, Faust discovered that "many committed suicide, some died as beggars on the street; the latter was the experience of a Hanoverian count . . ."[11]

Gustav Koerner visited the German settlements of Missouri in 1834 and decided that that state was a poor choice for German immigration. In the first place, there was no good public land left along the Missouri River, and secondly, the Germans, who for the most part refused to keep slaves, were greatly handicapped by their antislavery attitudes, since the Negroes were the only source of cheap labor and the Anglo-Americans had the advantage of possessing no such scruples. Timber was also scarce in that region, he noted. Furthermore, the prospects of the professional men in the Giessen migration were rather dim if they hoped to give up farming and return to the law, medicine, the pulpit or the classroom. In 1833, he observed, so many had abandoned their farms and tried to take up their old professional careers in St. Louis that the city was oversupplied. By that time St. Louis, with a population of less than ten thousand, had more than sixty doctors, far too many lawyers looking for a retainer while trying to master the English language and the American judicial system, and an overstock of teachers, astronomers, theologians, mathematicians, philosophers, Latin scholars and literary gentlemen. All in all, Koerner wrote in his *Memoirs*, the German coming to America had best subdue his culture-consciousness. "He who leaves Europe permanently," he warned, "must bid farewell to all museums, galleries, Gothic monuments, gardens and theaters, which have perhaps given him so much many-sided enjoyment, and must console himself with the thought that he must forever content himself with substitutes for these, with the green of thick forests and the flowering of the wide prairies."

The clash of cultures was evident in his account of how he and several friends made their stylish arrival in Belleville to settle on a nearby farm. Their small caravan halted in front of the Virginia House in midafternoon. "When we alighted a tall, lean, white-haired man, as straight as a pole, showed us into a small room . . . It was Major Doyle, a Virginian, who had evidently seen better days . . . After we had washed we bethought ourselves of having something to eat. I asked the Major very innocently for some lunch. 'Sir,' he said to me, 'supper will be ready at six o'clock. We have nothing in the house to eat between meals.' Mr. Engelmann grew somewhat angry. 'What — is this a tavern and we can get no kind of refreshment? You ought to take down the sign from your house.' While we were discussing the matter, Mrs. Doyle, a small round but very kindly looking lady, entered the room. Finding out what was going on, she remarked, looking up at the Major in a sort of beseeching way, that she could make us a cup of coffee. Of course, we accepted her offer. In the meantime, however, Mr. Engelmann thought it right to order a bottle of wine. The Major looked still more astonished. 'We keep no liquors in this house.' Mr. Engelmann now grew quite excited; for that in a tavern a man could get nothing to drink appeared to him the height of absurdity, the more so as the landlord bore the evident marks of being a hard drinker." The matter was straightened out when Koerner stepped across the way and bought a bottle of St. Julien for seventy-five cents. Once they understood each others' differing customs, the German newcomers found the Americans "all very kind and accommodating."[12]

It developed that many woolly-minded theorists among the Giessen migration and others, who were quicker with a Latin tag than learning how to pull stumps or drain bottomlands, survived mainly by raising a crop of sturdy sons and seeing that they kept *their* noses out of books. Herr Professor David Goebel of Coburg eked out a living in Washington County by teaching mathematics and going to St. Louis to lecture on astronomy, but his son Gert became a successful farmer, hunter and surveyor. For the Latin farmers it was a sort of reverse inheritance. German obsession with *Kultur* died out, of necessity, but the second generation replaced it with a fixation on hard work and success. The learned German father was a figure worthy of respect, but not of emulation.

In addition to the colonization attempts of the German intellectuals in Missouri, there was a similar but more practical scheme launched by the Philadelphia Society. The Pennsylvania Germans also proposed, in the mid-1830's, to establish a New Germany somewhere in the West. At first Texas was considered, but she had just won her independence (in 1836) and was regarded as too unsettled politically; then various sites in Wisconsin, Michigan, Illinois and Indiana — and even the Mexican state of Tamulipas — were surveyed but also found wanting for various reasons. The Philadelphia Society finally settled on Gasconade County, Missouri, where it bought large tracts of land. The society opened branch offices in various American and Canadian cities and advertised in German newspapers, offering its land to German-American, German-Canadian and native German migrants at very low rates. Hundreds of Germans were thus settled in the townships around Hermann, most of them with practical experience of farming. As an experiment in settling new land, the Philadelphia Society's plan worked well, but its underlying motive of founding a "New Germany" on Missouri soil was frustrated.

If the Giesseners were too impractical for such a scheme, the migrants forwarded by the Philadelphia Society were just the opposite. They were too hardheaded, too interested in their material well-being to care much about whether they lived in a New Germany or an Old Missouri. Furthermore they were alienated by what they claimed was a patronizing and arrogant attitude on the part of the society's headquarters. The society attempted a sort of remote control of the Gasconade County colony, and it didn't work. Finally all connections between the Philadelphia headquarters and the colony itself were severed with recriminations all around. The society itself was dissolved in 1840.

Individually, rather than as pan-German forerunners, the people who colonized parts of Missouri and southern Illinois prospered and sent down deep roots. They were lucky in that most of the malarial river bottoms and fever-ridden swamplands, which were the most fertile, had already been occupied by Anglo-American settlers, who became enervated by their agues and fevers and were accounted as "shiftless." The Germans settled on the prairies and the higher, less fertile but healthier ground and were wrongly credited, perhaps, with a greater industriousness simply because they weren't debilitated by annual bouts of parasitical disease. Their great handicap, as pioneers, was a lingering love of learning. Gustave Koerner recalled how, during a winter he spent on a farm at Turkey Hill near Belleville, he and his host tore down the rail fences to build up their fire so that it was bright enough to read by.

The "New Germany" idea in the Middle West was frittered away in just that spirit of impracticality. Its proponents had chosen the wrong locations for their experiment. "Unlike the Mormons in Utah," as Hawgood had written (the Mormons of course having been driven to that remote place), "they did not anywhere settle in an empty and undeveloped country, remote from all other settlements, where their geographical and political exclusiveness would stand a chance of being maintained long enough to have the desired results. Rather did they choose regions already partly settled, and their hope of obliterating all signs of the earlier settlers by the overwhelming size of the German settlement was defeated by the fact that the lands they chose . . . were among the richest and most potentially important in the whole of the United States. These were reasonably accessible, so they were bound to attract a vast new influx of native-born Americans from states further east as well as immigrants of other than German race."

The German migration to Missouri, no matter how misbegotten in concept, conflicting as it did with the American ideal of national integration, did have one historic consequence. The Germans were strongly antislavery, though they settled in a state that permitted slavery. The fact that so many of them failed at farming and settled in St. Louis, where their political cohesion was decisive and their determination to uphold the Union unshakeable, would constitute one of the major turning points of the Civil War.

SENTENCED TO TEXAS

Shortly after President Lyndon B. Johnson succeeded to the White House, he received Chancellor Erhard of West Germany on a state visit and invited him to his ranch home on the Pedernales. As one of his gestures of hospitality, the President took the Chancellor on a tour of nearby towns, particularly Fredericksburg, where he was welcomed by a turnout of thousands of blond, blue-eyed people the German dignitary could easily recognize as the descendants of people who had left Germany more than a century ago. Presumably the Chancellor was gratified by his glimpses of German-American faces and neat Lutheran churches. President Johnson himself claims a fraction of German blood in his ancestry and learned a smattering of German from his upbringing among the largely German-American people who settled the sandhill country of the Pedernales.

Germans began settling in Texas even while it was a Mexican province, many of them bearing theories of a "New Germany" to be established before Texas became a state of the Union. That dream died of inanition, but the thousands of Germans who settled in the state, particularly the western part, contributed their own distinctive elements to that still emerging figure, the "super-American," the tall-hatted Texan in his handmade boots and string tie, with his booming self-assertiveness and his own potent brand of patriotism.

The first German colony was organized by the Baron von Bastrop and located on the Colorado River. Bastrop, as the settlement was named, was the northernmost white settlement in the valley of the Colorado. It was also much too exposed to the Indians, and several

86

times had to be abandoned because of the persistent attentions of the Comanches. They stuck it out, however, and in succeeding years the country between the Colorado and the Brazos became a center of German settlement.

The earlycomers had not been infected by the "New Germany" propaganda. They were nonintellectual, as Frederick Law Olmsted described them in his classic account of the Texas frontier before the Civil War, and "of a somewhat humble and promiscuous description." Many were honest farmers and artisans, as Olmsted noted, but others were jailbirds and troublemakers who had been requested to leave Germany or face imprisonment. The majority of the migrants "had no other reproach than that of honest poverty," but "there was a certain number, as among the early settlers of Virginia, who were suffered to escape justice at home on condition of becoming colonists; who were, in short, sentenced to Texas." (The British used the same method in colonizing Australia, and there as in Texas the mother country's loss of its troublesome elements was the adoptive land's gain.) Further, "whatever of reckless energy was thus disposed of seems to have found for itself a natural and harmless vent among the rough demands of frontier life. The result, at least, favors an offer to every rogue of the chance to show himself the victim of circumstances; for it is certainly remarkable with what success the unpractical nation has joined issue with nature and the savages; and how here, where the comparison may every day be made, even Americans acknowledge the Germans their equals as pioneers."[13]

Following that somewhat raffish influx, Olmsted noted in his A Journey Through Texas, published in 1857, there came a more respectable and educated German migrant, "numbers of cultivated and high-minded men, some distinctly refugees, others simply compromised in various degrees by their democratic tendencies, who found themselves exposed to disagreeable surveillance, or to obstructions, through police management, in whatever honorable career they wished to enter, while others merely followed, from affection or curiosity, this current of their friends."

Once again, as in Missouri, there was the touchingly anomalous human, half-scholar and half-pioneer, often known to his untutored neighbors as an "educated fool," struggling to convert a patch of prairie into a homestead. Apparently the more astringent air of Texas was beneficial to those Germans who hoped to nurture a democracy in the open spaces of the Southwest and still cling to the culture and customs of the old country. Olmsted was struck by "how wonderfully some of them are still able to sustain their intellectual life and retain their refined taste . . . while under the necessity of supporting life in the most frugal manner by hard manual labor."

He found "something extremely striking in the temporary incongruities and bizarre contrasts of the backwoods life of these settlers," and described a fairly typical visit to a German home as follows:

"You are welcomed by a figure in a blue flannel shirt and pendant beard, quoting Tacitus, having in one hand a long pipe, in the other a butcher's knife; Madonnas upon log walls; coffee in tin cups upon Dresden saucers; barrels for seats; to hear a Beethoven's symphony on the grand piano; 'My wife made these pantaloons, and my stockings grew in the field yonder'; a fowling-piece that cost $300, and a saddle that cost $5; a book case half-filled with classics, half with sweet potatoes."[14]

Such incongruities would pass into "amusing traditions" with the advance of civilization, Olmsted believed, but life among the Germans on the Texas frontier was not all Gemütlichkeit and appreciation of the finer things. Olmsted observed that the Germans' worst faults, carried over from their disputatious student days in the Fatherland, were "a free-thinking and a devotion to reason, carried, in their turn, to the verge of bigotry" and also "an insane mutual jealousy, and petty personal bickering, that prevents all prolonged and effective cooperation — an old German ail, which the Atlantic had not sufficed to cleanse."

Between the more or less native Texans and the German newcomers there was "an unfeigned curiosity, often tempered by mutual contempt." The Americans had the "prestige of preoccupation, of accustomed dominance over Mexicans and slaves." The Germans were "quiet, and engrossed in their own business, by nature law-abiding and patient," and submitted to the American overlordship "with little murmuring." Besides what would later be known as "cultural shock" intervening between Americans and Germans there was a certain amount of economic rivalry. "The ordinary Texan wages for an able field-hand are $200. The German laborer hires at $150, and clothes and insures himself. The planter for one hand must have paid $1,000. The German with this sum can hire six hands. It is here the contact galls."[15]

It may also have "galled" the Americans that the German migration, organized by various colonizing societies both in the United States and Germany, was so comprehensive — men, women, children and all their possessions — as contrasted with the native American's more individualistic way of coming to a new frontier alone and with little but his boots, saddle and guns.

Most of the Germans came to Texas between 1836, when it won its independence from Mexico, and 1845, when it joined the Union. Because so much of the state was unexplored as well as unsettled, and also was populated by large and hostile Indian tribes, the conditions were right for organized colonies such as the Germans established. The loner didn't have much of a chance to survive, let alone establish himself as a farmer or rancher. By their collective effort the Germans thus had the opportunity — a much fairer one than in Missouri or later in Wisconsin — to try out their concept of a "New Germany." In many parts of west Texas they outnumbered the native Americans, and the population of San Antonio for many years was about half-German and half Anglo-Saxon. "Up to 1845," as Hawgood has remarked, "almost anything might have happened in Texas, and among many possibilities it is not entirely fantastic to imagine that region as a 'New Germany.' . . . Until annexation actually took place, the field was still an open one . . ."

The literary basis for the German influx to Texas was a book by J. V. Hecke published in Germany in 1821, in which it was suggested that Prussia, forming a spearhead modeled after the British East India Company, undertake the colonization of Texas. (Needless to say, such a venture had received no encouragement from the American government.) Such an enterprise, Hecke pointed out, would necessarily result in building up the Prussian navy and increase Prussian trade with North and South America.

The book sparked little interest in Prussia, which had other than naval fixations, but caught fire among Germans in the United States. Subsequently the Germania Society of New York decided to undertake the task of Germanizing Texas. In December, 1839, the vanguard of one hundred thirty-two migrants gathered together by the society was dumped on the fever-stricken coast near Galveston. Six months' rations and an assortment of building tools seemed inadequate for such a task. The "first division," as it was called, broke up soon after it struggled on its way to Houston, where the group voted to dissolve and the well heeled returned to New York, leaving the others to shift for themselves.

Other promoters soon entered the field, among them a Frenchman named Henri Castro, who received a large land grant west of San Antonio and founded Castroville with the help of a number of German, Swiss and Alsatian settlers. A year later, in 1842, several Hessian noblemen formed a company to transport their countrymen to Texas and settle them on a tract it bought along the San Saba River. Behind the promotion glimmered the old pan-Germanic dream of establishing an overseas Vaterland; furthermore the Hessian noblemen were determined that the rigid social castes of the old country be transplanted in their Texas colony. The Mainzer Adelsverein, as the company styled itself under the patronage of the Duke of Nassau and other princelings, insisted on payment of three hundred gulden per man, or six hundred gulden per family, in return for which each would be given one hundred sixty acres, a log house, transportation to Texas, and cut-rate prices on cattle and farm implements. Interest in the Adelsverein's enterprise was stimulated by the publication of Nathan der Squatter Regulator and Kajutenbuch, both novels by Charles Seasfield, the latter dealing with the Texas war of independence. Colonial promotion in Germany owed much to its industrious literary men.

The republic of Texas was so impressed by the Verein's promotional energy, or awed by its ducal sponsorship, that it instructed Colonel Daingerfield, its representative at The Hague, to enter into formal negotiations with the company. In September, 1843, the Colonel was able to report to his superiors in Texas that he had signed a contract for the migration of twelve hundred to ten thousand German settlers, and rather flutteringly added that it was being rumored that the proposed colony would include "a large proportion of the Dukes and Princes of the smaller German States."

In May, 1844, Prince Carl of Solms-Braunfels, the designated leader of the Verein's colony, started on his journey to Texas, with three ships bearing one hundred fifty families following him. The realities of the venture soon were impressed upon Prince Carl. An inspection tour of the San Saba River site proved to him that it was too remote and otherwise unsuitable for settlement. By the time the immigrant ships arrived he had bought another tract on the Guadalupe River thirty miles north of San Antonio, where the town of New Braunfels was founded on March 21, 1845.

Other complexities were impressed on Prince Carl shortly after his arrival. Undoubtedly he knew that the British government was said to be encouraging the German colonization of Texas through Prince-Consort Albert and his connections with the German nobility, because it wanted to prevent the annexation of Texas by the United States. Prince Carl himself had attended the University of Bonn with Prince Albert.

On December 3, 1844, Prince Carl paid a courtesy call on the United States consul, General Duff Green, at Galveston, and was told that "Mexico was pledged to invade Texas — to make it a desert, and to exterminate the inhabitants, men, women and children." Prince Carl immediately reported on this conversation — obviously an attempt by General Green to discourage any German immigration — not to his own company, but to the British consul at Galveston, William Kennedy. He informed Kennedy that he was convinced that the United States consul "wishes me and my good German Emigrants anywhere else but in this country." Further indicating that there was British encouragement behind the German colonization plan, Prince Carl pledged the British consul that the German settlement would arm itself and "stop American encroachment toward the South."[16]

Undeterred by veiled or unveiled threats transmitted by the U. S.

representative, the *Adelsverein*'s colony solidly established itself at New Braunfels. The first contingent was soon followed by a second. All of the newcomers were given to understand that old-country traditions would be maintained and there would be social classes ranking from the nobility (Prince Carl) downward to the bond servants. Prince Carl did not last long enough to enjoy his feudal privileges, however, being removed from his position as "General Commissar" of the colony on charges of having squandered its funds, and very soon New Braunfels, mercifully distant from any real guidance by the German aristocrats who were its sponsors, fell in with the American tradition of a pecking order based on economic rather than social position.

His successor was an abler, more energetic and farsighted man, Baron von Meusebach, who set about signing a treaty with the Comanches and in May, 1846, acquiring a second tract of land on the Pedernales, with the town of Fredericksburg as its center.

The settlements on the Guadalupe and the Pedernales prospered despite bouts of trouble with the weather, the crops and the Indians. They were planted there permanently, but the seed they brought with them, the *Adelsverein*'s hope of establishing an overseas colony for Germany, did not germinate. There were too many distractions, historic as well as agricultural. The Germans joined with the Anglo-Americans in the recurring punitive campaigns against the Indians, and in wholesale lots with the United States army during the war against Mexico in 1846. That war had the effect of further integrating German-Americans, in Texas and elsewhere, with the other nationalities less bemused by ideas of separatism. Whole regiments were composed of the German-born or German-descended, and a number of them distinguished themselves in the Mexican campaigning, including Louis Armistead, a future Confederate general; August V. Kautz and Samuel P. Heintzelman, the latter a West Point graduate, both to be prominent Union generals, and Brigadier General John A. Quitman, the son of an immigrant who had become a Mississippi planter and politician, who led his brigade at the Battle of Monterey and the storming of Chapultepec and was the first American to enter Mexico City's Grand Plaza the morning it fell.

Yet there continued to be two sources of tension between the German and the native elements in Texas. Despite the bombastic claims of the *Adelsverein* and other immigration societies, they had succeeded in bringing to the state only enough people to build a few scattered settlements. By 1857 Frederick Law Olmsted estimated that there were thirty-five thousand Germans in Texas, which made them a one-sixth minority, enough to irritate but not to prevail against the "nativist" politicians, who were further exacerbated by the Germans' all but total opposition to slavery.

After describing a near-riotous election meeting in Seguin, Texas, in a series of articles he wrote for a German-language paper in New York, August Siemering observed that in Texas as elsewhere "the fight is on between Whigs and Democrats, Abolitionists and Slaveholders, Foreigners and Know-Nothings, Temperancers and Beer-Drinkers." The Germans, of course, were Democrats, Abolitionists, Foreigners and Beer-Drinkers. A fanatical temperance movement, Siemering reported, was sweeping across Texas. "You must know that Seguin is Temperance fanaticism incorporated, is the richest field for the most extravagant Methodist stupidity, is the gathering place of all the Coryphees of Know-Nothingism, and is the centre for the Slave-holders and the Yankees of the West." The fact that Seguin was located near a large settlement of Germans, he observed, "pushes all its specific Americanism to a laughable extreme." (New Braunfels was about fifteen miles away.) Siemering believed that no fusion between Germans and Americans was possible in the South and that "the German colonies will remain German, with all their good points and all their bad ones, with all their wiseheads and their dunces, their fanatics and their philistines — they will remain German until, well, until they are Americanized. History knows nothing of fusion, it witnesses only victory and defeat."[17]

Olmsted in his 1857 reportage of the Texas frontier told of rising tension between the Anglo-Americans and the Germans on the slavery question. The Germans were adamantly opposed. "Among the Germans of the west," Olmsted said, "we met not one slave-owner."

He told of a meeting held by German-Americans in San Antonio in May, 1854, at which a resolution was adopted favoring the abolition of slavery. Other Texans were outraged, and an Austin newspaper suggested that all German abolitionists be drowned.

According to Olmsted, the editor of the German-language newspaper in San Antonio was repeatedly threatened with violence. One morning a huge Texan carrying a large club invaded his offices with a friend at his side. The dialogue, as reported by Olmsted, went like this:

"Are you the editor of this German newspaper?"

"Yes, sir."

"You are an abolitionist, are you?"

"Yes, sir."

"What do you mean by an abolitionist?"

"A man's who against the enslavement of other men."

The man with the club conferred with his friend, then announced, "Well, sir, we've concluded that you are an abolitionist and that such a scoundrel as you are ought to be thrashed out of town."

"Very well, sir," the editor said. "Try it."

The two Texans glared at the editor for a moment, then the editor opened the door and "the individuals walked out." Soon thereafter, the San Antonio German repaired to the more congenial atmosphere of Boston.[18]

The Germans of Texas were never reconciled to slavery and few of their names could be found on the muster rolls of Hood's Texas Brigade when the Civil War broke out. In succeeding wars, however, the German-American of Texas has always been found, like all Texans, more prominent than his numbers would warrant in the annals of armed combat. Two of the descendants of those Germans who came to Texas in its frontier days particularly distinguished themselves in World War II: General of the Army Dwight D. Eisenhower and Fleet Admiral Chester W. Nimitz. The Eisenhower family moved on to Kansas, but Admiral Nimitz was raised in Kerr County, Texas, before entering the Naval Academy and eventually becoming the quiet, unassuming strategist of the naval war against Japan.

THE GERMAN ATHENS

The failure to set up separate German republics in Missouri and Texas did not entirely dissuade their proponents from trying elsewhere.

Nor were they dismayed by the apolitical tendency of ordinary Germans, which has been noteworthy to the present and which probably grew out of the fact that Germany did not become a national entity until long after the United States. A relatively few intellectuals, mostly of a liberal cast, were intensely political, but the masses were more interested in their daily bread — or lack of it — and were stirred up only when the importunities of their greedy nobles, military press gangs and ubiquitous tax collectors became unbearable. Land, and secondarily, perhaps, the blessings of democracy, attracted them to America.

The third focus of the Germania-in-America movement was on Wisconsin, the emotional heartland of German-American culture, to which thousands of Germans began migrating in the 1830's and 1840's. In 1835, encouraged beyond discretion by the immigration statistics, the "New Germany" advocates petitioned Congress for the right to establish several independent German republics in the United States, one of them to be the territory of Wisconsin. The brash proposal was instantly rejected, but its backers hoped that the weight of numbers would result in an ex-officio "New Germany" over which they would have substantial political and economic control.

Wisconsin is usually regarded as the most Germanic state in the Union, but actually it has always been dominated by the Anglo-Americans (such as General Douglas MacArthur's family in Milwaukee) and the German-American contingent has never exercised — nor has it attempted — any measure of political supremacy. The great political hero of the Wisconsin Germans was Robert M. La Follette, Sr., not least because his was the most vigorous and eloquent voice raised in the Congress against American participation in World War. I.

During the green years of German migration, however, Milwaukee was proclaimed the German Athens of America, and more than St. Louis or Cincinnati, the other two German-American urban centers, it was the scene of burgeoning Turnvereins, lieder-singing societies, theaters presenting the German classics and German opera and German symphonies. It was the city that made beer plentiful and cheap, as well as famous, with the breweries of Pabst, Schlitz, Blatz, Miller sending out their rivers of foaming lager. It was also the dowdiest, most humdrum large city in the country.

For Wisconsin, settlement and attainment of statehood came with amazing swiftness. In 1830 it was an unorganized wilderness with a population of 3,600. Two years later the gates were opened to civilization when the Black Hawk War, that series of skirmishes from northern Illinois to southern Wisconsin in which Abraham Lincoln was a militia captain, cleared away the major Indian menace. In 1836 Wisconsin was granted territorial status, and a dozen years later it was admitted to the Union as a state. Two years later, in 1850, it had a population of more than three hundred thousand. Much of that growth was supplied by German migration.

During those years about forty thousand Germans, mostly from the South German states and many of them Catholic, migrated to Wisconsin. The romantic travelogues of Franz Loher (*Geschichte und Zustande*), with his descriptions of the lakes and forests of Wisconsin, the crisp winters, the dry air and the rich black soil, influenced many to try their luck beside the shores of Lake Michigan. Loher, as a New Germany standard-bearer, urged that Germans settle in what was then known as the "Northwest" because it would become the "ruling centre" of the Union. Irish immigrants tended to stay in the eastern cities, he noted, and most native Americans seemed to be heading for the Far West. That left the millions of acres of potentially rich farmlands of Wisconsin, Iowa and Minnesota, where the dry clear pine-scented air resembled that of the old country, open to German settlement. And if the Germans concentrated on one or two of those localities, he maintained, they could become politically supreme, socially dominant, economically self-sufficient, and establish a Teutonic enclave free of the barbaric influences brought in by other nationalities. Another favorable feature of migrating to Wisconsin was its liberal land policy. The United States government had granted Wisconsin four million acres for the benefit of the public schools and the University of Wisconsin; this was sold at $1.25 an acre, for some of the best farmland in the country, which meant that a settler could buy a whole section for eight hundred dollars.

As elsewhere, the German movement to Wisconsin was made along organized, family-by-family lines. Most Germans brought their whole families over, down to the last drunken uncle and wailing infant, while the Irish and many other nationalities favored sending over a strong young man who worked until he made enough money to pay the passage for his family. The *Arbeiter Bund* of New York organized one stream of migration from the eastern United States; its plan was to form a large, all-German colony along communistic lines, but the people it sponsored dropped the ideology almost the moment they broke the soil of their new farms in Wisconsin. A much stronger magnet for German migration was the activity of the Catholic church in Wisconsin. The early foundation of a Milwaukee bishopric, to which a number of young priests were dispatched as a mission, encouraged many Catholics to migrate to Wisconsin from the Rhineland, Bavaria and other South German states. "The presence of a German Catholic bishop in Wisconsin," wrote one historian of the movement, "gave the territory wide publicity in the Catholic states of Germany."[19] Undoubtedly it also provided Milwaukee with that easygoing blend of *Gemütlichkeit* and lawfulness which characterizes the South German people.

The German population of Wisconsin was concentrated in Milwaukee and a dozen other counties, but the state never came close to being a "New Germany" or even a "Little Germany." Along with the thousands of migrants from Germany during the nineteenth century came parallel streams from Ireland and the Scandinavian countries, later from Italy and Poland, and in the past few years even less Nordic people from Puerto Rico and Cuba, Negroes from the American South, until it is possible to walk into a Milwaukee tavern today and hear the *Schnitzelbank* catechism recited in Latin accents.

The utter failure of hopes for a "New Germany" developed within American territory was emphasized by one striking circumstance. It seemed so vainglorious a concept that Americans of other nationalities were not even stirred to resentment, let alone fear or anger. It was simply ignored, as by a man too preoccupied on a summer's day to swat a fly buzzing around his head.

97

4. FORTY-EIGHTERS AND KNOW-

NOTHINGS

The potato may be the homeliest and least exotic plant in the vegetable world, but it has more than once changed the course of history. In the nineteenth century millions of people in Europe depended on it as the main staple of their diet. The failure of a harvest could bring widespread suffering, cause unrest that toppled governments, and start waves of migration from the blighted fields.

The major consequence of mankind's dependence on the potato occurred in 1845. Spring and early summer that year were warm and dry, and farmers throughout western Europe planted more potatoes than ever before in hopes of an unusually bountiful harvest. In August the rumor began to spread that a mysterious blight had struck the potato fields. It was helped along by an article in the *Irish Farmer's Gazette* on July 12 predicting that the crop generally would be a failure — and who would know more about the potato than the Irish?

By late August all of Europe was shaken by the news that a mysterious disease was sweeping the farmlands. The new potatoes not only rotted in the fields, but those which had already been harvested and stored also became wet, stinking masses of corruption. There was little scientific investigation of the disaster, but plenty of wild conjectures. It was suggested that "static electricity" caused by the puffs of smoke and steam from the hundreds of railway locomotives which were just coming into widespread use, was the reason for the crop failures. Others theorized about "mortiferous vapours" issuing from "blind volcanoes" in the interior of the planet. Still others blamed the innovation of spreading the fields with guano, a newly imported manure from the droppings of sea birds.[1]

Many historians believed that the blight started in the Rhineland, then spread westward across Europe to the British Isles. Most of western Europe, at any rate, was affected by the disease and the crop failures.

The hardest hit of all, however, were Ireland and Germany, because both depended more on the potato than the other countries. Ireland began one of the first of a succession of starvation winters, and a million of its peasants starved to death before the famine was over. In Germany, grain stocks relieved the suffering at first, but by the time the winter was over it was apparent to thousands of German farmers that they would have to migrate or perish. The same alternative confronted hundreds of thousands in Ireland.

In the middle and late 1840's a great parallel stream of migration began from Ireland and Germany, further widened in the latter country by political upheavals a few years later. The nearest and most promising refuge was America. And by a tragic irony America in that decade had been undergoing a change of heart regarding further immigration, one of the most violent symptoms of which was the rise of "nativist" propaganda and the exclusionist movement known as the "Know-Nothings." The violence of that antipathy, principally among Anglo-Americans, has been overshadowed by the Civil War, but next to the slavery question it was the most divisive and emotional controversy stirring the nation in the middle of the nineteenth century.

PLAGUE SHIPS AND SWIMMING COFFINS

Mother Courage herself would not have been out of place in the procession that wound along the roads leading from the Rhineland, the grand duchy of Baden, Württemberg, the two Hessian provinces and the kingdom of Bavaria toward the "damned plague ships and swimming coffins" which would offer a possibility of escape overseas. Bertolt Brecht's fictional heroine of the Hundred Years' War would have found herself amid familiar scenes, though it was hunger and despair rather than plundering armies which drove along the refugees of the 1840's. A French writer quoted in *Chambers's Edinburgh Journal* described a highroad in Bavaria where whole villages were selling their property and setting out for the nearest port with their priest or minister at their head:

"It is a lamentable sight when you are traveling in the spring or autumn on the Strasburg road, to see the long files of carts that you meet every mile, carrying the whole property of the poor wretches, who are about to cross the Atlantic on the faith of a lying prospectus. There they go slowly along; their miserable tumbrils — drawn by such starved, drooping beasts, that your only wonder is, how can they possibly hope to reach Havre alive — piled with the scanty boxes containing their few effects, and on the top of all, the women and children, the sick and bedridden, and all who are too exhausted with the journey to walk. One might take it for a convoy of wounded, the relics of a battlefield, but for the rows of little white heads peeping from beneath the ragged hood."[2]

Many in those processions winding along the roads to the sea were driven by motives other than hunger. To American observers in Germany it seemed there was almost a mass impulse to escape from the Fatherland. George Bancroft, the United States minister to Berlin, reported to the State Department that "all Germany is alive on the subject" of emigration, that the movement would be even greater if it were not "limited by the amount of transports." Charles Nicholls, the American consul in Amsterdam, wrote his superiors that among the refugees there was a indefinable feeling that the potato famine only portended greater disasters, explaining, "All well informed persons express the belief that the present crisis is so deeply interwoven in the events of the present period, that 'it' is but the commencement of that great Revolution, which they consider sooner or later is to dissolve the present constitution of things . . ."[3] The rumblings they felt, of course, were the forerunners of the revolutions of 1848.

The knowledgeable *Chambers's Edinburgh Journal*, which for years had been specializing in immigration coverage, also perceived that it wasn't famine, or the threat of hunger, which alone were responsible for the swelling exodus. It noted that the "dread of destitution" was not the "principal motive" for the mass migrations: "This is clear from the fact that the emigration does not take place in those districts where there is most want, but exists equally where population is dense, and where it is thinly distributed . . . The Bavarians emigrate alike from the Rhine country, where population is thickly clustered together, and from the upland districts, where there are not eighty inhabitants to the square mile."[4] One reason, as in Ireland, was that the people hardest hit by the crop failures were those unable to leave because they didn't have passage money.

It was not only fear but hope which impelled the migration, the journal contended. "The one great cause of this almost national movement is the desire for absolute political and religious freedom; the absence of all restrictions upon the development of society; and the publication of opinions which cannot be realized at home. The great agitation in society, caused first by the French domination, and then by the compulsive rise against it, has never passed away. In that gigantic struggle, when everything rested on the popular soul, the bonds of privilege and class were tacitly abandoned, and could never thenceforth be reunited as before. The promises of having constitutional governments, at that time made by the sovereigns to their subjects, have been but partially fulfilled . . . there are many restrictions, and the young, the restless, and the imaginative thirst for their ideal freedom, and many of them seek for the realization of Utopia in America." The German governments were becoming alarmed at the outgoing tide of their peoples because they were taking an estimated million and a half pounds annually from the German states, and because "the Germans in America consume English, not German commodities, and remit nothing to Germany in the shape of produce." With little success, the

German states tried to divert their emigrating citizens to Hungary, "to balance the Slavonic element," as the *Edinburgh Journal* reported.

Even when they finally glimpsed the ports which promised their escape from the Fatherland, even after surviving the journey westward across the German provinces in their creaking procession of carts, the migrating Germans still faced the ordeal of obtaining passage, waiting in the streets of Le Havre, Amsterdam, Hamburg or Bremen until their ship was ready to sail, and somehow living through the hazardous voyage itself.

Bremen for many years had been the chief port of European emigration. An independent city-state, long a member of the Hanseatic League, Bremen had been making a living off the sea and its commerce for a thousand years; and cities which live by the sea are not notable for a humanitarian outlook. The inscription carved on the lintel of a fifteenth century sailors' home in Bremen expressed the city's tough-mindedness: *Navigare necesse est, vivere non est necesse.*

The last painful moments which Europe inflicted on those who were leaving her, bitterly remembered by the antecedents of millions of Americans, first the Germans, then the Russians and Poles and other eastern European peoples who also left via the North Sea port, were endured among the dike-protected lowlands where the Weser River leaves Bremen, widens and flows into the sea. Their last glimpse of Europe was of that bleak coastal country, always threatened by the sea from which it was reclaimed. "We are a free city," was Bremen's proudest boast. It took a tough, callous people to maintain that boast. Bremen was surrounded to the south by such postage-stamp duchies and principalities as Oldenburg, Lüneburg, Brunswick and others, and to the north by Hanover, which owned part of the Weser between Bremen and the sea; all of these exacted customs duties and tolls on the ships sailing to and from Bremen.

The traffic to the New World had long been a source of Bremen's prosperity, not only providing passage for the migrants leaving northern Europe, but provisioning the Hessian brigades sent to join the British expeditionary force during the American Revolution. (Bremen did not object to profiting from the movement of Hessian troops, but did hope for their defeat. Under Britain's Navigation Act of 1651, no European ships were allowed to trade with the American Colonies. When Britain lost those Colonies, it meant a large increase in Bremen's profits from the cotton and tobacco trade.) The richest profits, however, came from speeding emigrants on their way.

By luck and shrewdness, Bremen continued to exact a considerable profit as a port of immigration even after Congress, in 1819, passed the bill restricting the number of immigrants to two for every five tons of the ship's displacement. Until 1830 many migrants had passed through the ports of Le Havre, Antwerp and Rotterdam, but they were diverted from those places by the revolution which restored the Bourbon monarchy in France and by cholera epidemics which scourged Antwerp and Rotterdam. That left Bremen in command of the traffic, and she promptly took measures to insure her primacy. She built the new port of Bremerhaven, which was capable of handling more and larger ships than Bremen itself, and encouraged her shipyards to produce lighter and faster packet ships along American lines. By 1833 Bremen packets were casting off for America on a regular schedule, the first and fifteenth of each month. The eastbound cargo was tobacco from Virginia and the Carolinas; the westbound, human beings, who were accommodated to capacity by removing temporary flooring and installing bunks between decks and packing them in suffocating layers. Tobacco dealers all over Germany acted as immigration agents, since the more ships that went over with migrants, the more returned with cargoes of tobacco, for which there was a booming demand. A Baden newspaper complained that Germany was "caught in a net of Bremen agents," who received a fee of 25 percent for each migrant he forwarded to the shipowners.[5]

Only the slightest attention was paid to the welfare of the human cargo being consigned to America. The immigrants, wrote Friedrich Kapp, a prosperous New Yorker who served on the board of an immigrants' aid society, "were commonly treated with the least possible attention, with the utmost disregard of decency and humanity. With rare exceptions they were robbed and plundered from the day of their departure to the moment of their arrival at their new homes, by almost everyone with whom they came in contact . . . There seemed to be a secret league, a tacit conspiracy, on the part of all parties dealing with immigrants to fleece and pluck them without mercy, and hand them from hand to hand as long as anything could be made of them . . . If crosses and tombstones could be erected on the water, the routes of the emigrant vessels from Europe to America would long since have assumed the appearance of crowded cemeteries."[6]

Petitions signed by men such as Kapp, forwarded by charitable organizations and the city and state of New York, persuaded Congress to enact further legislation in February, 1847, which specified exactly how much *Lebensraum* each passenger was to have on the Atlantic crossing. For every passenger there was to be a minimum of fourteen square feet of horizontal space. Each berth must be six feet long and eighteen inches wide. On the orlop (bottom) deck each passenger must be given thirty square feet of space. Families were to be separated by latticework partitions which could be opened or left closed. Children under eight counted as half an adult, and infants were not counted at all. The passengers still had to provide their own bedding, and frequently the ships were so crowded that they were forced to sleep in the gangways or in wooden shacks erected on the top deck, often so flimsily that they were open to the North Atlantic gales.

Many of the German migrants, of course, were able to afford greater comfort than the steerage offered. For those traveling first class, it was smooth sailing. The American vessel *Victoria*, commissioned for the Atlantic migration business in 1843, described in its promotional brochure a first-class cabin fitted out for the well-heeled gentleman taking his leave of Germany as being "lined with satin wood, in panels, banded with rose and zebra woods and American bird's-eye maple, and the ceiling white and gold. There is a centre table of choice white marble. The apartment is lit through ground glass; and one of the large panes bears a picturesque view of Windsor Castle, and at the opposite end is Buckingham Palace, surrounded by the rose, shamrock, and thistle. The decorator has not, however, lavished all his taste upon this apartment, for the berths are fitted *en suite*; the ceiling is in white and gold and the handles of the doors are of glass."

Ships such as the *Victoria* carried cows for fresh milk, chickens for eggs and meat, pigs for fresh meat. A standard menu aboard the *Victoria* indicated that scurvy was not to be feared by anyone with the money for a first-class passage. For breakfast there were ham and eggs, cold mutton, bread, hot rolls, black or green tea, coffee or hot chocolate. At noon he could satisfy his appetite with bread, cold tongue, cheese, port, liqueurs. Dinner included soup, beef, pork, veal, fowl, fresh milk, plum pudding, preserves, oranges, raisins, almond, figs and prunes. Wine was served with lunch and dinner, champagne every other day, and there was a ship's orchestra for concerts and dancing. One first-class passenger reported that day and night he heard "the noise of calling the steward and drawing the corks."

In the holds of less luxurious ships it was a different and more squalid story. The New York *Journal of Commerce* condemned them as "damned plague ships and swimming coffins" in an editorial published December 10, 1853, a half-dozen years after Congressional legislation was adopted to safeguard the health of the thousands of migrants crossing the Atlantic.

A packet sent out from Bremen under the old Hanseatic code of the passenger-be-damned had just docked at Baltimore with a cargo of forty passengers. When checked at quarantine, the *Anna* was found to have suffered an epidemic of cholera, in which a dozen passengers had died at sea.

Conditions on another Bremen packet, the *Johanna*, were so outrageous that a number of passengers documented their accounts before a notary public in New York. "After two weeks," read one deposition, "the potatoes gave out; the peas were musty, the meat and butter spoiled and had to be thrown into the sea. The passengers lived on hard branny bread, prunes and watery barley soup. In New York, the cook jumped ship."

And there was the *Howard*, the home port of which was Hamburg, which arrived in New York after a voyage of ninety-six days with 37 out of its 286 passengers dead from cholera. More than a third of the surviving passengers had to be carried from their berths when the

Howard docked. During the last six weeks of the voyage they had been without water fit to drink under ordinary circumstances.

Despite such horror tales, the ships sailing out of Bremen generally provided better care for their passengers than the French and British vessels in the same traffic. In 1854, stirred to action again by reports in the newspapers of horrifying conditions on the emigrant ships, the United States Congress launched an inquiry into "Sickness and Mortality on Board Emigrant Ships." An investigating committee headed by Hamilton Fish compiled statistics showing that the vessels operating out of Bremen had the lowest cholera rate. Six percent of all ships arriving from Bremen were found to have cholera aboard when they were inspected by quarantine officers, compared with 12 percent of the ships operating out of LeHavre, 21½ percent of those from Liverpool, and 25 percent of those from London. One reason, the committee believed, was that French and British ships made their passengers in steerage cook their own meals while "the Bremen ships, so celebrated for the general good condition of their passengers, adopt this course [preparing the food for their passengers] and find it to work admirably."[7]

Neither cholera, cramped quarters nor bad food shocked the Fish committee so much as the evidence of sexual immorality on all the vessels bringing over immigrants. Ships built in the future for that traffic, the committee recommended, should be fitted with separate hatchways so that males and females could be kept segregated. Meanwhile, the committee had searched its soul for an answer to what was to be done about improving morality on the ships already in service, but could find none. "In coming to this conclusion," the committee report stated, "the committee feels with great regret, as they in common with all well-thinking persons, view with a feeling amounting to disgust and horror, the improper intercourse said frequently to exist, not only between passengers of different sexes, but between the crew and female passengers, whose situation renders them accessible to the advances of the dissolute and unprincipled." The committee apparently was not prepared to believe that in the simple annals of the poor, procreation was the only recreation.

The Fish committee also learned that there was only one toilet for

On the quays of Hamburg

Last look at the Old Country

each hundred passengers on most ships, and recommended that separate privies be maintained for male and female passengers. Even if the voyage was comparatively smooth and there were no epidemics of cholera and smallpox, no starvation or thirst because of an extended stay at sea, the migrants still suffered from lesser ailments — such as scurvy, trench mouth, body ulcers — because of the close quarters in which they lived. During storms, people in the unlit steerage, many of whom had been born and raised hundreds of miles from the sea, were thrown into a panicky, screaming, praying mass and often suffered broken bones from the buffeting. "A sudden heave of the ship," related the committee report, "often dislodged whole families from their berths and hurled them headlong among their companions who lay on the opposite side."

On a fast sailing ship of the Fifties the voyage usually took at least six weeks, often twice as long due to the vagaries of wind and weather. The food on a Bremen ship was usually edible but hardly came close to the excellence of the *Victoria's* cuisine. The dinner served steerage passengers became fairly standardized on German ships and went like this:

Sunday — salt meat, meal pudding and prunes
Monday — salt bacon, pea soup and potatoes
Tuesday — salt meat, rice and prunes
Wednesday — smoked bacon, sauerkraut, potatoes
Thursday — salt meat, potatoes and bean soup
Friday — herring, meal and prunes
Saturday — salt bacon, pea soup and potatoes

On this diet, all able-bodied passengers were expected to work in partial payment of their fares, swabbing down the gangways, helping the cooks in the galley, emptying the chamber pots, washing the bedclothing. The work details were supervised by the second mate. Life on a German ship was strictly regimented, and for their own sake passengers were required to stay on deck and take exercise except in the coldest or stormiest weather. No one was permitted to loll in his bunk and meditate on the pleasures of a sea voyage; even the sick were hauled topside.

But if the Germans thought they were treated no better than cattle, they had only to study the newspapers to learn that those who traveled on French or British ships had it a lot tougher — particularly the Irish starvelings who climbed aboard an English ship after handing over their last sovereign.* A Quebec newspaper report quoted by Mary Jane Cable in her account of the perils of the Atlantic crossing told, in 1847, of the arrival of the British sailing vessel *Larch* from the Irish port of Sligo. Of the 408 who had boarded her, 108 died along the way and 150 were seriously ill. Another British ship, the *Virginius,* sailed with 496, of whom 158 died, 187 were taken ill, and the remainder were so feeble they could hardly walk down the gangplank. "The Black Hole of Calcutta," the newspaper commented, "was a mercy, compared to the holds of these vessels. Yet simultaneously, as if in reproof of those on whom the blame of all this wretchedness must fall, Germans from Hamburg and Bremen are daily arriving, all healthful, robust, and cheerful."

A German clergyman with a touching faith in the legend of British excellence in maritime matters bought a second-class passage on the English sailing ship *Indiana* on being promised by an immigration agent in his native Baden-Württemberg that he would be given an iron bed with clean white sheets, fresh meat and bread daily and a generous daily amount of wine. Instead he found that he had to share a wooden plank, a straw mattress and a horse blanket with a companion in the *Indiana*'s hold. After the first day at sea, he was forced to subsist on a diet of salt herring, potatoes and weak coffee. There was space for only a quarter of the passengers to eat at one sitting, the rest were fed on deck in fair weather, in the gangways in foul. Worse yet for Teutonic pride, the clergyman reported, the sixty-four Germans aboard were treated like members of an inferior species and all realized that if the ship foundered the English passengers would get the few available places in the small boats.

German immigrants thus learned that they had little choice but to

* The Irish often arrived in America dead broke, while Germans, having suffered less from the potato famine, often had as much as a hundred dollars, according to a survey made in 1856.

throw themselves on the mercy of the Bremen shipmasters. Fortunately, Bremen, egged on by the American inquiries and legislation, began making an effort toward taking better care of the thousands of emigrants passing through the port city. The Bremen City Senate urged on the merchants and shipowners who profited from the traffic the necessity of policing themselves or facing greater American restrictions; it also arranged a treaty with the United States permitting each to do business in the other's ports without the red tape and various fees required of other foreigners. A considerable efficiency was brought to the problem of forwarding the emigrants by 1855, when Bremen was known as *Der Vorort New-Yorks*, the suburb of New York. They were met in Bremen by licensed agents who saw to it that they passed through the city without being robbed of their possessions or cheated by guides, porters or shopkeepers. Then they were conducted to the Weser ferry and conveyed to Bremerhaven, now the chief port of exit, where they were lodged in a huge dormitory operated by the state. The dormitory was equipped with two thousand beds and provided food and lodging for sixty-six pfennigs (about twenty-five cents) a night. "Often five thousand passengers arrived and disappeared in forty-eight hours," Marcus Lee Hansen has written. "As a further assistance to the travelers, the municipal authorities sponsored a society which maintained booths at the railroad station, the river dock and the market place, where lists of rooming houses were posted and bewildered peasants were given advice."[8]

A semiweekly newspaper, the *Deutsche Auswanderer Zeitung*, was published in Bremen as a guide for the emigrants. Beneath the logotype on the front page they were instructed in large type to go at once to the Information Bureau on their arrival in Bremen and with equal dispatch, on their arrival in New York, to the German Society at 85 Greenwich Street. According to Mrs. Cable's study of the newspaper, it was a valuable guide for the gullible peasants leaving the farms on which their families had lived for centuries without ever seeing any more of the world than the nearest market town. "There was also information about various immigrant colonies in the new world: 'Warning against the Peruvian Immigration Project, by a Man Who Has Been There'; 'The Terms of the Minnesota *Landverein* at New Ulm.' Then there were cautionary tales for immigrants: 'A German immigrant in Chicago was first made totally drunk and then robbed of $1,000 by a scoundrel by the name of Dunn Kerch. Kerch stole the German's money belt.' . . . Occasionally, a sort of public thank-you note would appear, which one hopes was not contrived by a public-relations man: 'In our new homeland we the undersigned passengers of the Bremen ship *Ohio* offer our thanks for a speedy and fortune journey and for wonderful care. We take this opportunity to recommend to our countrymen this ship and her captain, Herr Herrmann Renjes, who ran this ship with good food and drink and good care for the sick; and the ship's personnel earned our fond remembrances.' "

Steamships had begun plying the Atlantic, making the crossing in two or three weeks instead of the six to fourteen weeks taken by the sailing ships, but it would be another twenty years before their fares were low enough to accommodate the poorer emigrants. Even after the hazards of the Atlantic crossing had been surmounted, however, the emigrant had to face the strangeness of a new land. Until the mid-century he was comforted by the knowledge that America welcomed the newcomer, that she needed people to fill up her forests and plains, that she boasted an open, classless society in which each man was intrinsically as good as another. But times had changed in America, as the new arrival would shortly learn.

"WAS HE A WHITE MAN? NO, HE WAS A DUTCHMAN"

Just at the time when the European migration was cresting, native Americans were beginning to wonder how many strangers the continent could absorb without changing the nature of its institutions and decreasing the opportunities available to them and their children. Quite suddenly, it seemed, Americans were taking a new and skeptical and often hostile look at the creatures who were deposited, often penniless, ill or diseased, sometimes with records of crime or shiftlessness in the old country, on the docks of the eastern cities. There was some justification for the suspicion that the Old World was ridding itself of undesirables. A town in Hessen-Darmstadt emptied its prisons and poor-houses by paying the passage of every criminal and indigent to New York. An equally systematic purge of the poverty-stricken was undertaken in other German states. Many among the German emigrants during the early Fifties, according to Marcus Lee Hansen, were the chronically indigent "sent out at the expense of the communes to which they belonged, or perhaps subsidized by the government when the local organization could not meet the charge. Most of the states along the upper Rhine made appropriations for this purpose . . ."9

Personal liberty went to the heads of many Germans once they landed in this country, it was observed. The *North American Review*, which was not a nativist journal, published a long article by J. D. Angell in 1856 which took a coolly objective view of the results of more than a century of migration from Germany. Angell conceded that often "the son of a poor emigrant from the Rhine surpasses in American enthusiasm the descendant of a signer of the Declaration of Independence," that Germans had willingly, even eagerly allowed themselves to be assimilated by other nationalities and "their blood and ours flow together in the veins of thousands of fairhaired boys and girls." He also gave them full credit for helping develop the country and joining in fighting its enemies from the Revolution to the Mexican War.

A sea-change, however, seemed to have affected many of the newer emigrants and "has permitted the excessive development of some of the worst tendencies of their character. Errors which only germinated on the Continent, here bear the most poisonous fruit. License reaches the most daring recklessness and profanity. Vice swells into shameless crime. Democracy becomes lawlessness, and virtue but a name. The earnest and industrious mechanic of Nuremberg grows into the tumultuous haranguer and street-fighter of New York. The wayward boy of Stuttgart is the brawler and ruffian in Philadelphia. The free-thinker of Tübingen is here an editor, who regards none of the courtesies of our life, nor any of our most hallowed customs and beliefs."

The traditional permissiveness of American society was too heady a brew for many German immigrants, Angell believed, particularly when gulped down by people who had always known the iron-handed restraint of the German governments. "No hundred-handed police represses every budding vice. Even the reaction, which is natural after escape from governmental oppression, is not at all checked. Moreover, the wave of emigration always carries on its bosom many of the outcasts, who are bound by no ties to any place or institution. It is also well known that many of the workhouses and jails of Germany have cast their incorrigible and desperate inmates upon our shores."

The unassimilated Germans, such as those called the Pennsylvania Dutch, also distressed Angell. They had shut themselves off from the world and even "their knowledge of Germany is limited to the vague idea that wine is cheaper and life merrier than here in America. Their strongest passions are love of beer and hatred of the Irish . . . They seem to be anchored in the past, unmoved by the rapid stream of American life which rushes by them on every side."

Angell, like Frederick Law Olmsted in his survey of the German colonies in Texas, was struck by the "intensest hatred" Germans of differing persuasions exhibited toward each other. "The republicans have a deadly hostility to the Roman Catholics, and many of them dislike the Lutherans almost as bitterly. They regard the established churches of Germany as the greatest enemies to civil liberty, and they stamp kingcraft and priestcraft with a common brand of infamy . . . The great majority of the wealthy and educated are atheists or rationalists. They have control of nearly half of the German newspapers in the land . . . the irreligious influence of thousands of German infidels must be perceptibly felt by the children who come after them. They grow up as Americans, and it is sad to think of the heavy cloud which will rest on their hearts. This is a grave subject of meditation for the Christian patriot."[10]

Equally severe was the judgment of a German writer, Karl Buchele, in his inquiry into the prospects of the German emigrant in the United States. Buchele was dismayed at finding how many of his countrymen emigrated with the belief that they could "make their fortune quickly and easily" here, a mistake for which they "suffer in the hospital, in the poorhouse, and in the cemetery."*

* Statistics did not entirely bear him out. Many German emigrants, of course, were cared for by German emigrant societies in the eastern cities. The report of the New York City Dispensary issued just before Buchele made his journey of inquiry show that of 16,000 patients treated there as charity cases only 22 were German, compared with 10,070 Irish, 5,046 native American.

It wasn't the brash and ruffianly behavior of the German new-comers, such as that which distressed Mr. Angell, that intensely irritated Buchele — quite the opposite. The German, he observed, was much too humble in spirit and too slow to take offense, a flaw in his character which Buchele believed was traceable to "his love of the foreigner," a conclusion which latter-day Europeans (particularly between 1939 and 1945) would have found astonishing. The German's submissiveness had "followed him everywhere in life and history," Buchele declared. "The drunken and ragged Irishman, the irresponsible and dissolute French-man, the begging Italian, rank higher in the estimate of the American than the simple German immigrant . . . Whenever the German sub-missiveness, and obstinate, excessive modesty are contrasted with Amer-ican independence; stupid, clumsy German timidity with overbearing American self-confidence — whenever pitiable timidity is forced to give way to impudence — the fate of the German is sealed in spite of his thoroughness and competence in his trade. He is incapable of behaving in a free and easy manner, crowds fearfully into a corner when the American proudly struts about . . ."

Everywhere the German was regarded as the member of an inferior race. Buchele said he often heard the jibe expressed in the following bit of dialogue:

"Was he a white man?"

"No, sir, he was a Dutchman."

Even intermarrying with the Anglo-Saxons, in Buchele's pessimistic view, was not likely to advance the German's status. "Sometimes the German is granted the honor of being allowed to mix with Yankee blood, but later he is treated somewhat like a European parvenu who has married into an old, aristocratic family, and from then on is only the husband of his wife. He is obliged to let himself be branded a criminal by aunts and cousins because he is a German, and suffer patiently all the tortures of nativism. His own children show him little respect and are sure to disown him when they are fourteen. He does not even dare to reprimand them for calling him 'an old Dutchman' in his very presence. The children of such immigrant Germans are, therefore, also the worst 'natives' and, as a rule, exhibit the very height of cruelty and worthlessness."

The dissension among Germans themselves, so often noted by others, was also noted by Buchele. To him, however, the "great division" was between the old immigrants, the "Grays," and the newer arrivals, the "Greens." The Grays, as Buchele saw them, were uneducated people who had come to the United States to better themselves in a material way and showed "disdain for everything which is not directly instrumental in making money, arrogance toward those whose capital consists only in intelligence and knowledge"; they considered themselves "privileged to play the brute toward everyone who has not yet American citizenship papers in his pocket." In Buchele's view, the Greens, verdant with the Teutonic virtues brought with them from the Fatherland, were "enthusiastic believers in aspiring to higher things . . . carriers of new ideas which they want to put into practice." And in the Philistine atmosphere of America the Greens rapidly turned Gray out of an instinct for protective coloration. Culturally, after a few generations, the German became an average American dunderhead who confined his reading to "the Bible, a few other religious writings, and the almanac." His only cultural interest was in music, principally the glee clubs. There were eighty thousand Germans in New York City midway through the 1850's but the theater there was "hardly comparable to the smallest municipal theater in Germany." If any German distinguished himself as a painter, he was unknown to Buchele and "the encouragement to do this was certainly not extended by his countrymen."

Politically, too, the Germans were an inert mass, seemingly incapable of acting together in their own interests. Buchele did not mention the fact that such initiatives had always been withheld from them, for many centuries, in their former homeland. "Even where they form a majority, the power is in the hands of the Yankees . . . Were it conceivable that a capable personality should arouse the German citizens of the Union from their cowardice and unite them into a compact whole, then Pennsylvania and Ohio would from time to time have German governors and always a proportion of officials and representatives of the people in Washington would be one-eighth German, and the possibility that the United States would sometime elect a German as president would not be entirely out of the question." (Buchele was lacking in the talent for prophecy. President John Tyler, 1840–1844, had a mother of German blood. Two future Presidents were also partly German: Hoover who was Palatinate German and Swiss, and Eisenhower who is of Swiss, German and English extraction. Buchele was accurate enough in forecasting that German-Americans would never swing their proportionate weight in politics.) Honor at least would be gained by sending a German-American to the White House, Buchele urged, but "no money would be made thereby, and as the thinking of the majority of Germans would consider not the honor, but only the dollar, things will probably remain as they are; that means our German countrymen will continue to vegetate as those who are tolerated, and will act as miserable instruments of parties, while the Yankees represent the real life of the powerful body of states." The few political triumphs of German-Americans, such as Gustav Koerner's election as lieutenant governor of Illinois, were greeted with rejoicing in the German-American press because they were as "rare as white ravens."[11]

Buchele's harsh judgments on his fellow Germans who had escaped to America undoubtedly were tailored to fit the current mood of official Germany. By the time he returned to write his book, with its bleak picture of the human results of emigration, the various German governments had taken alarm at the number of their ablest and most promising young people who had given up hope of achieving a decent life in the homeland and fled overseas.

The "Forty-eighters," unsuccessful revolutionaries who fled the Fatherland when all hopes of democratic reform were crushed, and who comprised more political enterprise and civil courage than was left in Germany, also were given the back of Buchele's hand. The fact that, among others, the group was to produce such a glowing figure as Carl Schurz was of course unknown to Buchele in 1855, but he saw them as a collection of feckless visionaries and hopeless malcontents. They would never be able to break the iron cord to the old country because "the educated immigrant is bound to Germany . . . by all the ties of the heart, while only his intellect becomes familiar with the progressive movements of the New World . . . many a man becomes alienated from the goddess of liberty when he sees that she deserts her most ardent followers . . . it is more difficult for the educated man than for the tradesman to make his living in a strange land where he always lives only as an exotic plant."

He continued in this vein: "The whole impractical army of German philosophers, journalists, and literary men has to become altogether degraded here or at least resort to the lowest, most unaccustomed work. Men who are by profession political agitators of the lowest class, lazy tramps, and rascals, find in America the most thankless field.

"The man with capital who thinks he can enjoy idleness here will soon get rid of his good money as well as his illusions. The German philosopher who, on account of Weltschmerz, has here become a farmer, finds that the American axe is more difficult to wield than the pen, and that the plow and the manure-fork are very matter-of-fact and stupid tools. The German Romanticist is grieved because the speculating Yankee lacks all appreciation of the magic and fairy world of medieval poety, and the German titled landowner in New Braunfels, Texas, is vexed because no one but he himself uses his title of 'Herr von.' "[12]

With increasing eagerness during the 1850's, American politicians, publicists and professional patriots were willing to agree with Buchele's conclusion that German migration to America was a bad bargain for both the Germans and Americans.

To reassure themselves that they were not merely being bigoted or selfish but were showing a genuine concern for the future of the country, they had only to read their newspapers or the reports of various government agencies. The streets were becoming unsafe because of the hooliganism of the Germans as well as the Irish — sometimes both together. One incident widely reported in the press took place in Washington, D.C., and worse yet occurred at a polling place where neither Germans nor Irish appeared to appreciate the privilege of voting in an orderly and democratic manner. How it started was a matter of dispute, but according to the Washington *Star* there was "one version that a citizen, having had his place in the line of voters temporarily filled, on resuming it was dragged from the line by a German named Schaffer, which led to an attack on the German, and then on the Irish who were present and in the neighborhood; another, that the German and a native citizen were playing a little roughly with each other, when an Irishman was also struck, who resented the blow, when the general melee commenced."[13]

For further justification of views that the newest wave of immigrants contributed more than their share of pauperism, the native American could read the report of the Select Committee of the New York State Assembly, which investigated conditions in the tenement districts of New York and Brooklyn in 1857.

Conditions among the Irish and Germans living in such noisome sections of the city as Hell's Kitchen on Manhattan's West Side, the Five Points downtown and the tenement warrens of Brooklyn across the river were so deplorable that landlords, the report said, preferred to rent their houses and flats to Negroes because they were more responsible tenants. If that seems incredible to their descendants in New York today, the exact wording of the committee's report was that "in some of the better class of houses built for tenantry, Negroes have been preferred as occupants to Irish or German poor; the incentive of possessing comparatively decent quarters appearing to inspire the colored residents with more desire for personal cleanliness and regard for property than is impressed upon the whites of their own condition . . ."

The committee was particularly appalled at conditions in lower Manhattan and described a tenement row on Sheriff Street known as "Ragpickers' Paradise." It was inhabited by Germans who made a living of sorts at picking rags and bones. "The locality was infected for squares around by the effluvia of putrefying flesh, from numberless bone-boiling places, and bales of filthy rags stored in cellars and sheds. 'Ragpickers' Paradise' is inhabited entirely by Germans, who dwell in small rooms, in almost fabulous gregariousness, surrounded by scores of dogs, and canopied by myriads of rags fluttering from lines crossing their filthy yards, where bones of dead animals and noisome collection of every kind were reeking with pestiferous smells.

"One establishment contains more than fifty families . . . We are told of a colony of 300 of these people, who occupied a single basement, living on offal and scraps . . . Their means of livelihood, degraded as it is, is likewise exceedingly precarious, especially in severe winters, when snowstorms, covering the ground, hide the rags, shreds of paper, etc., on the sale of which they subsist. In such seasons, the children are sent out to sweep crossings or beg, and many of the most adoit practitioners on public charity are found among these urchins, who are generally marked by a precocity and cunning which render them, too often, adepts in vice at the tender ages."

The rag- and bone-pickers regulated competition among themselves through "a sort of internal polity, by means of which they preserve an amicable understanding, though competing in the same miserable business. For the purposes of their daily life the city is districted or partitioned into streets and neighborhoods, certain individuals or families being allowed their distinct fields, over the boundaries of which they must not pass, to trepass on another's. The colonies sally out at daybreak with their baskets and pokers, disperse to their respective precincts, and pursue their work with more or less success throughout the day." Filthy rags collected from hospital yards, gutters and "every vile locality imaginable" were boiled in the rooms in which whole families ate and slept. Their living conditions were characterized, the committee reported, by "personal filth, stagnant water, fixed air . . ."[14]

"I KNOW NOTHING . . ."

"A race of murderous sheep" is one of the more corrosive French characterizations of their neighbors across the Rhine. Peaceable as individuals, the Germans have so often herded together under spiked helmets and goose-stepped off at the command of their warlords. Yet in America they strikingly failed to demonstrate that self-protective herd instinct, even when they were under attack from the nativist, anti-foreign, exclusionist movement of the 1840's and 1850's. Most historians have emphasized the persecutions endured by the Irish immigrants, but

Hawgood has declared that the nativist crisis which stirred this country for almost two decades "had a more far-reaching effect upon the Germans than upon any other immigrant people, for not only was German immigration far and away above any other in numbers at the height of the nativist scare, but the only other nineteenth century emigration to the United States which had up to that time been of any significance had come from the British Isles and had consisted of people speaking the same language and possessing a similar cultural heritage to the Americans." The Irish were persecuted mainly because they were Roman Catholic. About half the Germans were also Catholic, and altogether they were more "foreign" in customs and appearance than the Irish.

The Irish met the nativist challenge aggressively, and took the political counteroffensive. The Germans met it, on the whole, supinely.

Regarding the Irish reply to the exclusionists, Hawgood has written, it was "characteristically, to return violence with greater violence, a procedure that even a Know-Nothing came to respect, and instead of seeking to operate as a foreign group in American politics in defense of their interests as foreigners, they preferred to enter the fight and capture the [Democratic] party machine as Americans. Having once done this it was easy to persuade the world that the typical American was simply an Irishman once removed. The hyphen never appealed to the Irish in their early struggles against nativism, and after early days they did not need it. It was all too often their opponents who later came to need protection. The Germans in America seemed convinced ('Pioneers of the West as we are') that the best defense against 'Americanism' was a stockade; the Irish thought the best defense would be a charge. The stockade behind which the Germans sheltered held firm, but the Irish went forth and captured the citadel of the enemy."[15] It was true, of course, as Hawgood does not mention, that the Irish were gathered together in the big cities, for the most part, and could take collective action more easily than the Germans, who preferred to "live scattered," and who did not find big-city political machines available for seizure.

During this period the American attitude toward the German newcomers was compounded of many sectional elements. In the South, the Germans' stubborn opposition to slavery was held against them. In the Middle West, their persistence in drinking beer on Sunday and otherwise breaking the Sabbath was heartily resented by their Anglo-Saxon neighbors; and it was said that Yankee mothers "greeted with horror" the beer gardens and taverns which sprung up in any neighborhood or district invaded by Germans, who seemed to divide their time between hard work and hard guzzling. Their guttural speech, even when superimposed upon the English tongue, was also repugnant. And their oncoming numbers were especially dismaying. In 1854, German migration reached its peak with 215,000 entering the United States.

Their sharp instinct for picking out the best land on which to settle, with plentiful wood and water, with the richest and best-drained soil, was also a matter for resentment. The fact that many German newcomers considered themselves cultured and highly civilized people bearing the torch of learning to the semibarbaric Yankees did not win favor for them. The Yankees, in fact, tended to believe that the educated German vastly overestimated himself; that his only real talent was for grabbing the best land. That view was adopted a half-century later by H. L. Mencken — a German-American but certainly not a characteristic one — in an article he wrote for a German periodical advising Germany not to lament the loss of all those hundreds of thousands of their countrymen who migrated to America. "It is a fact that, with the exception of the small group of intellectual revolutionaries of the year 1848, the overwhelming majority of the Germans who migrated to the States belonged to the landworking, handworking and small shopkeeping classes. These 'good' Germans play little or no part in the intellectual life of America, and bring nothing of the intellectual life of Germany with them. As Americans they are mere numbers . . . The influence of the Germans upon American life is very slight, and they have left no impression upon American ideas . . . In the political field they are as feeble as in the cultural." The only visible German contributions, in Mencken's professionally jaundiced view, expressed with his customary overstatement, were in the field of cooking food; that and a few words and phrases also connected with eating and drinking. Germany was well rid of them, he declared, and "I can see no reason why the Germans should waste their time bemoaning the loss of the German-Americans."[16]

Nativism, too, may have been increased by the "New Germany" idea propounded almost from the beginning of the German migrations. There was little mention of it in the English-language press, but word of that movement, exclusionist in itself, must have gotten around.

Nativism became a political movement when the so-called American party held its first convention in Philadelphia on the Fourth of July, 1845. Later they became known as the Know-Nothings because members, when subjected to questioning by outsiders, were instructed to reply, "I know nothing." Their views were clearly stated, in any case, in the "declaration of principles" adopted by the first convention, which read in part:

"The danger of foreign influence, threatening the gradual destruction of our national institutions, failed not to arrest the attention of the Father of his Country, in the very dawn of American Liberty. Not only its direct agency in rendering the American system liable to the poisonous influence of European policy — a policy at war with the fundamental principles of the American Constitution — but also its still more fatal operation in aggravating the virulence of partisan warfare — has awakened deep alarm in the mind of every intelligent patriot, from the days of Washington to the present time."

People of foreign birth, the American party held, were "imbued with foreign feelings" and were of "an ignorant and immoral character." Europe was sending "the feeble, the imbecile, the idle, and intractable," thus relieving itself of the "burdens resulting from the vices of the European social systems by availing themselves of the generous errors of our own." The United States was becoming the "lazar house and penal colony of Europe."

Neither the Whigs nor the Democrats could effectively combat the foreign influence because "if either of the old parties, as such, were to attempt an extension of the term of naturalization, it would be impossible for it to carry out the measure, because they would immediately be abandoned by the foreign voters."

The formation of a third party, oriented toward the aspirations of native Americans, would result in "resisting the progress of foreign influence in the conduct of American affairs, and the correction of such political abuses as have resulted from unguarded or partisan legislation on the subject of naturalization . . ."[17]

What it all boiled down to, at first, was that the nativists wanted to make it more difficult for immigrants to become American citizens and be given their voting rights.

Nativism and some of its more vicious aspects were spelled out at the height of the agitation, between 1852 and 1856, not only by the mob violence visited upon the foreign-born, almost invariably the Irish, in which incidents of religious bigotry were greatly in evidence, but in a spate of books, pamphlets and broadsides. A sampling of some of the more intellectually respectable propaganda efforts might include Samuel C. Busey's *Immigration: Its Evils and Consequences* (1856) which collected a number of documents in support of the charge that the Irish and Germans were trying to subvert American institutions. It included resolutions passed by the German Social Democratic Association of Richmond, Virginia, which demanded the abolition of the Presidency, a reduced term for acquiring citizenship, the right of the people to change the Constitution at will, and also quoted from the platform of the Free Germans of Louisville, who demanded, among many other things, "the right of free expressions of religious conscience," including the privilege of expressing antireligious convictions publicly. Busey quoted from an Irish handbill reading: "Irishmen to your posts, or you will lose America. By perseverance you may become its rulers." The Galveston *Zeitung* was quoted on August 19, 1855, as urging Germans "to form in every town where there is a sufficient German population one or more guard companies who shall furnish their own arms." Busey also quoted a Mississippi congressman who had observed an election in a Texas town: "On the day of election here, the Germans paraded their flag (instead of the national) through the streets. They marched in procession through the city, chanting German national airs . . . Yet, it is said, we have nothing to fear from German influence." Busey concluded that it was "high time that the birth-right qualification for office and voting should be established."

In *Sons of the Sires: A History of the Rise, Progress, and Destiny of the American Party* (1855), an author who signed himself "An American" proclaimed:

"A change in our Naturalization laws is absolutely demanded by considerations of our safety. It is an incontrovertible fact, that a large majority of these foreigners range themselves under the banner of socialism, of freethinkers, of Jesuits. All these classes are hostile to the interests of this land. Their principles are in conflict with those of a sound morality, and subversive of civil government. Their peculiarities and their designs will be more fully unfolded . . . their numerical strength is such as to inspire the thoughtful with apprehensions for our safety. A writer from the West recently stated in a communication to a leading periodical, that in a certain city there are 60,000 Germans, and an equal number of Irish in a population of 200,000. These, though divided in their religious sentiments, manifest a singular unanimity in their hostility to all the leading interests of America. Suffer this influx of foreigners to continue for ten years, and clothe them as rapidly as they arrive on our shores with the right of suffrage, and no man may predict the result."

There was, of course, a spirited reply to the propaganda of the Know-Nothings. *Putman's Magazine* was particularly energetic in defending the rights of the foreign-born, one of a series of dissections of their opponents being Parke Godwin's "Secret Societies — The Know Nothings." Godwin conceded that politicians had courted the immigrants and that "It was better to be an Irishman, or a German than a native American; a 'Mac' or an 'O' to one's name was the handle which lifted him to fortune — and an unpronounceable German patronymic was the handle which lifted him to fortune. No ticket was a complete ticket which did not contain a sop, in the shape of a candidate to the Irish interest or the German interest, and the suppleness with which senators and governors bent themselves in that direction set new lessons in the art of fawning. . . ." For this he blamed the "dastardly and unprincipled demagogues" of American birth. All that Know-Nothingism had to propose was the "political disability of vast numbers of men, on the ground of race or religion." Godwin reminded his readers that "we have already, in the midst of us, one class of outcasts, in the poor and degraded free blacks, and that . . . was sufficient to appease everybody's malignity, without striving to raise up another from the Germans, the Irish, or any other nation."[18]

The Know-Nothings' objectives assumed a more extremist aspect as immigration statistics reached rather alarming heights in the early Fifties. But just as the nativist elements were beginning to gather strength, the German-American population, in what Hawgood has termed its psychological "stockade" against the buffeting of the 101 percent Americans, received a moral and intellectual reinforcement from the old country. This was the fleeing band of Forty-eighters, trained and dedicated, but unsuccessful, revolutionaries.

For a few months in 1848 the peoples of Europe from France to Hungary had a brief foretaste of democratic freedom. There was another revolution in France, the shock waves of which caused popular uprisings in a number of German states. The various rulers of those states were so alarmed by the people's mood, which was excited by the rebelling intellectuals and student leaders, that they permitted the convocation of a parliament in Frankfurt on May 18, 1848. A national government was provisionally established. Less than a year later it was dissolved when the ruler of Prussia, King Frederick William IV, refused to reign over a constitutional monarchy. Instead the Prussian hegemony spread to South Germany, and thousands of able-bodied young men migrated to escape the Prussian army's recruiters. Germany would become a national entity two decades later but under Prussian authority and without the democratic safeguards the revolutionaries — democrats and socialists alike — had been working for.

Among the fleeing revolutionaries were Carl Schurz, Friedrich Hecker, Franz Sigel, August Willich and others who made their mark on American as well as German history. Many of them came to the United States hoping to return soon to a more democratic Germany. They were more interested in arousing German-American sympathy and support for the democratic movement in Germany than in participating in the current defensive struggle of the Americanized Germans. The German-Americans' plight, more a matter of nativist threats than any positive action taken against them, seemed inconsequential compared to the desperation in the homeland. An exception to this feeling was Carl Schurz, who had migrated first to France and England and did not come to this country until 1852 — but he came to stay, to become an American and take only a cursory interest in Germany's troubles. Many other Forty-eighters, as the democratic cause in Germany seemed progressively more hopeless, eventually threw themselves into American causes, particularly, of course, the struggle against slavery. August Willich was a fairly typical case. He was a Prussian, the son of a captain in the Hussars, whose university education caused him to break with family tradition and join the revolutionaries in Baden. He was forced to flee with Hecker and Siegel. When the Civil War broke out, he joined a German-American regiment in Ohio and eventually was given command of a brigade.

Rather than contributing their political talents to solving the German-Americans' problems with the nativists, many of the Forty-eighters only increased them. Their radicalism, particularly in religious matters, affronted the native Americans and many German-Americans, particularly since many of them were highly articulate and immediately plunged into journalism. A majority of the educated Forty-eighters, apparently, were freethinkers or atheists; they did not hesitate to disseminate their views and propagandized vigorously against both the Lutheran and Catholic Churches. "Followers of Hecker and Kossuth," the Reverend Anthony Urbanek, a leader of the Wisconsin Catholics wrote to the Archbishop of Vienna in 1852, "are most annoying and disgusting to Catholics."[19]

The visionary and utopian aspects of the Forty-eighters' political philosophy also militated against their being of much practical help to their compatriots. Much of their credo was as murkily romantic and high-flown as the talk around a *Brauhaus* table or a students' seminar, in which most of it originated. Somehow, it appeared, they hoped to erect a philosophical bridge between Old-World authoritarianism and New-World freedom (unrefined and unsophisticated as it was in their view). America would be the center — under their tutelage — of a worldwide democracy. They were pioneers of the One World philosophy, in fact, though the debt has not been acknowledged.

Their ideological concepts were aired, and given substance in print, at the Wheeling Congress of 1852. Sixteen delegates representing German revolutionary societies all over the United States, with Friedrich Hecker prominent in the leadership, met in the Virginia city and formed the People's League of the Old and New Worlds. Their objectives were set forth in Julius Goebel, Jr.'s *A Political Prophecy of the Forty-Eighters in America* and even more definitively in *The New Rome, or the United States of the World*, by T. Poesche and C. Goepp. In *The New Rome* it was proposed that the United States annex, step by step, all the other civilized nations of the world. Just how this annexation would be accomplished was not prescribed, but it would be propelled by increased immigration from Germany. The result would be an "American Empire that is at the same time a Democracy." Just how such a self-contradicting beast as an imperial democracy could be made to restrain itself was not made clear, except that its proponents apparently had a touching faith in the purity of American idealism. They might well have been advised to reread the experiences of their compatriot, Dr. Frankenstein, with his own homemade monster.

Subsequently the Forty-eighters also excited alarm and annoyance among conservative Germans as well as native Americans by holding various convocations along the Middle Border from Texas to Wisconsin. In 1853, they presided over a convention at Sisterdale, Texas, in which it was declared: "The latest events in American, as well as in European politics, show the necessity of a close adhesion of all Germans in the United States." This was not in accord with the "stockade" thinking of the older German-American elements, who had more faith in the durability of American institutions and believed they had less to fear from nativists than their own radicals.

By the mid-1850's, in any event, a larger storm than that stirred up by the Know-Nothings was gathering on the horizon. The agitation over Irish and German immigration was soon to be swirled away by the crisis arising over the extension of slavery. The passage of the Kansas-Nebraska Act and the repeal of the Missouri Compromise signaled it in 1854, especially when Senator Butler of South Carolina attacked the German-Americans for their opposition to slavery during the Congressional debate over the new measure. "The intelligent and judicious master, having his slaves around him in Missouri or Nebraska, would be as acceptable a neighbor to me . . . as one of these new immigrants" — by which, the senator added, he meant "Germans, coming from Bremen." He was even blunter, according to the Philadelphia *Ledger's* report of the debate: "Judge Butler declared frankly in his seat that he should prefer Negroes in Nebraska to 'emigrants from the land of the Kraut.'" Such contemptuous references led to an immediate disenchantment with the Democratic party, to which most Germans had offered their loyalty until now, and a meeting of Chicago Germans adopted a resolution reading: "We perceive a spirit particularly inimical to us Germans, pioneers of the West as we are; that we have lost our confidence in and must look with distrust upon the leaders of the Democratic party in whom, hitherto, we had confidence enough to think they paid some regard to our interests."

In the pro-slavery declarations of the Democrats, along with their new hostility toward German-Americans as a solidly antislavery element in American opinion, the Germans proclaimed that they had detected the "Devil's cloven hoof sticking out." Germans do not take the name of the Devil in vain. In German literature he is omnipresent, always ready to subvert a nation of Fausts.

From then on, German-Americans were watchful for evidences of the "cloven hoof" prints left by nativists and slavery advocates alike. It was a critical turning point for them and for the United States. The fact that they turned en masse to the newly formed Republican party, and wholeheartedly to the cause of the Union in 1861, was one of the pivots on which the outcome of the Civil War revolved.

5. "I FIGHTS MIT SIGEL"

The military exploits of the Irish in the Civil War earned them the title of "the fighting Irish," but all the sacrifices of the German-Americans only won them the catchphrase of "those damn Dutch." In view of the rivalry of the Germans and the Irish, these tags are not without significance.

The undoubted heroism of the Irish was established largely by the accomplishments of the Irish Brigade, particularly its gallant charge against the heights of Fredericksburg.

The suspected pusillanimity of the German-Americans was confirmed, particularly in the minds of surviving Know-Nothings, by what happened to the mostly German XI Corps at the Battle of Chancellorsville when the corps was taken by surprise and scattered in a pell-mell retreat by one of General Robert E. Lee's better-planned attacks. That the same disgraced German-American divisions a few months later charged up Lookout Mountain and won the "battle in the clouds" was not nearly so well publicized, since it was part of a bigger victory in the campaign for Chattanooga.

Whatever cold mathematical comfort that German-Americans could take in return for their tremendous sacrifices in the Civil War came four years after the war ended and Benjamin A. Gould, the actuary for the

United States Sanitary Commission, published his *Investigations in the Military and Anthropological Statistics of American Soldiers* (1869).

Using the census of 1860, Dr. Gould showed that the Germans supplied a larger proportionate share of volunteers for the Union army than either the native Americans — many of whom hired substitutes under the bounty system — or the Irish.

According to Dr. Gould's figures 176,817 Germans enlisted in the Federal army, which totaled 2,018,200 men, though they would have had to supply only 118,402 in proportion to their share of the population. Native Americans should have supplied 1,660,068 but actually only 1,523,267 were enlisted. The Irish, like the Germans, exceeded their quota, supplying 144,221 when their share would have been only 139,052. Since there weren't as many Germans as Irish in the United States by 1860, it was plain that the Germans exceeded them as well as other nationalities in their contribution to the Union armies.

Another striking indication of the Germans' greater devotion to the cause — and perhaps also their long indoctrination in obedience to civil authority, contrasted to the more volatile temperament of the Irish — was the diverse attitudes shown during the draft riots of 1863 in New York City.

The differing attitudes were epitomized by a snatch of conversation a New York *Sun* reporter overheard when he watched a mob of Irishmen congregating to demonstrate their violent disapproval of government policy. The reporter heard a fat amiable Bavarian, the owner of a lager saloon, ask an Irish friend:

"What makes you Irishers all the time fight?"

"Och, Schlosser," the Irishman replied, "don't bother me. You wouldn't understand if I was talking from June to January."

Perhaps not, judging by the passiveness of the German population of New York during those days when the Union itself was endangered by the outraged Irish. In the wartime Sixties the New York City population included 203,000 Irish and 169,000 Germans, most of them crowded into slums like Hell's Kitchen. The slum-dwellers were restive enough without the imposition of the Conscription Act of 1863, which was designed to gather in the family men, the only untapped source of manpower left to an army decimated by two years of war. No man henceforth could claim exemption from the draft on the grounds that he was the sole support of his family. Exemption could be purchased for three hundred dollars or avoided by providing a substitute, but this means of escape was available to few of the newcomers from Ireland and Germany.

The inequity of the system was baldly stated by George Templeton Strong, the patrician lawyer and diarist, whose feverish Unionism never betrayed him into enlisting in its armed forces. Strong would write scornfully of the "rough loutish Germans and Celts" he saw marching in the raw regiments parading down Broadway. In his diary of the war years in New York he denounced a large part of the population as "equivalent to that of coward, *fainé-ant*, serf and craven" and promised himself to "emigrate and become a citizen of some community of gregarious blue baboons in South Africa" if his fellow Americans didn't pull themselves together. Three sentences later Mr. Strong was unabashedly recounting that he had just paid $1,100 for a substitute to take his place in the ranks, smugly adding that "the big Dutchman [German] therewith purchased looked as if he could do good service."[1]

The worst rioting in American history broke out on July 13, 1863, less than two weeks after the Battle of Gettysburg. Irish mothers with large families told their men to fight it out in the streets rather than leave them to support their children on public charity. For four days Manhattan was virtually controlled by mobs totaling fifty to seventy thousand men; the whole island above Mulberry Street was in the hands of the rioters, and the police and their auxiliaries were able to protect only the financial and commercial districts downtown and the streets where the well-to-do lived. They were brought under control four days later only by the intervention of army regiments who smashed through the street barricades and sent volleys up the avenues of the West Side, by which time two thousand persons had been killed, eight thousand to ten thousand injured, and property damage was estimated at five million dollars. The rioting was stopped not so much by military force as by the appeals of the Catholic archdiocese and the promise (later vetoed by the Anglo-American mayor) that the Common Council would appropriate millions of dollars to purchase draft exemption for men with large families.

The astonishing thing wasn't that thousands revolted against the inequities of the new Conscription Act, but that only a handful of Germans, though they were equally victimized and were emotionally on the side of the Irish, joined the rioting mobs. The observant Mr. Strong fumed against the "Irish canaille" and "these Celtic outrages," and was not dismayed by the possibility that Know-Nothingism would be revived. The only obstacle was that "it would be obliged to discriminate between Celts and Teutons. The Germans have behaved well and kept quiet. Where they acted at all, they volunteered against the rabble, as they did, most effectively, in the Seventh Ward."[2] As Mr. Strong indicated, the Germans' docility during that civil insurrection was credited to their account. It was a negative virtue, however, compared to the decisive German-American support of the Republican party and of the war effort itself, which finally made German-Americanism a respectable element in American life.

GERMANS FOR LINCOLN

Abraham Lincoln, a practical politician before all else, was quick to recognize the importance of the German-American vote which had cavalierly been written off by the Democrats. Even in Illinois, where Stephen A. Douglas had counted on their support for years, the Germans abandoned the Democratic party because of Douglas's vote in the Senate for the Kansas-Nebraska Act. The trump discarded by Douglas was promptly snatched up by Lincoln.

In May, 1859, through an intermediary, Lincoln secretly bought the weekly German-language paper, *Illinois Staats-Anzeiger*, which was read by the downstate Germans, particularly those influential "Latin farmers" around Belleville. For four hundred dollars Lincoln acquired the German paper's type, press and other physical equipment; presumably, too, the deal included its support for Lincoln's understated political ambitions. Included in the transaction was the provision that Theodore

Canisius, the editor, would continue publishing the *Staats-Anzeiger* as a Republican organ. Much as he confided in his law partner, William Herndon, at least by Herndon's later account, Lincoln never mentioned the deal to him, perhaps because he realized how important it is for a man to keep the glare of Presidential ambitions carefully concealed until the strategic moment.[3]

Lincoln apparently decided to buy the paper after Canisius wrote him early that year asking him how he stood on the Massachusetts Act of 1859, which provided that no foreign-born naturalized citizen could vote or hold office until two years after his naturalization. It was one of the later triumphs of the Know-Nothings, and naturally the German-Americans didn't want to see the pattern repeated in other states. Lincoln replied to Canisius: "I am against its adoption in Illinois, or in any other place, where I have a right to oppose it." He had become notorious for his pro-Negro attitude, Lincoln added, and it would be inconsistent if he favored "any project for curtailing the existing rights of white men, even though born in different lands, and speaking different languages from myself." Canisius published the letter, which was reprinted by many other newspapers.[4]

Lincoln had begun his assiduous courtship of the German-American vote. A study of the United States Census of the following year surely confirmed him in that course. Of the 1,300,000 foreign-born in the United States, 700,000 were Germans, mostly settled in the northern states. In many states they represented the balance of power at the polls. One of Lincoln's closest political collaborators was Gustav Koerner of Belleville, who became a lieutenant governor and state supreme court justice. In 1856 Lincoln had helped the Germans to write a resolution adopted by the Republican state convention, which declared that "our naturalization laws, being just in principle, we are opposed to any change being made in them intended to enlarge the time now required to secure the rights of citizenship." The same resolution was adopted by the Republican national convention later that year.

What particularly alarmed the German-Americans, and caused Lincoln to reassure them and make certain of his own power base in Illinois and the Middle West, was that the Massachusetts Know-Nothing law was passed with the assistance of the Republican party in that state. There and elsewhere Republican leaders, by 1859, were flirting with nativist political theory, careless of its effect on German-American sentiment. "The Two Year Amendment of Massachusetts," one commentator wrote, "was as much of an outrage to the Germans as the John Brown raid was to the Southerners."[5] No sooner had they captured the German vote, it seemed, than the Republicans were intent on losing it.

The Germans stood by the Republican party largely through the ameliorating influence of Lincoln and William H. Seward, the eastern leader of the party, and also because there was no real alternative to the Republicans by that time. Their first Republican hero, however, was John C. Frémont, "the great pathfinder," who had explored the unmapped West but found the political and military trails back East trickier to negotiate. Most German-American leaders subscribed to his candidacy for the Presidency in 1856 after he published his platform, along with a translation of the United States Constitution, in a German-language pamphlet. When Frémont ran against Buchanan, the Middle Western Germans largely gave their support to the first Republican nominee for the White House. In that election Lincoln's running mate for elector at large in Illinois was Friedrich Hecker, the Forty-eighter.

A dozen years had passed since the Forty-eighters had fled from Germany, and by now they had recovered from their bemusement, had given up the idea of returning to the old country from "exile," and mostly had discarded their utopian schemes. Hecker, Schurz, Sigel and most of the others would operate within the framework of the Republican party; all of them, from the beginning, were close to Abraham Lincoln and his aspirations, which they regarded as akin to their own. Even Seward wavered at times in wondering whether the German-Americans and the more conservative Republicans could work in political harness, largely because of the Germans' pro-labor bias. In May, 1858, Seward wrote Francis Lieber: "Sometimes I despair — the natural course for the Germans to pursue is to sustain free labor — but except for myself all our free labor public men either directly or indirectly join the Know-Nothings in persecuting Germans, while the Democrats by patronage subsidize the papers which the Germans rely on for information and guidance."[6]

By 1860 it was apparent that Abraham Lincoln owed a large measure of his support to German-Americans as he maneuvered, with considerable guile, toward the nomination for the Presidency. Some of his strongest supporters were among those attending the preconvention conference of German Republicans at the Deutsches Haus on May 14 and 15, 1860, in the convention city of Chicago. A historian who had studied that conference claims that its deliberations were mainly responsible for the success of Lincoln's candidacy.[7] Its less clandestine purpose was to make sure that German-American principles — or at least those of the more liberal hue — were included in the Republican platform. The conference insisted that the platform, as in 1856, must be "most hostile to slavery," that liberal naturalization laws be kept in effect, that the generous Homestead Act be pushed through Congress (which would promote more German settlement of the western lands), and that Kansas be admitted to the Union as soon as possible as a free state.

The Republican national convention, of course, went along with these demands because it was believed that the German-American vote held the balance of power in Missouri, Iowa, Illinois, Wisconsin, Minnesota, Ohio, Michigan, Indiana, Maryland, Pennsylvania, New Jersey, New York and Connecticut — and possibly in California and Massachusetts.

With the backing of the German-Americans, Lincoln had no serious opposition by the time the roll was called for a Presidential nominee. Hostile sections of the American press were quick to take notice of the Teutonic influence on the Republican party in its second sortie on the national scene. Days before the convention was called to order, the Detroit *Free Press*, then a Democratic organ, remarked: "Since they [the Germans] hold the controlling power in the Black Republic Party, they consider it no more than right that the party should yield to their preference." Even earlier the Providence *Daily Post* had accused Lincoln of truckling to the German-American vote and sneered, "He is in favor of allowing foreigners to vote, even before they are naturalized."

F. I. Herriott, in his study of the German-American influence on the convention, declared that "the question of the status of the foreign-born naturalized citizen and *not* slavery was the major cause of dissension in the national Republican convention," and that the Germans' determined opposition to any of Lincoln's rivals who were not so outspoken on that issue was responsible for Lincoln's nomination.[8] Several years before the election Samuel Bowles, the acerbic Springfield, Massachusetts, editor, had predicted the historic impact of the German-Americans on the outcome. "When you get a German between slavery on the one side and Know-Nothingism on the other, you get a stubborn fellow in a very tight place, and he is quite apt to let slavery slide for this time in order to make his vote tell against the Know-Nothings.' "[9]

With Lincoln's election and the coming of the Civil War, the Germans were enabled to strike hard at the two elements they most detested in American life — nativism and its restrictions, which was largely a self-protective and materialistic objective, and slavery, which could be said to be an idealistic one. In at least one sector of the war against the Confederacy, both politically and by direct action, the intervention of German-Americans was of strategic importance. That was the struggle for Missouri, the key border state and officially a slave state.

THE FIGHT FOR ST. LOUIS

The Civil War honor roll was liberally sprinkled with German names among the high-ranking officers. Schurz, Sigel, Willich, Steinwehr, Wagner, Blenker, Kautz, Osterhaus, Schimmelpfennig and others were general officers. Gustav Koerner organized a regiment of Illinois volunteers, and Friedrich Hecker became a Union colonel, severely wounded at Chancellorsville, commander of the 82nd Illinois Volunteers in the Chattanooga campaign. The chief of staff of the Union army was Major General Henry W. Halleck, slow-witted but adept at politico-military intrigue, a Californian of German descent.

Whatever military glory attached itself to those names would have been meaningless without the staunch pro-Unionism of the German-American population of St. Louis, an antislavery colony surrounded by slaveowners and their adherents. It was one instance in which men of German blood could not be accused of lacking civil courage. They were determined to form a resistance against the secessionist designs of the state's governor, Claiborne Jackson, and stage an uprising if necessary. The main elements of that resistance were Captain Nathaniel Lyon, a West Pointer who commanded a company of United States infantry guarding the United States Arsenal at St. Louis; Francis P. Blair, the aggressive Republican leader of Missouri, and the German militia regiments organized by Blair and trained by Captain Lyon. Through a combination of Lyon's daring tactics, Blair's talent for taking political risks, and the intense loyalty of the Germans on whom their power was based, the designs of the Confederacy in Missouri were placed in jeopardy before they had a chance to evolve.

The winter before the war broke out Blair, whose father was President Jackson's closest adviser and whose brother Montgomery was a member of Lincoln's cabinet, started recruiting the somewhat illegal militia companies among St. Louis's eighty thousand Germans. They began drilling in their Turnverein halls, often under the unofficial supervision of Captain Lyon, a small, wiry and energetic Connecticut man with sandy whiskers and red hair. What both Blair and Lyon — as well as Governor Jackson — kept covertly watching was the United States Arsenal and its collection of 60,000 muskets, 1,500,000 ball cartridges, a number of outmoded cannon and lathes for turning more gun barrels. It had been well stocked by the pro-Confederate Secretary of War John B. Floyd, who expected that all its contents would fall into the hands of the Secessionists and would arm irregular forces which would seize Missouri and Illinois.

There were really three forces in opposition to each other in Missouri: the Germans and other Unionists, the Secessionists, and a large segment of the population that wanted to see the state stay neutral and out of the war, or was waiting to make up its mind. Nevertheless the slavery faction mustered enough votes to elect Claiborne Jackson to the governor's mansion, and he could probably have pulled Missouri into the Confederacy if he could have taken the arsenal (as Virginians captured the one at Harpers Ferry) and armed his supporters. Probably the majority of Missourians, as in other border states, would have stayed out of the war if their wishes had prevailed against the partisans.

Blair pulled wires in Washington to have Captain Lyon empowered to enroll ten thousand militia if it became necessary to protect government property. The nominal Federal commander of the military department was General William S. Harney, who tended to balk at extralegal measures and was called back to Washington for consultations while his very junior subordinate worked with Blair and his Committee of Public Safety to thwart Governor Jackson's plans. A German brewer named Hammer, who lived in a house overlooking the arsenal grounds, was one part of their security program. One morning a Hammer brewery wagon loaded with beer barrels was driven to the arsenal, and when it left the barrels were crammed with arms and ammunition. These were used to outfit a guard formed among the students of the Humboldt Institution, which was quartered at Hammer's house and was prepared twenty-four hours a day to rush over to the arsenal and help protect it against an attack by Governor Jackson's forces.

The probability of a clash between Captain Lyon's several hundred regulars, plus the home-guard battalions raised by the St. Louis Turner Societies, and the state militia under Governor Jackson's control quickened in mid-April. Jackson's intentions were soon tested by President Lincoln. On April 14, 1861, the day after Fort Sumter fell, the President informed Jackson that his state's quota for the volunteers being summoned to three months' service in the Federal army would be four thousand troops. "Your requisition," Governor Jackson replied with scant courtesy, "is illegal, unconstitutional, and revolutionary in its object, inhuman and diabolical, and cannot be complied with." Six days later Governor Jackson's state troops seized government supplies at Liberty, and in St. Louis the secessionist counterpart to the German home guard, the Minute Men, formed up and started to march on the United States Arsenal. They were dissuaded only when the mayor convinced them that the *furor teutonicus* of the home guards would descend upon them and the city might be destroyed in the fighting.

Meanwhile, the Turner battalions were holding a caucus and demanding that they be allowed to seize the arsenal and hold it for the United States government, since the few Federal troops available to Captain Lyon would not be able to defend it against a determined attack. Blair and members of the Committee of Public Safety tried to calm them, knowing that such an action would not have the faintest color of legality, knowing also that if it weren't taken quickly Governor Jackson himself wouldn't be so finicky about legality. Furthermore the leaders of the home guard informed Blair that unless he acted immediately the German battalions would march out of St. Louis in a body and offer their services to the United States government across the line in Illinois. At 4:00 A.M. on April 22, after conferring with Lyon, Blair permitted the Germans to march out to the arsenal and occupy it. More Germans were enrolled in the home guard and formed into regiments, one of which was commanded by Blair, another by Franz Sigel, and three others. Then Blair and Lyon, exhilarated by the risks they were taking, immediately dispatched thirty thousand muskets and ten thousand pounds of powder to Illinois for the arming of its volunteer regiments.

On May 3, Governor Jackson made his countermove. He called up seven hundred members of the state militia and put them into camp in Lindell Grove on the outskirts of St. Louis. Routine training, he told Blair and Lyon. Preparing to attack the United States Arsenal, they replied.

Legend says Captain Lyon dressed himself in black bombazine, with a sunbonnet to hide his red hair and a heavy veil to conceal his beard, and drove through the state militia's camp, now called Camp Jackson, in a buggy. Either in that romantic fashion — which historians intent on making all the fun out of history have tried to debunk — or more soberly through intelligence reports, Captain Lyon learned that the state militia under the command of Brigadier General D. M. Frost was drilling with muskets which had been stolen by Louisiana rebels from a government arsenal at Baton Rouge, and that the company streets had been named after Jefferson Davis and General Beauregard. He immediately proposed an escalation in the cold war, one that might make it very hot indeed. Before Blair's Committee of Public Safety he declared that it was necessary to surround Camp Jackson, disarm the governor's troops and take them prisoner. A hot dispute broke out in the committee, two members arguing that the stolen arms Captain Lyon claimed he saw should be recovered through action in the Federal Court. Blair and the others, however, sided in with Captain Lyon. General Frost and his troops were formally — though still extralegally — designated as enemies of the United States.

Under the anathema thus pronounced, Captain Lyon and what he called his "division" — a few companies of United States regulars plus the German home-guard regiments — marched out to Camp Jackson on the morning of May 10. He called upon General Frost to surrender, and the secessionist commander did so under protest. Lyons's regulars marched into the camp and disarmed the state militia while his German regiments surrounded the installation. The Jackson forces were then marched out under heavy guard, to be escorted to the arsenal and given their paroles.

Along this route toward the arsenal a large crowd of muttering and belligerent pro-secessionists began gathering. The mob would take up Governor Jackson's cause. At first it was merely an affair of name-calling. One of the German regiments called itself *Die Schwarze Garde*, which the mob freely and loudly translated into "Damn Dutch Blackguards." Other of the more printable epithets showered on the stolid home guards were "long-eared Dutchmen" and "mercenary Hessians." Discipline was preserved, however, until Captain Lyon's horse shied, bolted and left Lyon stunned on the ground. His column — prisoners marching between files of home guards and regulars — came to a halt. The mob seized that moment of uncertainty. It surged against the files of German militiamen, which hurled them back with excessive enthusiasm. Somebody in the mob fired a revolver and the bullet struck Captain Blandowsky, a Polish-German, upon which the crowd began attacking with clubs and paving stones. No one gave the order to fire, Lyon was still recovering his senses, but his troops leveled their muskets and opened up on the crowd. Before the shooting was over, twenty-eight bodies, two of them Lyon's militiamen, the others of the rioters, lay on the cobblestones and many more were injured. The march to the arsenal then was resumed.

That day it looked as though St. Louis, almost evenly divided in its sentiments, would have its own civil war. All saloons were closed by order of the mayor, and many of the wealthier citizens fled the city. But the city stayed fairly quiet that night. The five German militia regiments represented the power necessary to keep the Minute Men and other secessionists from fighting back. Meanwhile, it was plain to Blair and Lyon that General Harney, who had just returned to the city and kept insisting that Governor Jackson must be appeased, would have to go. An emissary, K. L. Bernays, editor of *Anzeiger des Westens*, was dispatched to Washington to urge this and other measures. On May 20, the War Department announced that General Harney was being removed and Captain Lyon was promoted to brigadier general.

Governor Jackson declared his own war, against the citizens of his own state, when peace talks with General Lyon failed. He had offered a state of temporary neutrality for Missouri if the Union general would disband his "Dutch blackguard" regiments, which General Lyon indignantly refused. Following that there was a period of bushwhacking and barn burning, in which Germans were driven from secessionist districts and vice versa.[10]

The German-Americans of Missouri rightly prided themselves on having saved a key state at a critical hour, but an inglorious anticlimax was to follow.

By midsummer their old hero, General Frémont, arrived to take over as commander of the western theater, with headquarters in St. Louis. He began awarding millions of dollars in war contracts, with which he won a lot more German-American loyalty. To General Lyon was left the job of dealing with the secessionist forces being gathered by Governor Jackson. With his untried regiments he drove down the state, chased Jackson and his troops out of the capital. Possibly he was unaware that Jackson and his new commander, General Sterling Price, were gathering strength as they retreated. By the time Lyon had pressed on to Wilson's Creek, about ten miles from Springfield, with less than six thousand men (three of the German home guard regiments, two volun-

141

teer regiments from Kansas and one from Iowa, all of whose three-month terms of enlistment had ended), the Confederate force amounted to twice their number.

Undismayed by the odds, if he had reckoned them, Lyon conceived a bold plan by which his second-in-command, General Franz Sigel, and his Germans would make a wide sweep around the Confederate right and attack from the rear. Such a maneuver might have worked if Lyon and Sigel had had the forces available; also, perhaps, if Sigel's military aptitude had matched his courage. But the result was a disaster, a western Bull Run. Sigel's "division" executed its flanking maneuver, then attacked the Confederate rear across woods and meadows. It was met by a sheet of rifle and artillery fire which sent them reeling away in an unabashed retreat just as Lyon was attacking the Confederates frontally. Lyon was killed, the day was lost, and more than a fifth of the Union forces were killed or wounded. It would take another and better prepared campaign to settle the score with Governor Jackson and General Price.

The important thing was that the German-Americans' fervent loyalty to the Union had saved St. Louis. The Union's first general-in-chief, Winfield Scott, had devised a strategy for winning the war called the "Anaconda Plan." The South's coasts were to be blockaded, then Union armies were to drive down the Mississippi to the Gulf and slowly constrict upon the Confederate armies. It was the plan, essentially, which won the war, though only after the "On to Richmond" enthusiasts had bloodily failed in more direct efforts. And St. Louis was the essential base for the western constrictions of the Union Anaconda.

THE TRAGEDY OF XI CORPS

From the beginning, the XI Corps of the Army of the Potomac, with fifteen of its twenty-six regiments listed as German, had been the "Cinderella of the army." The phrase is Bruce Catton's, in his definitive history of that army.[11] "It seems to have felt, collectively, like a poor ignored wallflower at a high school dance," Mr. Catton goes on to explain. "The corps contained many German soldiers, known to one and all as Dutchmen, a contemptuous title by which the soldiers expressed the national feeling — that men who talked with a foreign accent just did not need to be taken seriously. It is hardly going too far to say that what happened at Chancellorsville was the price the country paid for its indulgence in that feeling."

Many of the regiments in XI Corps had originally served under a German-born divisional commander, General Louis Blenker, another of the Forty-eighters who had found themselves, after many spiritual and philosophical vicissitudes, caught up in the idealism attending the start of the Civil War. Blenker had led the revolutionary forces of Hesse-Darmstadt against the Prussian occupation in 1848 and fled to America when that revolt was put down. At the start of the war he raised the 8th New York Regiment and commanded it with distinction at First Bull Run. Early in 1862 he was given command of a division composed of three brigades of German troops from the East and Middle West. It was a hard-luck outfit. In the spring of 1862 it was sent, under Blenker's command, on a march over the Blue Ridge to reinforce a Union army operating in western Virginia under the command of General Frémont, who had been transferred out of St. Louis when the smell of corruption around his headquarters could no longer be ignored but who had to be given another army command because of his political influence. Blenker's March may well have been the comic-opera masterpiece of the Civil War. His division floundered over muddy mountain roads, ran out of supplies and lost their way, no reliable maps having been supplied their leader. The countryside was filled with stragglers and looters. While crossing the Shenandoah River, a young lieutenant swamped his ferry and caused forty of his men to drown — merely one more incident in the hapless venture. Finally General Frémont had to send out a rescue mission and bring in the wandering Blenker division. The German regiments naturally were the object of scorn, Yankee soldiers sniffing in their presence and commenting, "The air around here seems to be rather Dutchy." Frémont undertook a mountain campaign which similarly ended in disaster, by the end of which he was relieved of his command, and Blenker died of a fall from his horse.

143

In the reorganization that followed, Frémont's small army, including Blenker's former division, was converted into the XI Corps of the Army of the Potomac. German morale was restored when command of the corps was handed over to General Franz Sigel. The old Forty-eighter was the first German-born soldier to rise to high command in the Union army, though two German-Americans, Halleck as commanding general of the western armies, later as army chief of staff, and General William S. Rosecrans, as commander of the Army of the Cumberland at Stone's River and Chickamauga, were to outrank him and all other German-born general officers. Germans were so proud of Sigel's elevation that all through the North the catchphrase was heard: "I fights mit Sigel."

But not, as it turned out, very much. XI Corps arrived too late to join the fighting at Fredericksburg, where the Irish Brigade brought great honor to its people on Marye's Heights. By the spring of 1863, when it moved up with the rest of the Army of the Potomac to grapple with Lee and Jackson along the Rappahannock, it was still demoralized and in disgrace. The Know-Nothing spirit was still abroad, in the army as elsewhere, and as Bruce Catton has written, "a country which hated foreigners almost as much as Negroes was now using the one to enforce freedom for the other and was suffering from emotional indigestion as a result. It may yet find that a fight to end slavery would also, in the end, be a fight to improve the lot of the immigrant, and that was something it had not counted on."[12]

Morale was not improved in XI Corps, or elsewhere in the army, for that matter, when Major General "Fighting Joe" Hooker took over command with his special blend of arrogance and ineptitude. General Sigel requested that his corps, the smallest in the army, be enlarged. Hooker didn't care much for foreigners and was pleased to turn down the request, then accept Sigel's resignation from command of the corps. The Germans in XI Corps probably would have resented anyone who offered himself as Sigel's replacement, but they disliked their new commander, General O. O. Howard, for other reasons as well. Howard was a stiff-backed Yankee, widely known as the "Christian general," who addressed a soldier as "my man" and was assiduous in passing out religious tracts. Many of the Germans were agnostic or atheistic, having brought over an anticlerical tradition from the Fatherland. In any case, the new corps commander and his troops, particularly those of German birth or descent, were out of sympathy with each other.

XI Corps formed the right flank of Hooker's army as it arrayed itself against the Confederates near Chancellorsville. And it was that soft spot, weaker than the other corps and in something less than fighting trim, which was to be struck at twilight by a daring and overwhelming assault by Stonewall Jackson and more than twenty-five thousand of the best infantry in the world.

Most of the troops were gathered around cookfires, their arms stacked, as Jackson and his Confederate assault columns completed their march across the Union army's front and prepared to swing around its right flank. The various units of XI Corps had scouts out prowling the woods and brush which screened their front, and toward dusk they brought back alarming reports of Confederate activity, of enemy skirmish lines closing in, of rabbits and deer rushing away from advancing men. The reports were sped back to divisional, then to corps, then to army headquarters, where they were promptly dismissed as the panicky reactions of those "damned Dutchmen." XI Corps was spread out for a mile, its positions thinly held, and knew it was vulnerable if an attack struck it on the flank. Its commander, General Howard, and his West Point staff officers spoke learnedly of a "rolling reconnaissance" — whatever that meant — from the enemy side, and diplomatically agreed with headquarters opinion that Lee was in retreat, which was exactly what Lee wanted his opponents to believe.

One of the first to take alarm was Colonel Leopold von Gilsa, the commander of a brigade in an exposed position, a former major in the Prussian army. The colonel received a message from his advanced elements saying the front was thick with the enemy and "for God's sake, make dispositions to receive him!"

Von Gilsa took the note to General Howard's headquarters and showed it to the commanding general. Howard shrugged it off, said the woods in front of von Gilsa's brigade were too thick to permit the enemy to launch a massive assault.

By the time von Gilsa returned to his own headquarters General

Carl Schurz, who commanded a division of XI Corps, had quietly and without consulting higher authority began redeploying his troops around the Wilderness Church, facing west, so they could meet an anticipated attack from that quarter. On his return von Gilsa was greeted by a colorful artilleryman, Captain Hubert Dilger, formerly an officer in the Baden Mounted Artillery, now commander of a battery in the First Ohio Artillery. Dilger, known as "Leatherbreeches" because he habitually wore a pair of doeskin pants, had gone out alone on a reconnaissance and had almost been captured by the advancing Confederates. As Dilger recounted his adventures to von Gilsa — typical as they were of the reception given German officers by their Anglo-American comrades — he had taken a long detour to avoid the advancing Confederates and hastened to army headquarters. The highest officer who would consent to talk to him there was a cavalry major, who informed Dilger that the commanding general did not care to interview mere artillery captains, particularly ones with a German accent and a German habit of getting scared in the woods. Dilger then repaired to Howard's headquarters, where he was brushed off by a staff officer who lectured him on the inadvisability of making unauthorized scouting trips and told him that his superiors were convinced that Lee was retreating and didn't want to be bothered by reports to the contrary. Dilger hastened back to his own battery and ordered his gunners to be ready to go into action at any moment.

Thus XI Corps was partly prepared, though not nearly strong enough, when Stonewall Jackson's assault columns came roaring out of the brush and descended on its positions. Part of two of its divisions, those commanded by Schurz and General von Steinwehr, had started changing front to meet the anticipated attack. Buschbeck's brigade of Steinwehr's division had just moved into new positions, facing the direction of Jackson's onslaught, and it held on for a few minutes against overwhelming numbers. Some of Schurz's regiments stood their ground for twenty minutes until they were overrun. Von Gilsa's brigade, formed in a skirmish line, managed a few volleys before the Confederates rolled over them. "Dilger's battery trains some of its guns down the road," wrote one observer after the battle. "The reserve artillery is already in position at the north end of this line, and issues spherical case [shot] with rapidity . . . As well oppose resistance to an avalanche. Buschbeck's line stubbornly holds on. An occasional squad, still clinging to the colors of its regiment, joins itself to him, ashamed of falling thus disgracefully to the rear. Officers making frantic exertions to rally their men; useless effort . . ."[13]

XI Corps was routed, crushed by the Confederates attacking in a mass one mile wide and four divisions deep. Instead of the rolling reconnaissance about which staff officers theorized well back of the line, it was a counteroffensive which folded up the Army of the Potomac from right to left and drove it back across the river.

Never was blame parceled out so quickly in military history as during the Civil War campaigns. The generals were quite shameless about ducking responsibility and nominating scapegoats. Each leading commander had laid his pipelines to a Congressional sponsor, a cabinet member, or a prominent newspaper editor, and the smoke had barely drifted away from a battlefield before the commanding general was rushing his version of victory or defeat into print. It was plain enough, as Bruce Catton has written, that "the real reason for the disaster was the fact that neither Hooker nor anyone else in authority would listen to the specific warnings which the unhappy Dutchmen had repeatedly sent in."[14] This view is supported by Lieutenant Colonel T. A. Dodge in his history of the battle: "It seems reasonably settled therefore that the [XI] corps retarded the Confederate advance for about a mile of ground for exceeding an hour. How much more can be expected of ten thousand raw troops telescoped by twenty-five thousand veterans?"[15]

General Howard, who had been as wrongheaded as Hooker in ignoring the warnings from his divisions commanded by Schurz and Steinwehr, was guilty of conduct unbecoming a Christian general when he obliquely assigned the blame to those who least deserved it by noting in his corps orders that he had a "feeling of depression" over the conduct of "a portion of this corps."

The German officers raged with indignation. General Schimmelpfennig complained that "the most infamous falsehoods" regarding the conduct of the XI Corps had been passed along to newspaper correspondents by members of Hooker's staff. General Schurz warned the War Department that the men of his division had taken all the official and unofficial recrimination they could stand. "We have been overwhelmed by the army and the press with abuse and insult without measure," Schurz wrote. "We have borne as much as human nature can endure."[16]

In New York City the German-Americans became so wrought up over the public humiliation of the men who had fought "mit Sigel" that they held a mass meeting to protest the injustice. Of all the speakers who tried to restore the XI Corps' honor that night, the most effective was an Irish-American. General Thomas F. Meagher, whose Irish Brigade was guarding the roads to the rear the night of May 2, told the meeting that of the many soldiers his men intercepted in their flight from the battlefield very few of them spoke with a German accent.

Vindication of the kind non-Germans could believe, even anti-Germans, came later that year on the heights overlooking Chattanooga.

HONOR RESTORED

That summer of 1863, XI Corps with the rest of the Army of the Potomac pounded up the long dusty roads toward Gettysburg to fend off Lee's invasion of Pennsylvania. During the early stages of the battle the corps was posted on Cemetery Ridge. Many of the German regiments were heavily engaged as the Confederates attempted to knock aside the Union vanguard and proceed with their invasion before the bulk of the Army of the Potomac arrived on the scene. General Howard, who commanded during the early phase of the long battle, praised the German artillerymen on Cemetery Ridge who "left their guns, and used sponge-staffs, handspikes or anything they could lay hold of" to beat back the Confederate infantry. Later the Confederates, with their greater numbers, broke through the Union positions and XI Corps was among the elements swept away. Once more "other troops were to complain that the miserable Dutchmen had let them down again, but the line simply could not be held."[17] In his report General Howard considered the XI Corps, among the other elements of the Army of the Potomac's vanguard which arrived at Gettysburg after forced marches and had to go into action without food or rest, had "done wonders" in that they "held the vast army of Lee in check a day; took up a strong position; fought themselves into it, and kept it for the approaching Army of the Potomac to occupy with them, so as to meet the foe with better prospects of victory."

But XI Corps was still a dubious element, a military question mark early in the fall of 1863. That was when it was sent west, like so many Americans in succeeding years, to begin a new life. The Army of the Cumberland, having been severely handled at the Battle of Chicka- mauga, was under siege in the railroad center of Chattanooga. Grant's Army of the Tennessee was dispatched to its rescue from Mississippi, and the War Department also decided to send XI and XX Corps of the Army of the Potomac. Both corps were placed under the command of a chastened General Hooker, who had been put on the shelf shortly before the Battle of Gettysburg. The Confederates held the high ground around Chattanooga; it would be the task of the reinforcing armies to drive them off Missionary Ridge and the towering summit of Lookout Mountain so the Army of the Cumberland could break loose.

Opening a supply route to the Cumberlanders' half-starved men and horses, then taking Lookout Mountain, would be the assignment of Hooker's corps. XI Corps, with the rest of Hooker's twelve thousand men, was transported by rail to Alabama, then marched to their jump- off positions for the opening operation. They seized Lookout Mountain Valley and, with the cooperation of General George H. Thomas's besieged army across the Tennessee River, opened up a supply route into Chattanooga.

On November 24 XI Corps took part in the action against Lookout Mountain, a key segment of the battle plan by which the Army of the Tennessee was to attack the upper end of Missionary Ridge and the Army of the Cumberland the rest of the ridge and sweep the Confeder- ates out of northern Georgia. Hooker's corps were ordered to "demon- strate" against the summit of Lookout to draw the Confederates' attention away from Missionary Ridge, and to assault it only if capture appeared possible.

At daybreak the men of Schurz's and Steinwehr's divisions, XI Corps, began the work of vindication. They scrambled up a zigzagging path along the eastern face of Lookout Mountain under heavy artillery fire from the summit. By noon they were close to the peak and exchanging fire with the Confederate rifle pits. The climax was a bayonet charge by the men of Schurz's and Steinwehr's divisions, up a steep 200-foot incline strewn with boulders, which broke over the crest of Lookout and drove the enemy off the mountain. To the Union generals below — Grant, Sherman and Thomas — it looked like an impossible operation, which was why they had instructed Hooker not to attempt the capture of Lookout unless his demonstration "developed its practicability." It was a battle afterwards beloved of military muralists, the "battle above the clouds." It seemed a miraculous ascent to the watchers below; at dawn the Confederate Stars and Bars had floated from the summit, then six or so hours later it was suddenly replaced by the Stars and Stripes. "Up and up they went into the clouds," as one poetic observer later wrote, "until they were lost from sight, and their comrades anxiously watching in Chattanooga could hear only the booming of cannon and rattle of musketry far overhead, and catch glimpses of fire flashing from moment to moment through the dark clouds, as if the old myth-maker's notion of the thunderstorm were realized, and elemental spirits were engaged in a deadly struggle for the dominion of the upper air." The victory atop Lookout Mountain opened the way for successes all down the Union line, Missionary Ridge was taken in a breathtaking charge, and the Union armies were free to begin their march into Georgia, toward Atlanta, then toward the sea.

It finally removed the stain of Chancellorsville from the battle flags of XI Corps, which went on to perform valiantly under Sherman in his subsequent operations.

Individually and by companies, regiments and divisions the Germans of the North served in the Union armies. XI Corps of the Army of the Potomac and later of the Army of the Tennessee was only a small, but widely publicized, portion of their military endeavors. In that same

Army of the Cumberland, which the XI Corps helped to enable to break out of Chattanooga, there was a strong representation of German-American regiments from all the Middle Western states which made their contribution to the special quality of that army, "possibly . . . the best army of the lot" fielded by the Union, as Bruce Catton has judged it. "It was unbreakable, somewhat plodding, with an unexpected volcanic capacity for exploding all over the landscape just when an explosion was most needed."[18]

In the charge up Missionary Ridge, which was made without orders from General Grant and seemed such an astonishing feat that Assistant Secretary of War Charles A. Dana credited it to "the visible interposition of God," there were a large number of wild-eyed German-Americans, most of them reared on Middle Western farms. In General Philip H. Sheridan's division there was Wagner's brigade composed mostly of Illinois, Indiana, Michigan and Ohio regiments with a largely German personnel. In Wood's division, which raced Sheridan's for the honor of capturing the Confederate rifle pits and gun positions which studded the crest of Missionary Ridge, there was the brigade commanded by General August Willich, a Forty-eighter, with mostly German regiments from Illinois, Indiana, Kansas, Ohio and Wisconsin.

At Gettysburg, as at Yorktown almost a century earlier, Germans fought Germans on both sides of the battle line. Many Pennsylvania regiments were included in Hancock's II Corps, which bore the brunt of the fighting in the battle's later stages. On the other side German-Americans of southern birth fought with equal enthusiasm for the Confederacy, particularly in the Virginia, South and North Carolina, and Georgia brigades. In Pickett's division, the victim of a ridiculously heroic and futile last throw of Lee's dice, Brigadier General Louis A. Armistead was killed at the head of his brigade. Armistead was the member of a prominent Virginia family of German stock; the name was originally spelled Armstadt. "In the last assault," as his final moments were described, "Armistead . . . pressed forward, leaped the stone wall, waved his sword with his hat on it, shouted, 'Give them the cold steel, boys,' and laid his hands upon a gun. A hundred of his men had followed. They planted the Confederate battle flags on Cemetery Ridge among the cannon they had captured, and for the moment held.

Armistead was shot down; Garnett and Kemper, Pickett's other briga-
diers, fell . . ."[19]

Brigadier James L. Kemper was also a German-American, whose
antecedents were among the earliest settlers of Virginia, members of the
colony at Germanna founded in 1714 under the auspices of the colonial
governor. A veteran of the Mexican War, Brigadier Kemper had fought
valiantly at Bull Run, South Mountain, Antietam and Fredericksburg
before being seriously wounded at Gettysburg. Later he commanded the
Confederate forces at Richmond and was a postbellum governor of
Virginia from 1873 to 1878.

A more dashing figure in Southern legend was the gigantic Prussian
named Heros von Borcke, an authentic baron who so identified himself
with the supposedly chivalrous aspects of the Confederate cause that he
ran the Union blockade to join the Southern army. Most fittingly,
considering his childish love of display and Munchausen-like accounts of
his exploits, he joined the staff of Jeb Stuart, who also regarded war as
fun-and-games on an adult scale. Von Borcke, commissioned a major
and given the grandiose title of "inspector general" of Stuart's cavalry,
wielded a saber heavy enough to wipe out an enemy cavalry troop. The
baron, as one student of the Stuart military circus has written, "provided high splashes of color and, with his German accent, unconscious
humor for that riotous group of young riding men and . . . wielded his
outsize saber to the admiration of all."[20] Baron von Borcke rode with
Stuart, plumed and braided and sabretached to the teeth, until the fatal
day at Yellow Tavern when a far less colorful aggregation of Middle
Western plowboys cut the Confederate cavalry to pieces at Yellow
Tavern and struck down its leader. He joined in singing "Rock of Ages"
as Stuart lay dying, and the mournful crowd gathered outside his
Richmond home knew Jeb had crossed the river when von Borcke came
out with tears streaming down his blond beard.

On the Yankee side, too, there was a self-conscious throwback to
knightly combat, though a far more ferocious one. He was the golden-
haired cavalryman, George Armstrong Custer, the great-grandson of the
Hessian deserter who settled in Michigan. His style undoubtedly
would have delighted any Visigoth warriors in his ancestry. Just out of
West Point, he bluffed his way to a staff appointment with General

McClellan, later obtained a cavalry command and attained the rank of brigadier general at the age of twenty-three. At the head of the Michigan Brigade he distinguished himself at Gettysburg and Yellow Tavern, served as Sheridan's chief collaborator in burning out the Shenandoah Valley — the sort of task to which he always lent his wholehearted enthusiasm, whether it was destroying a Virginia plantation or later the winter quarters of a tribe of starving Indians on the Washita. Destructive and greedy for fame and promotion, yes, but physically he was a gorgeous fellow, and knew it well. Broad-shouldered, wasp-waisted, six feet tall and a magnificent horseman, he elaborated upon his natural endowments by using cinnamon-scented hair oil on his long wavy golden hair; dressed himself in a tight befrogged hussar jacket and black trousers trimmed with gold lace, and looked, as a jealous comrade remarked, "like a circus rider gone mad." But it was the "cavalry dash" that caught the eye of his superiors, first McClellan, then Sheridan. At Beaver Dam Station he recklessly drove ahead and captured the rolling stock of the Virginia Central Railroad; at Appomattox Depot, in the last days of the war, he captured Lee's remaining supplies and cut across the Confederates' line of retreat. Such exploits provided him with that enormous conceit which was to prove his undoing on the Montana plain a dozen years later. All in all, the country probably had a better bargain in his fleet-footed, inglorious great-grandfather.

Other German-Americans distinguished themselves in the Union service, though none with quite the Custer panache. The first regular army officer killed in action was Lieutenant John T. Greble, 2nd Artillery, at the Battle of Big Bethel in June, 1861. Captain Hugo "Leatherbreeches" Dilger, with his six smooth-bore brass guns, was regarded as one of the ablest artillerists in the Union armies before he finished marching with Sherman to the sea and settled down on a farm in the Shenandoah Valley. Generals S. P. Heintzelman and Godfrey Wietzel commanded Union corps before the war ended. In the technical aspects of warfare, a number of them rose to prominence, including General Herman Haupt of the engineers' corps, who repaired railroads as fast as they were destroyed by Confederate raiders, and Count Zeppelin who came over from Germany in 1863 and served as a cavalry officer and engineer with the Union armies, made his first experiments in military aviation with the Yankee observation balloons, and went back to Germany to build his dirigibles, some of which bombed London and Paris in World War I. General Alfred Mordecai was chief of ordnance for several Union armies, and General August V. Kautz, born in Baden but raised in Ohio, led cavalry raids into southern Virginia in 1864. In addition, there were a number of professional soldiers, many of them titled, who swanked it around various army headquarters but contributed little to the cause but social glamour. Among those who came over from Germany as mercenaries was Prince Salm-Salm, whose consort became a dainty footnote to history by reaching up and kissing President Lincoln while Mrs. Lincoln fumed.

For all these varied endeavors and heroic labors, it cannot be said that the German-Americans won a commensurate share of glory. They did not become known as the "Fighting Germans." Most people believed that the darling of the cavalry, Custer, was of Anglo-Saxon stock, and the accomplishments of others did not partake of that quality which attracts legends and makes headlines. Perhaps Albert B. Faust in his comprehensive *The German Element in the United States* was right in assigning that lack of glamour to the innate sobriety of the German temperament. "The German soldier, as the German agriculturalist," he wrote in 1909, "contributed . . . those qualities which are not heralded by fame — patience, steadiness and persistence. These essential staying qualities were exhibited not alone in battle, but as often in camp, on the march, or in the tedious waits incident to military life."

Supporting proof of this thesis might have been found during the Spanish-American War a generation later. Shortly after United States troops had captured the Spanish blockhouse on San Juan Hill at the climax of the Cuban campaign, the war correspondents following the first wave of assault were making bets with each other that the first American into the captured blockhouse was a "red-headed Irishman."

They were quite disappointed to learn that the first soldier to reach the heart of the Spanish defenses was a matter-of-fact Middle Western farm boy with a German name. It didn't even make the papers.

6. CARL SCHURZ, THE GOOD, GOOD GERMAN

Courage is not a rare virtue; but the resolutely independent and discriminating courage of a Schurz, which made him ready in the name of principle to face any public clamor, and to turn against an old friend almost as quickly as against an old foe, is rare indeed.

— ALLAN NEVINS

Name any genuinely liberal cause between the Civil War and the turn of the century, and Carl Schurz invariably was to be found in its forefront. He was a leader in the Middle Western fight against slavery, one of the few "political generals" in the Civil War more interested in serving the Union than himself, a pioneer in American social reform, the advocate of more leniency toward the defeated South during the Reconstruction, the foe of corruption in the federal government, the standard-bearer for the movement to obtain a measure of justice and humane treatment for the Indians, one of the firmest and clearest voices raised against the American imperialism which engulfed Cuba and the Philippines a half-dozen years before his death. More than once he sacrificed his own political aspirations to pursue what he regarded as the right, though unpopular, course.

Schurz possessed both military and civil courage. He was so laden

155

with statesman-like virtues — a ruthless honesty, a clarity of vision, an independence of intellect that compelled him to abandon the party he helped to found — that it would be almost comforting to find a flaw or two in his character. He might, for instance, have suffered from an excess of self-righteousness, yet none could be detected. He was too sane and well balanced to be a fanatic, and possessed enough humor and insight to avoid priggishness. Nor did he tend to drift with so many of the university-educated German-Americans into a gloomy romanticism or an airy utopianism. His life could have served as a model for the successive panels of the Ages of the Modern Liberal: Student Revolutionary, Political Idealist, Uniformed Crusader, Self-Sacrificing Dissident, Incorruptible Bureaucrat, Farseeing Statesman, and finally, without bitterness but with great vigor, in the ultimate role of the man whose convictions have led him away from the mainstream, Commentator in Exile.

His three-volume *Reminiscences*, along with his two-volume biography of Henry Clay and his biography of Abraham Lincoln, form a classic study of the indelible process of Americanization, the transition of a fugitive European intellectual into a pragmatic idealist of a totally American mold. The remarkable fact was that his idealism remained, at the end of his seventy-seven years, undimmed and undiminished by the corrosive influences of the Gilded Age which made cynics and misanthropes of lesser men. It was a testimonial of sorts that Ambrose Bierce, the idealist turned sour, detested him with all the vehemence of a fallen angel for one whose faith remained strong.

Schurz was a product of the Rhenish seedbed of German liberalism. He was born on March 2, 1829, at Liblar, on the left bank of the Rhine. His father was the schoolmaster of the village a dozen miles from Cologne; he also opened a hardware store to earn enough money to educate his children. At the age of ten Carl was sent to the Catholic gymnasium in Cologne. Eight years later he passed the entrance examinations for the University of Bonn. During his first year at the university he fell under the spell of Gottfried Kinkel, one of those spirited young professors who aspired to build a New Germany by inflaming the revolutionary ardors of their students.

How Schurz himself was converted from a dreamy youth with ambitions to become a writer into an active revolutionary was described in his *Reminiscences* in his characteristically spare and direct style: "One morning, toward the end of February, 1848, I sat quietly in my attic-chamber, working hard at my tragedy of 'Ulrich von Hutten,' when suddenly a friend rushed breathlessly into the room exclaiming: 'What, you sitting here! Do you not know what has happened?'

" 'No; what?'

" 'The French have driven away Louis Philippe and proclaimed the republic.'

"I threw down my pen — and that was the end of 'Ulrich von Hutten.' I never touched the manuscript again. We tore down the stairs, into the street, to the market-square, the accustomed meeting-place for all the student societies after their midday dinner . . . There was no shouting, no noise, only agitated conversation. What did we want there? . . . But since the French had driven away Louis Philippe and proclaimed the republic, something of course must happen here, too . . ."[1]

Within a few weeks mass demonstrations were disturbing the peace of the quiet little university town, with Professor Kinkel marching at the head of throngs of students bearing the black, red and gold tricolor, the revolutionary flag forbidden by the Prussian rulers of the Rhineland. Subsequently the German rulers were forced to make concessions, and promised to bring about a more democratic form of government with constitutional guarantees. The promises were broken as soon as the Junkers and the Prussian army regained control. The surge of reaction, as Schurz recalled, produced among the students and their supporters in Bonn "a state of mind resembling that of the terrorists in the French Revolution."

Prussian regiments began marching into the Rhenish provinces to restore order. By that time, June of 1848, the students and others who were willing to fight for a more democratic Germany had been organized into battalions. After a number of rearguard skirmishes the revolutionary forces in which Schurz served as a subaltern were forced to withdraw into the fortress of Rastatt on the Murg River. Schurz was appointed adjutant to General Tiedemann, commandant of the fortress, while the Prussian troops brought the fortress under siege. "I had to spend certain hours on the highest gallery of the tower of the castle armed with a telescope, to observe the enemy and to make report of what I might see," he later recalled. "Then I had, periodically, to visit certain bastions and gates, and to inspect certain watches . . . To fit me for that duty I donned the uniform of a regular infantry lieutenant of the Badish army, which transformed me into a respectable-looking officer and gave me a sort of military consciousness which until then I had not possessed." (This, in fact, was the military experience on which was based the major general's commission he was eventually granted in the Union army.) When the garrison of Rastatt was surrendered at the demand of the Prussians, Schurz decided against being taken prisoner, certain that he would be shot by a firing squad if he gave up with the others. Besides, at nineteen, he was a flaming romantic and here was a chance to translate literary fantasy into adventurous actuality.

Just before the garrison was assembled to stack their arms and surrender, Schurz armed himself with a brace of pistols, a loaf of bread, two bottles of wine and a string of sausages and disappeared into the castle's sewage system. He escaped through the sewage tunnel, which led for miles under the town of Rastatt to a cornfield near the village of Steinmauern on the banks of the Rhine. That night he bribed a boatman with five florins to take him across the river. He fled through France to Switzerland.

At nineteen he was a penniless refugee living in a suburb of Zurich with a number of other fugitives from the aborted revolution. Like political refugees of all times, they lived on the hope that somehow the revolution would erupt again and overturn the established authority. Schurz, however, was not content to go on dreaming over his books and pounding the table in nightly sessions at the tavern frequented by the German fugitives. He had learned that his Pangloss, Kinkel, had been captured by the Prussians and sentenced to life imprisonment at the fortress of Spandau near Berlin. Kinkel must be rescued, and Schurz nominated himself as the man to do it.

Now he was back in his element. He returned to Germany, though he knew that he would probably be executed if he was taken into custody by the ubiquitous secret police, saw Frau Kinkel in Bonn and arranged to communicate with her through letters written in a "magic ink" he had bought in Zurich. The ink became visible when the letter was held over heat. There was no good reason for secret messages, but the idea was vastly appealing to a young man who had nourished himself on romantic literature.

Schurz then removed himself from German soil and made his headquarters in Paris while the Rhenish underground raised funds for an attempt to liberate Professor Kinkel from Spandau. The leader of that attempt was to be Carl Schurz. In August, 1850, armed with a passport taken out in his cousin's name, Schurz journeyed to Berlin and took up lodgings there while he scouted the vicinity of the fortress-prison and tried to work out a plan for the jailbreak. He soon decided it couldn't be done by force. "The armed guard of the penitentiary itself consisted only of a handful of soldiers and turnkeys on duty. It would therefore have been possible for a number of resolute men to storm the building. But it was situated in the center of a fortified town filled with soldiers, and the first signal of alarm would have attracted an over-whelming force." Other prisoners had escaped by tunneling their way out but Kinkel's lack of skill with his hands would probably make that method unfeasible.

Posing as a young physician, he took up quarters over a beerhouse and plotted with three other conspirators, using funds supplied by their supporters in the Rhineland, to liberate Professor Kinkel through bribery. An officer of the guard at Spandau was singled out, plied with wine and food, and persuaded to join the plot in return for enough money to take himself and his family to America if his participation in the escape was discovered.

On a dark night in November, 1850, Schurz and his collaborators made their move. Kinkel's cell was on the second floor overlooking an inner court. While several of his co-conspirators held themselves in reserve on the street corners nearest the prison to reinforce him if necessary, Schurz slipped inside the gate with two pistols in his belt, a dirk and a slingshot. The young desperado was admitted to the inner court by the bribed officer. The other officers of the night watch were celebrating the birthday of one of their comrades over a punch bowl. A rope had been smuggled to Kinkel. At the arranged moment the professor came sliding down the rope from a dormer window in the attic above his cellblock.

Schurz immediately led him to a carriage waiting in the street outside, and the two men, with a hamper of Rhine wine at their feet, galloped off into the night. A pursuit was launched within a few hours, but Schurz and Kinkel made it safely to the port of Rostock with the prearranged assistance of revolutionary sympathizers. They were smuggled aboard a schooner, which took them to Leith, the port of Edinburgh, under assumed names. Schurz was pleased to smuggle himself out of Germany under the alias of "Kaiser."

For this feat, Schurz became famous all over Europe (except, of course, in Germany). Years later he modestly wrote: "What I had done appeared to me as nothing so extraordinary as to merit all this ado . . . New legends were invented which if possible were still more fantastic than the old ones." All the publicity given the affair, he believed, might endanger the plans to liberate other prisoners of the Prussians. In Paris, where Schurz settled down to become a newspaper correspondent, he was acclaimed a hero not only by the German refugee colony but the blasé Parisians, who recognized in his feat an éclat they had previously believed was the property of the French. Novels and poems were published with the escape from Spandau as their theme.

Irksome as he professed it to be, celebrity also had its rewards. Although barely twenty-one, he was admitted to the councils of two other famous libertarians, Kossuth and Mazzini, and was welcomed as a visitor to England, to which he commuted frequently from Paris as a newspaper correspondent. Again he and the other German exiles were living on hope, principally that the French would revolt and ignite a spark across the Rhine as had happened before. That hope was extinguished late in 1851. He was sitting on a bench in London's Hyde Park one December day with Louis Blanc, the French socialist leader, when they heard the news of Louis Napoleon's coup d'état. They stared at each other and muttered, "C'est fini." The death of republicanism in France doomed the similar movement in Germany.

"The fatherland was closed to me," Schurz later wrote. "England was to me a foreign country, and would always remain so. Where, then? 'To America,' I said to myself . . . *Ubi libertas, ibi patria* — I formed my resolution on the spot. I would remain only a short time longer in England to make some necessary preparations, and then — off to America."

Before he left, however, "something happened that infused into my apparently gloomy situation a radiance of sunshine and opened to my life unlooked-for prospects." He called on a wealthy German exile living in Hampstead, who introduced him to his sister-in-law, Margaretha Meyer. She was the daughter of a prosperous Hamburg merchant, the sister-in-law of the exile on whom Schurz was calling. "A girl of about eighteen years . . . of fine stature, a curly head, something childlike in her beautiful features and large, dark, truthful eyes," as he described her. It was love at first sight for both of them. Dim though his prospects were, she agreed to marry him and go to America. That decision of Margaretha Schurz's eventually made an impact on American education almost equal to her husband's on American politics — and perhaps more lasting. Mrs. Schurz opened the first kindergarten in the United States several years later when they were living in Watertown, Wisconsin. Others were soon founded in New England and elsewhere.

Carl and Margaretha were married in the parish church of Marylebone in London in July of 1852, and a month later sailed for the United States. The first night they spent in New York they walked its streets and were amazed at "the very noisy bustle . . . the men, old and young, mostly looking serious and preoccupied, and moving on with energetic rapidity; the women also appearing sober-minded and busy, although many of them were clothed in loud colors . . . the people, although they must have belonged to very different stations in life, looking surprisingly alike in feature and expression as well as habit . . . ; no military sentinels at public buildings; no soldiers on the streets . . . no uniformed officials except the police." They were overwhelmed with delight at the startling absence of authority.

For several months the Schurzes lived in Philadelphia while he studied English by reading the Philadelphia *Ledger* daily from first page to last, as well as Thackeray, Scott, Dickens, Macaulay, and Blackstone's

Commentaries. He also studied American political institutions with an avid interest and visited Washington, where he was received by Secretary of War Jefferson Davis, who impressed him with his "entirely natural and unaffected" dignity, and Senator Shields of Illinois, a jovial Irishman who "welcomed me with effusive cordiality as a sort of fellow revolutionary — he himself, as an enthusiastic Irish Nationalist, being in a state of permanent belligerency against England . . ."

Everything he saw of the American system delighted the twenty-three-year-old Schurz, who no longer thought of himself as a German exile but as a future American. "The abuse of the good," he wrote a friend, "does not tempt an American to abolish it. The abuse of liberty does not tempt him to curtail liberty . . . There is only one shrill discord, and that is slavery in the South."[2]

Soon after his arrival in the United States he met with August Willich, the Baden revolutionary who also became a Union army general, on the question of converting the German "loan committees," which had been raising funds for overthrowing the Prussian rule of the German states, into a sort of political organization. He wrote his old mentor, Professor Kinkel, that "I soon saw with what illusions he had come . . . His whole agitation is a thoroughly bad business. The transformation of the loan committees into little political clubs seems to be purposeless, as in general all showy undertakings are, all noise-makings, all forcible digging up of old stories, and entirely out of place."[3]

He was determined to Americanize himself at speed, and that meant jettisoning all the attitudes of the exile and refugee. The plotting and dreaming and expostulating of the other Forty-eighters, which went on for years and encompassed not only the establishment of a German republic but plans for a separate German-American state, were all so much bootless "agitation."

He undertook a scouting expedition to the west before settling on Watertown, Wisconsin, as the place he wanted to make his home. Milwaukee struck him unfavorably because "it suffers from the presence of too many Germans. Wherever the German in this country has to live off the Germans things go badly for him. There [in Milwaukee] you can see in the morning as you pass through the streets, the German house-father in dress-gown and slippers, with his long pipe, standing in the door."

Schurz bought a farm near Watertown, apparently with the assistance of his own and his wife's family, and plunged himself into state politics. He was a Republican in a largely Democratic district, and when he was nominated for the state legislature in 1856 he was beaten by a two-to-one majority. He came to the attention of the party's national leaders, however, by campaigning throughout Wisconsin for John Frémont, who took the state's vote by a thirteen thousand margin. His partisan fervor was attested by the fact that the Watertown *Democrat* engaged him as its editor, then fired him after two weeks as being "too Republican." When the county seat was moved to Watertown, he was appointed commissioner of public improvements, the first office he held; meanwhile he was studying law and had become the president of an insurance company headquartered in Watertown. In 1858 he was admitted to the bar, and at twenty-nine was a considerable man of affairs. With all that activity, he also managed to establish his own weekly newspaper, the *Deutsch Volks-Zeitung*, largely as a platform for his political views.

During the several years before the election of 1860, he spread the Republican gospel from one border of Wisconsin to the other and was the principal agent in luring thousands of German-Americans away from their old loyalty to the Democratic party. "The ascendancy of the Republican party in this state may be said to date from the time the Germans began to cut adrift from the Democratic party," as the Milwaukee *Sentinel* observed many years later. "His [Schurz's] influence in turning the drift of German sentiment toward the Republican party has never been fully admitted."[4] And Alexander M. Thompson, the Wisconsin political historian, wrote of his ceaseless speech-making: "He made converts wherever he spoke, and thousands of his nativity were won to the true political faith by his eloquent speeches, and flocked to our standard."[5]

At the Republican national convention of 1860, under the Chicago Wigwam, Schurz was a supporter of William H. Seward's candidacy. In the Wisconsin delegation, as Schurz later wrote, there was no "real antagonism" to Lincoln. "He was universally recognized as a true anti-slavery leader who had done our cause very great service. We esteemed him most highly, but we did not favor his nomination, because we were for Seward . . . 'first, last, and all the time.'" Schurz and the other Wisconsin delegates stayed with Seward through the last ballot, on which Lincoln won the nomination.

Schurz was quickly converted into a Lincoln man, partly because of party loyalty and, as he wrote his wife, "I know Mr. Lincoln, and I am sure that his administration will very favorably disappoint those who look upon him as a 'conservative' man. His impulses are in the right direction, and I think he has courage enough to follow them."[6]

He took the stump and campaigned for Lincoln without letup until election day. One speech was delivered in Springfield, Illinois, with Lincoln on the platform and encouraging him with "a nod and a broad smile." Later Schurz was invited to the Lincoln home for dinner, and at that first lengthy meeting with his party's nominee "we conversed about the course and the incidents of the campaign, and his genial and simple-hearted way of expressing himself would hardly permit me to remember that he was a great man and a candidate for the Presidency of the United States."

Schurz was given a large share of the credit for swinging the vote of what was then known as the "Northwest" into the Republican column. He attended the inauguration and was informed that, as a reward for his efforts, he would be appointed United States minister to Spain.

Schurz protested to Lincoln that "it was much against my feelings to go to Spain as Minister and to spend my days in the ease and luxury of a diplomatic position, while the young men of the North were exposing their lives in the field . . . that, having helped, as a public speaker, to bring about the present condition of things, I thought I would rather bear my share of the consequences." In brief, he wanted a commission in the Union army, but the President insisted that diplomatic service might "eventually offer me a field of greater usefulness."

Before he left for Madrid, he started raising a volunteer cavalry regiment of five squadrons, the enlistment of which was completed by another man under whom it served as the 1st New York Volunteer

Cavalry. During those days he commuted between New York and Washington and was a frequent visitor to the White House, where one of Lincoln's secretaries, John Hay, was favorably impressed by his blazing enthusiasm. Apparently still in hopes of avoiding the diplomatic service, Schurz was urging, as Lincoln wrote his Secretary of War, that he be allowed to "go immediately to Fortress Monroe [in Virginia]; and if it would be an objection that, by rank, he would command the garrison there, he would, of choice, waive that." Schurz in his enthusiasms would have made a "wonderful land pirate," as John Hay observed, "bold, quick, brilliant, and reckless — hard to control and difficult to direct."[7]

Schurz had to be satisfied with a half-promise of a brigadier general's commission (". . . I cannot make it move smoothly just yet," as President Lincoln rather vaguely informed him) before he was packed off to Spain with his ministerial portfolio. He was only thirty-three years old when he took up his duties as envoy to Queen Isabella. His comparative youth did not inhibit him from offering advice to the Administration, via the Secretary of State, from his listening post in Madrid. In September, 1861, he was warning that European opinion was unsympathetic toward a war for the subjection of the southern states if it did not include the immediate emancipation of the Negroes, that the defeats suffered by the Union army were being attributed to a lack of moral faith in the Union's cause. Only great victories or "such measures as will place the war against the rebellious slave states upon a higher moral basis, and thereby give us the control of public opinion in Europe" would prevent the alienation of the continental nations.[8] He urged an immediate proclamation of emancipation.

He was overwhelmed by homesickness, as he wrote his parents, who had migrated to Wisconsin, and he disliked Spain, not least of all for its preoccupation with the mystique of bullfighting. It was a "hateful task," he wrote his parents, trying to represent a misunderstood America in a foreign capital. "I would ten times rather fight in America along with the rest than here in Europe to extenuate our defeats."[9]

He was too much the ardent republican to be impressed by the inbred Spanish aristocracy. "Great titles are as common as blackberries here; but there is ordinarily little behind them," he wrote in a letter home. ". . . I cannot endure people who abase themselves as they do here; and I am embarrassed when all manner of honors and reverences are hurled at my head. Nowhere can I feel right save in a country where the people stand erect in their boots."

While fretting to return to America and appealing to the State Department for his recall forthwith — a purpose for which he did not hesitate to pull wires, including those available to the influential Senator Charles Sumner — he studied the works of Jomini and Clausewitz and the campaigns of Napoleon and Frederick the Great (a neat balance of experts for a Rhinelander) against the day when Lincoln's half-promise would be fulfilled and he would be allowed to put on the uniform of a Union brigadier.

In January, 1862, he was finally granted a leave of absence from his post which he intended to make permanent. In Washington he spent a lot of time with Senator Sumner, also an all-out advocate of emancipation, "an enlightened doctrinaire" (as Schurz wrote in his *Reminiscences*), and recorded Sumner's bewilderment at how to cope with President Lincoln's oblique sense of humor. "Being entirely devoid of the sense of humor himself, Mr. Sumner frequently — I might almost say always — failed to see the point of the quaint anecdotes or illustrations with which Lincoln was fond of elucidating his argument, as with a flashlight. Mr. Sumner not seldom quoted such Lincolnisms to me, and asked me with an air of innocent bewilderment whether I could guess what the President could possibly have meant."

For all his pawky, backwoods style, Lincoln, as Schurz observed, possessed an absolute self-assurance. "He would have approached the greatest man in the world . . . with absolute unconcern . . . He therefore met great statesmen and titled persons with the absolutely natural, instinctive, unaffected self-respect of an equal . . ."[10]

Acting as a sort of tuning fork to catch the vibrations of public opinion, Schurz prepared a speech to be delivered at the Cooper Union in New York City March 6, 1862, in which he advocated emancipation. The President himself read and approved of the speech before it was given. In one of the great oratorical efforts of his career, Schurz declared that Secession began, not with the bombardment of Fort Sumter, but when the South first threatened to break up the Union. "Would rebellion have broken out, if slavery had not existed? Did the rebellion raise its head at any place where slavery did not exist? Did it not find sympathy and support wherever slavery did exist?" He proposed that "slavery, in the District of Columbia and wherever the Government has immediate authority, be abolished. Let the slaves of rebels be confiscated by the General Government and then emancipated, and let fair compensation be offered to loyal slave states and masters, who will agree upon some system of emancipation . . ."

It was the rebellion itself, not the rebels, which he regarded as supremely evil. He was willing to differentiate between crushing the Confederacy, yet sparing the individuals of which it was composed; a doctrine, whether propaganda or not, which was to be adopted by the Western nations in later wars. "The best revenge for the past," he told the Cooper Union audience, "is that which furnishes us the best assurance for the future."

With the triumph of that speech to his credit, Schurz was able to press his claims for a transfer from the diplomatic to the military service. Secretary of State Seward, for obscure reasons of his own, wanted to send him back to Madrid, but President Lincoln's decision that he should go into uniform prevailed. With no more to recommend him for such responsible command than his readings of the military textbooks and his weeks as a subaltern with the revolutionary forces in the Rhineland, much of them spent with a telescope glued to his eye on the upper ramparts of the fortress of Rastatt, he was confident that he could deploy and maneuver thousands of men in battle against a desperate and battle-tested enemy.

Was it only ambition, a thirst for glory which impelled him? Perhaps not; certainly he was motivated by an idealism which had already caused him to risk his life more than once for his beliefs. Happily ambition and idealism happened to coincide in his determination to serve the Union as a soldier. Yet he must have been troubled by a self-questioning of his motives, as when he protested a bit too forcefully in a letter to an old friend. "The main thing is: That in a position in life such as mine, a man should not permit himself to be ruled by a false ambition. The ambition to *do* something can be boundless, but it must free itself from the ambition to *be* something."[11]

He would both "do" and "be" something important in the Union army with President Lincoln as his patron. For a start, command of a division in Sigel's corps of the army operating in the Virginia mountains, to which he reported in June, 1862, after one of its usual disasters. General Sigel struck him as "reserved, even morose," perhaps because he was depressed at having yet another of the ubiquitous "political generals" commanding one of his divisions. One of Schurz's regimental commanders was Colonel Alexander von Schimmelpfennig, who had been his superior when they both served in the revolutionary army of the Rhine Palatinate. At the first divisional maneuvers Schimmelpfennig complimented Schurz on the briskness of his orders, adding, "You have studied well; now let us do as well when the bullets whistle."

The bullets soon whistled most menacingly at Second Bull Run, where Schurz's division performed creditably, and at Chancellorsville, where his troops and the rest of the luckless XI Corps were blamed by the high command for the defeat. For the rest of his life Schurz defended his conduct and that of his division at Chancellorsville against the graceless imputations of the corps commander, General O. O. Howard, that his men had let him down. In Schurz's opinion Howard should have "frankly shouldered the responsibility for that calamity, and exonerated his officers and men," since he had disdained warnings from Schurz and other subordinates that the corps was about to be attacked by an overwhelming Confederate force. Instead Howard accused his men of "panicking," of "bad conduct." Schurz was never able to learn exactly why his demands for a court of inquiry were ignored, and wrote in his memoirs: "Not for my own sake, but in the name of thousands of my comrades I asked for nothing but a mere opportunity by a fair investigation of the facts to defend their honor . . . against the most infamous slanders and insults circulated from mouth to mouth in the army, and throughout the country by the press; when the opportunity was denied me, was there not ample reason for the conclusion that there was a powerful influence working to suppress the truth,

Carl Schurz, epitome of German goodness

and that the Eleventh Army Corps, and especially the German part of it, was to be systematically sacrificed as the scapegoat?"

The powerful influence, undoubtedly, was President Lincoln. He could have ordered a court of inquiry, but he knew that the consequent mud-spattering and recrimination could only harm the war effort, even if it succeeded in cleansing the honor of a few thousand German-American soldiers. Apparently Schurz demanded such an inquiry of the President, because Lincoln wrote him shortly after Chancellorsville, with a bluntness he reserved for the most serious occasions, that some men thought as poorly of Schurz's military abilities as others thought of his own statesmanship.

Schurz was comforted subsequently by promotion to major general, his troops vindicated themselves on Lookout Mountain, and together they served under the abler leadership, and easier circumstances, afforded by General William T. Sherman and his army in the march through Georgia. Schurz took leave during the Atlanta campaign to make a speaking tour on behalf of Lincoln's candidacy for a second term. Before he set out on the campaign trail, he visited the President and spent the night at his cottage on the grounds of the Soldiers Home, which served him as a retreat much as Camp David has served Eisenhower, Kennedy and Johnson. The President unburdened himself to Schurz on that hot summer's night. Some of the party leaders were urging him "with almost violent language to withdraw from the contest," Lincoln said, "although I have been unanimously nominated, in order to make room for a better man. I wish I could. Perhaps some other man might do this business better than I . . . But I am here, and that better man is not here . . . It is much more likely that the factions opposed to me would fall to fighting among themselves, and that those who want me to make room for a better man would get a man whom most of them would not want at all . . ." Lincoln's eyes were "moist," as Schurz recalled, and "his rugged features working strangely." With all the tact and eloquence at his command, Schurz assured the President that "the people, undisturbed by the bickerings of his critics, believed in him." By the end of the evening Lincoln "became more cheerful."

With Lincoln's reelection, Schurz returned to his duties under

General Sherman, whom he considered the greatest of the Union generals and more skillful than General Grant. "Grant believed in hammering — Sherman in maneuvering."

During the several years after the war, he returned to journalism, first as Washington correspondent of the New York *Tribune*, edited by Horace Greeley, another liberal Republican whom he greatly admired, then as editor of the Detroit *Post*, and a year later as editor of the *Westliche Post* of St. Louis. During this exile from politics, caused partly by his lack of sympathy for a Republican leadership which demanded the harshest possible treatment of the ruined South, he worked for a greater understanding and sympathy for the former enemy. He had always been an abolitionist, but he could not be an avenger. At the Republican convention of 1868, which nominated General Grant for the Presidency, he served as temporary chairman and used the fleeting influence of that position to hammer in a plank recommending a general amnesty for those who had served the Confederacy. He was still a Republican but was becoming increasingly disaffected by the harshness of the "peace" imposed on the South by the radical Republican leaders who vaulted into the saddle the moment Lincoln stopped breathing.

Bad as things were in the United States, in those years when a display of the "bloody shirt" was all that a politician needed to make himself popular, when the whole spirit of the nation seemed to be corroded by hatred, self-doubt and corruption, those years of the "Flash Age" and the antics of the war profiteers spending their loot, Schurz did not regret having so thoroughly Americanized himself. A visit to his native Germany only made him more positive that the American democracy, for all its hideous flaws currently thrown into high relief by an almost suicidal civil war, would surmount its difficulties and justify the travail it had endured.

He was more or less flattered by an invitation to visit Chancellor Bismarck. For all his reputation as a Prussian advocate of "blood and iron," Prince Bismarck received him in a genial humor, pressed Rhine wine and Havana cigars on the ex-revolutionary, and roared with leonine laughter when Schurz said he half-expected to be arrested for having rescued Professor Kinkel from Spandau almost twenty years before. "Oh, no!" Bismarck replied. "I rather liked that. And if it were not highly improper for His Majesty's Minister and the Chancellor of the North German Confederacy, I should like to go with you to Spandau and have you tell me the whole story on the spot."

Bismarck wanted to know whether Schurz was still so ardent a republican, to which Schurz replied that he had not found America "so lovely as my youthful enthusiasm had pictured it" but "much more practical in its general beneficence to the great masses of the people, and much more conservative in its tendencies than I had imagined." Bismarck said frankly that he was born an aristocrat and could not be a democrat even if he was willing to try, adding, "To tell the truth, there was something in me that made me instinctively sympathize with the slaveholders as the aristocratic party in your civil war."

The military capabilities of the Americans also interested Bismarck, who had heard the remark of European professionals that both the Union and Confederate armies were simply armed mobs assaulting each other. "I had to admit," Schurz recalled in his memoirs, "that the state of discipline would in many respects have shocked a thoroughbred Prussian officer, and I told him many anecdotes of outbreaks of the spirit of equality which the American is apt to carry into all relations of life, and of the occasional familiarities between the soldier and the officer which would spring from that spirit. Such anecdotes amused him immensely, but I suppose his Prussian pride inwardly revolted when I expressed the opinion that in spite of all this the American soldier would not only fight well, but would, in a prolonged conflict with any European army, although at first put at a disadvantage by more thorough drill and discipline, after some experience prove superior to all of them." Perhaps the Iron Chancellor should have left a memo on Schurz's remarks for his successors, particularly those in office in 1914 and 1939.

During his student days in Bonn, Schurz had met another German whose influence was to exceed Bismarck's in the slow grinding of history: Karl Marx. In his memoirs Schurz did not compare the two men who stood at opposite poles of German thought, but evidently he was more taken by Bismarck as an individual. Marx, whom he identified as "the recognized head of the advanced socialistic school," was about thirty when Schurz met him and admittedly was "eager to gather words of wisdom from the lips of that famous man." He was disappointed. "Marx's utterances were indeed full of meaning, logical and clear, but I have never seen a man whose bearing was so provoking and intolerable. . . . Everyone who contradicted him he treated with abject contempt" with the result that "everyone whose feelings had been hurt by his conduct was inclined to support everything that Marx did not favor." From the Marxian encounter Schurz believed that he learned "a very important lesson," which was that "he who would be a leader and teacher of men must treat the opinions of his hearers with respect; that even the most superior mind will lose influence upon others if he seeks to humiliate those others by constant demonstrations of his superiority."

Generally he kept that lesson in mind when, in 1869, the state legislature of Missouri elected him as United States Senator for that state. He was the first German-born citizen to be seated in the upper house of Congress. Not only did he become that chamber's gadfly and eternal dissenter, but its voice of conscience at a time when most of his colleagues were too busy engineering schemes such as the Credit Mobilier to pay much attention to the national interest. He was the unfailing champion of liberal causes, and the unfaltering critic of the ineptitude and corruption of the Grant Administration. The enforcement of the Reconstruction laws under Grant's dictates, the stupidity with which they were administered, and the graft that accompanied them impelled him to break with his party. The cozy arrangements of his colleagues, such as the sale of arms to France during the Franco-Prussian War, not because of pro-French sympathy but because of French bribery, were exposed by Schurz on the floor of the Senate. He placed himself in opposition to President Grant's clumsy attempt to annex Santo Domingo.

It was not only his ruthless honesty but his effectiveness as a parliamentary prosecutor that made him feared and hated among the plump boodlers who sat in the Senate with him. He used facts as edged weapons, undulled by the contemporary self-indulgence in ornate rhetoric. "He was not only the most effective speaker in the Republican party, but the greatest orator who has appeared in Congress in our generation," the New York *Evening Post* observed. "Unlike many of his most distinguished colleagues, he never resorted to inflated or bombastic rhetoric and never stooped to any of the well-worn artifices with which demagogues from time immemorial have been wont to tickle the ears of the mob. . . . He was always sure of his subject and always full of it, and the natural consequence was that he always had something to say that was worthy of serious attention, even from those who might differ from him in opinion . . . To his other qualities he added a quick wit with a biting sarcasm, which could cut very deep without ever over-stepping the bounds of parliamentary decorum, and which made him formidable both in attack and in defense."[12]

Someone asked him why he insisted on striving for ideals that were as "distant as the stars," and he quickly replied:

"The stars are what we must sail by."

With Horace Greeley, who was even less earthbound, and star-struck to the point of eccentricity, he organized the Liberal Republican party in 1870 to offer an alternative to Grant in the next national election. A Democrat, so soon after the war's end, wouldn't stand a chance against the Union's leading military hero. In 1872 Schurz and his followers nominated Greeley, who lost in a predictable Grant landslide. From then on, he called himself an Independent, not a Republican.

He left the Senate in 1875, a departure which James Russell Lowell called a "national misfortune." When he returned to the political arena a year later to campaign for the Republican Presidential candidate, Rutherford B. Hayes, it was not because of a resurgence of party loyalty — and certainly not because Hayes and his wife were temperance fanatics who would not serve wine at state dinners in the White House — but because he believed in "sound money," then and for many years under attack from the inflationary forces which advocated an avalanche of greenbacks or "free silver" as a cure-all for the nation's economic ills. The uninflated dollar was Schurz's sole tendency toward conservatism. Practically all German-Americans, in fact, were united in the determination to resist the Populist demands for easy money. They were among the organizers and officers of such groups as the Sound Money League of Pennsylvania and the Reform Club of New York, of which Schurz and Henry Villard were members. "History will record it as a pregnant fact that the vast mass of Germans have been on the right side of the financial questions which in recent years have so agitated this country," as one prominent Republican stated in 1897. "Whether they have called themselves Republicans or Democrats, they have been almost to a man opposed to all wild fiscal experiments, to all financial tricks and efforts to outwit the eternal laws of nature, to the 'greenback craze,' to the 'silver craze,' and to all the outbursts of unreason which for a time have seemed to threaten the future of the country."[13]

Another reason Schurz campaigned for Hayes, reportedly, was that he had been promised that the federal bureaucracy would be brought under a civil service system. President Grant had appointed a commission to look into the possibilities, but the idea was dropped a year later under intense pressure from politicians of both parties for the most obvious reasons. Grant's defection on this issue was yet another cause of Schurz's disenchantment with his Administration.

Still another hidden factor in Schurz's temporary support of the Republican candidate in 1876 was indicated when, on winning his close election over Samuel J. Tilden, Hayes promptly appointed Schurz as his Secretary of the Interior. Thus Schurz took over the most notoriously corrupt, inefficient and mismanaged department of the executive branch. For years the Department of the Interior had been plagued by scandals over the bribery of Indian agents, the mistreatment of the tribesmen for whose welfare it was responsible, the theft of timber and mineral lands by powerful and politically protected interests, and the various evils of the spoils system operation in its widespread activities.

Immediately on taking office Schurz announced that none of the clerks in his department would be removed except for cause, and that no promotions would be made except for merit. He did not even bring his own private secretary with him. A short time later he set up a board of inquiry, composed of three clerks of the highest rating, to investigate and advise on all appointments, dismissals and promotions. He intended this system as a model for all the other departments of the government, as a forerunner of the civil service. Furthermore he made the death of the spoils system an issue which attracted not only the bitter enmity of professional politicians but a national sympathy for the cause of civil service.

Soon he was busy shaking the clinkers out of the whole department. The Indian Bureau was a mass of corruption, so he busied himself rooting out and firing Indian agents who diverted for their own profit the supplies supposed to be going to their wards on the reservations. He fought the War Department, with its unofficial premise that the only good Indian was a dead Indian, a policy implemented by allowing the complete slaughter of the buffalo herds so the Indians would be deprived of their food supply, and insisted that the tribesmen be treated more humanely even when, in their frustration, they strayed off the reservations. (His views were allowed to prevail, partly because President Hayes had his own humanitarian aspects and because the army's condign methods had proved imperfect in the campaign against the Sioux which resulted in the disaster at the Little Big Horn the year before Schurz became Secretary of the Interior.) There was, in fact, great bitterness against ex-Major General Schurz in the Indian-fighting army, whose leaders condemned Schurz's "soft" policy and who were supported by many of the settlers naturally fearful of new Indian outbreaks. Undeterred, Schurz was constantly engaged in guerrilla war with the army bureaucrats over the control and care of the Indian wards of the government.

He was also the first high government official to formulate a conservation policy to protect the natural heritage of the American people. The great forest, then being stripped in many sections of the Northeast and Middle West, must be protected. The activities of the lumber magnates, who exploited the vast lands often acquired through political influence and bribery in the statehouses, must be checked. He held that the government must assume immediate responsibility for the land and hand it up to future generations with something of its beauty and primeval splendor intact. Naturally this campaign for conservation, at a time when most people believed the resources of North America were limitless and its wilderness hardly scratched, did not arouse any great enthusiasm among his contemporaries; it did make him many powerful enemies, and after he left Hayes's cabinet he never held public office again.

His fight for the civil service, for decent treatment of the Indians and for conservation formed the noblest part of his career, the part for which he was most widely condemned; but it was all of a piece with his youthful vision of America — the vision which so many immigrants brought over with them, and which faded into obscurity in the competitive struggle that began the moment they boarded the ferry from Ellis Island — as a sort of Paradise Regained. He was moved until the end of his life by a passionate determination that Americans should live up to the best that was in them . . . and the strangest thing is that, against all the evidence of greed and self-seeking that surrounded him, he never lost faith that they would.

After leaving the government with the end of the Hayes Administration, he served as an editor of the New York *Evening Post* and then of *Harper's Weekly*; published his two-volume biography of Henry Clay in 1887 and completed three volumes of his *Reminiscences*, which took him only to the conclusion of his Civil War service and which were published the year after his death.

Meanwhile, he kept a sternly perceptive eye on politics and at least once intervened in a national election to strategic effect. That was the election of 1884. Two years earlier, thanks in part to the crusading of the National Civil Service Reform Association, of which Schurz was president, the Republican party had lost out in the Congressional elections in New York, Pennsylvania and elsewhere. The establishment of a civil service was now a national issue. When Grover Cleveland was nominated by the Democrats and promised to carry out such a program, Schurz led a nonpartisan movement on Cleveland's behalf. Without his support, as Allan Nevins has written, "Cleveland would probably have been defeated."[14] And Cleveland kept the faith when he assumed the Presidency; he refused to discharge any government workers simply because they were Republicans, even though his party had been out of power, nationally, for a quarter of a century and its leaders were eager to get at the spoils of victory.

The next great issue which absorbed Schurz, now approaching seventy, was American imperialism. He was against it. And, once more, against the current of majority opinion. The easy shattering of the Spanish empire in the Caribbean and the western Pacific encouraged dreams of an American colonial system; the country had become fascinated by a Kiplingesque vision of Americans, beaming with good-will under their sun helmets, spreading civilization among the little brown brothers whether they wanted it or not. From the quick conquest of Cuba, the United States army and navy turned to mopping-up operations in the Philippines. The Spanish were rudely dispossessed in the islands; then, with what seemed to be equal rudeness, the Filipinos objected to having their Spanish masters replaced by Americans. What followed was called the Philippine Insurrection, a polite term for fourteen years of guerrilla war that took hundreds of thousands of lives.

Schurz warned against it with all the vehemence at his command: we had no right to send our divisions thousands of miles across the Pacific to impose our rule, imperfect as it was, on a resentful race determined to preserve their own traditions. One of the great speeches of his career was delivered at a University of Chicago convocation early in 1899, the following excerpt of which was quoted in the United States Senate debate:

"It is objected that they are not capable of independent government. They may answer that this is their affair and that they are at least entitled to a trial. I frankly admit that if they are given the trial, their conduct in governing themselves will be far from perfect. Well, the conduct of no people is perfect, not even our own. They may try to revenge themselves upon their Tories in their Revolutionary War. But we too threw our Tories into hideous dungeons . . . we, too, have had our civil war which cost hundreds and thousands of lives and devastated one-half of our land; and now we have in horrible abundance the killings by lynch law . . . They may have troubles with their wild tribes. So had we, and we treated our wild tribes in a manner not to be proud of. They may have corruption and rapacity in their government . . . but Manila may secure a city council not much less virtuous than that of Chicago."

It was his last crusade, the echoes of which might be listened to today as America extends her hegemony over Asia. He died in 1906 at the age of seventy-seven, with ex-President Cleveland, Ambassador to England Joseph H. Choate, Booker T. Washington and other dignitaries participating in the memorial service. Not even those eloquent men could encompass the meaning of Carl Schurz's life as an American, his influence as a nondoctrinaire liberal, because they are part of a continuing tradition. He not only kept the faith, but passed it along with a new force and clarity and passion.

2

CITIZENS AND DISSIDENTS

7. THE WESTWARD MOVEMENT

Countless things testify to the German-American presence in the advance of the frontier, the waves of pioneering and settlement, the development and exploitation — and the plundering — of the land beyond the Mississippi. Wine flowed from German vineyards, gold from German-discovered mines, wheat from virgin prairie broken by diligent and skillful German farmers, and blood from Indians who fought the cavalry regiments with their large proportion of German troopers. German blood and sweat, to a large degree, nurtured the New Eden — and German ingenuity in science and industry helped turn it into something less than an Eden within half a century.

Germans are born colonizers, quick to organize and establish their own way of life, and what has been called their "stockade mentality" made adaptation to frontier conditions all the easier in places where the stockade was a necessary fact of life and not a mere figure of speech. They also had a certain steadiness of temperament, a dogged persistence and stolid durability that stood them well in the chanciness of a pioneer's life, whether it preserved them against Kansas cyclones, Comanche raids in Texas, dust storms in the Dakotas, drought in Nebraska, cattle-killing blizzards in Montana, or cowboy exuberance in the trail towns.

Some idea of how they moved in and quickly impregnated a

community with the Teutonic atmosphere may be gathered from the recollections of an admiring Anglo-Saxon who had preceded them to Syracuse, New York. "In 1840 there were very few Germans in the region about Syracuse. Then German peasants appeared, picturesque in their native costumes, settling about Syracuse and Salina. The next step was when the Germans became more numerous. They then formed a militia company, and their brilliant uniforms and military drill outshone anything that the native militia had accomplished. A Turnverein soon appeared. There was a church, which was Catholic, as could be told by the surmounting cross and the word 'Deo' written above the entrance. This rude board structure soon gave way to the brick building in Romanesque style, with its two typical towers." Soon the whole community hummed with that beelike sound, that orderly bustle of Teutons at work, with Sabbath interludes of beer drinking and beery singing which the Anglo-Saxon observer did not resent because while the Irish "on occasion drank whiskey, and when they took too much, became bad-tempered" the Germans became "more good-humored and fraternal" with every barrel of beer they emptied.[1]

With the same beelike instincts they swarmed west. Every Boot Hill and deserted cemetery in the western states, as well as the obliterated graves of those who died in the wagon trains along the way or were killed by the Indians in remote farms and settlements, testify to their movement westward. The German imprint on the Old West, and what it became, is indelible. The artifacts of that influence are almost too numerous and diverse to catalogue. They range from the Derringer pistol, that sneaky little gun which snuffed out so many lives in disputes over gaming tables, which was invented by a Pennsylvania German named Henry Deringer, Jr., to the wagons which bore the pioneers westward. The swaybacked Conestoga wagons which formed the pioneers' trains were developed and manufactured by Pennsylvania Germans; during and after the Civil War they were made by J. M. Studebaker, the son of a German-born blacksmith, and his brothers, whose company lasted well into the automobile age. Some of the best plows, harrows, corn planters and threshers used in the pioneering of the virgin lands were manufactured by German firms in Illinois, Ohio and Pennsylvania. The pianos laboriously transported on river steamers, freight wagons and pack trains to the parlors of newly culture-conscious westerners who had suddenly prospered were made by German-American manufacturers.

Much of the fascination of the pristine West, long before the Indians were herded onto reservations and the buffalo herds slaughtered, was conveyed by German artists and contributed greatly to the romantic illusion which attracted so many western settlers. Their work glowed with the impressions of a boundless and unspoiled paradise of misty waterfalls and distant snow peaks and verdant mountain meadows, peopled by a picturesque but not particularly ferocious breed of savages, and was not at all inhibited by the influence of the Romantic School of Düsseldorf. Lithographed copies of those massive works spread the gospel of the New Eden to every corner of the country.

Long before the mass pioneering began, the wonders beyond the Mississippi were propagandized by the work of Carl Bodmer, who accompanied the scientific expedition up the Missouri led by Prince Maximilian of Wied-Neuwied. A superb draftsman, Bodmer produced sketches and portraits of the Indians of the upper Missouri for a folio volume first published in Germany under Prince Maximilian's patronage, then widely reprinted in the United States. Emmanuel Leutze, who spent his boyhood in America and studied painting in Düsseldorf, contributed not only the famous *Washington Crossing the Delaware* but the panoramic "Emigration to the West," which forms one of the panels of the staircase in the Capitol in Washington. Other German-American painters whose work was reproduced and broadcast in *Harper's* and *Leslie's Weekly* included Rufus Zogbaum, A. R. Waud, Charles Schreyvogel, Charles Wimar and Henry Farney.

Wimar was brought to this country at the age of fifteen and began learning his profession by painting wagon panels and making signs for St. Louis merchants. He traveled out West long before the Civil War and did much of his best work while living with an old Indian chief who befriended him. Large crowds were attracted to the exhibition of such Wimar works as *Attack on the Emigrant Train, The Buffalo Hunt, The Buffalo Dance* and *Indians Approaching Fort Benton.* Farney was

Alsatian-born but was raised in Cincinnati and served as an apprentice to a lithographer. Later he went out West to produce a number of striking pictures, including the graphic and celebrated *Song of the Talking Wire*, showing a blanketed Indian leaning against a telegraph pole and bewilderedly trying to grasp its meaning — one of the classics of western Americana.

Charles Schreyvogel, born to an impoverished family on New York's Lower East Side, also served his apprenticeship as a lithographer. Two wealthy art patrons recognized his talent and sent him to study in Munich for three years. After his return to America he journeyed out West and produced *My Bunkie*, which made him famous overnight, attracted large crowds wherever it was shown and won him first prize at a National Academy exhibition. His specialty, however, was the United States Cavalry and most of his canvases were filled with the thunder of mounted charges, skirmishes with the Sioux and Apaches. An enthusiastic horseman, he seemed unable to paint anything without a horse at full gallop in the foreground. Another of his celebrated works, *In Safe Hands*, showed a golden-haired little girl being carried to safety across a wide prairie river after an Indian war party had attempted to kidnap her.

By far the most celebrated of the German-American artists who glamorized the Old West, along with Frederic Remington and Charles M. Russell, was Albert Bierstadt, who was born in Solingen in 1830 and raised in New Bedford, Massachusetts. Often his paintings, celebrating the grandeur of the western mountains on titanic canvases, brought him $25,000 apiece. He studied painting in Düsseldorf, and the influence of those romanticists was expanded to heroic proportions in his own work. At the age of twenty-eight he journeyed westward and began composing his massive landscapes capturing the temple-like solitudes, the primeval splendor of the Yosemite Valley, Mount Hood and the peaks of the Rockies. Today his work is coming into vogue again, Wagnerian thunder converted to oil and canvas. He became famous with his first exhibitions in 1860. Eight years later his landscape *In the Sierras* won him the gold medal at the exhibition of the Berlin Academy. Many who had been dazzled by the heroic impressions of such canvases as *Emerald*

Pool in the White Mountains must have been bewildered when they encountered reality out West and found nothing to match the splendors of Bierstadt's composite attempts to capture the enduring glory of the Rockies.

If German romanticism helped to lure many innocents on the trails westward, German practicality and ingenuity also eased their lot once they were confronted by the necessity of making something out of their life in the new lands.

There was, for instance, the stubborn faith of Wendelin Grimm in the possibilities of alfalfa as cattle fodder. Grimm had farmed in the Tauber Valley of Franconia before migrating to the United States, and was one of hundreds of Germans who settled in the rolling wooded valley of the Minnesota. Almost forty years old, he arrived with twenty pounds of alfalfa seed and just enough money to buy himself a fair-sized farm. Until then (1857) no one had succeeded in growing alfalfa anywhere in the United States but balmy California; both Washington and Jefferson, keenly interested in the science of agriculture, had tried to grow the stuff on their Virginia plantations but had failed. Tauber was convinced that anything that could grow in Franconia could also survive the Middle Western winters. Most of his first crop was winter-killed, but there was enough seed to plant another crop in the spring. He kept planting and experimenting for half a dozen years, until one day in 1863 a neighbor stopped by his farm and asked Grimm if his cattle were so fat and sleek because he fed them corn.

"No grain at all," Grimm replied, "just everlasting clover."[2]

Grimm distributed his seed to other farmers in the Minnesota Valley when they discovered that his clover was so hardy that it struck roots ten feet deep in the clay of Carver County. In 1874 his strain of alfalfa was so tough that it survived the harshest winter in thirty years. Eventually that hardy breed of alfalfa, known as Minnesota Grimm, was propagandized by the Department of Agriculture and contributed greatly to American farming and ranching. A monument now marks the Grimm homestead. Aside from that, Wendelin Grimm died in obscurity, though his persevering faith in the virtues of alfalfa, enduring through long and lonely winters on what was then the frontier, was worth any number of six-gun shoot-outs as a factor in civilizing the West. A Wyatt Earp would make himself famous behind a Colt .45, but the name of Grimm is still associated with fairy tales.

American wines, now slowly winning acceptance as potable after more than a century's struggle against the canards of the European winemakers, also benefited greatly from German-American efforts. Many German-Americans, along with the French and Italians, pioneered in the grape-growing valleys of northern California. One of the great American viticulturists was George Husmann, who was born near Bremen, brought to this country as a child and first saw the steep green valleys of northern California, where sun and soil resembling those of the Rhineland and the French vineyards caught his eye, as a youth participating in the gold rush. He had to return to the family estate in Missouri on the death of a brother-in-law, and after experimental grape growing on that land published his first book, Grapes and Wine, after returning home from the Civil War. About that time the vine disease called phylloxera began making its inroads in the European vineyards and eventually almost destroyed the winemaking industry of the Old World. Husmann and other growers, however, had developed a new stock of riverbank grape, crossbred with other varieties, with deep cordlike roots. It was so hardy that it resisted the phylloxera. Cuttings of that vine were dispatched to France and grafted onto the parent stock. European wines were saved from extinction, a debt the French repaid by sneering that American wines were fit only for making into vinegar.[3]

In 1881, Husmann moved out to California to take over the management of the Talcoa Vineyards in the Napa Valley, shortly before phylloxera began attacking the California vines, which grew from cuttings brought over from France and Germany. Once again he was instrumental in saving vast grape-growing interests by introducing grafts of the hardy Missouri riverbank crossbreed. His later book, Grape Culture and Wine-Making, became a classic in the field of viticulture, and his career was capped by the honor of selecting the California wines entered at the Paris Exposition, which were awarded a score of medals. And his was only one of many great German names in the early California wine industry, which included those of Kohler, Frohling, Dresel,

Gunlach, Krug, Rock, Roeding, Dreyfus — not to mention Jacob Schramm, whose winery at the north end of the Napa Valley produced so soothing a vintage that it temporarily cured the misanthropy of Schramm's freeloading friend Ambrose Bierce, who lived in a mountain cabin nearby.

The German name with all the misbegotten glamour, the one emblazoned on western history for all time, however, had nothing to do with nourishing the mind of body. It was connected with that most squalid of all human migrations, the gold rush. Even so, it was agriculture on a princely scale, not gold mining, which brought John Augustus Sutter to California in the late 1830's. He unwittingly and accidentally started the gold rush, and was the first man destroyed by it. A German-Swiss, Sutter chose a huge tract of land in the fertile Sacramento Valley after fifteen ill-starred years of wandering in the West. With the permission of the Mexican authorities at Monterey, he planned to establish a manorial estate with himself as its feudal lord.

With a labor force of docile Indians supervised by a few white overseers, he built a compound at the confluence of the American and Sacramento rivers and placed cannon on its walls. Less than ten years later his colony was flourishing with herds of cattle and sheep grazing the ranges and various small industrial enterprises operating near his compound. Early in 1847 he decided to build a sawmill on a site to be selected by one of his overseers, James Marshall, who picked a location in the valley of the south fork of the American. (Now the site of the town of Coloma.) On agreement with Sutter, Marshall took a party of workmen to the site. One day in January, 1848, Marshall found traces of gold in the riverbed. Four days later he took several ounces of gold dust to Sutter's headquarters. Sutter knew the value of the discovery and secretly dispatched a messenger to Monterey asking for a three-year lease on "ten or twelve leagues" of land around what became known as Sutter's Mill. Within weeks the "secret" was out and the rush was on. Goldrushers appeared by the scores, then the hundreds and thousands. They trampled over Sutter's domain, disregarded his and Marshall's claims, ruined his crops and slaughtered his cattle. He had no legal recourse in the California of 1849. The gold rush which made so many men rich left Sutter a bitter, broken and bankrupt man.

BIG TROUBLE IN SIOUX COUNTRY

One of the first large-scale invasions of the Indian country — specifically the domain of the eastern branch of the Sioux — took place in the valley of the Minnesota River during the 1850's. A number of Welsh and Irish had already settled there. They were joined by eighteen thousand Germans and twelve thousand Scandinavians as the population of the richly endowed valley increased by tenfold within a few years.

The center of German settlement in the Minnesota Valley was the town of New Ulm, about twenty miles downriver from Fort Ridgley. The town site was located after Frederick Beinhorn, a thirty-one-year-old cobbler from Braunschweig who was working as a day laborer in Chicago and studying English in night school, formed the German Land Association to find a place for resettling the hundreds of German immigrants then flooding the cheap labor market. Four of its members were sent to Minnesota and after various misadventures met an old French trader named Joe La Framboise who pointed out the future site of New Ulm as the best place to settle.

Within a year the 4,800-acre tract was surveyed and staked out, land was being cleared and homes were being built. The town itself was platted on six thousand acres of glacial bench under the river bluffs, with its planners somewhat grandiosely envisioning a city of 75,000 to 100,000 inhabitants. Around the town itself 494 plots of four acres each were set aside for vegetable gardens, and inside the town space was allotted for the parks which survive in the New Ulm of today. No other town on the frontier was planned so carefully.

Meanwhile, the New Ulm colony having come under the sponsorship of the Cincinnati Turner Society, parties of German immigrants began arriving on the *Frank Steele*, a steamboat built in Cincinnati for the Minnesota River trade. In and around New Ulm the land was being occupied, stores and homes built, churches established, singing societies organized — it was observed that as soon as six or seven German arrived in any place they founded a choir or singing group almost as quickly as they built a brewery — and the process of coloniziation proceeded at that steady, orderly pace so valued by the Germans.

If there was a cloud on the generally fair horizon of the German settlers, it was colored red. The color of the Sioux on reservations upriver. How long would the Indians stay peaceful as they saw the valley filled up with white men and hunting ranges rapidly converted into farms? And elsewhere in the valley non-German settlers were envious of the fact that New Ulm was the best town site on the river; they also professed to be shocked by the fact that in New Ulm, as a privately published book charged, "the Sabbaths are spent in drinking and dancing."[4] True enough, New Ulm's beer halls never closed and its families kept a perpetual open house. Its hospitality became so famous in the valley that soon the Irish, Welsh and other settlers were coming there for the *Sommernachtfests*, on which the summer nights were filled with beer-drinking, dancing and singing until the first light of dawn.

Early in 1857 came the first rumors of Indian trouble to disturb the growing prosperity of the valley. Down in Iowa the Sioux had struck back at the white invaders and killed thirty settlers in the Spirit Lake massacre. The band of outlaw Sioux then moved north to Jackson, Minnesota, killed two storekeepers and ambushed a party of white men rushing to their assistance. The whites in the valley struck back in haste and panic. A party of Welsh and Germans, armed mostly with scythes lashed to long poles, fell upon a Sioux village innocent of any participation in the Spirit Lake killings and chased the Indians across the prairie.

For the next several years the valley was peaceful enough. There were soldiers at Fort Ridgley, a company of infantry, to handle any minor disturbances. Then the Civil War started, and the federal army had to thin out the forces allotted to defending the frontier. It seemed possible that the Indians, so long kept in check partly by government rations and partly by the threat of armed force, might take the opportunity to strike back. Early in 1862 the Sioux upriver were definitely showing signs of hostility. An eloquent and ambitious young chief named Little Crow had risen among them with promises of revenge to be exacted from the whites. A year earlier Henry Thoreau,

191

traveling for reasons of health, had journeyed up the Minnesota on a steamer and visited the Sioux reservation at Redwood. "The most prominent chief was named Little Crow," Thoreau wrote his friend Horace Mann, Jr. "They [the Sioux] were quite dissatisfied with the white man's treatment of them and probably have reason to be so."

In midsummer news of the Union army's defeat at Second Bull Run reached the Sioux reservations in Minnesota. Many of his followers urged Little Crow, who until now had attended an Episcopal church every Sunday and was depended upon by the white authorities to keep his tribesmen under control, to lead an uprising. Five thousand Minnesota white men had marched off to join the Union army. That army, according to rumors heard by the Indians, was cracking up under successive defeats. Now was the time to kill all the whites they could reach, and drive out the remainder.

On the morning of Monday, August 18, 1862, Little Crow and his followers began their uprising. They struck first at the Indian Agency compound at Redwood, where a dozen government employees were killed without a chance of defending themselves. Throughout the Minnesota Valley, on that hot summer's day, men, women and children were slaughtered on the roads, in their homes and fields and woods.

At a German settlement near Sacred Heart Creek a few miles from New Ulm, one of Little Crow's bands swooped down on the home of fourteen-year-old Mary Schwandt and her family. Her mother and father, her two grown brothers, her pregnant sister and her brother-in-law all were killed, and her twelve-year-old brother August was tomahawked and left for dead. The unborn baby was cut from her sister's womb and nailed to a tree. Down the road toward New Ulm, in another house, the children were snatched from their mother's arms, swung by the heels and had their brains dashed out against the walls; they and their mother were hurled onto a funeral pyre made of bedding and broken furniture.

Mary Schwandt, after witnessing those horrors, was dragged off as a nubile captive to Little Crow's village and thrust into his tepee. Some time later Little Crow returned from leading the various massacres. "I was sitting quietly and shrinkingly by a tepee," the girl wrote some years later, "when he came along in full chief's costume and looking very grand. Suddenly he jerked his tomahawk from his belt and sprang toward me with the weapon uplifted as if he meant to cleave my head in two . . . he glared down at me so savagely, that I thought he would really kill me; but I looked up at him, without any care or fear about my fate, and gazed quietly into his face without so much as winking my tear-swollen eyes. He brandished his tomahawk over me a few times, then laughed, put it back in his belt and walked away, still laughing."[5]

Closer to New Ulm the roving bands of Sioux caught Anton Messmer and his family out in the fields harvesting their wheat, and killed them all. Nearby, also on the Milford Road, they wiped out John Zettell, his wife and five children. Before the day was over the Sioux killed more than fifty settlers on the Milford Road alone. To the Sioux warriors it was all part of war; killing an infant was regarded as worthy an act as killing an armed man. The warriors' societies under Little Crow had taken an oath to kill every living white human in the valley, to reclaim it from the traders they claimed had cheated them for years, the Indian Agency employees who had withheld their rations, the settlers who had dispossessed them.

All over the valley, that first day and during the night, when they hoped the roads would be safe, white families were heading for New Ulm or Fort Ridgley in their wagons. Thirteen German families loaded into eleven wagons waited until darkness to set out for the fort from their farms in the Sacred Heart Creek neighborhood. The fear-stricken caravan was led by Paul Kitzman, who had been friendly with some of the Sioux and often fed them when they dropped by his house. The wagons were about halfway to Fort Ridgley when they were stopped by a small band of Sioux. One of the war party had often visited Kitzman in his home, and he greeted the white man by throwing his arm around him and kissing him on the cheek, then shook hands with the others and assured them that the Chippewas, not the Sioux, were responsible for the day's massacres. The war party, the Indian assured Kitzman, would protect the caravan and guide it safely to the fort. Kitzman had no option but to agree to accepting the "protection."

A few miles down the road, the Sioux halted the wagons and demanded all the money in the settlers' possession. The settlers complied. Shortly after the wagons began rolling again, the Indians attacked.

Kitzman and all but three of the men were killed by their volleys. One of the survivors was Frederick Krieger, who tried to flee into the woods with his wife and their eleven children. Krieger was shot to death, his wife was brought down by a shotgun blast and four of their children were killed in the pursuit through the woods. Mrs. Krieger and seven of the children escaped with their lives, though Mrs. Krieger was slashed across the abdomen by an Indian searching the bodies nearby for loot. When she recovered consciousness, she crawled into the brush, hiding there until daylight.

In New Ulm that night the nine hundred residents of the town, then consisting of several brick houses and almost two hundred frame houses, prepared for an onslaught before dawn. They threw up barricades in the business section, and the women and children huddled in the darkened stores while the hundred men able to bear arms, with only forty rifles among them, manned the improvised defenses. About midnight a war party appeared on the heights above the town and began pouring rifle fire into the streets. The Indians did not attack at close range, however, and rode off when a thunderstorm broke over the town.

Next day, recovering from the shock of the massacres, the whites began organizing to defend themselves until help could come from the outside. Militia companies marched to Fort Ridgley, where Lieutenant Timothy J. Sheehan was in command. He was so short of ammunition that he set the post's blacksmith to cutting iron rods into small pieces for bullets. On Wednesday, August 20, Little Crow and his warriors appeared in force on the bluffs overlooking the fort and began attacking up the ravines on its approaches. The Sioux kept attacking, trying to reach the stockade, from 1:00 P.M. to dusk but were driven off by Lieutenant Sheehan's howitzers.

Meanwhile, Colonel Henry H. Sibley had been appointed to take command of an expeditionary force against the Sioux. He came up the river on the sidewheeler *Favorite*, picked up four companies of Volunteer infantry at Fort Snelling, disembarked at Shakopee with three of the companies and sent the fourth on to Carver. Colonel Sibley found the river road lined with wagons bearing settlers and whatever household goods they could carry off.

Before Colonel Sibley could take the field, however, the Sioux were attacking two points in the valley they must capture in order to drive the whites out. On Friday, August 22, Little Crow and eight hundred mounted warriors gathered to attack Fort Ridgely again and this time they got close to the walls of the fort. Musketry and fire from the fort's twelve-pounder kept them out of the fort after desperate fighting, and one of the Sioux leaders, Chief Big Eagle, later admitted, "We thought the fort was the door to the valley as far as to St. Paul, and that if we got through the door nothing could stop us this side of the Mississippi. But the defenders of the fort were very brave and kept the door shut."

The next day, deciding that door was too stoutly defended, the Sioux turned back to New Ulm. Certainly, with all their hundreds of warriors eager for rape and plunder, the Sioux would be able to break into that all-but-defenseless town. Charles Flandrau, though a Frenchman, had been elected by the largely German population to command the town's slender defense force. He watched the war-painted Sioux swarming down the bluffs to cut off any attempt by the townspeople to flee to the east. "They came in a close mass," Frandrau later reported, "at a moderate gait, until they came within about a double rifle shot from us, when they deployed to the right and left until they covered our whole front, and then gave a blood curdling yell, and sailed down on us like the wind."

Flandrau had a line of riflemen waiting in their positions just inside the town limits. The first assault by the mounted Sioux sent them reeling back to the barricades around the business section.

Most of the German townsmen had never fired a musket at another human or seen an Indian on the warpath, and Flandrau was not disheartened by the initial retreat. "White men fight under a great disadvantage the first time they engage with the Indians," he said later. "There is something so fiendish in their yells and terrifying in their appearance that it takes a good deal of time to overcome the unpleasant sensation it inspires." He might have added that any soldiers with a prepared position behind them are likely to take the opportunity to withdraw behind it.

Once behind the barricades, however, the citizen soldiers of New

Ulm had to stand and fight, or be wiped out and condemn their wives and children to death or captivity. When the next charge came, they blazed away at the Sioux attackers and held their ground. Time after time the Indians charged. The battle for the town went on all day. Twenty-six of the townsmen were killed while manning the barricades, but the Indians were finally repulsed at nightfall.

That night New Ulm was a scene of victory won at a ghastly price. One hundred and ninety of its two hundred houses were in flames, and more than a tenth of its families had lost a breadwinner. The towns downriver saw the flames reflected against the sky as a red glow and believed that New Ulm had been destroyed along with all its inhabitants. Instead Flandrau was evacuating the town. During the night he led a caravan of 153 wagons crowded with the town's whole population to safety. It was a "melancholy spectacle" to see his fellow citizens "who but a few days before had been prosperous and happy, reduced to utter beggary . . ." he wrote the governor.

While eastern newspapers that weekend were reporting that five hundred settlers in the Minnesota Valley had been slaughtered, and the governor's office in St. Paul was deluged with pleas from all over the state that Colonel Sibley's punitive expedition be hurled into action instantly, the program for punishing the Sioux and thereby preventing any more outbreaks such as had terrorized the valley for six days was slowly being organized. Sibley, an ex-fur trader who knew something of the Indian psyche, was determined that precipitous action be avoided. His first objective, always kept coolly in mind, was to reclaim the women and children who had been captured by the Sioux. Their lives would be forfeited, he believed, if his forces simply marched out and engaged the hostiles. His only hope or rescuing the white captives was to convince the Sioux of his superiority and persuade them to surrender their prisoners alive and unharmed. Furthermore, the fourteen hundred men he had gathered under his command were an unknown quality. Only a few companies of Volunteers had gone through a semblance of military training. All the rest were undisciplined militia and four hundred mounted men formed into various units.

The first action he allowed his subordinates to urge upon him was to send a force of 160 "cavalry" to the Indian Agency headquarters at

Redwood, bury the sixteen bodies they found rotting in the late August sun, rescue Justina Krieger, almost dead from hunger and loss of blood, and send out scouts to see whether they could learn anything of Little Crow's movements. At dawn the next morning they were attacked by a large war party, which was driven off only after twenty-two men in the command were killed. The only wagon that survived the attack was the one in which the unconscious Mrs. Krieger had been placed. She was brought out alive, and later reunited with her surviving children.

Four days later Sibley and his volunteers moved out to grapple with the Sioux, but only after Sibley sent Little Crow a message reading: "If Little Crow has any proposition to make to me, let him send a half-breed to me, and he shall be protected in and out of camp." Little Crow's reply was late in coming, disdained any talk of surrender and pointedly concluded, "I have a great many prisoners, women and children."

Sibley handled himself and his ragtag command with exactly the sense of discretion required. The Sioux attempted an ambush of his column but it was accidentally uncovered. After a two-hour pitched battle in which the Sioux for the first time found themselves out-numbered, Little Crow signaled the retreat. A vainer type than Sibley would have launched a hot pursuit, but he let the Indians withdraw from the vicinity of the Wood Lake battle. He cautiously followed. Several days of diplomatic maneuvering ensued, in which Sibley sent messages to several chiefs known to be less militant than Little Crow.

Three days after the battle the Sioux decided to surrender and allowed Sibley and his troops to march into their encampment. Thus 269 white captives were recovered. Little Crow and a number of other bitter-enders had fled before the rest of the Sioux surrendered.

Before that year was out, 307 Sioux chiefs and warriors were convicted by a military tribunal on charges of rape and murder. All but thirty-eight had their sentences to death by hanging commuted by President Lincoln. On December 27, 1862, the largest mass execution in American history took place, with all thirty-eight of the luckless ones hanged simultaneously on a huge scaffold.

Accounts were settled with Little Crow in rather ironic fashion. The following June, Sibley, now a brigadier, set out with a column five miles long to track down the fugitive. Before the troops could close in, however, the half-starved fugitive was surprised by a settler in his berry patch and shot to death.

His son grew up to be a YMCA leader, his grandson a Protestant minister.

For whites, if not for the Indians, who were soon being massacred in equally barbaric fashion at Sand Creek and later on the Washita, the "Sioux War of 1862" was the most horrible event in the history of the frontier. Most of its white victims were German-American settlers. Few, however, abandoned the Minnesota Valley, and in a matter of months New Ulm was being rebuilt and ravaged farms were being restored, with new graveyards nearby.

The horrors in and around New Ulm were widely publicized, not only in the press but by a traveling exhibition of what its promoter and fabricator, John Stevens, called "diaphanous painting." Actually it was a forerunner of the motion pictures. Stevens's roadshow consisted of scenes of the massacres and the mass execution painted on thin cloth, through which light was focused from behind and which was unreeled while musicians played appropriate accompaniment.

Thousands throughout the United States saw what Stevens advertised as The Great Moral Exhibition of the Age, and undoubtedly it contributed heavily toward the contemporary belief that the only good Indian was a dead Indian, particularly one of the panels captioned "Minnesota Fruit," which showed the slain infants falling out of trees to be caught in their mothers' aprons.*

A GALLERY OF TINTYPES

The massacre at New Ulm, Minnesota, perhaps because it was muted by the greater slaughters in Virginia and along the Mississippi in the

---

* Many years later the "diaphanous panorama" exhibited by Stevens was presented to the Minnesota Historical Society. It consisted of thirty-six panels, each six feet by seven, and was unreeled from a huge spool. It was again exhibited in 1919–1920, with Mary Schwandt Schmidt, Little Crow's fourteen-year-old captive, providing the commentary.

summer of 1862, failed to serve as a lesson. The westward movement was largely suspended by the war, in any case, and after it was over prospective migrants to the frontier were assured that the United States Cavalry, now accustomed to dealing with the late Jeb Stuart and other masters of mounted warfare, would have little difficulty in handling the tribesmen.

German-Americans joined the westward flow by the thousands soon after the war ended, many as members of the Indian-fighting frontier army, many more as settlers of the rich grasslands that extended almost to the Rockies. The Germans and the Irish, as newcomers most urgently in need of employment, made up the bulk of the cavalry regiments which saw the hardest service in the Indian campaigns. The Germans, many of whom had fled the *Vaterland* to escape compulsory military service, enlisted more out of desperation than any inherent warlike tendencies; even if they spoke no English they were acceptable to recruiting sergeants when other employers turned them aside.

No matter what conditions attended their departure from the Fatherland, many of the Germans in the frontier regiments evidently retained a certain feeling for the old country. Most of the regimental bands were composed of German musicians, often with a sprinkling of Italians, and in 1870 the post musicians in several garrisons blared forth with "Die Wacht am Rhein" to celebrate German victories in the Franco-Prussian War. French-born soldiers immediately responded by singing "Le Marseillaise" at the top of their lungs. The musicale ended in a flurry of fists and band instruments until the guard was called out and old-country passions were cooled.[6] (Elsewhere Germans in the West followed news of that war with a similar interest. Santa Fe, New Mexico, had a large German population. The files of the Santa Fe *New Mexican* for the summer of 1870 showed that extras were issued and many columns of type were devoted to news of that faraway war. The city was strongly pro-German, even though many of its residents had fled Germany in fear of Prussian domination of the German states. One story related that the German colony, led by the Hon. C. P. Clever, was grateful to the newspapers and the governor of the territory for their support. The latter had just delivered an address, doubtless with his supporters' prejudices in mind, rejoicing in the triumph of the Prussian war machine.)[7]

Most of the Germans who went out West, of course, were neither Indian fighters nor adventurers of any kind. The soil of the virgin prairies attracted them and made them risk their lives on the frontier; and the wheatfields of Kansas, the Dakotas, Nebraska, Wyoming and Montana are enduring testimonials to their diligence. For the most part the men who made themselves famous as peace officers and outlaws bore Scotch-Irish or Anglo-Saxon names. Germans distinguished themselves neither in defending nor in breaking the rudimentary laws of the frontier.

There were a few, however, who became notorious for something besides backbreaking toil and plodding industry. The few German-born criminals seemed to specialize, perhaps because of the Munchausen trait which runs erratically through the German character, in confidence games and other forms of verbal trickery. One issue of the Las Vegas, New Mexico, *Gazette* in 1878 published the following bulletin from an irate correspondent: "Your vicinity will, no doubt, be inflicted soon with the presence of one George Fisher, a German. He is not only a 'deadbeat,' one could understand that; but he is a petty-larceny thief . . . the golden-haired Teuton 'got away with our baggage.' He is a drunken, lying, thieving vagabond, who will doubtless use the names of parties he has victimized here, as a passport to the confidence of some other damned fool! There would be no use in describing him. He has no shame. Will not deny his name, and will boast of his friendship with gentlemen who have expelled him from their houses for theft. I will give $10.00 to the man who will warm up the basement of my trousers with my belt. Fisher stole both of them."[8]

Two German-Americans out West did manage to distinguish themselves sufficiently to be awarded considerable mention in the history of western crime, and both showed in their endeavors the same persistence and diligence which their neighbors noted in German farmers and ranchers. One was the most talented horse thief and cattle rustler west of the Mississippi, and the other was the most dogged and efficient of manhunters, so celebrated in Montana Territory that the newspapers referred to him only by his middle initial "X," which marked the spot of many an outlaw's grave.

Horse thieves, of course, ranked very low on the western social scale, slightly above a pimp and slightly below a gambler who used loaded dice, but a Pennsylvania German named Henry Born, alias "Dutch Henry," was accorded a certain amount of respect not only for his talent but his breathtaking venturesomeness. Wyatt Earp said he was "the most astute cattle and horse thief on the plains in a day when stock-stealing was a capital offense."[9]

Small, meek and mild, Dutch Henry had come out West to make enough money to marry his girl back home. In the years following the Civil War, the most profitable pursuit for a man without capital was buffalo hunting, and that was the trade Dutch Henry took up.

His career as an outlaw began more by accident than design, but mostly because like many quiet inoffensive characters he mightily resented being put upon. One day his camp was attacked by Indians. Dutch Henry escaped with an arrow lodged in the calf of one leg, but had to walk many miles to reach Fort Lyon for medical assistance. The commandant, as it happened, detested buffalo hunters. He ordered Dutch Henry to quit the post even before the surgeon could remove the arrow from his leg. Dutch Henry, a slow Teutonic rage burning inside him, obediently limped away from the fort. Hiding in brush along the banks of a river nearby, he removed the arrow himself and while waiting for nightfall swore a vendetta against all Indians and all military gentlemen of high degree. When night came, he slipped inside the fort, past the sentries, and made off with a span of government mules — and the commandant's fine saddle horse. From then on, no government mule, Indian pony or cavalry horse was safe from Dutch Henry's depredations. He regarded these thefts as just compensation for the way he had been treated by the Indians and the United States government.

Occasionally he took a breather from what he regarded as his righteous cause by engaging in what might be called group activities. Thus as a free-lance gunslinger he became involved in the Lincoln County cattle war, associating himself for a time with Billy the Kid and other reprehensible types.

A few years later he joined a buffalo-hunting expedition which included Bat Masterson and other reckless fellows who proposed to hunt far below the Arkansas River on land supposedly ceded to the Comanches and other tribes. Once again Dutch Henry was caught in a desperate bind. He and a score of other hunters were besieged by hundreds of Comanches and Kiowas in a battle that lasted several days at Adobe Walls in the Canadian River valley. They escaped with their lives only because their long-ranging buffalo guns and repeating rifles took a heavy toll of the attacking Indians.

That experience apparently convinced Dutch Henry that his true vocation, antisocial though it might be, was expropriating horses and cattle on the Kansas ranges. The Kansas papers were full of his activities. His notoriety was such that a one-line item in the Dodge City *Globe* ("Dutch Henry is again on his old stamping ground south of Dodge," August 6, 1878) was enough to send posses streaking over the prairie and stockmen to hire extra hands to protect their herds.

A few years later he faded from view, and there is no record of his having met the fate of most rustlers either formally on the gallows or informally in a noose slung over the nearest tree limb. Perhaps, in his quiet way, he simply gave up his desperado's career, went back to Pennsylvania, married his girl and died respectably with his boots off.

His counterpart on the other side of the law was also a Pennsylvania German, a stubby little man who spent twenty-seven years instilling respect for the law in Montana Territory. His name was John X. Biedler. If he didn't win the fame of a Hickok, it was because he preferred to work in obscurity. The joy of his labors, as with so many German-Americans, was recompense enough. Thus his career can be traced only in scrappy items in the territorial press.

He was a small man with cold gray eyes and a short graying moustache, who eschewed the fancy tailoring of a Bat Masterson, the two-gun flashiness of a Wild Bill Hickok and the tall-tale-telling of a Wyatt Earp, which may account for the fact that no film or television series has ever been devised with John X. Biedler as its hero. He went about his business as soberly as a plumber.

During the early days around Virginia City, the Montana mining boomtown, he acquired certain ideas about the efficacy of summary justice that made his methods seem rather severe, not to say unconstitutional, as the territory became more civilized. The first mention of him was as one of the Vigilantes who hanged the notorious Joseph Slade in Virginia City. Subsequently he became a deputy sheriff who specialized in solitary manhunts — since posses in his opinion only raised a lot of dust and legal quibbles over formal trials and executions — and kept on the trail of a fugitive no matter how far and how long it took him. When he caught up with his man, he simply tried him on the spot, rendered a quick verdict of guilty as charged, and hung him on the nearest tree.

An item in the Helena *Herald* during 1867 may have puzzled any outsider who read it ("We saw 'X' pull a man off his horse the other day, and — that's all.") but knowledgeable Montanans translated the cryptic sentence without effort to read that John X. Biedler had caught up with and disposed of another miscreant. No one, apparently, cared to question his methods of law enforcement.

Later Biedler became an express messenger and a United States deputy marshal. As an arm of the federal government he showed more respect for the formalities of the law. But people still knew that when Biedler got into his manhunting costume — an enormous white slouch hat, a loose coat with many pockets to accommodate assorted weapons and rations for his journey, a long knife and two Navy Colts strapped around his waist — somebody would soon be brought back dead or alive.

Old-time westerns particularly honored him for the way he put down the swaggering showman, Buffalo Bill Cody, whose several genuine exploits were greatly expanded by his press agents. On a visit to New York during the 1880's he was introduced to "Colonel" Cody, who looked down his nose at the runtish Biedler and dismissed him with, "I never saw you, sir."

Bristling, Biedler replied, "I suppose not, sir, for I have been out West."

"So have I, sir," Cody snapped.

"Yes, but you went out West in a palace car [Pullman], and I crossed the plains with a pack train twenty-five years ago."

THE RESPECTABILITY OF PLUNDER

The name was curiously un-Germanic, and with the passing of the generations it has even acquired the ultimate sanction of being erroneously regarded as English. It stands for gilt-edged respectability and social eminence, for the haughtiest and most exclusive element in American life. One tributary of the family even managed to establish itself in England, penetrate the aristocracy and acquire its organ-toned mouthpiece, *The Times* of London.

The name, of course, is Astor. The German birthplace of the family's founder was Waldorf, which has also acquired lustrous connotations. In time — a century and a half — the humble German beginnings have been papered over with an Anglican surface as durable as armor-plate. Undoubtedly the Anglicization would have amused the family's founder, John Jacob Astor, to whom power and money were all-important, social pretensions a lot of nonsense.

He was quite unoffended when people referred to him as an ex-butcher, even though it didn't happen to be true. He was the son of a butcher, who left his native village near Heidelberg in 1770 at the age of seventeen with enough education to read, write and "do sums." First he joined an older brother, George, who was selling musical instruments in London; then he decided that America presented a greater opportunity, and joined another older brother, Heinrich, who was prospering in a butcher shop on the Bowery.

His ship arrived off Baltimore in January, 1774, when the Chesapeake was covered with ice, which was threatening to crush the ship. The captain ordered all the passengers to assemble on deck in their roughest clothes prepared to be removed in small boats. Young John Jacob Astor, however, came on deck dressed in his only good suit.

"What," demanded the captain, "are you all dressed up for? A welcoming ball?"

"If ve are saved," replied the youth, "I haf my Sunday suit on. If ve are drowned, it von't make no difference vot kind of clothes I haf on."[10]

This sturdy sense of practicality, within a remarkably few years, made Astor the first German-American to acquire a great fortune and one of the first Americans to tap the wealth of the western wilderness on an entrepreneurial scale.

Astor knew what he wanted and went about getting it with a single-minded, driving intensity. Instead of marrying a German wife like his brother (Heinrich boasted of his wife that "Dolly is der pink of der Powery"), John Jacob chose Sarah Todd for his wife. She was not only a cousin of the eminent Brevoort family but brought him a dowry of three hundred dollars. Instead of going into the old family trade of butchering, he entered the fur business, believing that the outside of the animal would be more profitable than the edible innards. His subsequent rise was rapid. Four years later he was listed in the city directory as a "furrier," and two years after that as a "fur merchant." By then he had begun buying real estate and his wealth was estimated at a quarter of a million dollars.

All this was piddling compared to the vision which gripped him and which was embodied in the American Fur Company, the first monopoly on the continent. His aim was simply to control the entire American fur trade. In 1808, with capital of half a million, he incorporated the company and was ready to trap, skin and trade the pelt of every fur-bearing creature in North America. In addition, he was determined to gain his share of the shipping trade.

Shrewd, close-fisted and ruthless, he proceeded to accomplish his purposes. The records of various Congressional investigating committees and the labors of latter-day muckrakers both confirmed that Astor was a looter on the imperial scale. His method of trading with the Indians who supplied most of the furs at his trading posts in the Pacific Northwest and elsewhere was to debauch them with whiskey and cheat them out of a fair price for their goods. Astor compounded the profits from this villainous trade by slippery maneuvers in shipping and high finance. The merchant-historian Walter Barrett (*The Merchants of Old*

New York) admiringly described one phase of Astor's operations: "John Jacob Astor at one period of his life had several vessels operating in this way. They would go to the Pacific and carry furs from thence to Canton. These would be sold at large profits. Then the cargoes of tea [picked up in Chinese ports] would pay enormous duties which Astor did not have to pay to the United States for a year and a half. His tea cargoes would be sold for good four and six months' paper, or perhaps cash; so that for eighteen or twenty years John Jacob Astor had what was actually a free-of-interest loan from the Government of over *five-millions* of dollars."[11]

By 1835 John Jacob Astor was the richest man in North America, but socially he was beyond the pale. Quickly gained wealth, as the Goulds and others found out, had to be sanctified by at least one generation of penance. Astor himself cared little for the folderols of social rank. For a long time he had lived at 223 Broadway above his office, salesroom and fur warehouse in which his son and chief heir, William, could be seen beating the furs to keep the moths out. His uncouth manners, in any case, would have kept him out of the higher realms of New York Society. Albert Gallatin, a former Secretary of the Treasury, refused to manage his real estate holdings because, said Gallatin, "he dined here last night and ate his ice cream and peas with a knife." Some years later Gallatin's son reported that Astor was still not quite housebroken: "Really Mr. Astor is dreadful . . . He came to *déjeuner* today; we were simply *en famille*, he sitting next to Frances [Gallatin's sister]. He actually wiped his fingers on the sleeve of her fresh white jacket."

Miserly and unpretentious in other ways, John Jacob Astor was, however, determined to found a dynasty and he laid down its foundations with all the care he gave to his fur-trading and shipping enterprises. In exchange for a lump sum, his son's bride was required to sign away her dower rights to the Astor fortune. Nothing could have pleased him more than the fact that the House of Astor was not only first among all the great American families but made more money, largely through simple accumulation, and kept it longer than any of the others. In his declining years, the only nourishment his stomach could hold was

August Belmont, who knew
how to live

John Jacob Astor, out of steerage into the top drawer

milk from the breast of a wet nurse, but even in that infantile state he kept such a tight grip on his leading faculty, the acquisitory one, that he was able to recite from memory the name of everyone he rented property to and how much they paid.

His methods of exploitation set the pattern for the material conquest of the West. His manner of extracting every last penny from the bloodstained and whiskey-reeking fur trade served as the real fable, as opposed to Horatio Alger's homilies, for his time and the time that followed.

Fellow German-Americans were among those who assiduously followed the Astor example. None, certainly, with greater diligence than Frederick Weyerhaeuser, who as one historian remarked "joined the business of amassing tens of millions of dollars with the studious art of extreme reticence."[12]

Weyerhaeuser's ascent to the unwanted throne wished upon him by the newspapers — the role of "lumber king" did not suit him because he did not care to attract attention to himself or his holdings — started from the humblest of beginnings and was marked by a keen appreciation of the business value of personal friendship. He migrated from Germany as a penniless youth in 1852. For a time he worked in Illinois sawmills, until it occurred to him that he would never get rich sawing other people's lumber. With whatever money he had managed to save, he went into business for himself in St. Paul. Once that business was prospering sufficiently, he built himself a mansion next to that of James J. Hill, the masterful operator of the Northern Pacific Railroad.

Hill's friendship was valuable to Weyerhaeuser because the former's railroad ran through, and held the carelessly bestowed rights to, millions of acres of the richest timberland on the continent.

In the glow of that friendship Weyerhaeuser's lumber company acquired almost two million acres, four-fifths of which, according to a federal government report, he bought from the Northern Pacific. In 1900 he bought a block of nine hundred thousand acres from Hill at the bargain rate of six dollars an acre, that tract being a large chunk of the western section of the state of Washington. Such land was supposed to go to settlers at nominal prices, but instead it disappeared into the maw of the Weyerhaeuser Lumber Company. Frederick Weyerhaeuser's fortune was estimated at three hundred million dollars when he died in 1914, but he left more than that to his heirs — the same sense of discretion, of keeping the glare of all that money out of the public eye. When Frederick Weyerhaeuser's great-grandson, the nine-year-old George, was kidnaped in 1935, spokesmen for the family stated that the two hundred thousand dollar ransom demanded could be raised only with great difficulty. It was raised, however, and the boy was recovered. The Weyerhaeuser timber operations are still one of the Northwest's more gigantic enterprises.

Henry Villard, born Heinrich Hilgard in Bavaria, was another German-American capitalist who joined enthusiastically, but somewhat less successfully than Astor or Weyerhaeuser, because of a rudimentary social conscience remarkable in a man of his time and occupation, in the exploitation of the West. A man of culture and refinement, possessed of a sense of proportion, could hardly have come out on top in deadly grapples with Jay Gould and James J. Hill. The simpler and more single-minded the man, among nineteenth century predators, the greater the bite.

Villard migrated to the United States at the age of eighteen shortly before the Civil War, became a journalist and served as a war correspondent with the Army of the Potomac. After the war he decided to become a financier and make use of the connections he had formed as a newspaperman. His first venture was a journey back to Germany during which he persuaded the German bondholders in the Oregon & Pacific Railroad to appoint him as their representative in straightening out the line's tangled affairs. He was so successful that he assumed a similar assignment on behalf of German and American bondholders in the Kansas Pacific, for whom he acted as receiver. The railroad then was under attack by Jay Gould, that "most unscrupulous and most dreaded machinator" as Villard called him. Gould controlled the Union Pacific, whose line paralleled it to the north and competed with it for the lucrative wheat-hauling traffic, and now he wanted to swallow up the Kansas Pacific. Gould acquired a controlling share of Kansas Pacific stock, but could not take over completely so long as Villard opposed his plans for reorganization as receiver for the bondholders. First Gould tried to bribe him by offering him a chance to participate in the syndicate which would take over the K. P. Newspapers under Gould's influence "heaped slander and abuse" on him, Villard recalled in his *Memoirs*. Gould was "playing for a harvest of millions" and moved so adroitly and ruthlessly, succeeding in splitting the stockholders away from Villard's control, that Villard was voted out as receiver. He was still the legal representative of the bondholders, however, and held out for four years until Gould was forced to guarantee their financial safety.[13]

Villard thus had demonstrated, perhaps for the first time in United States financial history, that a man who refused to be corrupted or bullied could withstand the most powerful forces of capitalism. And there was considerable profit in his endeavors, enough to permit him to become publisher of the New York *Evening Post*. He also joined with Carl Schurz in organizing the Reform Club, being one of the first men of financial power to see that capitalism's abuses must be contained or the whole system might be smashed by the rising influence of political and social radicalism.

That premonitory feeling did not, however, greatly handicap him in dealing with his fellow capitalists. Villard became the moving force behind the construction of the Northern Pacific Railroad, which had been chartered by Act of Congress in 1864 and awarded, by way of encouragement, a land grant forty miles wide along its right-of-way from the Missouri River to the Pacific — as immense strip of the public domain totaling fifty-seven million acres. Obviously the Northern Pacific was a great prize. It caught the covetous eye of James J. Hill, whose Great Northern line paralleled it to the north, just as the Kansas Pacific had aroused the appetite of Jay Gould. Hill's first moves against Villard consisted of cutting rates in any territory where the two lines were competitive. Secretly Hill began buying stock in his rival while publicly claiming that "the Northern Pacific ran through a stretch of worthless country" — the best timberlands on the continent — that "its bad grades and high interest charges and operating expenses in general were such as to ruin it."

Hill waited until Villard had superintended the final phases of

Henry Villard, a modified
capitalist

Claus Spreckels, an immoder-
ate capitalist

construction, meanwhile with his collaborators steadily buying control of the Northern Pacific's stock. Along came the panic of '93, and the Northern Pacific, like many other railroads, was thrown into receivership. Hill then stepped in with his majority stockholdings and engorged a richly endowed rival at comparatively small cost to himself.[14]

Villard possessed the intelligence and determination to outwit and outmaneuver any of the period's robber barons, but as a man of sensibility he could not give over his entire life to the pursuit of money and power.*

The German-American, as an entrepreneur, typically operated from a solid base; he mastered the details of an operation before committing all his energies to developing it. Much more in the hard-fisted Astor tradition was another German-American, Claus Spreckels, who saw the same connection between the Hawaiian Islands and the sugar industry as Weyerhaeuser saw between the land-grant railroads and the lumber industry. Ham-handed and uproarious as he was in temperament, he set about making himself the "Sugar King" in the thoroughgoing Teutonic manner.

He was born in Hanover, Germany, in 1828 and came to the United States nineteen years later with his brother Bernard. After working in a grocery store in Charlestown, South Carolina, for a year and a half, he bought out his employer on credit, meanwhile marrying and fathering the first of his thirteen children. In 1856, with four thousand dollars saved from the grocery business, he joined his brother in San Francisco. The Spreckels brothers saw an opportunity for themselves in the sugar industry. In the East it was controlled by the Sugar Trust, but the western market was wide open and sugarcane was being raised in the Hawaiian Islands. Why not import Hawaiian sugar by ship instead of eastern sugar by rail?

Claus Spreckels restrained himself from plunging into the enterprise until he knew exactly what he was about. First he returned to Germany

---

* Villard's philanthropic activities served as an example to Rockefeller and others of the robber-baronial period when they decided to seek a better public image. He endowed a large number of educational and charitable institutions in the United States and his native Bavaria.

and worked in a sugar refinery in Magdeburg, where he learned how beet sugar was processed. Then he went back to California and with his brother established the California Sugar Refinery in 1863. Almost immediately he introduced several new wrinkles in processing and marketing: the sugar cube and granulated sugar. He also invented a process by which raw sugar could be refined in twenty-four hours instead of three weeks.

A steady and inexpensive source of supply was his next concern. Hawaii had the cane fields and cheap labor — and an utterly corruptible king named Kalakaua. Spreckels made friends with King Kalakaua and finagled the sugar concession in the islands. According to one story that drifted back to San Francisco, and was widely believed by those acquainted with Spreckels's buccaneering methods, Spreckels won the entire island of Oahu in a marathon poker game with the Hawaiian monarch.[15] That may not have been true — and in any case Spreckels must have given back the island — but he did return to the mainland with a lease on twenty thousand acres of cane-raising land, which was subsequently increased to one hundred thousand acres.

During the next two decades Spreckels also organized the sugar-beet industry in the United States to insure himself of a steady supply of the raw product. By then he had won control of the western sugar markets. The eastern Sugar Trust decided to smash him by sending its product into the western states and selling it at a loss. Instead of cutting his own prices Spreckels characteristically carried the war into the enemy's territory by building a five-million-dollar refinery in Philadelphia and selling at a loss in the East. The Sugar Trust finally had to back away, bought Spreckel's refinery and agreed to stay out of the western markets.

Spreckels, with new profits coming in through lifting of duties on Hawaiian sugarcane, spread out in all directions. He was one of the mightier and less inhibited tycoons of the post-gold rush San Francisco. In a few years he organized a California railroad, electric power and gas companies, and the Oceanic Steamship Company, which immediately seized a large share of the shipping to the Orient with regular sailings to Hawaii, Australia and New Zealand. Being a tight-fisted employer, he soon brought upon himself recurrent maritime strikes. When coal passers on one of his ships went on strike in protest against having to work during their off-duty hours in order to keep up steam, he simply cleaned out the entire crew and hired a gang of Chinese to replace them. Boilermakers working on an Oceanic line vessel under repair went out on strike in sympathy with the seamen. The union labor movement gained new recruits as a result, and the strong unionism of San Francisco today, particularly on the waterfront, dates back to the era of Spreckels's medieval concept of labor relations.

Even two of his sons, Rudolph and Charles, eventually turned against the hardheaded Hanoverian. Rudolph struck out on his own as an enlightened businessman, his career almost strangled at the start when his father forced the San Francisco banks to refuse him any financing. Rudolph Spreckels not only became a millionaire on his own, but around the turn of the century joined with the crusading newspaper publisher, Fremont Older, to clean up an utterly corrupt city administration, which his father supported. In 1905, however, Spreckels and his sons were reconciled, united in defense of the family fortune which on Claus Spreckels's death, three years later, was estimated at fifteen million dollars plus the city's first skyscraper, the Spreckels Building.[16]

Other German-Americans made their fortunes out West through fortunate marriages. In 1883, Baron Henry von Schroeder, a much-decorated veteran of the Franco-Prussian War, married Mary Ellen Donohue, whose father Peter built the gaslighting system for San Francisco's streets and made a four-million-dollar fortune. She was one of the first of the post-Civil War rich to marry a titled foreigner. Most such minglings of new money and old titles ended disastrously, but Mary Ellen's marriage endured.[17]

Another highly successful venture along the same lines was the means by which the King Ranch of Texas, the largest privately owned domain (half a million acres) in the world, became the Kleberg Ranch. Captain Richard King, an Irishman, built up an inland empire of one hundred thousand cattle, twenty thousand sheep and ten thousand horses with a thousand retainers. One of his daughters, Alice, married Robert Justice Kleberg III, an astute second-generation German-American lawyer, who assumed management of the ranch on his father-in-law's death. Kleberg and his heirs doubled the size of the ranch, developed the famous new breed of San Gertrudis cattle, built up a celebrated racing stable and expanded into oil production. One of President Johnson's first jobs was as a legislative assistant to Congressman Richard Kleberg. The history of the King-Kleberg family provides added testimony that what the German-American made out of his life in the New World, whether it was a Middle Western farm or a whole industry, he held onto with an iron grip, the prehensile quality of which he managed to pass on to succeeding generations.

The Charles Krug winery in the Napa Valley of California was also the product of a fortunate marriage. Krug, a freethinking Prussian, fled his homeland with the Forty-eighters, settled near Sonoma and pressed the first wine ever produced in the valley. He sold his own small place when he married the niece of General Vallejo, the largest landowner in those parts, and acquired a 540-acre vineyard as part of the dowry. Krug made his label the most famous of all California wines during the last century, but it passed into other hands on his death. Several of his employees, Carl Wente and the Beringer brothers, started vineyards which became equally celebrated for the quality of their wine and survive as family enterprises.

Many of the mining engineers and prospectors who located and developed the mineral wealth of the West were German-Americans. They were particularly active in opening up the silver and gold veins of the Arizona desert. One of the first prospectors to invade that Apache stronghold was Frederick Brunckow, a Berliner with a Russian father and a German mother, who had obtained a mining engineer's degree in a Saxon university, joined the revolutionaries of '48 and fled to New Braunfels, Texas, where he worked for a time as a shingle-maker. In 1856 he went to the mountains of southern Arizona and began prospecting on his own, despite the proximity of hostile Indians. He became convinced that there were sizable deposits of gold and silver around the district later known as Tombstone. Before he could prove his point, he was murdered while working his claim. He had managed to make friends with the Apaches, but hadn't taken into account his Mexican workmen, who killed him and made off to Sonora with the silver bullion he had extracted and smelted on the spot.[18]

About twenty years later Ed Schieffelin, a Pennsylvania German, wandered into the same hellishly desolate territory. Thirty years old, with red hair worn shoulder length in defiance of Indian scalping knives, he had prepared himself for a prospecting career through a long apprenticeship in the placer mines of Oregon, where he began working with a miner's pick at the age of seventeen. Striking out on his own, he went to southern Arizona with two mules and twenty-five dollars' worth of supplies. For weeks he searched the scorching desert floor for a likely place to start digging, avoiding the Apaches by riding in the bottom of arroyos by day and sleeping a half-mile from his campfire at night.

On August 1, 1877, he staked out two claims, the Tombstone and the Graveyard, then rode into Tucson to register them. His clothes were patched with flour sacking and rabbitskin, his broken boots held together by thongs, his red hair stuck out through the holes in his hat — and altogether he was such a seedy specimen of a familiar species, the desert rat, that the merchants of Tucson refused him credit. Too bad for them. Ed Schieffelin had struck one of the richest ledges of silver on the continent, assaying $1998 to the ton. One of his mines, the Tough Nut, produced eight million dollars' worth of silver ore.[19]

8. ANGEL VOICES IN THE

WILDERNESS

When Rapp the Harmonist embargoed marriage
    In his harmonious settlement which flourishes
Strangely enough as yet without miscarriage,
    Why call'd he "Harmony" a state sans wedlock?
Now here I've got the preacher at a deadlock.
          — LORD BYRON, Don Juan, Canto xv

Most Germans coming to America were impelled by nothing more idealistic than an ancient yearning for land of their own, relief from the yoke of petty tyrants and tax collectors, escape from the press gangs of ducal armies. Only a comparative few specifically sought participation in the continuing experiment known as democracy. Aside from the idealistic Forty-eighters, there was one other grouping of immigrants who hoped for their various utopias in the American wilderness, the religious sectarians abhorred by their more orthodox Lutheran and Catholic countrymen. They were people who banished the thought of the twentieth century from their minds — the world would end long before the new century wheeled through time — and were intent upon preparing themselves immediately for the afterlife. New Jerusalems, not new opportunities in a new world, were the visions which brought them here.

They established themselves in colonies, based on a Christian-communist ideology, which endured longer than most such experiments in utopianism and for years, as one observer wrote, "sometimes seem as isolated as 16th Century duchies." But they were duchies of the spirit, rather than the realms of hedonistic princelings who were quick to suppress any such tendencies in Germany; they were expressions of the Teutonic strain of Calvinism which so often had been more fervent than the Anglo-Saxon. Eden came down with a crash because Adam and Eve were lured into sexual congress; therefore many of the German Puritans were determined to live in celibacy.

Children, future generations, the continuity of human life were unworthy of consideration in a world about to be swept away. "Their only affiliations were with the past," one historian has noted. "They felt the greatest correspondence between, not themselves and others burning like the dry thorn in the wilderness, but themselves and God, who had spoken out of the burning bush, themselves and the children of Israel, themselves and Saul, David, Solomon, Job, Job's turkey, and Tobit's dog. They were aristocratic. They converted, consciously or not, hallucination into fact and fact into hallucination, wherever they could. . . . They were self-isolated. Undoubtedly, few gave a thought to the poor Indian, who was already, like natural man, a dwindling order — though no celibate, for he had more papooses than imaginary pearls or onions on a string. After all, it is easier to comprehend eternity than the multitudinous operations of that vaster complexus, the experience of man."[1]

From Pennsylvania to the Middle Border, they established their enclaves and made themselves impervious to the clangor of a new nation being forged in war and peace. The clatter of Conestoga wagons heading West was only a momentary distraction. The Civil War was a distant eruption of no interest to people more concerned with Armageddon; the freeing of the slaves a bootless thing compared to the freeing of mankind from sin and error. And if the twentieth century, despite all prophecies of an immediate Final Judgment, did wheel into place, it only meant that the ultimate reckoning had been delayed.

Such colonies, stubbornly resisting the modern world, have left their quaint and inverted traces on American life. Perhaps it is one more piece of testimony to the phlegmatic solidity of the Teutonic spirit that Amish buggies still roll across back-country roads in Pennsylvania, Ohio, Iowa and now Kentucky; that the Plain People still consider themselves beyond, if not above, the laws governing other Americans; that hex signs still ward off witchcraft on the barns in the rolling countryside of Bucks, Lebanon, Lehigh and other Pennsylvania counties, and that a whole literature, fictional and documentary, has evolved from the inbred life and customs of the Pennsylvania Dutch. Jets streak east and west overhead, and traffic roars along the turnpikes a few miles away, but something of the agricultural Eden their ancestors sought still exists in sections closely bypassed by what other men call progress.

No matter what they called themselves — Moravians, Amish, Bethel-Aurora Germans, Pietists, Old Lutherans, Rappite-Harmonists, Stephanists — something of the religious ecstasy that sent them from Germany to the New World has managed to survive long after Puritan doctrine was pronounced dead and misbegotten.

NEW JERUSALEM — INDIANA?

Angelic visitations are rare in American folklore, which inclines more toward ghosts and demons when it comes to the supernatural. For some years, however, the footprint of an angel was preserved in the fields along the Wabash, where that muddy stream provides the southern borders of Illinois and Indiana. The footprint was on the Indiana side, naturally, because that was where a people had settled early in the nineteenth century in the utmost certainty that angels watched over them with considerable approval. The angel, it was testified, descended upon Indiana soil sometime between 1815 and 1824. He was seen in the barley fields, and he left his footprints in a slab of stone. An ethnologist named H. R. Schoolcraft, a literal fellow guided by the disciplines of his science, examined the footprints, measured them, studied them, tried to make earthly sense of them, in the year 1826.

Mr. Schoolcraft apparently was unwilling to accept the story of a heavenly visitation. The footprints, he decided, were those of a man who stood upright with heels turned inward. The toes were pressed out and the foot was flat, which suggested that the man had never worn shoes. Obviously they were the prints of an aboriginal creature who had walked this earth before the Indians came. Mr. Schoolcraft, with all his measurements and learned deductions, still was unable to suggest how the footprints happened to be preserved in a ten-foot slab of limestone. Nor could any other disbelieving men who saw the footprints, the right foot imprint clearly defined well into the twentieth century before the elements weathered it away, offer any definitive explanation.

The idea of angels calling upon so commonplace a locality as Posey County, Indiana, was unthinkable. Miraculous visions are reserved for the deserts of the Middle East, where most of the world's religions first shimmered in the heat waves. Then, too, if that section of the Wabash country was sacred territory, how come the man who saw that angel, or said he did, was succeeded by another prophet, who bought him out for hard cash and established a colony dedicated to free love and easy living?

The man who said he saw the angel was "Father" George Rapp. He was the sole eyewitness but he spared nothing in describing the angel. It was a towering figure with a rainbow on its back, seven stars in its right hand, seven gold candlesticks in its left hand, and its linen robe was girded by rubies, sapphires and emeralds. Taller than an oak, it spoke in a voice that roared like the wind. As an angel it had both masculine and feminine attributes ("For in the resurrection, they neither marry, nor are given in marriage, but are as angels of God in heaven").

The angel's voice thundered that ungodly places like New York, Philadelphia, Pittsburgh, Rome, Paris, not to mention Württemberg, the hometown of Faust and Father Rapp himself, all were to be destroyed. God was sick of their ways. He would send flame from heaven and poisonous gases from the center of the earth to sear and kill everything that lived on the planet. Only Rapp and his followers would be saved, and their colony would become the New Jerusalem with ten gates of jewel-studded gold.

Then the angel vanished, leaving only its footprints, and the sky darkened suddenly and a heavy rain fell.

Not long after that one of Rapp's followers, a carpenter, saw an angel himself, but it vanished without speaking to him. The carpenter was very drunk, whiskey being one of the several consolations allowed in the New Jerusalem, and besides authentic visitations came only to the prophet and leader.

The man in whom angels confided, who believed that he was appointed to transmit God's wishes to the elected, had the immense advantage of looking like an Old Testament patriarch. It mattered little that the King of Württemberg, investigating his claims to divine inspiration, dismissed him as merely another of those Lutheran schismatics, of the same breed that removed themselves to the shores of the Caspian Sea in search of a closer communion with God.

George Rapp was tall, with a commanding presence, an apron-like beard and a halo of white hair. By retailing his visions of a world about to be destroyed by heavenly wrath, by convincing other Württembergers that they were living in a modern incarnation of Sodom and Gomorrah (rather a stodgy replica, it must have seemed, without orgies or dancing girls), he gained a following of seven hundred souls eager to be saved from the holocaust to come. His biographer, Marguerite Young, believes that he was simply a colonizer, another Daniel Boone, with apocalyptic trimmings. Other German schismatics might "seek other frontiers on eternity . . . Let poets dream what they would. Father Rapp chose America first — not because he believed that God's voice would speak out of the marsh more clearly than it had spoken out of the vineyards of Württemberg — but because the land was fierce and cheap. Father Rapp had a Bible in one hand and an ax in the other . . ." The seven hundred faithful to his commandments were no weak, watery-eyed mystics or addled spinsters but sturdy artisans, good farmers, shrewd traders — "a community of businessmen who acted like oiled saints."[2]

Father George and his son, John, who presumably was born before Rapp was convinced that God would spare only the celibate, made the journey to America as the Lord's advance agents early in 1804. He located his first New Jerusalem in Pennsylvania, and that summer his disciples came over on three storm-battered ships. In the Pennsylvania wilderness, sleeping on the ground at first, they worked like people possessed and inside a year had built the town of Harmony, a settlement of sixty log houses, shops, sawmills, a tannery, and churches. The distillery was one of the first buildings erected, since whiskey was excellent for trading with the Indians and was also a balm to those afflicted with inner doubts about the virtues of celibacy. They saw nothing wrong about selling whiskey to the Indians, even if it sent them out on the warpath against other white settlements. Those godless settlements would be destroyed, in any case, when the great day came.

Rapp kept his community hard at work and all the profits flowing to him under a contract signed with every member. Rapp would provide for them in sickness and old age; in return they would turn over to him all the fruits of their labor and agree to obey all his laws. It was hardly a communistic arrangement. They did not share with each other, but handed everything over to Rapp. In essence, they had removed themselves from the kingdom of Württemberg to the even more demanding kingdom of Rapp, and yet, so compelling was the man and so dire his warnings after a vision came to him at appropriate moments, they were slow to realize that they had fallen under the rule of yet another petty tyrant.

Then a strange and terrible thing happened, considering that the first commandment of Harmony, Pennsylvania, was Thou Shalt Not Fornicate. The wife of John Rapp, the prophet's son, swelled with pregnancy. Worse yet, John Rapp was openly, gloatingly, even maliciously gleeful about it. If he was allowed to get away with fatherhood, how long would Harmony live up to its name? Father George grimly assumed the biblical role of Father Abraham. John Rapp was crudely emasculated out by the piggery, and bled to death. The wielder of the knife was said to be Father Rapp himself. The erring wife simply disappeared after giving birth to a daughter. Since she did not take the child with her, it was assumed by people in the surrounding settlements that she too was killed.

Soon after that, in 1814, Father Rapp had one of his fortuitous consultations with the Almighty and revealed to his congregation that a voice had commanded him to take his flock farther west. Perhaps another voice, less heavenly, told him it would not be wise to stay at the place where his own son had proved to be such a weak vessel.

Thus the community was moved to the banks of the Wabash, where the land was even better and the opportunities for trade much greater. Within ten years New Harmony, as it was called, flourished in a manner astounding to its neighbors on the frontier. Rapp, of course, continued to be the steward of all the funds collected in its various endeavors (which apparently averaged about twelve thousand dollars a year) and still accountable for them only to the Lord. The Rappites established stores, sold whiskey, hides, furs, livestock, shingles, butter, flax, hops, tobacco, hemp, furniture and fruits of all kinds. In 1820 the settlement at New Harmony was valued at one million dollars, firm testimony of Rapp's acumen as a colonizer and businessman.

But what of the souls of the people he had elected to save, and of the quality of life in New Harmony? Curious neighbors could see that the place hummed like a beehive, with all its cottage industries, its brewery and distillery, its mills and furnaces and small factories — but were the people content merely with hard work and waiting for the New Jerusalem and its golden gates?

A man named John Woods, who lived twenty miles up the Wabash, lurked around the colony for a few days in the summer of 1820. What amazed him, as an unregimented American, was the insect-like uniformity of the people of New Harmony, their meek submission to Father Rapp's dictates. "They were amazingly similar. The men wore jackets and pantaloons, very wide, of vivid Prussian blue, with coarse flat hats like pancakes. The women wore jackets and petticoats, a darker shade, with skullcaps and straw bonnets . . . The Rappite people, marching in unison, two by two, waved their sickles in distant greeting as they passed, as if they had been given a signal to do so." Woods saw a herd of cattle going to pasture, and was struck by the similarity between them and the zombie-like humans who were held in thrall by Rapp's visions and commandments.[3]

An English traveler who visited the colony was amazed at the solidity of what Father Rapp had ordained and built in the wilderness. Surrounding settlements were squalid, often decayed and abandoned a few years after being established. The discipline, or superstition, with which Rapp held his people together and kept them at their tasks had produced a model community in the physical sense. Rapp himself lived in a turreted and gabled red-brick mansion, and God lived, or manifested Himself, in a structure even more lordly, a cruciform church with colonnades and immense walnut pillars. There was probably no more stately building west of the Alleghenies in the early 1820's. The colonists themselves lived in comfortable homes, every moment of their days governed by the striking of the church bells. At nine o'clock they all went sexlessly to bed.

Father Rapp spared his people the vexations of citizenship. He cast all their ballots in the local and state elections. He fought the banking laws and — this may have seemed ironic to anyone capable of ironic reflection — against Negro slavery. The good father also relieved them of all anxieties regarding the future of the colony, which he assured them would endure long enough to claim its heavenly heritage. Since the birthrate of New Harmony was zero, its population was kept in balance by the immigration of carefully selected newcomers from Württemberg and other parts of Germany where Father Rapp's success as a prophet-businessman had spread.

Bountiful as they had found southern Indiana, the Rappites were removed back to Pennsylvania in the spring of 1824, leaving an inscription on one of the buildings which read: "In the twenty-fourth of May, 1824, we have departed. Lord, with thy great help, and goodness, in body and soul, protect us." Why Father Rapp decided to move is still a mystery. New Harmony was a going concern, and Father Rapp himself was seventy years old. Various reasons have been advanced. There was recurrent malaria and attacks by other fevers which took their annual toll. There was also the possibility that the Rappites were becoming restless — particularly the women, who in all the nineteenth century utopias caused the most trouble with their inability to comprehend the virtues of universal, as opposed to human and individual love — and that their leader had to give them something else to think about, new tasks to which they could bend their backs while waiting for the resurrection, now twenty years delayed. At any rate it must have taken internal pressures of considerable force to persuade Rapp that it was necessary to uproot the community. He sold the colony, valued several years before at a million dollars, for only one hundred fifty thousand dollars to Robert Owen, a Scotsman. The price included everything the Rappites couldn't carry with them — even the footprints of the angel in the slab of limestone. And not the least painful part of that bargain, if Rapp believed an iota of what he professed, was that New Harmony would now become a permissive paradise — the direct opposite of what it had been — governed by rationalism and free love. Those fields in which the angel had walked would now become the scene of lewd chases through the hops and barley, followed by couplings which would, under the previous order, have caused Father Rapp to run his thumb reflectively over the edge of his castrating knife. "The German prototype of American Puritanism," as Marguerite Young has remarked, "was to be followed by the French Revolution in miniature."

Doubtless with a heavy heart, Father Rapp relocated his colony on the Ohio River, in Beaver County, Pennsylvania. The new community was named, perhaps more accurately than the old, Economy. And once again, within a few years, a new settlement was raised and in full production, adding to the treasury over which Rapp alone presided.

Five years after the move back to Pennsylvania, in the summer of 1829, a serpent began gliding toward the new Eden. A beautifully plumed serpent, it announced its coming in a letter addressed to "Aged Patriarch George Rapp" and was signed by John George Gantgen, "Private Secretary of Count Maximilian de Leon." The Count, as his secretary proclaimed, was "the Great Ambassador and Anointed One of God," who had descended from "the Stem of Judah and the Root of David." He was suffering spiritual anguish over the corrupt state of European civilization, Gantgen related, and begged the opportunity to offer his purse, his services and indeed his soul to Father Rapp. Instead of taking alarm at the grandiloquent tone of the letter, Father Rapp was flattered. He began corresponding with Count Maximilian without inquiring into his aristocratic credentials or his pretensions as a spiritual leader who had wearied of trying to convert the pagan and heretic in Europe.

In the autumn of 1831, while Rapp's herdsmen blew lustily on their horns, the Count and his secretary arrived in two gilded coaches. As the assembled population of Economy cheered, the secretary, Herr Gant-gen, stepped from the first in a sable robe. From the second, in a costume of green and purple broadcloth, emerged Count Maximilian with all the lordly airs of a Cagliostro and the con man's talent for impersonation which had transformed him from Herr Bernard Mueller, traveling salesman, into a member of the nobility who had left a trail of deflated hopes and flattened purses throughout western Europe.

Father Rapp, now perhaps on the brink of dotage, welcomed him with open arms as a fellow messiah. In his replies to the Count's letters, he had suggested that Maximilian de Leon would perhaps like to stay in Economy for two or three days, touring the colony and conversing with its leader. Soon his instincts, so drowsy until now, were bristling with alarm. The corpulent and smooth-talking Count showed no dis-position to abandon the hospitality of Economy. Instead he wandered around the colony, talking to Rapp's followers, telling them of the pleasures of the great world outside — and damned little of all those spiritual agonies he claimed to have suffered — and even reading from a document which was on Father Rapp's private Index — a copy of the Constitution of the United States. The Rappites were astounded to learn that as American citizens they were entitled to the pursuit of happiness, that all men were created equal and entitled to the fruits of their labors.

Rapp awakened to the fact that a dangerous interloper had been admitted within the fold when the Count began asking pointed ques-tions about where the money went, how much the Rappites shared in the bounty of their harvests, why Rapp lived in a big house while they made do with small cottages, whether celibacy was really so holy a practice. His worst fears were realized when, six weeks after he came, six weeks of diligently gathering information about every detail of life in Economy, Count Maximilian mounted the pulpit and proclaimed the new order in Economy. The sermon, from Rapp's viewpoint, came straight out of the mouth of hell.

Count Maximilian told the Rappites that he had come to Economy as "the Ambassador of God" to deliver them from an unduly harsh bondage. Father Rapp's strictures, while divinely inspired, had been too inhumanly applied. Count Maximilian, as God's messenger, had arrived with a revised text to guide them. Henceforth man and wife would mate as God had intended for all His creatures. They would also enjoy a share in what they had produced. With an immodesty equaled only by Father Rapp's in his prime, Count Maximilian announced that he would now assume the burden of leading Economy out of the error of its ways.

In the old days, Rapp would probably have taken after the fat pretender with one of his large knives, but now he was confronted, in his increasing feebleness, by a revolution. Many voices were raised in favor of Count Maximilian's new dispensation. The colony was bursting with controversy. Those whose sexual instincts and capabilities had not atrophied after a quarter-century's obedience to Father Rapp's first commandment were naturally in the forefront of the Count's following.

George Rapp, even in his decay, was not the man to allow his colony to be split asunder. He and his disciples were greatly cheered when a winter storm of Old Testament proportions howled down on Pennsylvania and tore the roof off the distillery, striking at the very center of the community's solace for its labors. Father Rapp pronounced that the storm and the unusually severe winter that followed were a sign from God that He was displeased and was letting the Rappites know that the Count was a bearer of false tidings.

Nevertheless, come spring, more than a third of the Rappites, about two hundred fifty in all, announced that they wanted to break away under the benign leadership of Count Maximilian. There was nothing for Rapp to do but strike a bargain with the dissidents. An agreement was made whereby the Count and his private secretary would leave within six weeks, his followers within three months, and that they would take $105,000 of Economy's treasury with them — that is, the Count, no man to duck responsibility, would take it in trust. Furthermore, within six months the Count and his erring flock would leave Pennsylvania altogether.

It didn't work out that way. The Count did not want to lay out a lot of money for traveling expenses, so he settled his people only twenty miles away from Economy. The stern leadership of George Rapp was only one of the missing elements when it came to founding a new colony. It took promises of hellfire and poisonous gases, it seemed, to bring out the best in the Teutonic spirit. Mere latent energy, without order or compulsion, was of little use in colonizing. And so much of that energy apparently was diverted into new channels: almost immediately the women who had followed the Count into the new wilderness swelled with child. All that summer the Leonites camped out. By fall, they had raised nothing but a crop of babies, with no roofs to shelter them. About the time of the first snowfall the Count, his private secretary and his gilded coaches had vanished down the roads southward. The $105,000 committed to the Count's stewardship had been flung away in Pittsburgh gambling houses and betting on cockfights.

Early in the winter the Leonites tried to make a forcible reentry into the Eden from which they had banished themselves. Father Rapp got word of their coming and sent all his men into the woods because he intended to repulse the Leonites without bloodshed. The Leonites crept into what appeared to be a deserted settlement late at night. They made a rush for the storehouse and battered down the doors. Inside they found the Rappite women waiting in an Amazonian fury to repel them with hot coals, scalding water, brooms, switches, pitchforks, buggy whips and brickbats. The Leonites were chased out of Economy and never came back.

Some settled in celibate communities elsewhere, and at least one, Jacob Zundel, went whole hog in the opposite direction and joined the Mormons in Utah, whence he kept writing his former brethren in Economy that polygamy was a lot more fun than celibacy. Bernard Mueller, alias Count Maximilian de Leon, died of the cholera in Louisiana about a year after he abandoned his own disciples. Judgement of God, said Father Rapp with satisfaction.

Economy continued to prosper, no more serpents came gliding in from the evil world outside. Visions still appeared before Father's clouding eyes and voices still spoke to him when problems arose. In his ninetieth year, one August day in 1847, the patriarch called his people together to announce a new transmission from on high. God had ordered him to lead his people to the banks of the Euphrates. In Mesopotamia, Father Rapp would live to be a hundred years old and his people would make the desert bloom. Before the Rappites could be uprooted again, however, Father Rapp died.

Economy did not die with its founder. The idea of a communisitc society bound together by religious fervor seemed to work for the obedient Germans, and it was favored, too, by sheer luck and circumstance. Shortly after the Civil War oil was found on its extensive land, coal was mined, and large stands of timber were cut. With all its holdings, it was probably the most prosperous community in the United States. A succession of managers from the "evil outside" took over its affairs and its finances were managed by a board of trustees. In 1877 the colony's books showed such a large cash surplus that $650,000 was invested in the stock of the Pittsburgh & Lake Erie Railroad.

A retired official of that railroad became the spiritual and financial leader of the community. Father Henrici, as he was called, was eighty-seven years old but vigorous enough to play the organ and direct the choir in addition to his managerial duties. A reporter for the New York *World* who visited Economy in the early 1890's found that the community was flourishing as amazingly under Father Henrici, the business-man, as under Father Rapp, the prophet of imminent catastrophe. Ecclesiastical communism still "reigned supreme," the reporter observed. Most of the inhabitants were working twelve hours a day in the silk and woolen factory. "No person is seen strolling along the streets during working hours. The corner lounger is absent." Others were working the 3,000-acre section of farms around the town. Oil pipelines crisscrossed its fields. But it was apparent that Economy was dying; economically it flourished, but did not increase. Celibacy, rather than Father Rapp's prophecy of the Final Judgment, finally closed out the experiment.

In 1903 there were only three women and one man left, and all but eight acres were sold to a Pittsburgh syndicate for two-and-a-half million dollars. A few years later the last of the Rappites were gone.[4] They vanished, in fact, long before that angel's footprint in the Indiana limestone.*

---

* Among similar experiments in religious communalism was that of Father Ochswald of Baden, whose beliefs brought him in conflict with the Catholic hierarchy. He brought 113 Catholic colonists from Baden to St. Nazianz, Wisconsin, in 1854. There he established the Spiritual-Magnetic Association of the Holy St. Gregor of St. Nazianz. After his death in 1873, the Catholic schismatics fell to bickering among themselves, but the colony stayed in existence after the Milwaukee archdiocese reconverted its members to a less exotic Catholicism.

MARTIN STEPHAN'S SEVEN HUNDRED

Something in the German psyche seemed to respond fervently to mystic fuehrers holding forth in the dark bower of their forests. Perhaps it was the racial memory of past centuries when Teutonic tribes roamed the great European forest, never clearing it for settlements and seemingly shunning the open sky. An eloquent and perceptive Saxon named Martin Stephan had observed that tendency in his countrymen, as well as their susceptibility to the cultish and clandestine. He had set himself up as a religious mystic in Dresden during the middle 1830's. At first he proclaimed himself a Pietist, but then began introducing modifications of his own.

Stephan was a Lutheran minister, a magnetic speaker whose influence spread beyond his congregation to the workingmen's clubs he addressed in his out-of-parish hours. He began delivering sermons on contemporary matters, which pleased his audiences but displeased the authorities. The king of Saxony and his catchpoles were always suspicious of clerics who addressed themselves to temporal affairs — such tendencies gave off a whiff of revolution — and the Lutheran bigwigs, always conscious of how their own church had been founded by the great schismatic himself, were naturally quick to smite any leanings toward dissent.

The Reverend Stephan, at the risk of defrocking and possibly jail, began sneaking off into the Saxonian forest with his followers. This was illegal, but he had news to impart which could not be broadcast from the pulpit. The fact was, Stephan said, that modern Germany was becoming a Sodom and Gomorrah; it was destined to be scourged by fires from heaven. (Undoubtedly he was well versed in the history of New Harmony under the leadership of George Rapp.) The only salvation was to migrate, sell out, pack up and follow him to wherever Providence suggested.

The police caught him holding one of his arboreal meetings outside

Dresden. He and his followers were herded off to jail, and in the fall of 1837 his religious superiors suspended him from the ministry.

That winter, on his release from jail, he began secretly formulating plans to remove himself and his followers from Germany. At first he considered migration to Australia, but decided it was too remote and primitive. America was his second and final choice. Stephan followed the usual pattern, by which his disciples were required to hand over all their savings, a procedure which kept possible backsliders and the fainthearted committed to his purposes. The money was placed in a "common fund" to pay the costs of transportation and buy the land to be colonized, but Stephan, like other colonizers with a religious bias, kept the key to the treasure chest. None of the prophets of doom were ever so carried away by their own doctrines, their preachments against worldiness, that they loosened their hold on the purse strings and risked losing power over their adherents.

Like Father Rapp, Stephan chose the able-bodied and comparatively well-heeled for his colony. Many were well-established artisans and professional men. Stephan wanted to enlist people sturdy and skilled enough to build a prosperous settlement while they awaited the end of the world which he prophesied.

In the summer of 1838 the Stephanists' migration was announced publicly. The authorities decided not to forbid it, perhaps glad to rid themselves of a troublesome element. The first contingent left Dresden in October, and the scene of leave-taking was commemorated by an artist whose picture was exhibited at the Leipzig Fair and attracted much attention to the Stephanist movement. It was further dramatized by uncertainty over whether Martin Stephan himself would be permitted to leave Germany. The authorities withheld permission, in fact, until after the last groups of Stephanists had set out for Bremen. Then Stephan made a dramatic dash overland to join his followers at the port of exit.[5]

On November 19, 1838, five ships lifted anchor from Bremen with Stephan and his seven hundred followers. They landed safely — but not entirely amicably — in New Orleans. Their leader, it was being whispered, conducted himself in an unseemly manner with some of the female members of the contingent. Was it possible that the virus which had caused the destruction of Gomorrah was being carried by the man who had inveighed against it and inspired the journey to America?

During the journey, Stephan proposed himself for election as "bishop" of the colony-to-be. Dissenting voices were raised, but Stephan beat down the opposition by pointing out that all the colony's funds were in his keeping.

The Stephanists proceeded up the Mississippi to St. Louis, where arrangements were made for the purchase of ten thousand acres in Perry County, about a hundred miles from the city. Meanwhile "Bishop" Stephan insisted that he be formally installed and talked the Episcopal Bishop Jackson Kemper into loaning his cathedral so the ceremony could be made as impressive as possible. Many a blond Saxon head whirled with doubt and confusion at witnessing that spectacle — a supposed Protestant adorning himself with the mitre and robes so reminiscent of the Papist hierarchy in an atmosphere of bells and incense reeking of Rome!

That bit of self-indulgence in the St. Louis Episcopal cathedral cost Martin Stephan dearly. Dreamy Württembergers might accept George Rapp as the personal representative of God on earth, but down-to-earth Saxonians were damned if they'd swallow Martin Stephan as a "bishop." The charges that Stephan had attempted or succeeded in trifling with the women of the party were brought out into the open. A trial was held, at which a number of his subordinates testified that Stephan had indeed misconducted himself. Stephan's followers voted to depose him as bishop and expel him from their midst. Plans to establish the colony in Perry County, which was already named Stephansburg, were carried on without their moving spirit. Hundreds of other Saxonians had been planning to join the colony, but the news of Stephan's expulsion was widely published in the Saxon newspapers and new migrations were temporarily halted.[6] Within a few years, however, the news drifted back to Germany that Stephansburg without Stephan, and indeed with Stephanism, was prospering, and more Saxonians departed to join the colony in Missouri. It was a happier experience than that of the Rappites, but it was achieved only because the Stephanists were quick to abandon the beliefs which brought them to the New World.

PLAIN PEOPLE

Other and less fanciful efforts to establish religious communities succeeded while the Rappites, through following the dictates of their faith, made themselves extinct and the Stephanists simply disavowed their leader and got on with the business of becoming Americans. Those who have succeeded in resisting the homogenizing influence of American society — the most stubbornly resistant elements in the nation — include the Dunkards, or German Baptists, and the Amish, an offshoot of the Mennonites, who follow the strictures of Jacob Amen, a seventeenth century Mennonite of the sternest rigidity. The Amish, the Plain People, in particular are regarded as eccentrics by people who forget that one man's eccentricity is another's orthodoxy.

Another successful and enduring attempt at religious colonization was the establishment of the seven Amana colonies near Cedar Rapids, Iowa, which still flourish on the banks of the Iowa River. What began as the "Community of the True Inspiration," an offshoot of German Pietism which blossomed into a pre-Marxist communism, was finally killed off, along with so many capitalistic enterprises, during the depression of the 1930's. Christian communism was converted into a more sophisticated profit sharing, and as one observer has written, the members of the Amana colonies now are "a bunch of capitalistic corporation stockholders, every one."[7]

The mainstay of the Amana true believers was their faith, contradicting formal Lutheran doctrine, that divine inspiration may come in modern times. An advance guard was sent over to buy land in Iowa, first a tract of five thousand acres on which the eight hundred colonists built their villages. Later these holdings were expanded to twenty-six thousand acres of the most fertile farming country in Iowa. A council of elders was elected to govern the villages. A constitution was adopted with provisions that everything but clothing and households goods were to be held in common. The theory was that only through this mild form of communism could the colony be held together and the old, the feeble and the poor provided for.

The membership increased to a peak of eighteen hundred and by 1921 its property was valued at $2,100,000. In each village the cooking and baking were done in "kitchen houses" for the whole community; each with its one long street was patterned after a German *Dorf*. The villagers dressed plainly though not uniformly, and followed the tenets of their sober faith by prohibiting card-playing, dancing and other worldly pastimes. "Eloquently the simple, silent, clove-scented Amana cemetery with its incense-breathing hedge of cedar speaks of the many sacrifices of personal ambition, of material prosperity, and of individual pleasures dear to the human heart . . ." wrote Amana's historian.[8]

In 1932, however, a younger group less eager for those sacrifices and alarmed by the inroads made by the depression in the outside world succeeded in forcing an abandonment of communism. The Amana holdings were reorganized as a corporation. Since then, the colony has maintained its standoffish attitude to the "outside," except in matters of commerce. One Amana woman says they "don't speak English except to customers." Tourists are welcome to walk the old-fashioned streets, have Sunday dinners served family style at the Yoke Inn in Amana or buy rhubarb wine from the fifty-gallon barrels in the general store at Homestead. They are quiet places out of synchronization with the rush of American life, their streets lined with neat brick houses, with the small factories and barns of the communal enterprises on the outskirts of the towns. Profit sharing works, and life is placid in the deliberately created and preserved backwater of the Amana colonies.

Not always so placid has been the experience of the Amish in the United States. There are too many of them, an estimated fifty thousand settled in twenty states, to be ignored in their desire to pursue their own way of life. They shun automobiles, the telephone and electricity as attributes of the world's evil, but it is their abhorrence for the public school system which brings them in conflict with the authorities.

The Amish, adamantly insisting that "we are different," a "peculiar people," refuse to venerate the American flag or admit to any supremacy but God's. Their lives are governed by thrift, hard work, honesty — and apartness. And life is different among the Amish. In the back-country roads and lanes where the Amish have settled, the only signs read "Eggs Sold — Except Sunday." No beer cans glint from the roadsides — alcohol is also forbidden. Even in their own countryside one catches only fleeting glimpses of the Amish, who seem to treasure invisibility as well as unostentation. On a winter's day a file of children, dressed black as crows, can be seen running across the stubble of a cornfield. At a cattle auction an Amish farmer, bearded, wearing a black-brimmed round hat, speaks only when it is necessary to make a bid. At night a black buggy, illuminated only by its battery-powered headlights, trots down a deserted road in almost ghostly fashion.

They have skipped two centuries and are determined to live in the style ordained by the founders of their faith. In addition to the Bible, *The Martyr's Mirror*, a collection of accounts of the horrible persecutions suffered by their sect during the Reformation, which reminds them of the world's evil, governs their daily lives. They wear black clothing except for brightly colored shirts and skirts, never striped or patterned. Their clothing is fastened by hooks and eyes, since buttons, in the old country, two centuries ago, were reserved for the military and for the rich and worldly. Their biweekly church services extend for almost four hours, and their hymns are slowly chanted so that four verses can take twenty minutes. They are not sung to music, since music too is worldly and therefore evil.

Dr. Charles Spotts, a professor of religion who has studied their customs, says: "They live under communal monasticism. Loyola said, 'Give me the child until he is five and he will be a Catholic for life.' So with the Amish. After dinner the father gathers his children around him and reads from Luther's Bible, explaining and always making the pitch 'We are different.' "[9] The Bible readings are conducted in Pennsylvania Dutch, a Low German dialect.

To most Americans, in the rare moments when they are conscious of the Old Order Amish and their quaint refusal to partake of the general affluence, the pleasures of the discothèque and the freeway and the nightly watch before the television screen, they are merely something to read about, periodically, in a *National Geographic* essay, or to gawk at while touring through Amish country in Pennsylvania or elsewhere. To the officials of at least half a dozen states, however, they do not seem quite so inoffensive.

Educational bureaucracy's war with the Amish revolves around the

235

Plain People's insistence that their children attend little one-room schoolhouses without plumbing, electricity, teaching aids, standard curriculum or teachers with more than an eighth-grade education; that they end their schooling with the eighth grade.

It is a bitter and pathetic struggle. It is fought with legal and sometimes physical force on the part of bureaucracy; with passive (but glacial) resistance on the part of the Amish. The educational law which requires high school attendance is circumvented, wherever possible, by the Amish sending their children to school a year later than is customary, repeating the eighth grade, then sending them to "vocational high schools," which some states refuse to recognize as anything but an attempt to evade the law. Undoubtedly Amish education is substandard by the guidelines of the public school system. In 1959–1960 the Ohio Department of Education conducted a survey of twenty-two Amish elementary schools and reported that all were in violation of eighteen of the state's thirty-nine minimum standards for private schools, and that only one requirement, that relating to the length of the school day, was met by all twenty-two. In a similar survey of nine Amish "vocational high schools" all were found to violate seventy-nine requirements for such schools. Recent studies of the Amish schools in Ohio have shown that they have not improved their curricula since then.

"But contrary to a common view," Donald A. Erickson, a University of Chicago professor of education, has written, "this noncompliance represents more than stubbornness or stupidity. It is calculated to preserve the highest Amish values. At the heart of the Amish culture, reinforced by religious tenets and a long history of persecution, is the view that the larger society is evil. The Amish are taught to keep themselves peculiar — a separated people.

"They are knit together by kinship, common unquestioned values, and customs that mark them off visibly from everyone else. By emphasizing mixed farming as a way of life, they limit the need for outside contacts. Reliance on horse-and-buggy transporation keeps the basic social unit small, facilitating surveillance of behavior. Community norms prescribe ways of acting in such detail that most early symptoms of rebellion are detected. The *streng meidung* — the strict shunning of those who violate Amish rules, even by spouses and other members of the immediate family — is a powerful enforcer of obedience.

"Like other social systems, Amish society is organismic, composed of mutually dependent parts. Alter one component and the rest will change in response, often in irreversible, self-reinforcing fashion. Allow automobiles, radios, telephones, and modernized clothing, and the individual feels less distinct from the dominant social order and starts to internalize its values. Take away farming as the predominant occupation, and exposure to alien folkways is vastly increased, for more complex callings demand more formal education and bring interdependence in their wake. Inure the child to the consolidated public school, replete with such luxuries as bus rides, plumbing, and electrical devices, and he is less likely to tolerate the taboos of his culture as an adult; furthermore, his peers and teachers will often influence him to defect. Give him a modern secondary education, or even too elaborate an elementary education, and he will frequently gain aspirations for, and access to, pursuits that are outlawed for an Amishman. Expose him too long to the lure of learning, and he will yearn for the higher education that will alienate him still further from his origins."[10]

The Amish are acutely aware of the dangers suggested by Erickson. Their resistance to the education laws is nonviolent but anguished and unremitting. A year or two ago the state of Iowa decided to bring the Amish into line. In the full glare of publicity, unfortunate from their standpoint, the Iowa authorities forced their way into an Amish schoolhouse. They were greeted by fathers kneeling in prayer, mothers sobbing, and children chanting "Jesus Loves Me." Then the truant officers chased the Amish children through the surrounding cornfields while others were dragged, weeping and protesting, to buses which would take them to the consolidated schools they had been taught to fear as brimming with all the evils of the non-Amish world. The reaction from people all over the United States, watching those scenes on television news programs, was prompt and overwhelmingly adverse. Conscious of the encroachments of bigness and consolidation in their own lives, they protested with as much vehemence as if they had watched a reenactment of the United States Cavalry's similar experiment in consolidation with the Ghost Dancers of the Sioux reservation at the Battle of Wounded Knee.

Public opinion, in fact, has begun to swing from indifference to positive support of the Amish in their determination to lead their own lives. The emotions aroused by the controversy are somewhat akin to the organized campaigns to save architectural landmarks before everything even faintly reminiscent of pre-1900 America is bulldozed and jackhammered into oblivion.

Erickson, unusually sympathetic to their case, considering the stand taken by the educational bureaucracy, has declared that the Amish education, virtually limited to the three R's, is adequate for children who will follow the Amish way of life. In fact, he points out, the very successes of Amish education have brought down upon the Plain People the envy and hatred of the bureaucrats, whose own methods have certainly not been entirely successful. "Their success in training the young to be farmers has impressed many agricultural experts. Unemployment, indigence, juvenile delinquency, and crime are surprisingly infrequent. Amish prosperity and self-sufficiency are legendary. These are not the characteristics of a preparation for adulthood that has failed."

In the conflict between the state of Iowa and the Amish, county officials were reported to have said, "We are going to assimilate these people whether they want to be assimilated or not!" Erickson adds, "When asked about the ethics and constitutionality of such an approach, the officials replied that they couldn't see what was the problem. Part of the antagonism was occasioned, apparently, because the Amish put too much money into ironware crocks and not enough into local purchases. When the cash registers stopped ringing, businessmen became conscience-stricken over the limited educational opportunities of Amish children nearby."

For the time being it appears the contest between the Amish and the bureaucrats who insist that their children be educated in the standard manner is at a standstill. Eventually the Amish will probably have to bring their own schools to the norms of the public school system or send their children to the public schools. Though they might be received with sympathy by a United States Supreme Court sensitive to libertarian causes, they will not defend themselves in court because litigation too is among their taboos.

The world keeps intruding on the Amish way of life, rooted in the eighteenth century and marked by a pathetic but doomed desire to be left in peace as they leave others in peace. Often the infiltration has been accomplished under the genial, all-conquering dollar sign. Recently a number of Amish in Kansas abandoned the faith by selling their oil-bearing land, shaving off their beards, discarding their round hats and black clothes, and disappearing into the conformity of modern America.

Amish youth have taken to secretly buying transistor radios and listening to rock-and-roll music, the devil's own pipers if ever there were any. In such Amish centers of Lancaster County, Pennsylvania, as Intercourse, Bird in Hand and Smoketown, other satanic influences are at work. Young Amish men have been secretly buying automobiles and keeping them in barns or town garages out of their elders' sight. Much of this alien influence has been carried into Lancaster County by tourists in everlasting search of quaintness. Two million tourists a year invade Lancaster County, with the Old Order Amish the main attraction. They leave behind fifty million dollars annually . . . and winter memories for Amish youth of girls in mini-skirts and other temptations to "go gay," as the old Amish put it.

The Amish have also become alarmed recently by the reports of a high incidence of congenital defects among their people, including six-fingered dwarfism, hemophilia, muscular dystrophy and infant anemia. Scientists of the Division of Medical Genetics at Johns Hopkins University School of Medicine believe these defects are caused by intensive intermarriage. Most Amish marriages are between people living in the same settlement, who are usually related in some degree. Inbreeding was inevitable, since all the Amish are descended from about two hundred original immigrants.[11]

Dr. John A. Hostetler, a professor of sociology at Temple University, whose father was expelled by the Old Order for exhibiting modernist tendencies, believes that the Amish are "resigned to coping with their genetic difficulties . . . The cure, of course, is prevention, by providing young Amish the opportunity to range outside the immediate neighborhood — beyond the horse-and-buggy range."[12]

If the Amish do accept the automobile and venture beyond the horse-and-buggy circumference of their farms and hamlets, and if they still hold on to their faith, they will prove themselves to be the most tenaciously unhomogenized element in American society.

9. THE "JEWISH GRAND DUKES"

AND OTHERS

Mutual persecution between Catholics and Protestants hastened the migration of hundreds of thousands of Germans to America. Protestants were forced to flee Catholic districts, happy to escape with their lives. Similarly Catholics were driven from the largely Protestant provinces. Members of the Pietist sects, regarded by good Lutherans as more heretical than any of the Pope's followers and by the Catholics as more satanic than Martin Luther himself, were hunted down and driven out with equal enthusiasm by Protestants and Catholics alike. All these good Christians, Catholic, Protestant and Pietist, so harassed each other it was a wonder that they had enough energy left to maintain a rigorous repression of yet another religious element in their midst: the Jews.

In the patchwork of German principalities, the Jews were treated as nonpersons, not persecuted as the Catholics and Protestants persecuted each other, but penned up in ghettos and deprived of what few civil liberties were granted the Gentiles by the petty tyrants who ruled them. They were all but invisible to their Christian neighbors. Their treatment varied from province to province, city to city. Frankfurt was harsh, Hanover relatively tolerant. When a Jew crossed the Main to enter Frankfurt, he had to pay the "Jew toll." Along the way he would be greeted by Christian urchins who shouted at him, "Jew, do your duty!"

upon which he would be required to step aside for the children, take off his hat and bow low. The Frankfurt ghetto was a dark alley called Judengasse (Jew Street), located as Goethe related "between the city wall and a trench." At its entrance was a barrier of chains manned by Hessian soldiers, through which every Jewish resident had to pass before nightfall. The Jews of Frankfurt were under the strictest of municipal controls. They were forbidden to take up any agricultural pursuits, from engaging in the handicrafts, from dealing in what were regarded as "nobler" goods — weapons, silk, fresh fruit. Another municipal ordinance limited the ghetto to five hundred Jewish families and to no more than twelve marriages a year.[1]

From so restricted a life, the bottom layer of a rigidly stratified social and economic system, the German Jews would depart with an eagerness exceeded only by that of their coreligionists fleeing the pogroms of eastern Europe. Thus the German Jews began migrating to America only a little later than German Protestants and Catholics. Once across the Atlantic they breathed the air of religious and political freedom for the first time in centuries.

Acceptance as a fellow human being by members of another faith was a new experience, which came in many different ways. There was the day in 1817 when Joseph Jonas, a watchmaker, later the leader of the Jewish community in Cincinnati, wandered into an Ohio frontier settlement to be confronted by a gaping and astonished crowd.

A Quaker woman, more daring than the others, circled Jonas and carefully examined him from worn bootheels to wide-brimmed hat. At a greater and more cautious distance her fellow settlers stared at the newcomer without hostility but with unconcealed curiosity.

Finally the Quaker woman, having satisfied herself that Jonas in all his aspects was indeed a fellow human, addressed him: "Thou art no different from other people. Would thee care to sup with us?"

AUGUST BELMONT, INSTANT ARISTOCRAT

In pre–Civil War America there was little overt anti-Semitism. Even in high society a Jew with polished manners and other appurtenances of wealth was regarded as perfectly acceptable, as all historians of the fashionable world from Amory to Wecter make clear. A recent work on the subject, Stephen Birmingham's *Our Crowd*, was published after this book was completed; it tends to bear out the conclusion that if the rich German-Jewish families of New York clung together it was more out of original preference for their own society than exclusion. As Cleveland Amory has written, "No Families in America have more genuine claims to Aristocracy" than the Jews, "particularly the Sephardic Families, notably the Baruchs and Cardozos," but "almost equally firmly . . . the German Jewish Families, notably the Strauses, the Warburgs, the Lehmans, the Schiffs, the Loebs, the Morgenthaus, the Ochses, the Sulzbergers, the Seligmans, the Goldmans, the Sachses, the Bernheimers and the Blumenthals."[2]

Those families, mostly predominant in private banking, were called the "Jewish Grand Dukes." The term was used by their fellow Jews, and not without admiration. Their style, no matter how recently or quickly acquired, was both grand and ducal; their attitude and manner were aristocratic even if the seed money of the Straus and Seligman fortunes, for instance, came from the founder's initial ventures into the business world with a peddler's pack. At first the ducal families were "extremely self-contained and intramural" when it came to marriage. Later, when some intermarried with Gentile families, it was usually with those of similar interests and equally solid holdings.* As this process of assimilation continued, Otto Kahn, the banker, philanthropist and patron of the arts, whose two daughters married into eminent Gentile families, would smilingly refer to himself as "the fly-leaf between the Old and New Testaments."[3]

The social pattern of the Jewish nabobs was cut for them by August Belmont, whose long and strikingly successful life served as a model of social acceptance, quick assimilation and instant Americanization. The first Belmont showed them how it was possible for a man to rise from a

* Examples of their matrimonial tendency have been cited by Mr. Amory in his *Who Killed Society?* Paul Warburg, originator of the Federal Reserve System, took Nina Loeb, daughter of a Kuhn, Loeb & Co. partner, as his bride while Felix Warburg married Frieda Schiff, the daughter of Jacob Schiff. In a later generation, John Schiff married Edith Baker, of the Gentile banking family, and Gerald Warburg married Natica Nast of the publishing dynasty.

German ghetto and become a feather-footed cotillion leader in the New World before the first gray hair frosted his head.

In one generation he established himself as the founder of a family of the highest social rank, as the leading spirit of the "Belmont Clique" in which the grandfather of Sir Winston Churchill was merely a satellite, as a founder of the Manhattan Club, president of the American Jockey club, United States Minister to The Hague and to Austria, leading financier and sportsman and social arbiter. August Belmont did not push himself into society's dress circle; he created his own magnetism and became the accepter as well as the accepted. He had a perfect grasp of the role of a social aristocracy created within a political democracy, and never valued the one above the other. In 1860 he wrote:

"I prefer to leave to my children, instead of the gilded prospects of New York merchant princes, the more enviable title of American citizen, and as long as God spares my life I shall not falter in my efforts to procure them that heritage."

But that heritage, as he saw it, was more American than Jewish. By the time he wrote those words the more orthodox among his fellow German-Jewish-Americans questioned whether he was a Jew at all, except by ancestry. How could a Jew also be an Episcopalian? By then Belmont had left Jewishness far behind. It was his apparent belief that quitting the synagogue for a Christian church and marrying a Christian wife were no more reprehensible than crossing from Ellis Island to Manhattan. The Belmonts, in fact, became so un-Jewish that it was widely believed they had never been Jewish at all, or even German, since Belmont is a French name.

His descendants followed the founding father's example, and it may be only an ironic coincidence that the family thereupon slipped from national prominence and financial importance almost as quickly as the Goulds, who denied they were Jewish although their common ancestor was one Nathan Gold, declined after the death of Jay Gould. "Since the first August Belmont set foot in America," Dixon Wecter wrote, "no member of that Family has ever married a Jewess, but invariably a Gentile of social standing. In this way, plus an exchange of the synagogue for Episcopal communion, a constant association with non-

Jews, and the adaptability of Nature which has given Belmonts scarcely any Semitic cast of feature except in their patriarchal age, a complete break with their Old World background has been successfully effected. In social acceptance no later Jewish Family can compare with them."

From the moment of his arrival in America, in fact, August Belmont was incomparable as a devotee of assimilation. He was rather stout and short, with round Teutonic features and shrewd dark eyes; in appearance more the typical South German than Jewish. Born in the Rhenish Palatinate in 1816, he was sent to work in the Rothschilds' Frankfurt bank as an unpaid apprentice at the age of thirteen. Subsequently he was sent to work for the Rothschilds' interests in Naples and Havana. At the age of twenty-one he came to the United States during the financial panic of 1837. Though he had little capital of his own, he opened a small office on Wall Street and established August Belmont & Company. Within three years he was rated one of the three leading private bankers in the United States. The reason for his meteoric success was simple enough: he had the financial backing of the Rothschilds and acted as their American agent.

It was also apparent that he was adopting the Rothschilds' method of breaking away from the ghetto mentality and adopting the style and manner of their Christian financial peers. There was no landed gentry or titled aristocracy with which to identify himself, as the Rothschilds did in France and England, but Belmont found suitable substitutes among the high-living, sportive element in Wall Street. The older and more staid New York families would probably have closed ranks against him, but he had no taste for their company in any case. His natural element was the sporting-life group which abandoned the countinghouse on all possible occasions and conducted business in the clubs, on the hunting field or racing sloops. They followed the later dictum of J. P. Morgan that "you can do business with anyone, but you can go sailing only with a gentleman."

Belmont effortlessly converted himself into that type of gentleman. In 1849 he strengthened his claims to social standing by marrying Caroline Slidell Perry, the daughter of Commodore Perry, whose squadron opened the ports of Japan to the trading nations of the West, who was imperiously beautiful and had elegant French-schooled manners. Several years before that his gentlemanliness was tested, and not found wanting, under the terms of the code duello. Over "a subject too trite to be mentioned," as Belmont so stylishly put it, he fought a duel with Edward Heyward in South Carolina. His honor was satisfied, but he carried a bullet in his thigh for the rest of his life.

Two years after his marriage Belmont climbed to country-gentleman status by purchasing the Nursery Farm near Babylon, Long Island, where he gathered with his friends to fish and play whist. Two brooks fed Belmont Lake, which was stocked with trout, and elsewhere on the 1,300-acre estate a preserve for quail and deer was established. Subsequently he built a one-mile track on which his racehorses could be worked out, and raised pigs, which were fed on Jerusalem artichokes to improve the flavor of the bacon. A pork-eating Episcopalian, August Belmont was now a total loss to the orthodox among his former coreligionists.[4]

By the time the Civil War began, he and Mrs. Belmont and their sons were established in a Fifth Avenue mansion and he had begun acquiring the paintings and porcelains, the fast horses and trim boats which certified him a man of wealth and taste. His political activities during the war did not lighten the burden of the German-Jews in America, however, at a time when overt anti-Semitism made its first appearance. It was openly charged in the press that Jews, "the accursed race who crucified the Savior," were destroying the national credit by speculating in gold and smuggling essential supplies to the Confederacy.

Belmont was singled out as a leader of the alleged conspiracy because he was chairman of the Democratic National Committee and therefore suspected of being a Copperhead and traitor to the Union, even though he had raised and equipped a Union regiment and was exerting his influence on behalf of the Union cause in European financial circles. During the election campaign of 1864, the anti-Jewish sentiment rose to an alarming crest and there was considerable agitation in the press and from street-corner demagogues against Belmont and "the whole tribe of Jews."[5]

With the end of the Civil War, Belmont, in his lusty middle age, really began to enjoy himself. The Flash Age, which lasted from the end of the war until the panic of '73, did not at all dismay him with its vulgarity and ostentation. Nor would he have been greatly affronted by the comment of George Templeton Strong, the lawyer and New England moralist transplanted to New York, in his celebrated diary: "This community is devoid of moral sense. It has proclaimed an extra Beatitude of greater influence than all the others put together, namely, 'Blessed are the smart.'" Strong was referring in particular to what had become known as the Belmont Clique, most of whose members were Wall Street speculators. It included the Jerome brothers, Leonard, Lawrence and Addison, who were born on an upstate New York farm and came to the city to make, and lose, several fortunes; Henry Clews, an English-born broker and author of the uninhibited *Fifty Years in Wall Street*; William Travers and Addison Cammack, both noted for their wit and unconventional manners. A little later the group took in a new and frighteningly madcap recruit named James Gordon Bennett, Jr., the son of the publisher of the New York *Herald*.

Now a multimillionaire, Belmont was able to devote much of his time to the sporting pursuits of his group. With Leonard Jerome and several others, he organized the American Jockey Club and established a racetrack on the old Bathgate estate which was renamed Jerome Park. The purpose of the club, as it announced in a high-minded prospectus, was to "promote the improvement of horses, to elevate the public taste in sports of the turf, and to become an authority on racing matters in the country." Well, possibly. It was noted by cynical journalists, however, that on opening day of Jerome Park in September, 1866, there were a number of raffish characters present and prominent in the bunting-draped boxes, who could not be expected to subscribe whole-heartedly to the Club's program of keeping horse racing a sport for gentlemanly idealists. True that an air of surface respectability was provided by Belmont, the Jeromes and their friends, along with Lieutenant General Ulysses S. Grant, but rubbing elbows with them were Boss Tweed of Tammany Hall, John Morrissey, the Bowery gang leader who brought out most of the Irish vote for Belmont, the Jeromes and other more respectable Democrats; Josie Woods, who operated the city's most exclusive and beautifully appointed house of assignation; William Travers, who wondered aloud what insignia should be inscribed on the silver buttons of the liveried footmen attending Miss Woods; and a Mrs. Ronalds, whose association with Leonard Jerome was mentioned only in whispers. It was a matter of great relief to Belmont and Jerome that Madame Restell, who operated an abortion mill in a brownstone at Fifth Avenue and Fifty-second Street and would have met many of her best customers at the gala opening day, did not show up for the occasion.

Belmont later became president of the American Jockey Club, owned one of the finest stables in America and established the Nursery Stud at Lexington, Kentucky, to breed the champions which carried the Belmont colors of scarlet and maroon.

He was also a founding member of the Coaching Club. The sport of coaching had been revived in England recently, and American sportsmen were quick to follow the English example. Every swell in New York yearned to emulate Belmont, Bennett and the Jeromes as they dashed through the streets with their coaches-and-four. Belmont sallied forth in lordly style with his footmen dressed in maroon livery with scarlet piping and silver buttons bearing the Belmont crest. The wheels of all the Belmont coaches and carriages were painted maroon with a scarlet stripe. Their owner did not, however, adapt himself to the more extreme coaching styles of Leonard Jerome, who dashed around the city with his coach laden with gay young women, or Jimmy Bennett, who sometimes became so exhilarated by the sport that he stripped off all his clothes, tore along country roads in Connecticut stark naked in the box, and drove his horses until they dropped.

Nor did Belmont, who combined geniality with a certain caution and tough-mindedness, plunge over the financial brink with Leonard Jerome and other clubbable fellows when their speculations in the Pacific Mail steamship line's stock ended disastrously. Lawrence Jerome had to sell his seat on the Stock Exchange and his brother Leonard was unable to scrape up a respectable dowry for his daughter Jennie when she married into the Churchill family. Belmont, as a private banker, was too sophisticated to join in speculative enterprises. He not only survived the panic of '73 in fine shape, but four years later was able to participate in floating the $260,000,000 United States government bond issue of 1877, which Gustavus Myers (*History of the Great American Fortunes*) characterized as "one of the very worst cases that had ever been known of the people being betrayed over to a few bankers." The sale of the government bonds was allotted to a syndicate composed of Belmont, the Rothschilds, J. & W. Seligman Bros., and Drexel, Morgan & Co. Belmont and his partners "at once sold the bonds at an advance of from one to four percent above the price which they had paid to the Government. The profits of the syndicate reached into the tens of millions of dollars," in return for which the syndicate had done "nothing more or less than acting as licensed speculative middlemen for a Government which could have disposed of the bonds without intermediaries." In addition, the participants were "able to get the bonds for themselves at 'bargain prices' and then through associated national banks carry on the familiar practice of exacting double interest — one interest from the Government, and another for the use of the currency issued on the basis of those same bonds." Scandal ensued, the bond transactions were hotly debated in Congress, but Belmont and his partners were allowed to make off with their excessive profits.[6]

With the money rolling in by the millions, August and the beautiful Caroline were enabled to make a sizable splash in the newly fashionable resort of Newport. New Yorkers discovered the Rhode Island watering place and moved up the coast in a lemming-like migration, shouldering their way in among such literary Bostonians as Dr. Oliver Wendell Holmes, Henry Wadsworth Longfellow and Julia Ward Howe. The quiet style of the place was considerably enlivened when the Belmonts built "Bythesea" at Newport and began entertaining in royal fashion. Older Newporters were particularly taken aback by the flashiness of the Belmont equipage. Mrs. Belmont took the sea air in a *demi-daumont* imported from Paris, the carriage being drawn by four horses with no coachman at the reins but the two near horses driven by postillions costumed in short jackets, tight breeches and maroon jockey caps.

With the Belmonts and their friends came the ten-course dinners with liveried footmen in attendance which brought an unholy whiff of

Sybaritism to the plain-living and high-thinking Bostonians who had preceded them to the resort. One Bostonian, summering in a one-story cottage maintained with the help of a single servant, had the depressing experience of hiring a maid who had formerly been employed by the Belmonts and who kept complaining about the contrast between her old and new positions. "Mr. Belmont keeps ten servants . . . Mr. Belmont keeps twenty horses," she kept telling her new mistress. Finally the latter could stand it no longer, and snapped, "Mr. Belmont keeps everything but the Ten Commandments."[7]

Undeterred and undismayed by the disapproval of Jews and Christians alike, moralists and reformers, Congressional investigators and journalists, August Belmont lived until 1890, and enjoyed every moment of his seventy-four years. He loved the game of money-getting, but enjoyed money-spending even more. It would have dismayed him not in the least that his descendants were more notable for the latter than the former, or that the power of the Belmont fortune began and ended with him.

"THE RICHEST AND RANKIEST OF THEM ALL"

August Belmont, of course, was no more typical of the quarter-million German Jews who migrated to the United States than Carl Schurz or Baron von Steuben of the non-Jewish Germans. For most of them the problem of assimilation was much more painful and difficult, nor did they possess the backing of the Rothschilds, the savoir-faire to make themselves acceptable in the highest social and financial circles, the worldliness to make themselves the leaders of fashion. Most came over under circumstances as desperate as the German peasants who were forced to leave their holdings and set out for the nearest seaport with all their possessions in a two-wheeled cart or on their back. If they possessed one advantage over their Gentile countrymen, as Dr. Rudolf Glanz has pointed out in his 1947 study of the relations between German Jews and non-Jewish Germans in the United States, it was in being "more farsighted and optimistic" about the possibilities of America.[8]

The German-Jews who migrated here before the Civil War identified themselves strongly with their fellow Germans in America. The passenger lists of the sailing ships which brought them from to this country show, as Glanz has written, that "Jews and Germans sailed together for America on the same ships . . . Ties formed which grew stronger with time and led the Jews to the Germans' cultural milieu." His investigations of the early Jewish communities demonstrated that "in great things and in small we encounter the Jews as companions of the Germans," in which "social intercourse between Germans and Jews plays a great part." The German-Jew, as Glanz emphasized, "wished to spend his life in the German-American cultural milieu," to become "an active element in the whole life of the German-American community."

An amity forbidden them by the racial laws of the various German principalities sprang up between German Jews and non-Jewish Germans from the earliest years of the American Republic. Conrad Doehla, a Hessian officer, observed in his diary that in America "the Jewish women have their hair dressed and wear French finery like the women of other faiths. They are very much enamored of and attached to Germans." Jewish-Americans, astonishingly enough, "live in mutual trust and unity . . . Jews and Christians do not hesitate to intermarry . . ."[9]

Many Jews served in the Revolutionary armies, some as officers, including Major Benjamin Nones, Captain Jacob de la Motta and Captain Jacob de Leon, all of whom were attached to Baron de Kalb's staff at the battle of Camden. When the huge Franconian brigadier was mortally wounded and deserted by most of his troops, it was the three Jewish officers who, at the risk of their own lives, carried him off the battlefield.[10]

The German Jews, whose emigration increased in pace with the German Gentiles, tended to settle in the established German-American communities after the Revolutionary War. Thus Cincinnati, even more than New York, was the capital of the Jewish-American dream. In the Ohio city, heavily populated by other German-Americans, they found the kind of atmosphere best suited to them. The first congregation, the Sons of Israel, was organized in 1824. In Cincinnati, too, the first Reformed congregation was established a half-century later with the noted Dr. Isaac Mayer Wise as its first rabbi. It was his descendant, Isidor Wise, who expressed so feelingly their appreciation of Cincinnati as the first Jewish homeland in the New World:

"Cincinnati is the pioneer city of the West; so far as the Jews are concerned, she is the pioneer city of the world. To the long-suffering children of Israel, she is indeed the Queen City, and so will ever remain, though she may lose her commercial preeminence ten times over . . . how many of her children, scattered through the new and vast territory beyond the Mississippi, may cry with the Maccabees, 'If ever I forget thee . . . may my right hand be withered.'"

Many German-Americans were grateful to the Jews of their homeland for helping them to escape during the religious persecutions. German Jews contributed heavily to funds raised for the Salzburgers harried from their lands by a Catholic prince. In Hesse-Cassel alone the Jewish communities contributed four thousand thalers toward assisting the Salzburgers in their struggle to reach America. When that straggling column of Protestant refugees passed through the Rhenish provinces, Jews helped to tend the sick and feed the starving at considerable risk to themselves. The Rhenish Catholics were forbidden by their bishops even to give a Salzburger a glass of water if he dropped on their doorstep.[11] Thus Jews migrating to Georgia and South Carolina found a warm welcome awaiting them from the Salzburgers who had preceded them and remembered their compassion. One of those welcomed Jews was Isaac Friedlander, who was brought to South Carolina at the age of eleven in 1835 and grew up "as ardent a Southerner as if the blood of a Thornton or Crittenden ran in his veins." A towering six feet seven, he joined the gold rush, settled in San Francisco and became known as the city's grain king, the father of three beautiful daughters and a leading member of the community. An Englishman visiting the city in 1860 recorded his amazement at Friedlander's dignity, which matched his size, his polished manners and his erudition.

In following the pattern of German settlement in the United States, German Jews naturally found themselves fighting on both sides of the Civil War battle lines, just as other German-Americans did. The Jewish social system in the South was divided into an upper layer of Jewish planters (and slaveowners), mostly Sephardim, and the German Jews, many of them peddlers or small traders, but both committed to the Confederate cause. Thus the Confederacy's Secretary of War was Judah P. Benjamin, so intimate an adviser of President Jefferson Davis that he was often called the "brains of the Confederacy." One of the great German-Jewish-American families, the Strauses, also was nurtured on southern soil. The founder, Isidor Straus, was born in the Rhenish Palatinate in 1845 and brought to this country at the age of nine. He was raised in Talbotton, Georgia. When the Civil War broke out, he was just about to enter the United States Military Academy, but joined a company of the local militia instead. He was elected a first lieutenant, though only seventeen, but the company was disbanded for lack of equipment.

His elders so valued Isidor Straus's intelligence that he was dispatched, at the age of eighteen, to London as the representative of the Georgia Export Company, a purchasing agent for the Confederate Government Commissioners. In England he bought supplies to be shipped to the Confederate ports on blockade runners and sold Confederate bonds there and in Holland to pay for the purchases.

Reconstruction was as irksome to the Strauses as to any other Southerners. Isidor's financial precocity had been employed in operating a pottery and porcelain importing firm, but the family moved to New York, where Isidor and his brother became partners in the R. H. Macy department store, later buying out other interests and entering into a partnership in the Brooklyn department store of Abraham & Straus. By the turn of the century Isidor Straus was fifty times a millionaire. He was a prominent philanthropist, a founder of the Reform Club, and his friendship with President Grover Cleveland, his sympathy for that statesman's well-intentioned but largely ineffectual gestures toward social justice at a time of economic upheaval, resulted in his election to the House of Representatives in 1894.

His ending, like the rest of his life, was touched with grace. On an April morning in 1912, he and his wife Ida, long and idyllically married, boarded the R.M.S. Titanic for her maiden voyage from Southampton to New York. When the Titanic struck the spur of an iceberg and began sinking fast, Straus and others tried to persuade Mrs. Straus to take her place in a lifeboat, but she would not leave without her husband and Straus, a man of honor to the end, would not leave while there were still women and children in steerage unable to be rescued. "We have been together many years," Mrs. Straus said quietly. "Where you go I will go." They were last seen strolling back to their cabin, where they awaited death together.

It was during the Civil War that German Jews — as did the Gentile Germans of XI Corps — learned they were the objects of prejudice. A strong current of anti-Semitism began running through the North (but not, ironically, the otherwise race-conscious South). Until the Civil War, as the historian Morris Schappes has recorded, the Jews occupied a "secure, stable and untrammeled place in American society."[12] Another historian concurred that "throughout the antebellum period Jews continued to enjoy almost complete social acceptance and freedom."[13] In the northern armies, as well as the southern, Jewish men fought with valor and seven were awarded Congressional Medals of Honor. Their sacrifices, however, did not stem the rumors spreading throughout the North. Rich Jews like Belmont, Democrats in the bargain, were enriching themselves in financing the war and covertly trading with the enemy; poor Jews were all sutlers, selling cheap whiskey and otherwise cheating the boys in blue.

On December 17, 1862, General Grant, as commander of the Army of the Tennessee, took up the refrain. He signed the infamous Order No. 11 in a moment of vexation with cotton smugglers and other dealers in contraband, some of whom, undoubtedly, were Jewish, as a Jewish-American historian concedes. The order read: "The Jews, as a class violating every regulation of trade established by the Treasury Department and also department orders, are hereby expelled from the department within twenty-four hours upon receipt of this order. Post commanders will see that all of this class of people be furnished passes and required to leave, and anyone returning after such notification will be arrested and held in confinement until an opportunity occurs of sending them out as prisoners, unless furnished with permit from headquarters. No passes will be given these people to visit headquarters for the purpose of making personal application for trade permits."

General Grant's order, said the New York *Times*, caused "one of the deepest sensations of the war." Protest meetings were held in many eastern cities, at which speakers demanded to know whether, in a war fought at least partially for the emancipation of one race, Jews, as Jews, were to be oppressed; and "the Old World specter of mass expulsions stood up and stared at the Jews of America." But not for long. Less than three weeks after the order was issued, it was curtly rescinded on orders from President Lincoln. General Grant tried to defend the order on the grounds that "the Jews seemed to be a privileged class that can travel everywhere" and pointed out that cotton prices fell from forty to twenty-five cents a pound the day after the order was issued. Later, when Grant was running for President, his apologists claimed that it had been foisted on him by his staff. Grant himself could only lamely confess that he regretted issuance of the order.

After the war, German Jewry, which had resisted the separatist movements of other German-Americans, began experiencing an internal and theological movement toward separatism. In those years, elsewhere as well as in the United States, the Jewish faith was being fragmented by modernist tendencies. Eventually it was split into the Orthodox, Reform and Conservative elements, the Conservative being a sort of compromise between the other two.

Reform Judaism had started in Germany as a counter to the increasing number of Jewish converts to Christianity. With all the surviving social and legal restrictions placed upon German Jewry — though they had been successively relaxed under the influence of the Emancipation of 1791, with the French Revolution followed by the Napoleonic Code conferring citizenship for the first time on Jews living in western Europe, followed by greater educational and other opportunities in Germany — a professed Christian still stood a better chance than an Orthodox Jew. Baptism, as the poet Heinrich Heine, himself a Christian convert, mockingly explained, was "a passport to European civilization." Reform Judaism, however, failed to halt the movement toward nominal conversion in Germany, and as one leader of the faith said, "We must reform ourselves, not our religion."

The Reform movement was introduced in the United States by Rabbi Isaac Mayer Wise as an "Americanized" version of the faith.

Fittingly enough, his congregation was established in the "pioneer city" of American Jewry, Cincinnati, in 1875. The pace of American life was too brisk, Rabbi Wise believed, for the six hundred rituals, governing every moment of the waking day, practiced by the rigidly Orthodox. In the new temples sermons were to be delivered in English instead of Hebrew and Sabbath services were to be held on Sunday instead of Saturday. (Subsequently Reform Judaism returned to Saturday worship.) The various taboos regarding food were also discarded. Another element of American Jewry believed that Orthodox practice was too rigid, Reform too progressive, and started a third sect calling itself the Conservative, which retained much of the ritual but did away with the physical separation of the sexes during worship in the synagogue.

The schismatic tendencies, perhaps inevitable in transplanting the faith to the New World, have continued to blur the theological boundaries of American Jewry. They are united, however, in secular organizations such as the American Jewish Committee, the American Jewish Congress and the Anti-Defamation League, which provide an umbrella sheltering those of Orthodox, Reform, Conservative or no formal allegiance at all. Even in the synagogues and temples, a recent survey has shown, it is difficult to sort out the believers into the three main elements of Jewry. A questionnaire distributed in a Baltimore synagogue of the Orthodox persuasion disclosed that only 63 percent of its members considered themselves Orthodox, 28 percent said they were Conservative, 3 percent replied they were Reform, and the rest as "none."[14]

During the post-Civil period, as the number of Jewish communities in the United States rose from one hundred fifty in the mid-1860's to four hundred in 1874, mostly German-Jewish, there was little anti-Semitism in evidence. It was never a serious problem in the German-American community as a whole. In Cincinnati and other German-American centers, Jews were welcomed into the *Pionierverein*, German pioneer societies, as freely as any other applicants qualified by their native-son status. There and elsewhere the practice of interfaith pastoral visits sprang up, with Protestant ministers appearing in the "Israelitish temples" and rabbis before Protestant congregations.

A measure of the Gentile German regard for the German Jew was expressed in the most vigorous terms by Carl Schurz when he took note of the German-Jewish contributions to American life. Observing that the Jewish fraction of the German-American population was only a third in New York City, 100,000 out of 350,000 as of 1885, Schurz praised the German-Jewish-American community because they "give three times as much for their charitable institutions as the Germans." In addition, he said, the German Jews assisted "with a liberal hand the German welfare enterprises."[15]

Social historians of the period observed that German Jews as well as German Gentiles were addicted to beer-drinking, playing cards on Sunday, and other customs brought over from Germany.

In the nineteenth century and well into the twentieth, as Cleveland Amory has written, Jews "belonged to the most fashionable city clubs in Richmond. New Orleans, too, was a particular ornament of American tolerance; in 1872, a Jewish businessman, Louis Salomon, was the first king of the first Mardi Gras. Such facts contrast sharply with the all-inclusive upper-echelon anti-Semitism of a later day." The eccentric pattern of latter-day anti-Semitism was studied by John Higham in three cities with sizable German-Jewish populations, Minneapolis, St. Paul and San Francisco, with these findings:

"By 1920, the Jews of Minneapolis lay under a singularly complete ostracism. It was perhaps the only city in the land that shut out Jews from the service clubs (Rotary, Kiwanis and Lions), to say nothing of the local realty board and the numerous civic welfare boards. Across the river, the twin city of St. Paul behaved somewhat more decently. Jews could at least belong to the local service clubs and the Automobile Club. San Francisco presented the other extreme. There acceptance of Jews extended very widely in elite social organizations, civic activities, and even residential patterns. This discrimination has been strong in Minneapolis, moderate in St. Paul, and weak in San Francisco, as in the whole South. Yet all three cities had concentrated Jewish districts produced by recent immigration, and the ratio of Jews to the total population in 1930 was highest in San Francisco (6.5 percent) and lowest in Minneapolis (3.5 percent)."

Even in the period between the Civil and World Wars, when anti-Semitism was muted in the few places where it existed, there was an occasional indication of the social discrimination to come. The most celebrated incident involved Joseph Seligman, the financier, friend of Grant and Lincoln and leader of New York City's Jewish community. For years Seligman and his family had spent their summers at the fashionable Grand Union Hotel in Saratoga Springs. Then came a change of managers, occasioned by the death of A. T. Stewart, the department store owner and operator of the Grand Union. The new manager informed Seligman, when he arrived with his family in June, 1877, that there had been a change of policy and "Israelites" would no longer be permitted to stay at the Grand Union. Seligman and his family quietly decamped, but the news of their rejection reached New York and became front-page news. The result was that Jews boycotted the Stewart department store, which went into a rapid decline. A short time later it was sold to John Wanamaker.

Until 1881, however, there were few such marsh-gas flareups in the bogs of racialism to concern the Jewish communities, or any internal dissensions aside from occasional set-tos between temple and synagogue. The leaders of German-American Jewry were "like the peers in *Iolanthe* — 'the richest and rankiest of them all,'" as Marion K. Sanders has designated the founders of the American Jewish committee, the Warburgs, Schiffs, Lehmans, Rosenwalds, Strauses and allied families.[16] All were of German extraction, and all prided themselves on partaking of the superiority of German culture.

But 1881 . . . that was a year to remember, a time of self-questioning for every Jew who had already established himself in America.

DARK SHADOWS ACROSS THE GOLDEN DOOR

The trouble began in Russia in April that year. It was the month in which Czar Alexander II was assassinated and succeeded by his son, Alexander III. Retribution was immediately levied upon the most convenient and helpless scapegoat, the Jews penned in the Pale of

Settlement and treated far more harshly than they had ever been in Germany or any other part of western Europe. Obviously under central direction from St. Petersburg, pogroms were organized throughout the Ukraine, then in the Warsaw ghetto and elsewhere in Poland and Russia. All the flaying and killing were excused by the czar's government on the grounds that the revolutionary movement slowly expanding underground, which was responsible for Alexander II's death, was the creation of Jewish conspiracy. Accordingly, the Procurator of the Orthodox Church announced a simple but rigid formula: one-third of Russia's Jews would be forced to emigrate, one-third would be allowed to "accept" baptism, and the remaining third would be starved to death.

After a year of pogroms mostly carried out by Cossack cavalry wielding knouts and sabers, less violent means of repression were ordained. The reason for calling off the Cossacks was pressure from the outside world, a clamor that penetrated even czarist Russia. Diplomatic representations were made by the United States State Department and other Western governments. A huge protest meeting was held in Paris under the chairmanship of Victor Hugo, and after a similar mass meeting in New York over which Mayor William R. Grace presided a petition was signed by a hundred leading American Christians. The list of signatures was headed by that of General Grant, the repentant author of General Order No. 11.

Petitions and protests did not, however, spare the Russian Jews from the "May Laws," promulgated that month in 1882, which forbade Jews from trading in or even entering the villages within the Pale of Settlement and severely limited the number of Jewish children admitted to the schools and universities.

The result was a mass exodus. Jews had lost all hope of attaining a decent life under the czars and began migrating. A few headed for Palestine, others for a Spain anxious to atone for its own record of medieval repressions and announcing the refugees would be welcome within the Spanish borders. For most of them, however, America was the first and last hope. From 1881 to 1914 approximately two million Russian Jews migrated to the United States.

They were even poorer than the Irish and German millions who had preceded them by less than half a century, but fortunately they landed in an America that was between depressions, the period of the Elegant Eighties. The country prided itself on being the City of Refuge for all oppressed peoples — and now that boast would be tested again. That feeling was most poignantly expressed in the verse of Emma Lazarus, a poetess of Sephardic ancestry, which was to be inscribed on the Statue of Liberty: ". . . I lift my lamp beside the golden door!"

Keeping that lamp lit, and that golden door open, was not always easy. Eventually, in the 1920's, the golden door was all but slammed shut by immigration quotas which favored migration from northern and western Europe. Long before that, partly stimulated by the influx of Russian, Polish and other eastern European Jews, anti-Semitism began growing and was nurtured by such instances as the Dreyfus case, the "scientific" anti-Semitism of Houston Chamberlain and his French and German disciples, and the charge by New York Police Commissioner Theodore A. Bingham in 1908 that 50 percent of New York City's crimes were committed by Russian Jews. (A study of the 175,000 persons arraigned before police magistrates showed, however, that only 7 percent were "Russians.")

The great influx from eastern Europe came as a shock to the sensibilities of the quarter-million Jews, mostly of German extraction, already in the United States, most of them comfortably established and sure of their place in American society. The newcomers, obviously, threatened that secure place. Conscience and the teachings of their faith told them they must accept and welcome their coreligionists from the East, but they were also strongly conscious of a cultural superiority. "Between them and the new immigrants from Eastern Europe," as Irving Howe has written, "there soon arose — it could not be avoided — a grating hostility, in part the continuation of cultural struggles from the Old World and in part a result of mass toe-stepping by harassed immigrants upon settled residents."[17]

Even their fellow Jews called the newcomers "kikes," and were repelled by their long beards, their strange language and all the evidence of poverty and oppression they bore with them. Even their profiles seemed "different," more Oriental. And there was the curious, incredible "gallows humor" which had sustained them in the Pale of Settlement, the black humor their grandsons would develop into a literary fashion seventy or eighty years later. Its quality, which German Jews found difficult to absorb with their progressive Western attitudes, was strikingly suggested by Shalom Aleichem, who concluded a long and woeful tale with the words, "And now let's talk about something cheerful. Tell me, what news is there about the cholera in Odessa?" German Jews were affronted by the idea that tragedy, instead of being confronted and overcome, should be turned aside with a shrugging, wry, defeatist humor.

Russian and German Jews were "divided by sharp differences of conviction and caste," Marion K. Sanders has noted. "Far less opulent Jews" than the great merchant princes, financiers and philanthropists "had no doubt that they were superior to the hordes from Russia, Poland, and other eastern European countries . . ."[18] Instead of scattering throughout the United States, as most German Jews did, the Russian Jews clung to their port of entry and made the Lower East Side of New York their new homeland. It was a natural choice, considering the circumstances of their life in eastern Europe, but it prolonged and impeded the process of assimilation which German Jews valued so highly. "Unable to live wholly by the ways of the Old World but not yet ready to yield wholly to the ways of the new," as Irving Howe has described that subculture of lower Manhattan, "the Lower East Side chose to improvise a world of its own . . . It jumbled together Europe and America; it forced Messianism and mercantilism into an inconceivable union; it refused the option of euthanasia that history was preparing and would soon administer."[19]

It was also a matter of affront to many German Jews, who were wedded to the middle class, its fears and prejudices, that Russian Jews often were quickly infected by the socialism which was then endemic in the American working classes. Non-Jewish German-Americans had formed the backbone of social reform — not only the socialist prescription but anarchism and other more exotic remedies; but in this tendency toward political radicalism they had never been joined by sizable numbers of German-Jews, Education, not social revolution, was the totem of the German Jews; not only for their own people but all Americans.

The Russian and other eastern Jews, however, were the bottom layer of society at the turn of the century and most were condemned to labor in the sweatshops. They had found that the rumor that American streets were paved with gold was not even remotely true, but they also learned that they were not completely shut off from opportunity. "In the United States," Irving Howe wrote, "even during the worst years of the sweatshops, there were far more tempting possibilities than had been known in eastern Europe for economic success, social mobility, educational advantage, cultural release — so that people trained for centuries to a life apart from history and power suddenly found themselves facing the temptations, small as these might at first be, of worldliness."[20]

The German Jews slowly learned to understand the ways of the eastern European Jews, but for many it was almost as difficult as for a Prussian field marshal to make friends with the Polish peasants on his estate. Marion K. Sanders has recorded her family's consternation when her cousin Bertha married a Polish Jew as late as the 1920's. "Sam was an embarrassment not only because of his national origin. He had an 'accent'; furthermore he was a Socialist and a Zionist, which meant that he was basically un-American or un-Americanizable. Bertha and Sam settled in Boston while I was a student at Wellesley. During a weekend visit my parents invited them to lunch at the Copley. It was a ghastly confrontation. Bertha arrived wearing some sort of peasant smock while Sam's unruly hair was crowned by a ragged peaked cap which he considered suitably proletarian headgear. In my memory the hatcheck girl was almost as flabbergasted as my father, who was something of a dandy in matters of dress. He was a generous and faithful contributor to causes for the relief of poor Jews in the slums of New York or the ghettoes of Europe. But Sam's physical and public appearance was something else again."[21]

Gradually a mutual identification was established. The pressures, however, came from the outside rather than inside the Jewish community as a whole. If, in a sense, the eastern European newcomers were a psychological threat to the established, they also had to meet, together, a greater threat from bigotry and a revival of Know-Nothingism.

For the first time, in 1897, Congress passed a bill requiring a literacy test for adult immigrants. This, of course, was directed mainly at the floodtide of Russian-Jewish migration but also at the widening stream of Italian and Balkan immigrants. President Grover Cleveland vetoed the bill, holding that a literacy test certified only a person's past education not his future capabilities or value as a citizen. Under pressure from the Immigration Restriction League, the bill was reintroduced at the next session of Congress. By now the immigrants of earlier years had organized the Immigration Protective League and compaigned vigorously against the bill. One reason for the bill's second defeat was a proclamation from one hundred fifty German-American societies that the golden door must be kept open, that efforts to shut it were a sign that the Know-Nothings had returned to life.

The snobbishness evidenced by German Jews and others toward the Russians also received a sly rebuke from the period's leading humorist, Finley Peter Dunne, whose Mr. Dooley commented in 1902: "As a pilgrim father that missed the first boat, I must raise me claryon voice again' the invasion iv this fair land be th' paupers and arnychists in Europe. Ye bet I must — because I'm here first . . . In thim days America was th' refuge iv th' oppressed in all the wurruld . . . But as I tell ye, 'tis different now. 'Tis time we put our back again' th' open dure an' keep out th' savage horde."

And there were other less gentle reminders that anti-Semitic discrimination was not selective, that to the bigot there was little or no difference between a cultured, philanthropic Jew of German or Sephardic origin and a Russian Jew laboring in a sweatshop. The recognition that a Jew was a Jew was forced upon them in various ways. Something more jolting than any cultural shock was the lynching of Leo Frank, a prosperous Jewish manufacturer, in Georgia in 1915, after he was wrongly convicted of murdering a Christian child. A year later there was the publication of The Passing of the Great Race by Madison Grant, the chairman of the New York Zoological Society, with a preface by Henry Fairfield Osborn, professor of zoology at Columbia University.

The book claimed that the Nordics — Anglo-Saxon, German, Scandinavian — were racially superior to all other breeds and destined to rule the earth; that other races from eastern Europe and the Mediterranean littoral were "human flotsam" who "lowered and vulgarized" the whole tone of American social and political life. The same theme absorbed one of the era's most popular novelists, Jack London, who believed that "my race is the salt of the earth," which was destined to be ruled by Nordic supermen. Anti-Semitism was becoming intellectually fashionable. After World War I, American Jews of all origins were reminded once again of the necessity for self-defense when Henry Ford published the *Protocols of the Elders of Zion* and for seven years performed as a Jew-baiter in the columns of his Dearborn *Independent*.

SAM DREBEN AND OTHERS

Shortly after the United States entered the First World War, a *Manual of Instructions for Medical Advisory Boards* was issued for the draft boards. One sentence warned that "the foreign born, especially Jews, are more apt to malinger than the native born." Once again organizations such as the American Jewish Committee had to swing into action to defend the patriotism of its people. The manual was promptly destroyed on orders of President Wilson, but the rumor that all Jews were shirkers, who either dodged the draft or found a safe berth in the Quartermaster Corps, persisted both in the army and on the home front.

Such rumor-mongers were lucky not to encounter Sam Dreben. He was one of those rare creatures, the Jewish soldier of fortune, and had fought in the Boxer Rebellion, the Spanish-American War and a number of Latin American revolutions before enlisting in the American Expeditionary Force. In France he became one of the A.E.F.'s legendary heroes by rushing a German machine-gun nest and killing twenty-three of the enemy.

The records of the A.E.F., aside from Dreben's example, showed that Jewish Americans did their bit. A total of 225,000 served in the

United States armed forces, and statistics of the various ethnic groups showed that a higher proportion of Jews than any other group served in the infantry. Forty percent of the "Lost Battalion," an outfit recruited in New York, and which fought its way out of the Argonne forest, was Jewish.

One side effect of the war was the detachment of the German Jews from their formerly cozy, special relationship with the German-American community as a whole. Many German-Americans opposed American participation in the war; a minority actively supported the cause of Germany and her allies. In this crisis of alienation, German Jews suffered no traumatic wounds over loyalties divided between America and Germany. In leaving Germany their antecedents, like most Gentile Germans, were shaking off the chains that bound them to a system of petty tyrannies. The difference was that the Jews had suffered more from the medieval restrictions of the old country, and remembered them more keenly. Sympathizing with Germany in her struggle with half the world seemed ridiculous to them, and furthermore the British, with the issuance of the Balfour Declaration, promised the establishment of a Jewish homeland in Palestine.

There was no open rupture between German Jews and others of German extraction, but a division of opinion over the war only speeded the process begun when the great migration of eastern European Jews started early in the 1880's.

Whatever lingering affection or nostalgia existed among German-Jewish-Americans for Germany as a wellspring of culture was obliterated by Nazi genocide. For almost a century many German Jews had looked back to the old country, granting that their people had been injustly treated there, yet regarding it, in a cultural way, as a sort of substitute Palestine. It was natural enough, considering that so much of German culture was built up by Jewish intellect. That feeling of inheritance was destroyed forever in the concentration camps.

Late in 1966, however, there appeared one of those historical footnotes, no larger than a flyspeck in the American press, which may have far-reaching effects. Its ironic aspects need not be elaborated upon, but a reverse flow of educational technique, so long the proud preserve of the German, has begun from the Jews in the United States. Conceived and sponsored by the American Jewish Committee, a pilot project designed to give West German schoolchildren a better understanding of democracy is now in full operation. The plan calls for distribution of new textbooks to replace those which skipped over the Hitler regime and failed to show how Nazism destroyed German democracy. It also provides for bringing over groups of German educators to learn how social studies are taught in American classrooms.[22]

In the long view of history, it may be the first step toward a reconciliation not easily imagined little more than a score of years since Hitler's concentration camps were burst open.

10. THE PURSUIT OF EXCELLENCE

The American nation is full of enthusiasm for education, believes thoroughly in the dissemination of knowledge and in the importance of education for citizenship . . . All this is admirable and excellent, and yet it cannot reach the ideal aim and cannot perform the wonderful miracle . . . what is needed still more is the spirit of belief in the value of knowledge . . . One of the greatest European scientists on returning home from an exchange year at an American university condensed his impressions into the remark that he had never heard from university colleagues so much talking about education and so little about scholarly problems.

— HUGO MUNSTERBURG

Henry Adams recalled his experiences as a young Harvard instructor transmitting the results of his own partial education in a German university in his usual wry and deprecating fashion. Writing of himself in the third person in *The Education of Henry Adams*, he said: "He made use of his last two years of German schooling to inflict their results on his students, and by a happy chance he was in the full tide of fashion. The Germans were crowning their new emperor at Versailles, and surrounding his head with a halo of Pepins and Merwigs, Othos and Barbarossas. James Bryce had even discovered the Holy Roman Empire. Germany was never so powerful, and the Assistant Professor of History had nothing else as his stock in trade. He imposed Germany on his students with a heavy hand. He was rejoiced; but he sometimes doubted whether they should be grateful."

The "tide of fashion" Henry Adams remarked upon was the great prestige Germany was enjoying abroad following her victory in the Franco-Prussian War, not only for her military successes but for all the evidence of scientific and educational superiority on which they were founded. The superiority of rapid-fire German artillery testified to the excellence of the German universities. In the United States, remote as it was from the menacing efficiency of the Prussian war machine, all things German were particularly admired. After the two World Wars, in fact, it is difficult to believe how pervasive the enthusiasm for German science, education and culture were in the United States as well as Britain. The Germans knew how to make things *work*, and that quality has always engaged the attention of the pragmatic American.

Decades before the Prussian armies swarmed across the Rhine, however, the symmetry, exactitude and discipline of a German university education had begun making their impression on upper-class Americans able to gain a higher education. Boston, as the self-conscious center of American culture, early had adopted a worshipful attitude toward the Germany of the scholars and philosophers, the poets and musicians; the Germany of the ferocious barbarians who topped the walls of Rome having receded into the historic mists, the Germany of the goose-stepping armies still so far in the future that it could not be perceived by even the most prophetic minds. In his Phi Beta Kappa address at Harvard in 1837, Emerson urged any educator "anxious to spare himself the mortification of reading to empty benches" to keep up with the scholarly times, "striking out exploded errors, incorporating new discoveries." Their inspiration, Emerson indicated, must be Teutonic: "The German brain is prolific. The sight of the semi-annual catalogue of new publications in Germany is enough to unhinge the strongest mind. The professor must keep abreast with the swelling tide."

The prestige of the German educational system, which resulted in the transformation of the American system from kindergarten to graduate school, naturally cast its flattering glow on the German-American community as a whole between the Civil War and World War I. Ten thousand Americans, it has been estimated, were educated in German universities up to 1900. The old-country educational and cultural magnificence contributed to an impression that German-Americans must come of a superior stock, and they were not slow to accept that secondhand tribute, undeserved as it often was. It also built up the self-assertiveness of the German-American minority to the pitch of over-expectation which resulted in the numbingly swift and bitter deflation of their credit balance as a nationality group during the years of the First World War.

In the beginning the interest of the rudimentary American educational establishment was more a necessity than an infatuation. It began in the 1820's, when the more natural links with the French and British institutions were broken. The War of 1812, of course, resulted in a general Anglo-American estrangement, deepening the disruptive effects of the Revolutionary War. Until the second decade of the nineteenth century, the British influence had been replaced by the French, whose political and military power naturally encouraged this development up to the last shots fired at Waterloo. Intellectual dominance in the early years of the American republic was represented, for the most part, by Thomas Jefferson. And Jefferson, as a scholar in French literature, a strong sympathizer of whatever French democratic institutions survived Napoleonic authoritarianism, was an all-out Francophile.

Napoleon's final defeat, however, effectively closed out French intellectual and cultural influence: Americans have always been overimpressed by success. "Waterloo was almost as conclusive of the ending of the French era," Charles Franklin Thwing has written in his survey of German educational influences in the United States, "as the Massachusetts Concord was of the English. The majesty and picturesqueness of Napoleon ceased to captivate, and the force of his ambitious schemes to dominate." In those years America was "coming to national and academic self-consciousness," and the only remaining example to which it could turn was the German. That turn, as Thwing has pointed out, was accomplished with difficulty because "Germany was far more remote to most Americans than was either England or France. The German language was a more foreign tongue than the French. German literature did not, and indeed could not, receive the recognition in America that French literature possessed . . . The number of scholars who could read German was few."[1]

The earliest known instance of what would later be known as a cultural exchange between America and Germany took place in 1709, when the fire-eating and fire-promising Boston theologian Cotton Mather sent a collection of one hundred sixty books and tracts on the subject of Pietism to the German religious reformer, August Hermann Francke, in the university town of Halle. In reply, Francke wrote Mather a letter of sixty-nine pages in Latin. The correspondence between the two theologians continued until their deaths, and was carried on by their sons.[2] During the next century, however, there was little intellectual communication between America and Germany.

That it suddenly began flourishing in the 1820's was due largely to translation of Madame de Staël's famous and largely sympathetic work De l'Allemagne, which publicized to the world the burgeoning glories of the German intellect, first in France, then in England, when the book was translated in 1814, and swiftly thereafter to the United States.

"Possibly a few Bostonians could read and speak French," as Henry Adams later commented; "but Germany was nearly as unknown as China until Madame de Stael published her famous work."[3]

Four young Americans of later celebrity were inspired to investigate the possibilities of applying a German finish to their American educations largely under the inspiration of Madame de Staël's unqualified declaration that "all the north of Germany is filled with the most learned universities in Europe. In no country, not even in England, have the people so many means of instructing themselves, and of bringing their faculties to perfection — the literary glory of Germany depends altogether upon these institutions."

THE GÖTTINGEN GRADUATES

The four young men were George Ticknor, George Bancroft, Joseph Green Cogswell and Edward Everett, the latter being more celebrated for his political career, his fame as an orator and finally for providing the background music to Abraham Lincoln's Gettysburg Address, but in a quieter way influential in attracting American attention to the virtues of the German university system. All attended the great Hanoverian university of Göttingen, which lacked the glamour of Heidelburg but had the most learned faculty and one of the finest libraries in Europe. The pioneering quartet was followed to Göttingen by Emerson, Longfellow, John Lothrop Motley, Francis J. Child and other future luminaries; George William Curtis and Timothy Dwight chose the University of Berlin. Various reasons impelled them to seek a German polish on the Harvard patina, but the prime motive was probably that which animated Ticknor's journey to Göttingen, as provided by his biographer: "The literary poverty of this country at that time cannot be better illustrated than by the fact which Mr. Ticknor gives, that when he wanted to study German he was obliged to seek a textbook in one place, a dictionary in a second, and a grammar in a third; the last two very indifferent in their kind. There are now, doubtless, more facilities in New England for the study of Arabic or Persian than there were then for the study of German."[4]

It was not easy for the young Americans to adjust themselves to the German intellectual climate, far more rarefied than the atmosphere of the Harvard Yard. "As the large body of instructors," George Bancroft wrote home in 1819 regarding the Göttingen faculty, "have passed their lives exclusively among their books, they have something exceedingly cold in their deportment, and a person must have become quite intimate with them before he can find out that they are capable of feeling." Everett wrote home that America had much to learn from Germany, little from England. Cogswell, however, believed that Göttingen's leading passion, the "formation of scholars," was not necessarily to be imported wholesale to the United States, just a sufficient quantity to inspire Americans with a respect for and capability of scholarship. Seedlings, not massive transplants, were the requirement. "It is true that very few of what the Germans call scholars are needed in America," Cogswell remarked in a letter from Göttingen; "if there would be only one thorough one to begin with, the number would soon be sufficient for all the uses that could be made of them, and for the literary character of the country. This one, I say, could never be formed there, because, in the first place, there is no one who knows how it is to be done; secondly, there are no books, and then, by the habits of desultory study practiced there, are wholly incompatible with it."

With a youthful sternness, Cogswell, who a half-dozen years later founded the Round Hill School at Northampton, Massachusetts, in association with George Bancroft, advised his friends in Cambridge that they would not prove themselves worthy of a higher education by attendance "at your dinner-tables, at your suppers, your clubs, and your ladies, at your tea-parties (you perceive that I am aiming at Boston folks) . . . most of these gratifications must be sacrificed to attain the objects of a scholar's ambition . . ."

Ticknor, also by way of providing an example for the graceful but laggard men of Harvard, wrote back home of spending much time with his professor of Greek history, "still a young man of hardly thirty, and yet has been called as professor to three universities . . ."

George Bancroft sent one of his Harvard perceptors a schedule of his daily routine at Göttingen, a heroic regimen indeed; based on the German theory that a student should apply himself eighteen hours a day:

5 a.m.–7 *Hebrew and Syriac.*
7–8 . . . *Heeren in Ethnography.*
8–9 . . . *Church history by the elder Planck.*
9–10 . . . *Exegesis of the New Testament by old Eichorn.*
10–11 . . *Exegesis of the Old Testament by old Eichorn.*
11–12 . . *Syriac by old Eichorn.*
12–1 . . . *Dinner and walk.*
1–2 . . . *Library.*
2–4 . . . *Latin or French.*
4–5 . . . *Philological Encyclopedie by Dissen.*
5–7 . . . *Greek.*
7–8 . . . *Syriac.*
8–9 . . . *Tea and walk.*
9–11 . . . *Repetition of the old lectures and preparation for the new.*[5]

The disciplines acquired in Germany by Bancroft, Everett, Cogswell and Ticknor and introduced on their return to the United States "exerted a formative influence, if not over Harvard, at least through Harvard College, upon American literature and higher education," Professor Thwing observed. "They helped to bring European scholarship to America. They aided in breaking up the isolation of American life. They enriched American thought. They stirred up American scholars unto an appreciation of the unique worth of German learning and teaching. They gave a vision — and a gloomy one — of the poverty of American literature. They aided in inspiring college administrators and teachers unto the appreciation of their own limitations. They were the early prophets who prepared the way for the unique growth of American colleges and universities in the decades following their return to America."[6]

Various historians of American education have noted that the emphasis on religion and ethics applied in early American colleges, many of them founded by religious groups, was not generally a part of the German academic design. Whether or not that was a flaw, it was also noted that Americans in Germany often returned with a more dogmatic approach, if not the arrogance that often marked their German "Herr Doctors." Thwing believed that Americans finishing their education in Germany also were deprived of an appreciation of good taste. Another American academic observer decided that "German higher education . . . concentrates itself too exclusively on the intellectual side." The German-educated American was all too likely, in brief, to be turned into an intellectual boor. And not the least of German crimes of the intellect have been their imprint on historiography, the weightiness, the labyrinthine narrative, the footnote-dappled and aggressive quibbling of it all, as contrasted with the frequent astringency of the English, the aphoristic wit of the French. It was a pity that German thoroughness could not have been leavened by other influences during the most formative years of American education. On balance, however, the thoroughgoing German approach probably worked best for a young nation intent on building a monolithic industrial society within a few generations.

The German educational influence continued almost to the First World War. The University of Michigan, founded in 1837, was reorganized along Germanic lines a dozen years later, when the religious denominational influence was banished. Johns Hopkins University, established in 1876, used the German university as its model and most of the members of its first faculty boasted German degrees. Horace Mann's reform of the public-school system in Massachusetts, which spread to other states, was largely motivated by his survey of German elementary schooling. Before the end of the century, Daniel C. Gilman, the first president of Johns Hopkins, was to assert that "as Latin was the language of the scholar during the Middle Ages, so the knowledge of German is now indispensable for anyone who claims the name of a student and scholar."

Many German professors came over on an exchange basis, and others as emigrants. They followed by some years the aggressively liberal Forty-eighters, who were mostly student revolutionaries rather than pedants, and many brought with them a nostalgia for *Der Vaterland* which would have provoked derisive outcries from those who fled the political oppression that preceded federalization (and continued, but in a more subtle form, under that Machiavelli of the North, Bismarck). Many of those later imports, wittingly or not, served as propagandists for the new Imperial Germany.

A vivid example of the process by which German scholarship and propaganda were exported to America in the same beguiling package was Kuno Francke, a literary scholar and a descendant of Cotton Mather's correspondent. He was born in Kiel in 1855, received his doctor's degree at Munich in 1878, and six years later migrated to the Harvard Yard. He immediately busied himself with the Germanic Museum, which was to "illustrate by reproductions of typical works of the fine arts and crafts the development of Germanic culture from the first contact of the Germanic tribes with the civilization of the Roman Empire to the present day."

That might have encompassed a less energetic man's lifework, in addition to his teaching duties, but Francke also turned out a stream of books and articles portraying the splendor of the new Germany. Francke was wildly optimistic about the growth of personal freedom in the Kaiser's Germany. On returning from visits to his homeland he produced glowing tributes to its "ardent life and intense activity in every field of national aspirations."

Although he did not make much mention of the thunder of jackboots on every parade ground or the steady increase of army corps, he stressed the nobility of the German soldier and thrilled to "the magnificent Army with its manly discipline and high standards of professional conduct." It symbolized "the wonderfully organized collective will toward the higher forms of national existence." Just how the "collective will" and the growth of personal freedom could stay off a collision course he did not elaborate upon. Instead he hymned the glories of work and order for slothful and easygoing America. "Healthfulness, power, orderliness meet the eye on every square mile of German soil." He also pointed with pride to "these flourishing, well-kept farms and estates, these thriving villages, these carefully replenished forests . . . these bursting cities teeming with a well-fed and well-behaved population . . . with proud city halls and stately courthouses, with theatres and museums rising everywhere, admirable means of communication, model arrangements for healthy recreation and amusement, earnest universities and technical schools." The social and civil life was characterized by the "orderly management of political meetings," the "fight for social betterment," the "respectful and attentive attitude toward all forms of art."[7]

And Francke was only one of the earnest Herr Doctors imported from Germany who contributed to the chestiness of the German-Americans during the years before the First World War. They had long ago abandoned the schemes of separatism, but the size and power of their minority convinced many that they were destined to exert a specifically German influence on the course of American history, a course that would keep America out of the Anglo-French orbit and guide it toward closer association with Germany. The residual chauvinism, though a transplant, was a hardy breed, as Peter Finley Dunne's barroom philosopher Mr. Dooley ruminated on the German-Americans:

"I'm not prejudiced against thim, mind ye. They made good beer an' good citizens an' mod-rate policemen, an' they are fond iv their families an' cheese. But wanst a German, always Dutch. Ye cudden't make Americans iv them if ye called them all Perkins an' brought thim up in Worcester. A German niver ra-aly laves Germany. He takes it with him wherever he goes. Whin an Irishman is four miles out at sea he is as much an American as Presarved Fish. But a German is niver an American excipt whin he goes back to Germany to see his rilatives. He keeps his own language, he plays pinochle, he despises th' drink iv th' counthry, his food is sthrange an' he only votes f'r Germans f'r office, or if he can't get a German, f'r somewhan who's again' th' Irish. I bet ye, if ye was suddenly to ask Schwarzmeister where he is, he'd say: 'At Hockheimer in Schawbia.' He don't ra-aly know he iver came over to this counthry. I've heard him talkin' to himsilf. He always counts in German."[8]

ON A HUMBLER LEVEL

While beard-stroking savants and chalk-dusted pedants were providing higher education with a German accent, a number of German-Americans were conducting their own pursuit of excellence on a less exalted level. Their diverse efforts resulted in striking advances in popularization, in the education of the masses. From them stemmed, among other institutions and innovations, the Chautauqua movement, the Turnvereins, the linotype and the development of the political cartoon as a potent force in civic reform and the comic strip as a means of communication of mixed blessings but great popular appeal.

The graphic arts, beginning with Guttenberg, have always attracted the genius of the Germans. Thus the greatest advance in printing technology since Gutenberg first went to press was the invention of the linotype by a German-American. The stark and effective simplicity of the line drawing has employed talents as various as those of George Grosz, whose savage caricatures captured the bitter essence of Germany between the two World Wars before Grosz migrated to America; of Thomas Nast, whose political cartoons have never been

276

equaled in their effect; of Carl Emil Schultze, who produced one of the first ("Foxy Grandpa") cartoon strips around the turn of the century, which attracted a mass readership to the newspapers and greatly increased the power of the press as a time when it was unchallenged as a means of communication; and of Charles Schulz, of the present generation, whose "Peanuts" has become the godhead of a youthful cult.

When Thomas Nast took up his lancelike pen against New York's municipal corruption, the city was filled with hundreds of thousands of semiliterate Irish and German immigrants. It was under the incredibly oppressive and corrupt domination of Boss Tweed and Tammany Hall, a microcosmic dictatorship so brazen it could throw a man into jail and keep him there without charges being filed against him, so pervasive that under its protection Jay Gould and Jim Fisk were able to loot the Erie Railway and print their own stock certificates without interference. With his steel-tipped pen and his pot of India ink, with his ability to convert invective into a line drawing whose implications could be grasped even by the illiterate, Nast was able to make himself chiefly instrumental in overthrowing the most powerful political conspiracy to seize an American city.

"Nast was one of the greatest statesman of his time," said J. Henry Harper, publisher of the weekly which employed his calefactory talents. "I have never known a man with surer political insight. He seemed to see approaching events before most men dreamed of them as possible. His work was entirely his own and generally in his own way. He never could bear interference or even suggestion. I never knew him to use an idea that was not his own."

Some of that insight was evidenced when Nast invented the elephant as the symbol of the powerful but sluggish Republican party and the Tammany Tiger as the symbol of that political beast of prey, when he forecast the total eclipse of the second Napoleon in his cartoon "Thrown into the Shade," which showed a picture of Napoleon III with the shadow of Germany's Wilhelm I falling across it and covering it completely.

Thomas Nast was born in the Bavarian Palatinate and brought to America in 1846 at the age of six when his father, a musician, joined the

New York Philharmonic Society's orchestra. Young Thomas attended evening classes at the Academy of Design, and while still a teen-ager boldly marched into the offices of magazine publisher Frank Leslie and asked him for an illustrator's job. Leslie told him to go out, find a suitable subject and bring back a drawing which would prove his capabilities. The next Sunday, Nast joined the Sunday throngs taking the ferry on an excursion to the Elysian Fields, beyond Hoboken, and the following day presented Leslie with a drawing that conveyed the excursionists' carefree mood so exactly that Leslie hired him at a salary of four dollars a week. His first venture into political satire was a cartoon deploring one of the recurring police scandals.

In 1860, when he was only twenty years old, the New York *Illustrated News*, a short-lived premonition of the tabloid, sent him to England to send back illustrations of the Heenan-Sayers championship prizefight. On his own, he wandered off to Italy and took part in Garibaldi's war of liberation, returning to New York a year later with sketches published in various newspapers and magazines.

His political education under Garibaldi prepared him for the galvanic events then taking place on the American scene. With his usual directness, he immediately decided that abolition was a cause worth fighting for — at least with his pen — and became one of the Union's most effective advocates. It was then he joined the staff of the like-minded *Harper's Weekly* and produced the long series of drawings underlining the righteousness of the Union's war aims, the worthiness of the North's sacrifices in preserving the Union and ending slavery. This series, as one historian wrote, "exerted an enormous influence far beyond the eloquence of any single orator."[9] The drawings also caused President Lincoln to say: "Thomas Nast has been our best recruiting sergeant; his emblematic cartoons have never failed to arouse enthusiasm and patriotism, and have always seemed to come just when these articles were getting scarce."

One of Nast's drawings, drawn in a rare moment of sentiment, was clipped from the Christmas issue of *Harper's* in 1862 and pasted on the walls of thousands of homes and barracks throughout the North. It was a double-page picture which seemed to arch like a rainbow from war front to home front: on one side a sentry pacing beside a watch fire, on the other his wife kneeling beside the cradle of their child.

He became nationally famous late in the Sixties and early in the Seventies for the cartoons in which he almost weekly tore strips off Boss Tweed, his corrupt magistrates and city officials, and the financial powers allied to them. The first time he used the symbol ever afterward associated with Tammany Hall was in a cartoon titled "The Tammany Tiger Loose." It showed a prostrate female, the Republic, being torn to pieces by a tiger labeled Tammany. At that time *Harper's Weekly* and Horace Greeley's New York *Tribune* were the only journalistic voices raised against Tweed and his gang. Time after time he spurned offers from Tammany to multiply his five-thousand-dollar salary from *Harper's* if only he would turn his attention to something else. When Tweed was finally deposed and his henchmen jailed or scattered in flight, the New York *Times* having finally roused itself and published a definitive series showing just how the Tweed Ring worked, with whom and for how much, Thomas Nast was rightly given a large share of the credit for the belated triumph of civic virtue.

Unappeased, Nast continued to flay those who had profited from association with Tweed, particularly the Gould-Fisk plunderbund operating the Erie Railway. When Jim Fisk was shot to death in a more or less romantic triangle, Gould hinted to the Erie stockholders that the company's treasury would be safer now that his partner was dead. Nast neatly punctured that trial balloon by publishing a cartoon under the title "Dead Men Tell No Tales." It showed Gould and his henchmen dropping crocodile tears on Fisk's grave. Beneath it was the caption:

Jay Gould: "All the sins of Erie lie buried here."

Justice: "I am not quite so blind."

In no other way, perhaps, could the immigrant masses of New York City be made to see how a political machine could misuse the democratic process, oppress the people whose votes it cajoled or purchased, and rob them of their savings through alliances with corrupted bankers and piratical financiers. Few immigrants ever served their country better than Nast, and no American political cartoonist has equaled his talent for ridicule, fortunately endowed also with the instinct to choose the targets most worthy of his educated malice. There were no Pulitzer Prizes during Nast's long career. If there had been, he would have been the perennial winner. Instead he was rewarded, at last, by the capstone of so many nineteenth century literary careers, the appointment to a consulship by President Theodore Roosevelt.

If Nast contributed to the political education of the immigrant masses, another German-American concerned himself with increasing the cultural quotient of their second and third generations. Americans have always been fascinated by the painless and palliated acquisition of knowledge, from the era of the magic lantern to educational television. In the latter decades of the nineteenth century and the earlier ones of this century, there was no more satisfying way of soaking up a sugary concoction of culture and knowledge than attending the Chautauqua; for half a century the mammoth tents, the lecturers (including the indefatigable William Jennings Bryan) and all their paraphernalia blossomed on the summer landscape of America and brought a highly moral season of edification, a form of intellectual vaudeville, to millions of people. Chautauqua was the university of the Bible Belt.

It would be easy to sneer at Chautauqua as a manifestation of the mass cult mentality at its most pathetic — if most successful on its own terms — stage of development. But it probably did less harm than good at a time when most people's education began and ended in a one-room schoolhouse.

The prime mover behind the Chautauqua movement was Lewis Miller, born in Greentown, Ohio, in 1829, the son of a German immigrant. As a second-generation American himself, he understood the aspirations of that group to rise above the illiteracy of their fathers. He was only in his middle twenties when he invented the Buckeye Mower, a reaper, and became a partner in a farm equipment manufacturing company. Wealthy and successful at so early an age, he turned his attention to a life of good works. The idea of self-betterment on a massive scale aroused his inventive instincts. In the future, it seemed to him, the working day might well be reduced from ten or twelve hours, as it then was, to eight, and when that workingman's millennium arrived he must be prepared to spend his leisure in a worthwhile manner.

The Chautauqua movement was his inspiration. In 1873, he and the Methodist bishop John H. Vincent of Akron journeyed to the village of Chautauqua, in western New York, to locate a sort of part-time university and universal Sunday school. At the first assembly that summer the studies were confined to the Bible and the training of Sunday school teachers, but in the next few years its purposes were widened. The Chautauqua Literary and Scientific Circle was established, then an unaccredited college of liberal arts, a reading circle and a music school. The Summer School, with lectures, classes and outdoor recreation, was founded in 1878. Along with the summer classes, those who attended were expected to continue their part-time education by a course in home reading during the winter. Soon the Chautauqua idea engrossed much of the nation, particularly its middle sections, with roadshow units of the parent organization carrying the virus of instant self-improvement to the hinterlands. Eventually it attained the status of a communications medium, a combination of instruction and entertainment, lectures and music and general uplift, that reached into all but the stateliest homes; a precursor of educational television. The home of Chautauqua is still a going institution, attended by thousands each summer. For many years, though the despair of intellectual snobs, it provided a ray of enlightenment for millions in its peculiarly American, earnest and innocent way.

Even more pervasive in a different sense was the impact of the invention of an automatic typesetting machine, which revolutionized the newspaper industry and book publishing. For years, and at a cost of hundreds of thousands of dollars, it had shimmered dreamlike across the vision of Mark Twain, who might better have been occupied by his literary career. Twain backed a typesetting machine developed by James W. Paige, which supposedly was an improvement on an earlier device, the Pianotype, invented by Henry Bessmer, who also produced the iron converter on which the steel industry was based. The basement of the London *Times* was reportedly a storehouse of such machines which had been tried out and found wanting.

Into this rather crowded field came a German immigrant named Ottmar Mergenthaler. He was born in Württemberg, and migrated to the United States in 1872 at the age of eighteen. Apprenticed to a manufacturer of musical instruments in Baltimore, Mergenthaler began tinkering with the invention of a typesetting machine which wouldn't be so cumbersome (the earlier ones being the size of grand pianos) that they couldn't be accommodated in newspaper composing rooms, nor so susceptible to breakdowns, nor so costly to operate. The newspapers, with their circulations bounding upward, needed a technological breakthrough. Mergenthaler, though a late entry, worked night and day to perfect his machine.

After a decade of lonely perseverance, he interested Whitelaw Reid, the publisher of the New York *Tribune*, in his machine. Reid became a majority stockholder in the syndicate formed to back Mergenthaler, and allowed the young man to install his machine in the *Tribune's* composing room and continue his efforts to perfect it there. Compared to the machine backed by Twain, which had eighteen thousand different parts, Mergenthaler's was much more compact and simply constructed. It set a line of type from its own brass matrices, which were then redistributed automatically; the lead in which the lines were cast later was thrown back into the melting pot beneath the machine to be endlessly reused. The Linotype, as Publisher Reid christened Mergenthaler's machine, worked continuously and without frequent breakdowns.

Its great day was July 3, 1886. A battery of twelve Linotypes had been fabricated and installed in the *Tribune* composing room. That day they were used to set most of the issue. From then on Mergenthaler had a clear field, though for several years Twain and his partner clung to their hopes, claiming the Linotype was a racehorse trying to compete with a locomotive. The locomotive, or Paige typesetting machine, never did make its run down the tracks. Not the least of the Mergenthaler machine's contributions to mass culture was the fact that its success dissuaded Twain from his industrial ambitions and sent him back to the work at which he was superlative.[10]

With all their diligence in perfecting public education and wistfully edging toward cultural and intellectual status, the German-Americans were convinced that they were elected to make yet another contribution to American life. What use was a brilliant mind in a slack body? Heeding the Latin tag about a healthy mind in a healthy body, they introduced the gymnasium. Outdoor sports were an Anglo-Saxon development, indoor the German. Nothing was more soothing to the German psyche than the spectacle of large numbers of muscular youths, lathered in sweat, flying and flipping and flinging themselves around a gymnasium — preferably in unison. The result has been the gymnasium attached to every sizable secondary school in the land, an edifice which threatens to overshadow the other functions, and compulsory physical education, which has now been endured by five or six generations of youth not necessarily enthused about wrenching their muscles on parallel bars and trapeze rings. The *compulsory* aspect is truly the Teutonic touch.

All who recall the torments of the physical education period in their secondary schooling may curse the name of Friedrich Ludwig Jahn, not unexpectedly a Prussian.

Jahn was a student of Tacitus, but a patriot even more. He read the Latin historian's descriptions of Teutonic barbarians, so huge and muscular as they bounded out of the forest that even Caesar's legions quailed at the sight. Then he was bemused by the contrast between those ferocious ancestors and the defeated, sundered Germany of the post-Napoleonic years.

The way to restore the German nation and build up the physique of its men, he believed, was through violent exercise. Healthy minds in healthy bodies would turn to healthily patriotic thoughts. He built his first gymnasium in a village near Berlin and began preaching the gospel of his *Turnverein*, gymnastic exercises, and the Turner movement spread throughout Germany. Its toy monarchs and miniature despots were naturally alarmed by any movement not initiated by themselves. Jahn a patriot? More likely a revolutionary! Around 1820 he was arrested and charged with demagoguery, a breach of political manners in more sophisticated climes but a high crime, verging on treason, in the Germany of *Turnvater* Jahn's time. Eventually Jahn was released from the Prussian prison, but for twenty years — so dogged and faithful to their duty were the secret state police — he was shadowed wherever he went night and day. The surveillance was finally lifted, and Jahn was granted freedom of movement throughout Germany, when Frederick Wilhelm IV took the Prussian throne. Two years later, grasping what Jahn was striving for, the king issued an order through his cabinet that the Turnverein be given official encouragement and appointed a Herr Director of Prussian Gymnastics with headquarters in Berlin. That post was not given to Jahn, but his credo was responsible for turning modern Germany into a nation of part-time gymnasts.

A number of Jahn's disciples were among the educated refugees who subsequently migrated to America. The first gymnasium, modeled after Jahn's, was built in the United States at the Round Hill School, founded by two young Americans educated at German universities, Joseph Cogswell and George Bancroft, when its faculty was joined by Carl Beck and Carl Follen. Beck, the school's Latin teacher, supervised the construction of the gymnasium shortly after arriving in Northampton late in 1824, and Beck translated Father Jahn's *Deutsche Turnkunst* into English, upon which it became the gospel of American enthusiasts of physical education. Three years later the distinguished Francis Lieber, whose academic field was international law and social ethics, introduced gymnastic training to Boston and also established a swimming school there. New ideas did not easily penetrate through the layers of Boston tradition, but Lieber's program was enthusiastically taken up by Dr. J. C. Warren of the Harvard Medical School. Dr. Warren tried to obtain the services of Jahn himself as director of the Tremont Gymnasium, but the Prussian secret police couldn't bear to part with the *Turnvater* so the appointment was given to Lieber.

The *Turnverein* soon became a feature of the American cityscape, the center of its German neighborhoods. The first Turner hall in America was opened in New York City in 1850, the same year that Turner Society representatives from New York, Baltimore, Boston and elsewhere convened in Philadelphia, with all their organizational instincts aroused to the true Teutonic pitch, to found *Die Vereinigten Turnvereine Nordamerikas*. In addition to dedicating themselves to the muscle tone of American youth, the Turner Society representatives, by now heavily infiltrated by Forty-eighters who could recite Marx by the page, resolved that they would propagate "certain political ideas of a social-democratic nature." Soon they were coming out vigorously in support of the Free Soil movement in Kansas and in opposition to the Know-Nothings.

Within three years there were sixty *Turnvereins* established throughout the United States, along with a *Turnlehrerseminar*, an academy charged with producing more gymnastics teachers, and a *Turnzeitung* to carry on its propaganda. One of the early successes of all this energetic organizing and propagandizing was the introduction of gymnastics at the United States Naval Academy. Soon graduates of the *Turnlehrerseminar* were being dispatched to public and private schools throughout the United States. A little more alarming, perhaps, to fellow citizens who were neither German nor gymnastic, were the sounds of military drill which began issuing from the *Turnvereins*. Marching and musketry were hygenic exercises, too, weren't they? Non-German citizens of Cincinnati were understandably taken aback when whole legions of clumping Turners seemingly sprang out of the pavements, gorgeous in scarlet and blue uniforms, hussar's capes and guardee manners to match, and rejoicing in such militant titles as the Jackson Guards, the Lafayette Guards, the Jagers.

During the yahoo years of the Know-Nothings, the *Turnvereins* in some cities became citadels for German-Americans determined to defend themselves against rowdyism, Clashes between Turners and Know-Nothings occurred in Covington, Kentucky, where the mayor ordered the Turners to surrender their weapons but was overruled by a German-born judge, and in Baltimore. In the latter city the volunteer fire companies were largely manned by ruffians, thugs and gangsters who warred on foreigners when they weren't dashing to fires and robbing householders unwise enough to summon them. A rival fire company was formed by the Baltimore Turners. One of the city's more stirring spectacles was the Turner fire company and the "Liberties" racing each other to the scene of a fire, then engaging in hand-to-hand combat against a background of burning property. The Turner "self-defense" companies also turned out whenever any of their landsmen was set upon by Know-Nothings, rescued him, and then battled with any police who came to rescue the Know-Nothings.

Aside from such extramural activities, the American *Turnvereins* also sent teams of gymnasts to compete with the Germans and in 1880, at the Frankfort *Turnfest*, proudly returned with seven of the twenty-two prizes, although they had sent a team of only nine men. The *Turnvereins*, during the latter decades of the nineteenth century, also produced a crop of athletes who made names for themselves on the college football, track, baseball teams and rowing crews, particularly at Michigan, Cornell, Dartmouth, Yale, Pennsylvania and the Naval Academy. One of these was A. B. Lueder, a Cornell football star who later built all the bridges for the Uganda Railway in central Africa.

Until a few decades ago the *Turnvereins* were as ubiquitous in any German-American community as the *Bierstubes*. They have all but disappeared, along with that once notable German-American muscle tone.

PORTRAIT OF A PEDAGOGUE

German influences on the American educational system, particularly before World War I, comprised an awesome record of achievement. "Germany obsessed the American educator," as Sir Shane Leslie, an astute Irish observer, commented. "The democracy of letters seemed resident beyond the Rhine."[11] It should not be imagined, however, that all the German educators who came to the United States were men of massive intellect or overwhelming persuasiveness.

One of the notables who came to the United States with the intellectual rebels of '48 was Professor Friedrich Knapp, who established a boys' seminary in Baltimore. One of his more skeptical pupils in the late 1880's was Henry L. Mencken, who remembered the professor with more tolerance than admiration. Considering the ferocious reputation of the German schoolmaster, Professor Knapp was a "very mild and even amiable man," as Mencken recalled him in his memoir *Happy Days*.

Professor Knapp invariably wore the classical uniform of the German schoolmaster — "A long-tailed coat of black alpaca, a boiled shirt with somewhat fringey cuffs, and a white lawn necktie. The front of his coat was dusty with chalk, and his hands were so caked with it that he had to blow it off every time he took snuff. He was of small stature but large diameter, and wore close-clipped mutton-chop whiskers. . . ."

The quality of education, as Mencken looked back on it, had declined considerably at Knapp's seminary, and the institution was beginning to suffer from the competition of the public schools. Professor Knapp, fortunately for his peace of mind, lacked any talent for prophecy and "believed firmly, and often predicted, that the public schools would collapse soon or late under the weight of their own inherent and incurable infamy. They were fit, he argued freely, only for dealing with boys too stupid, too lazy, to sassy or too dirty to be admitted to academies such as his own, and it was their well-deserved destiny to be shut down eventually by the police, if not by actual public violence. As for sending girls to them, he simply could not imagine it; as well shame and degrade the poor little angels by cutting off their pigtails or putting them into pants."[12]

11. DOWN WHERE THE WURZBURGER FLOWED

The Germans, when they weren't stirring up various kinds of trouble, brought a generous measure of joviality to American life. To the dour, Calvinistic outlook of the Anglo-Saxons, and to the rather desperate frivolity of the Celts, they and the Poles and the Italians added a Middle European sensibility of how to enjoy life without inhibition. The Germans brought with them the tradition of *Fasching*, the hedonistic festival that preceded Lent; the *Sommernachtfests*, the bock beer celebrations just after Easter, and most impressively of all, the sentimentalized (though not as yet commercialized) observance of Christmas. It all went under the heading of *Gemütlichkeit*: the cozy, all-inclusive reveling in which everyone from toddlers to great-grandmothers participated, with beer and wurst for all, and a brass band oompahing in the background, spelled by the strumming of zithers and the homely melodies of the accordion. In their homes the Germans tended to keep to the family circle, but when the bungs were tapped out and the wine uncorked all nationalities were invited to join in the singing, dancing, drinking and feasting.

Before the Germans brought the Christmas tree and the Santa Claus tradition to America, historians have noted, the Christmas celebrations

288

were usually rowdy affairs attended by whiskey-drinking and fist-fighting. The Germans made it a family occasion, the climax of which was Christmas Eve rather than Christmas Day. Naturally it was celebrated in a thoroughgoing fashion, with much attention paid to the logistics and preparations begun long in advance for the blazing Yule log, the hard little *Pfeffernusse* (cookies baked like bullets), the decking and lighting of the tree, the hanging out of stockings. Thus, unconsciously, the jovial figure of Santa Claus was superimposed on the image of Christ's birth in the manger and much of its significance effaced.

Christmas preparations, as Herman Hagedorn, the eminent biographer of Theodore Roosevelt and others, has recalled from his boyhood, began with the preparations for the *Honigkuchen*, one of the many Christmas cookies required for the occasion. "Those golden-brown cookies were an essential part of the show. You couldn't imagine Christmas without them. Mother made them by the barrel and though she gave them away generously, we generally had some well into February . . . I don't know what went into the composition of the *Honigkuchen*, except that, parodoxically, honey was not among the ingredients and it was molasses which contributed the color. The dough was mixed and set aside for two weeks to ferment; *garen* was the word. It was another great day when Mother finally rolled out the dough, dusted it with flour and stamped it with little tin forms into diamonds and circles and stars. We youngsters had a share in that, and in the further business of plastering an almond in the center of each cookie. We might help bake the cookies, but . . . that was the last we saw of them until Christmas."

Mr. Hagedorn also recalled that a room called the *Weihnachstube*, the Christmas room, was set aside and sealed off from the children, not to be opened until Christmas Eve. "The suspense of that final hour before the giving of the gifts, the *Bescherung!*" Then, on a command from his father, they all marched upstairs to the Christmas room singing "Silent Night" and "O Tannenbaum."

Christmas had not yet become an orgy of department store competition and "most of the gifts would be useful, the sort of thing Mother would have had to buy for us in the course of the winter anyway, but, finding it there, under the blaze of lights, gave it an aura. And then there were always things that were not utilitarian, a sled, perhaps, and lead soldiers and stamps and books; and on every table, always a soup plate full of the *Honigkuchen* and another full of nuts and raisins and tough, jaw-cracking *Pfeffernusse* and *Aniseplatzchen*."[1]

Young as he was in those years before World War I, when the German-American was secure in his *gemütlich* world, Mr. Hagedorn admittedly reveled in the Germanic aspects of his boyhood. But he came to realize later that there was a flaw in that beautifully ordered world: the insistence on "uncritical respect for the judgments and opinions of elders. The first duty of a young man, Father told me, was to be *bescheiden* — modest — in the presence of his elders . . . Ridiculous as it may seem, I was actually in my thirties before I fully realized that a man with gray hair might conceivably know less of a given proposition than I, or be less dependable in judgment."[2]

Underneath all the surface jollity, and the cheerfulness of the beer gardens and summer night festivals, there was that anxious regard for authority, whether bestowed by seniority or social and economic position. The German-American knew his place and valued it. His greatest fear was that others wouldn't know theirs and disruption would result; order was his passion. In much of their writing and music Germans have demonstrated their awareness that things did not fall apart at the center, as Yeats wrote, but around the fringes; that the terrors of disorder lurk in the outer shadows waiting for men to forget their places in the scheme of things. *Lèsemajesté* was a crime not only against kings but the people themselves.

The somber awareness of how important it was to behave "correctly" — the word "correct" was used with the same hushed respect by nineteenth century Germans as by modern Russians — was forgotten only in one special circumstance. That arose when authority interposed itself between a German and his beer. Or whatever he chose to drink. Confronted by any form of prohibition on his drinking habits, he succumbed to the *furore teutonicus* which had so frightened the civilized world in past centuries.

In 1855, when the Know-Nothings and the prohibitionists were collaborating against the foreign-born, the authorities in Davenport,

Iowa, confiscated several barrels of beer with which the local Germans and Irish were planning to while away a Sunday afternoon. A riot erupted, and the Germans and Irish reclaimed their beer.[3]

Earlier that same yaar the "lager beer riots" broke out in Chicago. The city had just elected Dr. Levi D. Boone, a Know-Nothing, as mayor. Almost half the city was foreign-born but Mayor Boone immediately antagonized the Irish by decreeing that all policemen must be native Americans. He then set out to cure the Germans, 25 percent of the population, of their beer-drinking. Native bluenoses had been especially offended when the Germans established a beer garden, which they tactfully called a "tea garden," across from St. James's Episcopal Church. Parishioners leaving the morning services or returning to the Anglo-Saxon religious citadel for vespers were outraged by the blare of a brass band, the lusty malt-mellowed singing and the uproar of hundreds of Germans emptying and banging their steins on the oaken tables. Germans may well be the noisiest drinkers in the world — next to the Japanese.

Mayor Boone came to the rescue of his Anglo constituents by raising the fee for liquor licenses by 600 percent. This was designed to put most of the German saloonkeepers out of business. The mayor then decreed that the Sunday-closing ordinance be enforced, but made it clear that this applied only to those places which sold beer and not the establishments which sold only whiskey. That meant the Anglos could drink their whiskey on Sundays but the Germans were deprived of their beer on their only day of rest. The North Side, then so heavily Germanic that it was called the *Nord Seite*, was in an uproar.

The first Sunday the beer-drinking prohibition was enforced about two hundred German saloonkeepers were arrested for violating it. Their case was called for the morning of April 21, 1855. An hour before the hearing, the saloonkeepers and about three hundred of their best customers marched in a body to Courthouse Square to the music of fife and drum. They shook their fists at Squire Henry Rucker, the magistrate assigned to arraign them, then marched away to Randolph and Clark streets, in front of the Sherman House, where they took over the intersection and blocked traffic. The police arrived and drove them off. Across the river, several hours later, they re-formed and were reinforced by hundreds of other partisans, many of them Irish and most of them armed with shotguns, pistols, rifles, clubs, knives and shillelaghs.

At three o'clock that afternoon the demonstrators, about a thousand strong, moved down Clark to recross the river. Mayor Boone temporarily balked the armed mob by ordering the bridge opened. Meanwhile he had one hundred fifty special deputies sworn in and all the off-duty police collected downtown, having been informed that the mob intended to storm the City Hall and tear it apart brick by brick. An hour later, confident that he had assembled enough force to handle the demonstrators, Mayor Boone ordered the bridge reopened. The mob surged down Clark Street toward City Hall. Police and deputies met it in a massed formation. One of the rioters fired a shotgun and blew the arm off a policeman, and firing began on both sides. One rioter gave up his life for the lager-beer cause, and a number of others were wounded. Again the mob was dispersed. That evening the city was tense with rumors of civil insurrection. The army hauled up field guns to cover the approaches to the City Hall. There were only scattered outbreaks of violence that night, however, and the beer riots were over.[4]

Mayor Boone, sensibly enough, yielded to second thoughts about the evil of beer-drinking, Sundays or any other time, and the North Side quieted down. On many other occasions, however, the German-Americans testified to their devotion to Gambrinus, the legendary inventor of beer. In 1867 they even cooperated politically with the Irish to vote down a law that would have closed the saloons on Sunday in New York City.

From the beer gardens of Yorkville to those on the outskirts of San Francisco, the Germans were kept cheerful, orderly and amicable so long as the Wurzburger, the Pilsner, the Dortmunder, the Löwenbräu and all their American tributaries were kept flowing.

LOYAL SUBJECTS OF KING GAMBRINUS

There are no statistics available for the amount of beer consumed in the United States up to the time the Volstead Act dried up that mighty foaming torrent, but they would probably be astounding. German-Americans, in particular, seemed to regulate their lives by the ebb and flow of the beer seasons. Many came from South Germany, where beer was as indigenous as mother's milk. Those from the wine-growing provinces of the Rhineland naturally favored Moselle and other wines, while Prussians and others from North Germany clung to the more potent schnapps, a quarrelsome brother to whiskey.

The lamentably brief season during which bock beer, that "dark and ripened beverage" which usually flowed from the breweries just after Easter, was available gladdened millions of hearts.

"We know that while bock beer lasted the *Eltern* [elders] would be gayer, kinder," as Lucille Kohler remembered from her childhood in St. Louis. "We knew that while bock beer lasted pretzels would be free at all beer saloon counters, and patrons, moved to song, would grow hoarse in *Sangerfests*. We knew that while bock beer lasted, there would be many who would marry, some even for a second time; and second weddings were twice as much fun. We knew that with bock beer and pinochle the grown-ups would let the evenings stretch and give us our fill of games and peanuts."

In the German sections of St. Louis, towheaded children raced for the nearest beer saloons Easter Sunday morning for the first of the bock, which "hailed the Risen Lord and the end of the Lenten season." Each child carried a bucket and a chip, which cost four cents. At Hermann Klein's the proprietor was so exhilarated by the bock season that he would order his pet rooster, named Hindenburg, to march on command for the children "just like I used to march in the guard back in Baden." The German beer saloon was as respectable a place, as family-oriented, as the corner grocery.

During the several weeks during which the bock flowed, as Lucille Koller recalls, a carnival atmosphere prevailed for children as well as adults. "From after supper until dark we might follow a Little German Band from beer saloon to beer saloon in our neighborhood, listen to the singing, and reap pretzels and soda water . . . we attended charivaris, pinochle and *klatsch* fests, a concert at Liederkranz Hall, and never did we see our beds before nine, even ten, o'clock."

It was a sad day when the bungstarter tapped the last barrel of bock, but at Hermann Klein's saloon the end of season was properly and gratefully observed. "The first twelve steins" of the last barrel "he gave away . . . Then he put on a steaming lunch that was the end of two days' cooking for Frau Klein. He hired the Little German Band for all afternoon and all evening and himself led the singing of all the slattern verses of 'Ja, Das Ist Ein Schnitzelbank.' "[5]

Cincinnati and Milwaukee were the other two leading centers of German-Americanism and equally governed by the *gemütlich* spirit.

In Cincinnati, so Germanized that all the German states, including the Free City of Lübeck, had consuls stationed there, the Teutonic heartland was the section across a canal called the Rhine, a jumble of short narrow streets in the north part of the Basin. In the so-called "Over the Rhine" section lived most of the city's forty-nine thousand (in 1870) German-Americans, whom the German-Jewish mayor, A. Julius Freiburg, characterized as "frugal, honest and truthful." The front steps of each of the brick row houses were whitewashed every Saturday, there were potted plants in the windows and tiny garden plots in the rear. The clock towers of its red-brick or stone churches resounded with Bach chorales. With Teutonic bluntness St. Peter's Roman Catholic Church alluded to the one great sin of its patron; its spire was crowned by a gilded rooster, symbolizing the cock which crowed thrice when Peter denied his Lord. A half-dozen German language newspapers kept the "Over the Rhine" residents informed of daily events. Their parochial slant was indicated by the style in which they reported the news. "A German was badly beaten by two soldiers on 7th Street," they would report in doleful tones, but when it came to something discreditable the style would change: "A *foreigner* was robbed of $17 last night by a person whom he had met in a house of ill fame." (Italics supplied by the present writer.) What little dissension arose in that tidy enclave usually was traceable to the hard feelings between South and North Germans. When the Hungarian patriot Kossuth came to Cincinnati, he had to address separate meetings of the two geographic factions. Cincinnatians of German descent were particularly agile in finding reasons to celebrate. May Day, Whitsuntide

Down where the Wurzburger flowed — on the corner

Honus Wagner, the brick wall at shortstop

and the Fourth of July were proclaimed *Volkfests* in addition to other holidays and feast days, attended by lashings of Rhine wine and frothings of lager and by the singing of the Männerchor, the Young Männerchor, the Dresden Gesang, the Sangerbund and the Harmonic Society. On such occasions Mecklenburg's Gardens and Grammer's Café were crowded to capacity.[6]

In all the German theaters and concert halls, beer and wine were served during the performances. The most respected men in the German community, naturally, were the brewers. During the panic of '57, many Germans drew their savings out of the banks and deposited them in the safes of the breweries, which they regarded as so many impregnable fortresses (which, indeed, they architecturally resembled).

During those worrisome days, one German withdrew his two hundred dollars in savings and gave it to a brewer for safekeeping. Shortly after midnight the depositor woke up and began fretting over whether the brewer was as honest as everyone said he was. He worried for hours, then shortly before dawn went over to the brewer's magnificent town house and banged on the door until the brewer came down in his nightshirt. On second thought, the man said, he'd like to have his two hundred dollars back. The brewer went to the safe in his library, got out two hundred dollars of his own money and hurled it at his caller, shouting, "Raus! Put your Gottverdammt gelt in der bank und neffer ask me again!"

The tranquillity of the "Over the Rhine" district was seldom disturbed, but there were occasional ripples on its placid surface. The various singing societies quarreled over which was superior and occasionally came to blows. Their only truce was declared in 1870 when the huge Middle Western *Sangerfest* was held, with twelve thousand inside the auditorium built for the purpose and two thousand outside listening to the lieder singing. There was considerable agitation when the Women's Christian Temperance Union launched a membership drive in 1874 and invaded the "Over the Rhine" saloons with its preachments until German saloonkeepers were forced to post signs reading "No Crusaders Allowed."

The section was united in support of the bishop of Cincinnati, a fellow German-American, when Clara Longworth, the member of a prominent Cincinnati family, asked him for a priest to perform her marriage ceremony. Miss Longworth, possibly unaware of how the Germans felt about their old-country neighbors, was about to marry a French nobleman, the Count de Chambrun. The bishop refused on the grounds that he didn't approve of "mixed marriages," and Miss Longworth had to find a priest elsewhere.[7]

In Milwaukee, too, there was a mellow atmosphere compounded of beer, wine, music and the smell of thick German sausages. On winter Sundays the proper culture-minded German turned out for the weekly concerts of Christian Bach's West Side Turnerhalle. "It is not proper to miss it," as Ernest L. Meyer, the son of a German-language newspaper editor, later reflected. "Besides it costs only fifteen cents on a season ticket, and the music fits in with the slumbrous Sabbath feeling that follows a dinner of *Knodel* and *Sauerbraten*. It is that kind of music, soothing and sensible . . . Also, the setting is meant for relaxation. There are tables and chairs on the floor, and when we come in the hall is already misty with cigar smoke that drifts in layers in the shafts of light from the high windows. A door off to one end leads into the long barroom, and from it bustle waiters laden with steins, while from a kitchen in the rear waitresses bring trays of coffee and cakes for the women and children.

"The air is comforting with the fragrance of hops, coffee and tobacco. Combined with the music of Suppe and Strauss it induces a benign expansiveness in which one feels like taking the world to one's bosom, even including Old Petrus Grimm, who sits alone at a table with his dour eyes fastened on his beer mug. Petrus is the neighborhood bear, and everybody blames his bitterness on a blighted troth in the Old Country, though it is more likely due to liver and gout."[8]

The children were particularly fascinated by the antics of Direktor Bach (no relation to *the* Bach) on the podium. He was a short, elderly man who worked himself into a frenzy at the more spirited passages of the music he was conducting. "At such times his wig turns half way around on his head and protrudes at such a curious angle that few can blame the children for tittering, even though such levity is sternly rebuked. The musicians have learned not to smile at these crises, for Herr Bach has a peppery temper. He has been teaching them music since they were in knee-pants, and his son, Hugo, a splendid cellist, will carry on after him, and so on and on, world without end." After the concert everyone adjourned to Mamma Memmler's *Gasthaus* on Sherman Street, where the walls were frescoed with fat monks, troubadours and mottoes urging the virtues of the conspicuous consumption of beer, wine and food, and also the framed original copy of a poem composed on the spot when Eugene Field, the poet, wandering newspaperman and drinker nonpareil, tarried there while temporarily employed on a Milwaukee paper. Artists, musicians and journalists each had their separate tables at Mamma Memmler's.

In the summer the Sunday and holiday festivities took place in Schlitz Park, "a place of pavilions and picnics, of long open-air tables and benches where lusty Männerchor roared drinking songs between rounds of steins, and children frolicked on the carousel. The merry-go-round was operated by an ancient brewery-wagon horse, once a tremendous Percheron in glittering harness, but now old and thin . . . but needing no ship or spur to keep him jogging amiably in the round-and-round routine that was the life of horses and of men."

Young Ernie Meyer, like most boys of German descent, was required to spend Monday evenings practicing with the Männerchor. His group of forty voices convened in a meeting hall over a saloon in which the older men lubricated their throats. Young Ernie's voice "croaked," but he enjoyed attending the rehearsals because of the diverse characters on view. "Most of the bassos are enormously stout, though the fellow with the deepest voice is Weizenpfeffer, who is a skinny string bean with a long neck and great, bobbing Adam's apple and who can boom like a bull fiddle. Everybody envies Weizenpfeffer for there is a tradition that bull-fiddle voice indicates great virility, and the first tenors always look a bit sheepish even though they're strapping fellows enough."

The leader of the Männerchor, a Herr Schildkrot, was "a choleric man with a bristling black dyed moustache and startling bright black eyes that bore right through one when he is enraged . . . in his home he is a martinet. He works himself and his family furiously. He directs three singing societies, including our Orpheus, for very little pay. Our dues are twenty-five cents a week for each member, part of which goes to pay hall rent, part for musical scores and the director's pay, and the rest is put into a Bummelkasse to pay for our annual family beer-picnic. Besides the three singing societies, Herr Schildkrot directs two orchestras and a string quartet, and he's always dashing from one to the other of his many appointments with a worn briefcase spilling with music scores."

Herr Schildkrot was outraged when his daughter Katie ran away with the Hungarian who led the band at one of the palm gardens downtown, and swore she would never darken his door again. A year later Katie returned to Milwaukee with a baby boy. "Frau Schildkrot," Ernie Meyer recounted, "gave her money and sent her to a friend, fearing that her husband might do her harm, but she kept the baby in the house. It had a funny hawk nose and black hair and eyes just like the Herr Direktor, and maybe that is why Schildkrot's heart melted. He forgave his daughter in a noble speech, and she returned home . . . They lived together quite happily, these four . . . the Herr Direcktor was late at a good many rehearsals because he lingered too long in the nursery singing old cradle songs to the baby. And when he did get to rehearsals he was no longer so peppery as he had been in past years. So we were all glad for Katie's baby, even though its gypsy father was a *Taugenichts* and when last heard from had run through the fortune of a Cincinnati widow . . ."[9]

Every Wednesday night from October to May the Milwaukee Germans trooped to the Pabst Theater. It was the night on which German-language dramas were presented, some of them trilogies fifteen acts long and taking three nights to play. No matter, the red plush seats of the Pabst were comfortable and Germans were willing to endure much in the name of culture. The *König Heinrich* trilogy especially stirred the depths of the German psyche; it was the story of the kingly pilgrimage to Canossa, the three days in which the red-bearded king hungered in the cold before he was admitted to beg the Pope's forgiveness. Catholic and Lutheran alike wept at the final reconciliation.

Germans were proud of the Pabst and its avant-garde tradition.

"What has the English stage to offer?" Meyer asked himself as a boy theatergoer. "They sometimes lag far behind. Don't you know, for example, that Shaw's famed play *Pygmalion* was produced for the first time in America, not in English, but in German, and in this same red-plushy old Pabst Theater named for a brewer? Yes, that is so, even though it is difficult, to say the least, to create a German heroine speaking London cockney."[10]

It was a good, hearty, close-textured life in the German-American enclaves of the American cities. Its German-ness would endure forever, the bearded sages agreed over foaming seidels, stoutly ignoring such premonitory evidence as signs in store windows reading "English Spoken Here," the agitation for prohibition and women's suffrage, and the growing possibility that England and Germany would go to war and force a conflict of loyalties among the Germans in an America that might not escape involvement.

CULTURAL IMAGES

To the non-German part of America the Germanic element, its character and customs were hilariously defined by the ubiquitous "Dutch" comedians in vaudeville, burlesque and musical comedy. The "Dutch" caricatures represented the German-American as an ineffably thickheaded fellow, full of slapstick bellicosity, who would never manage to speak English correctly. Sensitive as they were about their cultural background, the Germans apparently did not resent the caricature; perhaps it was too broad to be taken seriously, and in any case they could always laugh at the vaudeville conception of the Irish as equally stupid, intemperate and bellicose bog-trotters or the Jews as cunning and greedy knaves. The outrageous racial slurs may, in fact, have been cathartic. If you can laugh at a man, you can't hate him too much.

By far the most successful practitioners of taking off the Germans were (Joe) Weber and (Lew) Fields, who were born on New York's Lower East Side and prospered so greatly as "Dutch" comics that they later incorporated themselves as the Weberfields Co. "There had been German-dialect comedians before but no such interchange of twisted, strangled speech as this," their biographer wrote.

They would back on stage from the opposite wings, then greet each other with feigned surprise.

WEBER: "I am delightfulness to meet you."
FIELDS: "Der disgust is all mine."
Almost immediately they would fall into a raging argument.
WEBER: "Don't poosh me, Myer."
FIELDS: "Didn't I telling you, watch your etiquette?"
WEBER: "Who says I et a cat?"

This was only the polite prelude to their act. Soon they were engaged in a knockabout brawl. Fields, as the "bully," would set upon his short stout partner, choking him, kicking him in his padded stomach, swatting him with a pool cue. Weber would end the bullying by hooking his cane around Fields's neck and hauling him offstage sputtering with rage.[11]

By the turn of the century they had replaced Harrigan and Hart, the Irish comedians, as the biggest names in the comedy field. They invented the famous who-was-that-lady? gag and got off one of the choicer insults in the best tradition of American comedic violence: "Your family got t'rown out on the street so many times that your mother had to buy curtains vot matched the sidevalk."

Anyone so thin-skinned as to be offended by the preposterous Weber and Fields representation of the German-American could turn to contemplating the more visually delightful image of Fritzi Scheff. It was true that the dainty but sweetly curved Fritzi, with her grand-opera voice and what one theatrical historian has called her "operetta spirit," usually played French girls on the musical stage, but she was the heroine of the German-American community — and not only the men. For German women she helped destroy the cliché that they were all plump little homebodies with a scrubbing brush in their hands.

Better yet, from the German-Americans' viewpoint, she rose to fame in collaboration with a man somewhat mistakenly claimed for one of their own — Victor Herbert, the manufacturer of musical sugarplums in the Viennese tradition. That Victor Herbert was raised and educated in

Germany, that he wore a Kaiser Wilhelm-type moustache upswept at the ends, that he spoke with a German accent and had a name that sounded as though it might be German, that he consumed Pilsner and sauerbraten in quantities that would win the respect of any trencherman from Hamburg . . . all these convinced most German-Americans that he was one of them. They disregarded contrary evidence when Herbert became a prominent member of the Friendly Sons of St. Patrick. By blood, Victor Herbert was 100 percent Irish, though he often admitted that he must be part-German by absorption.

A short, cheerful, beefy and beery little man, he composed the music that America hummed for at least two generations. Sigmund Spaeth has called him the "Irish Johann Strauss." There were many German-American composers of great and serious merit, but none of them won so much popular acclaim as the Dubliner who looked, talked and wrote music like a German.

Victor Herbert was born in Dublin in 1859, the grandson of the Irish novelist and poet Samuel Lover. His father died shortly after he was born, and his mother married Dr. Wilhelm Schmid of Stuttgart. At the age of seven he was taken to Stuttgart and educated there as a musical prodigy. His half-brother, Willy Faber as he was known professionally, became famous as an actor in the German theater.

In his mid-twenties, while performing as first cellist at the Stuttgart Opera, Herbert fell in love with the company's prima donna soprano Therese Foerster. The romance developed across the footlights from orchestra pit to stage. In 1886, when he and Fraulein Foerster became engaged, the celebrated German-American conductor Walter Damrosch was touring Germany and Austria on a hunt for new singers for the Metropolitan Opera. Damrosch offered Fraulein Foerster a contract, but she refused to sign it unless Victor Herbert was brought along as the Met's leading cellist.

With the American contract in hand, Herbert and the younger singer immediately got married and sailed for America. Herbert may have seemed an appendage to her career when they migrated, but circumstances reversed their positions, happily enough for both.

Therese Forester made her American debut in *Aïda*. It was not an overwhelming success, and she soon retired in favor of being, simply and solely, Mrs. Victor Herbert. Her confidence in her husband's talent was slowly but surely justified. He became conductor of the Pittsburgh Symphony Orchestra and on the side began turning out operettas in the romantic, lighthearted German-Austrian vein. His first several efforts were produced, but not with any great success, on the Broadway stage. He was in his early forties before inspiration swept him along to fame and fortune.

The inspiration was provided, in part, by the young soprano who appeared with the Pittsburgh Symphony in a concert one night in 1902. She was Fritzi Scheff, then twenty-two years old but already a veteran with sixteen roles at the Metropolitan Opera behind her. Herbert was struck by her brunette beauty, her lively dark eyes, her grace and stage presence. The liveliness and sexual magnetism of the young soprano was wasted, to a large extent, in grand opera.

The next year his *Babes in Toyland* was a considerable success but he was already working on a vehicle for the talents of Fritzi Scheff. It was called *Mlle Modiste* and included a waltz titled "Kiss Me Again." Produced in 1905, it was a smashing success. Fritzi, twirling around in her daringly backless gowns, sang "Kiss Me" with such fervor that overnight she elbowed aside the blond and buxom figure of Lillian Russell, twenty years her senior, and "every stylish woman in America dreamed of changing places with her." Fritzi Scheff became the dream girl of pre-World War I America. At the end of a long and creditable career, propelled in large part by the parts and songs Victor Herbert and his collaborators created for her, she sang "Kiss Me Again" when a bronze plaque was dedicated in 1951 over the table at Lüchow's restaurant where Victor Herbert spent so many happy hours stuffing himself with German food and beer.

One thing Herbert had acquired "by absorption" in Germany was an almost feverish industriousness. "He always seemed to work at high pressure when there was no need for it," Harry B. Smith, who wrote the lyrics for a number of his show tunes, recalled. "He would dash across a room merely to get another piece of paper, across a street simply to get on the other side."[12]

To the musicologist Sigmund Spaeth, he was "probably the best trained musician ever to write for the Broadway stage. His technique of composition was thorough and masterly, with a complete command of orchestration, harmony, and counterpoint, in addition to an apparently inexhaustible inventiveness."[13]

Herbert himself was as modest about his talents as he was open-handed with the money that flooded into his bank account. "Don't kid me," he would scoff when complimented on his musicianship. "I'm a good tunesmith. Six months after I'm dead no one will remember my name."

In creating and performing, there were many lustrous German names in American music, of interest chiefly to musical scholars and historians, but in popular impact few could equal those of Oscar Hammerstein (the elder), who revolutionized opera much against its stodgy inclinations, and Bix Beiderbecke, one of the heroes of the Jazz Age.

Oscar Hammerstein was a natural-born impresario, just as his son Oscar Hammerstein II was a born lyricist, with the true entrepreneur's two leading characteristics: flamboyance and daring. The career which, as Gilbert Seldes has written, "revolutionized the production of grand opera in America," began in Berlin, where Hammerstein was born in 1847. All his extravagance went into the production of his plays and operas; no fur-collared coats and diamonds glittering on every finger for him. Most of his years in New York he and his wife lived in the one-room garret over the Victoria Theater, which contained only a bed, table, several chairs and his personal cigar-rolling machine. The magnificence to which his fortune entitled him, before it evaporated, was placed on view only behind the footlights or diverted to the pockets of his star performers (he once offered the unemployed Sultan of Sulu twenty-five hundred dollars a week to appear in vaudeville for him).[14]

Hammerstein ran away from home at the age of seventeen when his stern Berliner father beat him for going skating instead of practicing on his violin. He sold the violin, in fact, to pay for his passage to England, then worked his way on a ship to New York. His first job as a teen-aged immigrant was as a cigar maker. Soon he invented a process for stripping

Fritzi Scheff, envy of the
housewives

Madame Schumann-Heink, the all-American
mother

tobacco by machine and sold the patent to the American Tobacco Company.

With the tobacco company's money he bought a part interest in two German-language theaters in New York, the Germania and the Thalia, and in 1870, at the age of twenty-three, he acquired ownership of the Stadt Theater. He also built the Harlem Opera House and a dozen apartment houses in Harlem, then a white residential neighborhood. These properties included an apartment block on Seventh Avenue between 136th and 137th streets, which he named for Kaiser Wilhelm. He also raised a public outcry when he installed a statue of the Kaiser on the cornice of the block-long apartment house.

Hammerstein plunged into the production of vaudeville shows and musical comedies, undeterred by such mishaps as losing three thousand dollars a day while presenting Anna Held in *La Poupée*.

In 1906 he built the Manhattan Opera House and declared war on the Metropolitan Opera, which had long been held in thrall by German and Italian opera. Hammerstein thought the American opera should be livelier and introduced a more modern, chiefly French, repertory. He was also unafraid of bringing an element of showmanship to the stuffy confines of the opera stage. The Met began to suffer when he presented *Thaïs, Louise, Herodiade, Elektra, Pelléas et Mélisande* in the more vibrant and realistic French style of acting and singing.

Nor could he see any reason why all female opera stars should be dreadnoughts in size and temperament. Except for Tetrazzini, he never engaged any singer in the florid Italian tradition. He made a star out of the red-haired, trimly beautiful Mary Garden and did not hesitate to brawl publicly with her when success made her difficult to handle.

Miss Garden informed the press that Hammerstein had wounded her deeply by calling her a loafer.

Asked for his comment, Hammerstein simply replied, "Mary Garden, the distinguished songbird, *is* a loafer."

But he made her famous as *Salome*, shedding her veils with an enthusiasm and a shamelessness that shocked the Edwardian audiences and brought them back for more shamefulness night after night. The Met was so shaken by his venturesome competition that it was forced to buy off Hammerstein under a contract which paid him $1,500,000 in return for agreement not to produce grand opera in New York for the next ten years.

Next he decided to challenge the equally stately and tradition-bound Covent Garden in London. He built his own opera house and opened it with a gorgeous production of *Quo Vadis*, during which Rome was burned on stage, but he made no dent in the English operagoers' affection for the Covent Garden. "I'd rather be dead in New York," he snarled on leaving England, "than alive in London."

He got his wish only five years later. Returning to New York in 1914 and breaking his agreement with the Metropolitan Opera, which he charged with violation of the antitrust laws and which bedeviled him with lawsuits to the end of his life, he opened the Lexington Opera House. Evidently he had lost his touch. His first bill included one act of *Aïda* and one act of *Faust*, with a pioneer war film, *The Last Volunteer*, presented in between — and it was a disastrous flop. He died in 1919 in his garret room on top of the Victoria Theater, but his sons would carry the name to the musical stage well into the century.

A few old records are all that survive of the legendary jazz musician, Leon Bismarck Beiderbecke, "Bix" of the golden horn and prototype of the "cool" hero of a later era. He fulfilled all the requirements: lived fast and died young, blew his heart out on a cornet, played only what he loved and was satisfied with the obscurity of smoky nightclubs and Chicago speakeasies. He didn't become a celebrity in fact until after he died in 1931, and then his posthumous fame was based on a few records in a few passages in which the purity of his notes shone through.

Bix was born in Davenport, Iowa, in a family that would rather have seen him join a Salvation Army band than make himself famous as a jazz musician. Easten Spurrier, a boyhood friend, remembered that Beiderbecke learned to play the cornet given him by an uncle by putting records on a Victrola and playing along with them.

Bix was still going to school in Chicago, where his family had moved, when the New Orleans beat was imported by Louis Armstrong. He used to skip school to play his cornet in speakeasies. The first jam session, according to the jazz historian Mezz Mezzerow, was played in a Chicago speakeasy called the Three Deuces on North State Street in the late Twenties. The leading participants, Mezzerow says, were Bix Beiderbecke and Bing Crosby, both of whom were appearing on the bill at the nearby Chicago Theater.

"The best of Bix isn't on records," his boyhood friend Easten Spurrier cautions. "You want to remember the bands of that era weren't all recorded . . . There are no records of the sessions when we had Bix playing for us by the hour . . . He never, you must realize, had a chance to play anything he wanted to on any of the records we have of his. He was too individual . . . you couldn't get anybody else to come and hear him when he was alive. Nobody cared . . . He had the truth. He never played anything except what he thought."[15]

His legend, in any event, was memorialized by one of the better novels about the jazz world, Dorothy Baker's *Young Man with a Horn*.

In literature, both popular and of the more substantial kind, German-Americans lagged noticeably behind the other minorities. No great German writer arose from the millions who came to the United States in the nineteenth century, and one of the few popular novelists of German blood was the Pennsylvania-born Owen Wister, author of the durable quasi-classic *The Virginian*, which was much admired by President Theodore Roosevelt and survives today, in a rather anemic and effete fashion, on the television screen.

The sole German-American who distinguished himself in modern American literary history was Theodore Dreiser. English professors approve of him, but it is hard to imagine anyone reading him for pleasure. The man who discovered him and approved of his anti-Puritan onslaughts on a literary world dominated by the standards of William Dean Howells was H. L. Mencken. And even the articulate Mencken confessed that he was "disconcertingly hard to explain." The reason that he has been sanctified by literary historians and examined in detail by literary biographers is that he formed the spearhead of the realistic novelists. He grew up on a southern Indiana farm in a family which included his playboy brother Paul Dresser, the songwriter who produced "On the Banks of the Wabash" and other sentimental successes. Early rebellion against his family's Catholicism, drifting through the newspaper business, editing magazines in New York, much solitary and morose reflection on the inequities of American life finally led to the production of such massive Zolaesque works as *Sister Carrie, Jennie Gerhardt, The Titan, The Financier* and *An American Tragedy.*

Mencken called him the Hindenburg of the American novel, explaining that "in his manner, as opposed to his matter, he is more the Teuton, for he shows all of the racial patience and pertinacity and all of the racial lack of humor. Writing a novel is as solemn a business to him as trimming a beard is to a German barber. He blasts his way through his interminable stories by something not unlike main strength; his writing, one feels, often takes on the character of an actual siege operation, with tunnelings, drum fire, assaults in close order and hand-to-hand fighting."[16]

The traces of that influence can be found in few other American writers. Certainly not his fellow German-Americans. John Steinbeck, part German, may have similarly probed the lower depths, but in a far more lively and impressionistic style. German names are hard to find among contemporary German-American writers and several of the more promising — Kurt Vonnegut, Jr., and Thomas Berger among them — have veered far away from Dreiserian social realism.

AN APTITUDE FOR BASEBALL

One way for a minority to win acceptance in the American scheme, among its generally sports-mad fellow citizens, is on the athletic field, baseball diamond or in the boxing ring. The athletic prowess of a few raises the self-esteem of a whole race or nationality. Thus the Irish, and later the Italians, were tremendously uplifted by the example of the prizefight champions they produced. Germans, however, showed little aptitude for fighting with their fists padded. But baseball, the "American pastime" as it once was, with its geometric order, its requirement of technical skills as well as brute strength and quick reflexes, its disciplined pattern, appealed to something in the German psyche. Perhaps there was something soothing about contemplating its orderliness. A ball park has a *gemütlich* atmosphere, with none of the bloodthirst and venality of the fight arena.

Some of the greatest stars in baseball history were of German descent — Babe Ruth, Lou Gehrig, Honus Wagner, Rube Waddell, Frank Frisch — not to mention the German-Irish Casey Stengel with his Teutonic syntax and Celtic garrulity. An all-star German-American team composed of the following would be hard to beat: Lou Gehrig, first base; Frank Frisch, second base; Honus Wagner, shortstop; Heinie Groh, third base; Heinie Manush, left field; Bob Meusel, center field; Babe Ruth, right field; Ray Schalk, catcher; and Rube Waddell, pitcher.

The impact of Babe Ruth, born George Herman Erhardt in Baltimore, on the game is all but incalculable. He was, as Paul Gallico, then a sportswriter, remarked, "purely an American phenomenon . . . an American Porthos . . . a Golem-like monster . . . the greatest single attraction in the entire world of sports . . . Ruth's nickname, 'Babe,' is so much a part of our national consciousness that the strange message spelled out in letters six inches high across the top of any afternoon newspaper, 'Babe Conks No. 36' or 'Bam Busts Two,' is not, as an English or French crypotologist might imagine, a code for 'Come home, all is forgiven,' but a very simple presentation of the news that Ruth hit his 36th home run, and that he has made two homers in one game."[17]

When Babe Ruth fell violently ill from eating a dozen hot dogs and drinking an equal number of bottles of soda pop, it was a national disaster. He "hung between life and death for many days — on Page One. Bulletins were issued from the sickroom. Little boys brought nosegays, or congregated outside the high walls of the hospital, and looked up at the window of the room wherein lay the stricken hero. The presses lay in wait with pages of obituaries, and editorials announced the impending catastrophe as a national calamity . . . He recovered, he convalesced, and the nation sent a great sigh of honest relief." The newspaper files from those trying days, with banner lines reporting every word leaking from the Babe's sickroom, testify that Mr. Gallico was not merely expressing himself in the lawful hyperbole of the sportswriter.

For Babe Ruth, with his sixty home runs in one season and his status as a national idol on a par with Charles Lindbergh and Sergeant

York, by himself made baseball a corporate endeavor, an industry, out of what once had been a carefree pastime. An orphan and a reform-school graduate, boyishly irresponsible, the Babe was the last man in the world to have brought about the big-business evolution in baseball as a matter of calculation.

Until he came along, the game was dominated by a casual, prankish atmosphere suitable to an endeavor employing grown men in short pants to bend all their efforts toward striking a small leather-covered ball with a length of wood.

The greatest player in the game until Ruth came along was John Peter (Honus) Wagner, a squat, bowlegged Pennsylvania German, whom a scout discovered heaving chunks of coal around a railroad yard at Carnegie, Pennsylvania, and whom he described thus: "He walks like a crab, plays like an octopus and hits like the devil." His lifetime batting average was .344, two points higher than Ruth's, and for seventeen consecutive years as shortstop for the Pittsburgh Pirates he batted over .300. He stills holds several all-time batting records.

"Honus could play any position except pitcher and be easily the best in the league at it," Rube Marquard, the great New York Giants pitcher, recently recalled. "He was a wonderful fielder, you know, terrific arm, very quick, all over the place grabbing sure hits . . . You'd never think it to look at to look at him, of course. He looked so awkward, bowlegged, barrel-chested, about 200 pounds. And yet he could run like a scared rabbit. He had enormous hands and when he scooped up the ball at shortstop, he'd grab half the infield with it . . . Talk about speed. That bowlegged guy stole over 700 bases in the 21 years he played in the big leagues. A good team man, too, and the sweetest disposition in the world. The greatest ballplayer who ever lived, in my book."[18]

Aside from great technicians like Wagner and box-office attractions like Ruth, the German-American contingent in baseball also produced some of its wildest eccentrics.

Rube Waddell, a masterful pitcher when he felt like working, made a habit of disappearing on epic beer benders or simply to go fishing. There was always great suspense over whether Waddell would appear on a given day, and his appearance in a ball park was often highly dramatic. As Sam Crawford, the Detroit Tigers celebrated power hitter, recalled, Waddell's appearance would be preceded by a commotion in the grandstand and shouts of "Here comes Rube!" Waddell would come racing through the stands and then "he'd jump down onto the field, cut across the infield to the clubhouse, taking off his shirt as he went. In about three minutes — he never wore any underwear — he'd run back out on the field in uniform all ready to pitch . . ."

Waddell's battery-mate was an equally frolicsome catcher named Ossie Schreck (originally Schreckengost). They were also roommates and Schreck once had their manager, Connie Mack, insert a clause in Waddell's contract forbidding him to eat animal crackers in bed.

Probably the drollest fellow in organized baseball was Herman "Germany" Schaeffer, who enlivened the Detroit Tigers for a number of years after the turn of the century as a particularly frolicsome second baseman, and various saloons around the circuit of American League cities, along with his teammate and playfellow Charley O'Leary (with whom he partnered in a comedy act in burlesque off season).

Germany Schaefer simply refused to take baseball seriously. Once during the 1906 season he came to bat as a pinchhitter. Just as he was about to step into the batter's box, he paused, then stepped back, took off his cap and addressed the crowd:

"Ladies and gentlemen, you are now looking at Germany Schaefer, better known as Herman the Great, acknowledged by one and all to be the greatest pinch hitter in the world. I am now going to hit the ball into the left-field bleachers."

A chorus of jeers arose from the stands, but on the second pitch Schaefer hit a home run into the left-field bleachers.

He also distinguished himself by becoming the only man in baseball history to steal first base, an event which shocked baseball purists and caused a hurried rewriting of the rules of the game. This instance of his endless efforts to enliven the game occurred during a game between his Detroit Tigers and the Cleveland Indians in the 1908 season. Sam Crawford came to bat in a late inning with Schaefer on first and Davy Jones on Third. Schaefer flashed the sign for a double steal. The Cleveland catcher hung onto the ball, however, and Jones stayed on third while Schaefer stole second. "On the next pitch," as Davy Jones has recalled, "Schaefer yelled 'Let's try it again!' And with a blood-curdling shout he took off like a wild Indian *back to first base,* and drove in headfirst in a cloud of dust. He figured the catcher might throw to first — since he evidently wouldn't throw to second — and then I could come home same as before.

"But nothing happened. Nothing at all. Everybody just stood there and watched Schaefer, with their mouths open, not knowing what the devil was going on. Me, too. Even if the catcher *had* thrown to first, I was too stunned to move . . . But the catcher didn't throw. In fact, George Stovall, the Cleveland first baseman, was playing way back and didn't even come in to cover the bag. We just watched the madman running the wrong way on the base path and didn't know what to do.

"The umpires were just as confused as everybody else. However, it turned out there wasn't any rule against a guy going from second back to first, if that's the way he wanted to play baseball, so they had to let it stand.

"So there we were, back where we started, with Schaefer on first and me on second. And on the next pitch darned if he didn't let out another war whoop and take off *again* for second base. By this time the Cleveland catcher evidently had enough, because he threw to second to get Schaefer, and when he did I took off for home, and *both* of us were safe."[19]

Immediately after that episode the officials of the American League met in emergency session, determined not to let Germany Schaefer and his odd ideas wreck the national pastime. The league's president, Ban Johnson, solemnly announced a new rule, which might be called the Schaefer Decision, providing that men on base had to run counter-clockwise and not reverse themselves on a whim. The game was saved for the corporations, eventually including the Anheuser-Busch Brewing Company and the Columbia Broadcasting System.

12. THE IMAGE DARKENS

In Germany, impassioned hearts are divorced from logical heads. And so the honest Teuton is never slow to assume the existence of anything whose existence appears to be desirable.

— STENDAHL

A good case could be made for the proposition that the Germans — no matter how sedate and amiable their present reputation — were the most dangerously volatile addition to the ethnic mixture which makes up the American. Certainly there would have been a few non-Germans who would have cared to take the negative side in any debate on that issue, not seventy or eighty years ago when most of those publicly identified as trying to pull down the foundations of the Republic by anarchic or Marxist means bore German names.

It almost seemed to their fellow Americans that the German element had been stirring up trouble ever since their arrival. Their separatist movements had caused more irritation than serious concern, yet the suspicion lingered that many Germans would have been happier with a large chunk of the Northwest labeled on the maps, "Republic of Germania" or "Independent State of Teutonia" or something like that.

Yet another element among the German-Americans disturbing to their neighbors everywhere was the large number of the anticlerical and antireligious among them. They were not of the familiar "village

314

atheist" stamp, the disgruntled old man sneering at God from his cracker box, but were aggressive partisans of their nonbeliefs. In many communities with a sizable German population they impressed their ideas on their citizens quite forcefully and tactlessly. In New Ulm, Minnesota, for many years it was an unwritten law that the school board consist of two Catholics, two Protestants and two freethinkers.

No less disturbing to those with property to protect and businesses to operate were the outspoken radical tendencies of so many German-Americans. Most of the Marxist socialists in the United States were of German extraction. Germans also were energetically organizing trade unions. And when they weren't raising the Red Flag of Marxism, all too often they were marching under the black banners of anarchy. The philosophy of anarchy may seem in disharmony with the Germans who herded so obediently into the armies of Prussia in 1870, who fought so long and hard for the Kaiser in World War I and succumbed to the mass impulse toward self-destruction under the Nazis — but the Germans, perhaps more than any other people, are tugged and torn by inner contradictions. In the decades after Civil War, German-born or German-descended anarchists were among the most disruptive elements in American society. The Anglo-Saxon majority and the non-German minorities regarded the Germans as bomb throwers, rabble-rousers and dangerous dissidents, although this was true of only a small minority of the Germans themselves.

The fear of those activist Germans was heightened by the fact that Populism, with its own radical prescriptions for the economic injustice and political corruption of the Gilded Age, was sweeping large sections of the West and Southwest. The Germans, mostly those newly migrated, matched rural Populism with urban Marxism and anarchism and added a dangerous ingredient — violence.

THE REDDISH "GREENS"

The Marxist infection was first brought to the United States by the Forty-eighters, perhaps two thousand of whom were university graduates or students or teachers who had been studying Marx — often with *Der*

Grossmeister himself — clandestinely in Germany. Many of them were journalists, or hoped to be, as well as writers, poets and others with an aptitude for spreading propaganda. Their first objective on arriving in America was to destroy the influence of the "Grays," the intellectual and political leaders of the older immigrants, particularly Gustav Koerner, "der Graue Gustav," as the Forty-eighters ("Greens") called him. They attacked the Grays for their lack of culture, their political passivity in failing to end Negro slavery and destroy Know-Nothingism, and their "slavish clericalism."

The Greens were radicals, reformists, activists, rebels waiting impatiently for the millennium. America seemed ripe for an overturn; with all its resources and with its exploitable restlessness of minorities resenting Anglo-Saxon domination it could be turned upside down and the capitalist republic replaced by the workers' state. Many were so impatient, in fact, that they returned to Germany within a few years when they saw that it would take a long struggle indeed to persuade the Americans to abandon democracy. Others reluctantly gave in to the necessity of making a living for themselves; marriage and family responsibilities damped down the ardor of many, and some were tamed by the struggle to hack a place for themselves out of the wilderness, a struggle for which they were ill-prepared. One flaming revolutionary cooled his passions while cutting corn with a sword which one of his relatives had wielded against the French in 1813. L. A. Wollenweber and Carl Dominique, two activists who had acquired their ideas about the dignity and sanctity of human labor, sweated out some of their former principles while laboring with pick and shovel on the construction of the Schuykill Canal. Others no doubt were overawed by the vast uninhabited stretches of the continent, or disheartened by that amorphous quality of American politics which tends to ooze over extremism and somehow encompass and engorge it.[1]

The "Greens," with their reddish complexion, were also dismayed at the thought of plunging themselves into the American political game. It seemed to them to be entirely lacking in dignity, whether one viewed it from the spittle-slick floor of a national convention or at the level of ward and district conniving. It appeared to be a shady business conducted by Neanderthal types in the back rooms of saloons, all shirt-sleeves, tobacco cuds, cigar butts, back-slapping, false bonhomie and emotional oratory empty of substance. It was true that there was no police surveillance — incredibly enough the national government did not even have a force of secret police to find out what the people were thinking — but there was plenty of watchfulness from nosy neighbors.

Most worrisome of all was the political unawareness, the refusal of the average American to be stirred by economic and social issues. Even the German-born, within a few years, seemed to lose interest and walk away yawning from anyone who tried to arouse them.

But the Forty-eighters did their best. Within a few years after the migrations of '48 a rash of communist newspapers erupted across the United States. All of them were published in German for the benefit of the German-born or -descended working class in the cities. Many of the migrants who stayed in the cities were made to feel inferior, partly because of their poverty and partly because they couldn't speak English, which, as one historian has written, "prepared them for the message of socialism." They were therefore "ripe for the intellectual leadership which the communist element of the radical Forty-eighters offered."[2] That leadership was largely composed of those with a journalistic bent.*

New York City had a communist weekly, the short-lived *Zeit*, even before the Forty-eighters came over. It began publishing in 1844. Two years later the *Adoptivburger*, a communist-labor organ, was founded in Philadelphia. In 1847 *Der Reformer* began weekly publication in St. Louis under the sponsorship of the local communist club.

Soon after the migrations of 1848 began, the weekly *Kommunist* sprang up in Cleveland and *Der Kommunist* in New Orleans. Other communist or socialist publications appeared in Milwaukee, Cincinnati, New York and other centers of the German population. Some, like *Arbiterzeitungen*, were simply in favor of the workingman throughout the country, without being dogmatically Marxist. Some were anti-Marxist but in favor of land reform. The journalistic spectrum ranged

---

* According to a survey by A. E. Zucker, 74 of the intellectual Forty-eighters were journalists, 67 soldiers, 37 physicians, 25 teachers, 16 authors, 11 diplomats, 11 musicians and eight poets.[3]

from a violent red to a very few of reactionary black, but most leaned toward radical solutions for the situation of the working and farming classes in America.

In all the radical parties which rose during the 1870's and 1880's there was a strong German representation. For fifteen years after the Socialist Labor party was founded in 1877, the German language was spoken at its conventions. The executive board of the First International's branch in the United States included three Germans, two Irishmen, two Frenchmen, one Swede and one Italian. The directors of the First International considered that the Germans were the ablest theorists while the Irish supplied the organizing ability.[4]

Perhaps the leading Marxist-influenced intellectual who came over during the 1840's was Wilhelm Weitling, who was born in Magdeburg, Prussia, in 1808. A tailor by trade, he had traveled all over Europe agitating among the workingmen's clubs. For a time he traveled the ideological path broken by Marx and Engels, but they soon came to suspect that his convictions were more of the utopian than the communist variety, and they also envied his influence with the working classes which, as intellectuals and theorists, they found it difficult to attain.

Because he refused to adopt all the principles of Marxism, the movement's leaders read him out of the party. Marx and Engels criticized him for "meekness" and "brotherliness," qualities they evidently regarded as unworthy of a true-believing communist, labeled him a reactionary and a deviationist, and tried to undermine his influence among the European workingmen's clubs. Some of their followers believed that Marx and Engels were also motivated by the fear that Weitling, a younger man, might succeed them in the leadership of the communist movement.

In 1846, as an outcast shunned by his former comrades, Weitling migrated to the United States. He energetically set about organizing the *Arbeiter Bund* (Workingmen's League) in New York City. Many of its principles are now part of the Social Security system. On the side he edited the German-language Free Soilers' weekly. When the revolution of '48 broke out in Germany, he hastened back to the Fatherland to participate, but returned to the United States two years later as the attempts to obtain a constitutional monarchy were smothered out of existence.

On his return to New York, Weitling established the national weekly *Die Republik der Arbeiter* as the organ of his Workingmen's League. He saw that other nationalities would have to be drawn into the movement and organized the Central Committee of United Trades to include non-German workingmen's groups. He was still enough of a Marxist to urge the abolition of all capitalists. The state, he said, should serve the "ethos of work." His wide-ranging organizational efforts even took in New Jersey farmers and Negro laborers in New York. Largely through his efforts the first General Workmen's Convention was held in Philadelphia in the fall of 1850. It was attended by forty-four delegates claiming to represent 4,400 members in the United States. The delegates were urged by Weitling to throw all their efforts into establishing a "World Republic," under which all countries would be governed by those who worked with their hands. Aside from world federalization, Weitling also obtained the convention's support for a workers' colony to serve as the pilot model of his utopian vision of a world in which labor would be supreme.

He bustled about to make his dream come true, raised the funds to buy a thousand-acre tract in Iowa which was to be called Communia. The only entrance requirements were the sum of ten dollars and a willingness to work. Forty men were selected to flesh out Weitling's conception of an ideal society. But politico-economic utopias foundered on the same rock that sundered the religious colonies: the perversity of human nature. In Communia debts accumulated, chores went undone, and the members spent most of their time quarreling with each other and, by mail, with their anxious patron in New York. Despite Weitling's exhortations at a distance, Communia broke up and was disbanded less than a year after it was established.[5]

Weitling was thoroughly disillusioned. Like so many other German radicals, he gave up in disgust and decided that his best course was to look after himself and allow the rest of mankind to stumble along on its own. He became a clerk in the Bureau of Immigration and spent the rest of his life, outside the bureau, studying astronomy. The stars, at least, were constant and far removed from irksome unsaveable humanity.

UNDER THE BLACK FLAG

While traveling in the wake of Napoleon's armies, Stendahl observed, "In Germany, impassioned hearts are divorced from logical heads. And so the honest Teuton is never slow to assume the existence of anything whose existence appears to be desirable." If communism was conceived in Germany, however, it was also true that anarchism had its philosophical birthplace in Stendahl's native land; its violent activism stemmed from Czarist Russia. While Marx and Engels worked and propagandized for government by the working classes, Pierre Proudhon and his Russian disciple, Michael Bakunin, were developing the theory that all forms of government must be destroyed and swept away before humanity could achieve the happiness it deserved. The perfect society, Proudhon declared, would be "An-archy," and he further proclaimed:

"Whoever lays his hand on me to govern me is a usurper and a tyrant; I declare him to be my enemy. Government of man by man is slavery . . . To be governed is to be watched, inspected, spied on, regulated, indoctrinated, preached at, controlled, ruled, censored, by persons who have neither wisdom nor virtue . . . Under pretext of the common good it is to be exploited, monopolized, embezzled, robbed and then, at the least protest or word of complaint, to be fined, harassed, vilified, beaten up, bludgeoned, disarmed, judged, condemned, imprisoned, shot, garroted, deported, sold, betrayed, swindled, deceived, outraged, dishonored. That's government, that's its justice, that's its morality!"

The "abstract idea of right," he believed, would make a revolution unnecessary. Men as reasonable creatures would control themselves in a society without being governed. Here his disciple Bakunin, with his experience of Czarist repressions, differed with Proudhon. Violence, erupting on one of the more backward countries, would be necessary to overthrow the governments, and for that purpose revolutionaries willing to use rifles, bombs and any other means of persuasion must be trained and organized.

Anarchy was given its economic as well as its philosophical slant by M. Proudhon when he asked his rhetorical question, "What is Property?" To which he supplied the answer, "Property is theft." Another disciple, Enrico Malatesta, elaborated on this principle in his *Talk Between Two Workers* when he demanded, "Do you not know that every bit of bread they eat is taken from your children, every fine present they give their wives means the poverty, hunger, cold, even perhaps prostitution of yours?" Bakunin had already listed the prime oppressors of mankind as all "priests, monarchs, statesmen, soldiers, officials, financiers, capitalists, moneylenders, lawyers." A milder and more optimistic theorist was Peter Kropotkin, born one of the princes of Smolensk, who had been thrown into the fortress prison of SS. Peter and Paul for his beliefs. He believed that the "galloping decay" of the various governments would hasten their collapse, but favored a forcible overthrow if necessary. So airy was his vision that Prince Kropotkin, one of the few anarchists who gave much thought to what would happen after governments were destroyed, believed that all property and possessions could be pooled and each man would "decide for himself what he needs for a comfortable life" and draw from the communal pile whatever he wanted without unduly aggrandizing himself.

German-American radicals absorbed these doctrines without adding anything of substance to the theoretical bases of anarchism. They were content to help make it work. With Teutonic practicality, they published pamphlets in English and German on how to go about overthrowing the government. The only thing required was a sufficient quantity of high explosives placed in strategic locations. "Dynamite!" exclaimed one manifesto of the German-American anarchists hymning the joys to come. "Of all the good stuff, that is the stuff. Stuff several pounds of this sublime stuff into an inch pipe . . . plug up both ends, insert a cap with a fuse attached, place this in the vicinity of a lot of rich loafers who live by the sweat of other people's brows, and light the fuse. A most cheerful and gratifying result will follow. A pound of this good stuff beats a bushel of ballots all hollow . . ."[6]

All German-American anarchists, of course, did not go along with

Bakunin, the bomb throwers and dynamite planters. Many were also socialists who believed that social justice could be attained through peaceful means. Among these were Ernest L. Meyer's parents, who were married in France after his father, newly impressed into the German army, "pummeled a Prussian lieutenant with the flat of the officer's own sword." Though provocation was clearly established, his action was considered highly indiscreet, and he barely escaped with his life. Immediately after migrating to the United States, the Meyers joined a group of philosophical anarchists because "even in Germany as a youth father leaned to the theory that the individual must not yield his liberty to the state and his very soul to the potsdammer *Herrenvolk*, a conviction which accounted for father's explosive reaction when the Prussian lieutenant called him a fathead, a guttersnipe and a pig-dog because one button of father's tunic was unbuttoned during maneuvers under the eyes of no less a god than His Majesty."[7]

Anarchy was anything but philosophical in Chicago during the Seventies and Eighties, when the bulk of the population was composed of newly arrived immigrants. Jobs had become scarce as a result of the depression of '73 and there was great economic pressure on both the immigrant and the longer established families. Few of the newcomers spoke English but most could make themselves understood in German, the "universal Latin of European radicalism." Seeking distraction from their troubles, they had to find places where German was spoken. "Entertainment in the German theaters was expensive; even the beer gardens were beyond the means of an unemployed worker who had spent his life's stake on the trip to the New World," a Chicago historian has noted. "The only diversions accessible under these conditions were the free labor meetings, in reality socialist rallies, where skilled orators spoke eloquently in German of the workers' millennium. A dramatist could not have created a more roseate picture than the visions of these outdoor spellbinders, who captured both the hearts and the minds of their audiences. If the men who heard these speakers had not been out of work or isolated by the barrier of language, they might have found other sources of amusement. But they were essentially a captive audience and soon came to believe the speakers on the platform were the only real champions of the workingman."[8]

The Image Darkens

In addition, the German-speaking immigrants' chief reading matter was the *Arbeiter-Zeitung*, a daily newspaper edited by August Spies, a militant anarchist of the Bakunin school. "A pound of dynamite is worth a bushel of bullets!" Spies preached to his readership. "Police and militia, the bloodhounds of capitalism, are ready to murder!"

Another anarchist periodical in wide circulation was *The Alarm*, published by Albert Parsons, who ran for mayor on the Socialist Labor ticket and was the prime mover in the International Working People's party. He was the son of Confederate General W. H. Parsons. One of his leading collaborators was Samuel Fielden, a Lancastershire Englishman who drove a stone wagon and was both a fervent Methodist and a fanatical anarchist. With Publisher Spies they made up what some Chicago newspapers called the "Danton, Marat and Robespierre of the American Revolution."

The seeds of their agitation, in print and on the platform, fell upon fertile ground. No one else seemed to be concerned with the plight of Chicago's unemployed immigrants, most of them German or German-speaking. There was a sizable labor organization called the Knights of Labor, but its leader, Grand Master Workman Terence V. Powderley, was so conservative that he opposed strikes (local assemblies usually struck at his displeasure), and he was naturally engrossed in the plentiful injustices inflicted on his own members.

There were no voices of moderation speaking in a language the immigrants could understand. March under the black flag of anarchy or starve unprotestingly seemed to be the alternatives. The result of this lack of communication between prosperous men of goodwill in Chicago and the unemployed masses was a series of riots and disorders. In the winter of 1873 the first floor of the City Hall had to be turned over to ragged families of the unemployed who had no other place to sleep. During the railroad strikes of 1877, a mob of rioters roamed the downtown streets and could not be brought under control. They broke into pawnshops and stores selling guns and collected an arsenal of weapons for street fighting. The authorities meanwhile were organizing special police units composed of volunteers, and the younger members of the city's wealthier families formed an unofficial militia. The police also mounted a field gun on an express wagon and used it as mobile artillery to drive off mobs firing rifles and throwing stones at trains passing under the viaduct on South Halstead Street. On a hot summer's night a protest meeting was called at the Turners' Hall. The police decided to disperse the several thousand persons gathered there, and a riot broke out in which two policemen were wounded, one rioter was killed and an unknown number injured. Federal troops were rushed to the scene. Passions cooled that summer, but the socialists and anarchists began organizing themselves into military companies which marched under black and red flags.

A show of strength was ordained by the radical leaders when the new Board of Trade Building, symbol of all their hatreds and resentments, was opened. The tenement districts were flooded with pamphlets sneering at the ceremonies with which the building would be dedicated. "After the ceremonies and sermons, the participants will move in a body to the Grand Temple of Usury, Gambling and Cut-Throatism, where they will serenade the priests and officers of King Mammon and pay honor and respect to the benevolent institute. All friends of the bourse are invited." Uninvited, the anarchists, with Spies, Parsons and Fielden at their head, marched to the Board of Trade Building and were confronted by two hundred police. The anarchists surged against the police lines, and a Board of Trade member and his wife, late in arriving for the ceremonies, were stoned and dumped out of their carriage.

From then until the year 1886 there was constant unrest, part of it caused by continuing underemployment and genuine grievances against the city's industrialists (particularly the streetcar companies and the McCormick reaper factory) and partly also by the exertions of the anarchist leaders and propagandists. The activists began making bombs. In January, one was placed against the doorstep of a judge's home, but it was defused before it could explode. A few days later another was found in the Burlington Depot and similarly disposed of. Tension grew in February when there was a walkout at the McCormick plant by workers demanding an eight-hour day and increased wages. The strike dragged on, and in May the McCormick factory began bringing in strikebreakers, whereupon there was a strike against the Pullman Company and seven thousand packinghouse employees walked off their jobs at the stockyards. The Knights of Labor, always timorous, refused to assume the leadership of the eight-hour-day movement, and the anarchists moved in to fill the vacuum.

Strikers charged a group of "scabs" trying to enter the McCormick factory. Their police protectors fired, leaving six dead and many wounded. Within a few hours the plotters at the *Arbeiter-Zeitung* seized upon the occasion and produced bundles of pamphlets which were distributed throughout the North and West Sides by a man on horseback. The pamphlets were printed in German on one side, English on the other, and read: "REVENGE! WORKINGMEN TO ARMS! They killed six of your brothers at McCormick's works this afternoon because the poor wretches had the temerity to disobey the supreme will of your bosses. *To arms! We call you to arms!*"

Next morning the streets were filled with the angry proletariat, goaded on by that morning's editorial in the *Arbeiter-Zeitung* in which August Spies called upon them to "rise in your might and level the existing robber rule with the dust." A few hours later there was another wide circulation of leaflets calling for a "great mass meeting at the Haymarket," on Randolph Street between Desplaines and Halsted. "Good speakers," the leaflet promised, "will be present to denounce the latest atrocious acts of the police — the shooting of our fellow-workingmen yesterday."

At 7:30 P.M. on May 4, in obedience to the summons from the anarchist leaders, two or three thousand people began filling the Haymarket. It was a warm, damp, cloudy evening. At the Desplaines Street police station a block away a force of about two hundred policemen were assembled and issued new revolvers and long riot sticks made of hickory. They were to be kept in readiness in case the crowd in the Haymarket became disorderly or threatened to march on the more prosperous residential districts.

Police detectives infiltrated the crowd and listened as Spies, Parsons and Fielden exhorted the working classes to protect their own interests, answering violence with violence if necessary. Also listening on the fringe of the crowd was Mayor Carter Harrison. He had grown wealthy on real estate, loved fine Havanas and silk underwear, but had exhibited a considerable amount of sympathy for the strikers. Nine out of ten of Chicago's citizens, he had been quoted as saying, supported the movement for the eight-hour day. He strolled back to the police station and remarked to the chief of police, "I have no right to interfere with any peaceable meeting of the people. Let them talk. So long as they are orderly, I will not interfere."

Mayor Harrison thought he had made himself understood and left the Desplaines police station with the chief of police. The man left in charge of the police battalion was, however, the strongly antianarchist and antistriker Inspector John Bonfield. He itched for a showdown. Shortly after the mayor and his own superior departed, Inspector Bonfield listened to reports from his detectives, who quoted Samuel Fielden as telling the crowd that the law must be "throttled, killed and stabbed."

That was enough for Bonfield. He ordered his phalanx of police to move on the Haymarket.

They marched up just as Fielden was finishing his speech. A police captain stepped forward and shouted, "You're all to disperse in a peaceable manner!"

There was a moment of ominous silence, then Fielden replied, "Why, Captain, we are peaceable."

A second or two later an unknown hand, holding a large bomb with sputtering fuse, was raised above the heads of the crowd. It arched into the massed ranks of the police — the first anarchist bomb to be hurled in the United States and, according to the experts, of the same design as that which had killed Czar Alexander II of Russia several years before.

The bomb had been fashioned by an expert. There was a terrific explosion which killed seven policemen and injured sixty others. "Charge!" shouted Inspector Bonfield. "Fire!" The surviving police fired in all directions, shooting down people in the crowd and their fellow officers alike. The shots sounded like "the falling of corn on a tin pan or the rolling of a drum," wrote a Chicago *Daily News* reporter. Police estimated that two hundred were killed or wounded, but had no way of telling because the crowd quickly hauled away their casualties.

That night the city was in a state of shock. It was incredible that

Thousands riot in the Haymarket of Chicago

Anarchists battle under the Black Flag

Old World anarchism could erupt in all its most violent manifestations; most people had believed, with Mayor Harrison, that the anarchist leaders were "only talking." Now the word had become the deed. Panic and hysteria followed. Bomb-carrying anarchists were reported lurking in alleys and plotting more terrorism in basements throughout the city. Police squads ranged over the North and West Sides throughout the night, arresting several hundred workingmen suspected of conspiring and bomb-making in "dynamiters' lairs." One city official hastily rigged a wire barricade across the second-floor landing of his home to prevent any bombs from being hurled into his family's sleeping quarters.

Early that morning a heavily armed police squad broke into the offices of the *Arbeiter-Zeitung* and, sure enough, found a large quantity of explosives. August Spies and his assistant editor, Michael Schwab, were arrested, along with Samuel Fielden. Albert Parsons had fled the city, but surrendered himself later. In short order the police also arrested Louis Lingg, an officer of the carpenters' union, whom police claimed was the manufacturer of the fatal bomb; George Engle, a painter; Adolph Fischer, a printer, and Oscar Neebe, an organizer for the beer-wagon drivers' union. Of the eight men brought to trial for the Haymarket bombing, six bore German names. Among non-German Chicagoans there was an understandable wave of anti-German sentiment, and a continuing fear of what the anarchists might do in protest against the swift justice ordered for the defendants.

The prosecution's case against all eight was weak. No evidence was presented as to who threw the bomb. Two of the principal elements of the state's case were the "To arms!" pamphlets published by Spies and the fact that the site of the meeting had been moved from Desplaines Street to the Haymarket. The prosecution contended the meeting was moved to "set a trap for the police," though just how the square was more of a trap than the street it bordered on was unclear. Undoubtedly the chief unseen factor in the trial was the public sentiment in favor of quick and conclusive punishment, particularly in that segment which contributed to election funds.

In August, 1886, all eight defendants were found guilty. Judge Joseph E. Gary sentenced seven to be hanged. The eighth, Oscar

Neebe, whose only apparent crime was owning stock in the *Arbeiter-Zeitung*, was sentenced to fifteen years in prison. A request for a new trial was refused. The seven condemned men then asked for the privilege of addressing the court and, by extension, the newspapers.

Fielden, the ex-Methodist preacher, was the most eloquent. "I have loved my fellow men as I have loved myself . . . If it will do any good, I freely give myself up." The others were less inclined toward Christian forbearance. The death sentences, cried August Spies, were part of a conspiracy to "stamp out the labor movement." Lingg said he would gladly die on the gallows "in the sure hope that hundreds and thousands of people to whom I have spoken will now recognize and make use of dynamite. In this hope I despise you and despise your laws. Hang me for it."

Parsons fumed that the trial was "the sum totality of the disorganized passion of Chicago" and charged that the jury had been bribed. He also chanted a hymn to the blessings of dynamite as the agent of social justice. "Dynamite is the equilibrium. It is the disseminator of authority; it is the dawn of peace; it is the end of war." Michael Schwab, Publisher Spies's young assistant, offered a definition of anarchism as "a state of society in which the only government is reason."

Four of the seven men sentenced to the gallows were hung on November 11, 1887. Just before that the sentences of Fielden and Schwab were commuted to life imprisonment by the governor. Louis Lingg, the youngest, handsomest and perhaps the most fanatic of the lot, acted as his own executioner by exploding a dynamite cartridge, smuggled into his cell on death row, between his teeth.

As he stood on the gallows, Spies cried out, "There will be a time when our silence will be more powerful than the voices you hear today." Parsons quietly pronounced his own benediction: "Let the voice of the people be heard."

It was not heard, certainly, by the people who counted in Chicago. They busied themselves with appeals to the federal government to establish a military post close enough to the city to protect them and their property in case of further terrorism. For that purpose they even provided a tract of six hundred acres twenty-six miles north of Chicago on the shore of Lake Michigan, and thus Fort Sheridan was established as a guarantor of peace. It came in handy.

"OH, WILD CHICAGO"

Anarchists in the United States and Europe capitalized, if that is not too harsh a word, on the four Haymarket martyrs. For years afterward anarchist literature frequently bore the colophon of four men hanging from the state of Illinois gallows. They provided radicalism's cause célèbre, "suitable martyrs," as the late Stewart H. Holbrook has written, "to what left-wing orators for many years never referred to other than the Cause of Labor, though, no matter who tossed the bomb,* the Haymarket affair was really a disaster to the cause of labor. It set radical and conservative elements bitterly at odds with each other. It prejudiced the public against labor, organized or otherwise. It presented employers with the best kind of excuse for almost any action they cared to employ against unions. It stopped the rising eight-hour movement dead in its tracks."[9]

The Haymarket bombing, as Mr. Holbrook pointed out, was to result in one more martyrdom — that of the German-American named John P. Altgeld, governor of Illinois from 1893 to 1897. Altgeld was a liberal of the stature, if not quite the charismatic appeal, of Carl Schurz. When he came to office in the much-troubled year of 1893, the "Haymarket martyrs" still alive — Neebe, Fielden and Schwab — had been in prison for almost seven years. Not only from the left had come a continuing clamor for their release. Almost any objective study of the trial records indicated there were glaring imperfections in the state's case against all the defendants, hung and unhung.

Altgeld, the "eagle forgotten" as one of his biographers has called him, was a hardheaded, self-contained yet passionate man. His ambi-

---

* In his lively history *Fabulous Chicago*, Emmett Dedmon has recorded: "All those who could settle the question" of who threw the Haymarket bomb "are dead, but their descendants say they heard from their fathers . . . that the actual bomb was thrown by Rudolph Schnaubelt, who fled to Europe, lived on anonymously, and died quietly in his sleep."

tions, rising at a time when the German element in the United States was still growing in size and political importance, seeking a clear voice and a young leader, undoubtedly encompassed the White House. Yet he would not sacrifice his principles — particularly his cold hard passion for justice — to attain them; and a politician tugged by the centripetal force of principle and the centrifugal force of ambition is likely to find himself at a standoff. Both Schurz and Altgeld, with that curious intermingling of Teutonic practicality, which allowed them to get things done, and stubborn romanticism, which would not allow them to compromise, died the deaths of politically honorable men.

John Peter Altgeld was born in Germany in 1847 and brought to this country by his parents at the age of three months. He spent his boyhood in Mansfield, Ohio, until at the age of sixteen he marched off to the Civil War as the drummer boy of an Ohio regiment. Later he worked as a manual laborer while obtaining enough education to pass his bar examinations. He became state's attorney for Cook County, made himself reasonably wealthy in real estate deals and developed political aspirations with the encouragement of Mrs. Potter Palmer, who was not only Chicago society's most glittering personage but a woman whose interest in social justice matched his own.

He ran for governor of Illinois in 1892 as a Democrat and what one historian has called "an almost demonic liberal." One of his campaign pledges, attractive to the resentful masses of laboring men to whom the "Haymarket martyrs" were a living cause, was to correct the injustice of the "drumhead" trial at which they were convicted.

His first act on being elected was to order a close study of the trial record. For weeks he pored over the transcript himself. Then he sat down to write an eighteen thousand-word document justifying the pardon of Michael Schwab, Samuel Fielden and Oscar Neebe, the three men who had escaped the noose but were still in prison. His decision to free the men came at a time when anarchy was again the cause of widespread fears: the Russian-born anarchist Alexander Berkman had tried to kill Henry Clay Frick at the height of the Homestead steel strike.[10]

More dangerously still, Governor Altgeld, so soon after taking office, had not only decided to pardon the three "martyrs" but to indict the law itself for inflicting an injustice upon them. There would have been no great furor over the pardons because, as Barbara W. Tuchman (*The Proud Tower*) noted, "many prominent Chicagoans, uneasy over the death sentence, had worked privately for pardon and had in fact been responsible for the commutation of the sentence of the three defendants now still alive." (Actually only two of them had been condemned, the third had been given a fifteen-year sentence.) In his harshly uncompromising way, however, Governor Altgeld was determined to indict the indicters. And when "Altgeld displayed publicly the cloven hoof of the law, he shook public faith in a fundamental institution." There would have been little controversy, probably, if he had simply turned the three men loose as an act of forgiveness.

His determination not only to right a wrong, but to show in his explanation of the pardons that the jury which convicted them had been "selected to convict," that Judge Gary had been openly and injudiciously hostile to the defendants, aroused the respectable people who believed that the system which protected them was under serious attack.

His action was, as Stewart Holbrook said, "as courageous as any ever performed by a man in public life."

The decision accompanying the pardons, with its inferential condemnation of the society which permitted the original sentences, was excoriated in the press, from the pulpit, from the mouths of outraged "leading citizens." He had encouraged "the overthrow of civilization," declared the Toledo *Blade*. The New York *Sun* gave vent to its feelings in splenetic verse:

> *Oh wild Chicago . . .*
> *Lift up your weak and guilty hands*
> *From out of the wreck of states*
> *And as the crumbling towers fall down*
> *Write* ALTGELD *on your gates!*

The Haymarket pardons might well have doomed his political career in any case, but Altgeld proceeded in his uncompromising way to do, not what was politic and tactful and easeful, but what he believed was right. In 1894 came trouble in the medieval fiefdom of Pullman City. The men who built the Pullman Palace Cars for George Pullman lived under a harsh paternalism, in a company town, on a wage scale which in some cases paid them as little as seven cents a week in cash. A delegation of workers which ventured to protest to Mr. Pullman was fired to the last man. In came the organizers for the American Railway Union, and out went the workers on strike.

There were bitter clashes throughout Illinois when strikers and their sympathizers tried to cut Pullman cars out of trains proceeding through the state. Now was the time for Fort Sheridan to prove its usefulness to the upper class. A more or less liberal Democrat, Grover Cleveland, was in the White House but his attorney general, Richard Olney, a founder of the General Managers Association, wanted federal troops to provide an armed excort for the trains. Rail traffic had come to an almost complete stop. Governor Altgeld vigorously protested any such interference from Washington. He had sent state troops to control the situation in Cairo, but his political enemies, gaining the ear of President Cleveland and Attorney General Olney, whispered that he could not be trusted because of his "advanced social views." (One thing held against him was his advocacy of prison reform. In 1890 he had published a book titled *Our Penal Machinery and Its Victims.*)

To his protests against federal troops, President Cleveland replied by sending in 2,000 regulars and deputizing a force of 3,600 toughs and desperadoes as "deputy United States marshals." Governor Altgeld wired the President: "The railroads are paralyzed not by reason of obstruction but because they cannot get men to operate their trains. I ask for immediate withdrawal of Federal troops from active duty in this state."

To which President Cleveland coldly replied: "We are confronted with a condition, not a theory."

The strike was broken, at a cost of a dozen lives.

Also broken was the political career of John P. Altgeld. His action in setting himself against his party's leader, reviving the old suspicions that he was a dangerous radical, resulted in his defeat for the governership in 1896. His career proved that political courage and personal conviction, despite legends to the contrary, often pay off in defeat, with self-satisfaction their only reward.

JOHANN MOST, HIGH PRIEST OF VIOLENCE

Johann Most often said that his greatest ambition was to be an actor. Probably, if circumstances had permitted, he would have been a great one. Unfortunately for peace and order in the United States, that true ambition was thwarted and his histrionic energies were channeled into a career which made him, for some years, one of the most feared men in America. He migrated to this country at a time when anarchy was a real and present danger throughout the Western world. The Haymarket bombing in Chicago was followed by a two-year reign of anarchistic terror in France beginning in 1891 and political assassinations in other countries. By 1885 it was estimated that there were seven thousand anarchists in the United States and many others who could be classified as unorganized sympathizers.

Very early in his life Johann Most was infected with a hatred of society. He was born in Augsburg, Bavaria, the illegitimate son of a governess and an impoverished clerk, and was raised by a stepmother whom he hated. Some time during his boyhood he suffered a jaw infection which was improperly treated. It left his face permanently scarred, twisted in a bitter expression, which he later imperfectly concealed with black whiskers. The ugliness of his face not only doomed his acting ambitions but made it a perfect, if heartless target for caricaturists seeking to epitomize the most dangerous and hateful aspects of anarchism. Yet something of what he might have been, had not only his face but his character been twisted by his early experiences, was indicated by a woman who heard him speak and said his blue eyes were strikingly sympathetic and radiated "both hatred and love."

Early in his youth Most was apprenticed to a bookbinder but abandoned that settled way of life to wander from town to town, job to job, an outcast and an object of ridicule because of his malevolently twisted features. As an expression of his contempt for the society which cast him out, he began writing for the underground revolutionary press in South Germany. At first he was a Social Democrat and achieved enough prominence to be elected to the Reichstag in 1874, when he was thirty-two years old. After one term as a deputy, he revolted against any gradual reform of society, established a radical weekly in Berlin and was repeatedly jailed and questioned and hounded by the Prussian secret police. The German Socialist party expelled him from its membership.

Most continued his violent opposition to anything but the principles of the First International until he was exiled from Germany in 1878. Britain next was given the benefit of his person and his inflammatory opinions of king, clergy and government. He established the radical Socialist weekly *Freiheit* in London and soon learned that English tolerance would not endure forever his calefactory dissenting opinions against established thought. In the columns of *Freiheit* he applauded the assassination of Czar Alexander II with undue enthusiasm. Regicide was not popular in a monarchy, which naturally feared its spread, and Most and several like-minded comrades were sentenced to eighteen months in prison.

While he was still serving his sentence, Lord Frederick Cavendish was assassinated in Dublin by Irish rebels. Most promptly smuggled out of prison his considered opinion that killing Lord Cavendish was an excellent way of promoting Irish freedom. The authorities retaliated by announcing that they would no longer allow the publication of *Freiheit*.

On his release from the English prison in 1882, Most immediately embarked for America, which he hoped would be more fertile ground for his ideas. The agitation for an eight-hour day and the rising influx of immigrants from Russia and Italy, he rightly believed, would provide him with thousands of followers. He reestablished *Freiheit* as a national anarchist weekly in Rochester, New York, and busied himself with preparations for the coming overthrow of the United States government.

High explosives, having been perfected just at the time when they would be most useful not only in extending railroads through the western mountains but in furthering the terroristic program of the anarchists, attracted his attention at the outset of the American phase of his career as a revolutionary. What good, he wondered, was a lot of agitated pamphleteering if his fellow revolutionaries did not understand the political potential of dynamite, TNT, nitroglycerin and all the other "good stuff"?

Under an assumed name he obtained a job in an explosives factory in Jersey City. His secret researches there resulted in the publication of a manual titled *Science of Revolutionary Warfare*. It was not a pre-Leninist work of subversive theory, as its title may have indicated, but a practical handbook for the dedicated man intent on destroying the physical foundations of the present order. Its subtitle more accurately conveyed its author's purpose: "A Manual of Instruction in the Use and Preparation of Nitro-glycerine, Gun-cotton, Dynamite, Fulminating Mercury, Bombs, Fuses, Poisons, Etc."

Johann Most's real flair, however, was not for making and setting off bombs but for pamphleteering journalism and for arousing the masses of newly arrived immigrants, particularly those jammed into the tenement districts of New York City. The German-Americans, by now, had begun turning away from anarchic solutions, and his greatest appeal was to the Russian Jews who had so recently suffered from the persecutions and pogroms of constituted authority in their homeland.

Among those roused to a new hope for perfecting human society by Most's *Freiheit* was a girl named Emma Goldman who had recently come to this country with only five dollars and a sewing machine and who had quickly learned how brutal life could be even in America if Emma Lazarus's "golden door" was, in reality, the door to a sweatshop on the Lower East Side. She was a worshipful reader of *Freiheit*, the fulminations of which seemed like "lava shooting forth flames of ridicule, scorn and defiance." She was overwhelmed by Most's attacks on "existing class rule" and inspired by his advocacy of "relentless revolutionary action." The eight-hour day, Most was telling his readers, was a piddling issue. The real goal for any working man or woman with guts was the destruction of capitalism and the building of a new and more equitable order.

By then Most had seized command of the left wing of the Socialist party and made himself the ideological link between socialism and anarchy. With the Socialist Labor faction — the far left of the First

International in America — as his instrument, he began driving for unchallenged leadership of the radical movement. Aside from his pioneering researches in the technique of employing high explosives, he added little of philosophic or ideological content to the movement. The Pittsburgh Manifesto of 1883, which formalized the marriage of radical socialism and anarchism, was a restatement of Michael Bakunin's writings. It did, however, attract enough attention to Most for Henry Jones to use him as a model for the mysterious Hoffendahl in his novel *Princess Casamassima* published in 1886.

Emma Goldman, twenty-one years old, went to hear him speak one evening in 1890 — the beginning of a love affair almost as explosive as a capsule of fulminating mercury.

The occasion was a memorial meeting for the Haymarket "martyrs," at which Most was the principal speaker. Miss Goldman was taken to the meeting by her constant companion, Alexander Berkman, a young Russian émigré of middle-class background. There was so much "tension and fearful excitement" in Most's oration, she later wrote, that she sought "relief" in lovemaking with "Sasha." Soon thereafter she managed an introduction to Most, who was then twice as old as she, and with a surpassing ugliness that was forgotten only when he was blazing forth on the platform. Almost immediately she became his mistress as well as Berkman's.[11]

There were emotional complications to the triangle, even though all three were dedicated to the revolutionary principle that sex was subject to comradely sharing. For a time, however, all three lived together in Worcester, Massachusetts, where, on the solemn word of Miss Goldman's biographer, they were engaged in operating an ice-cream parlor.[12]

Their three-cornered love affair broke up, as it turned out, not on the issue of sexual jealousy but, appropriately enough, on a matter of doctrine complicated by ideological loyalty. The older he got, the less of an activist Most became, the less willing to believe that the social struggle could be resolved by violence. He was turning from Bakunin's teachings, which had formerly inspired him to advocate the literal blasting apart of the state, to the gentler doctrines of Prince Kropotkin.

His solidarity, both ideological and personal, was severely tested in

July of 1892 when "Sasha" Berkman made the Word become the Deed, as anarchists would put it. A strike had broken out at Andrew Carnegie's steel plant in Homestead, Pennsylvania, upon which the self-styled humanitarian repaired to his summer home in Scotland and left his general manager to deal with the strikers. The manager, Henry Clay Frick, a steely-eyed and tough-minded Pennsylvania German, could be relied upon to take stern measures. He hired a large force of Pinkerton men to escort strikebreakers into the plant. Fighting broke out in which ten men were killed and seventy wounded. The Pinkertons were replaced by eight thousand state militiamen. On July 23, Berkman, posing as the agent of an employment office, gained admittance to Frick's office. He shot Frick twice with a revolver and stabbed him several times with a dagger before he was disarmed. Police found two dynamite caps on his person with which, in emulation of Louis Lingg of the Haymarket "martyrs," he intended to kill himself. Since Frick recovered from his wounds, Berkman was given a prison sentence of twenty-two years.[13]

The anarchist world was shocked — and none more than Emma Goldman — when a month after Berkman's attempt on Frick's life Johann Most denounced the deed in the August 27 issue of *Freiheit*. Some of his followers believed he had been frightened into apostasy by the wave of public revulsion that spread across the country. At that moment antiradicalism was stronger even than during the weeks following the Haymarket bombing. Others, including Emma Goldman, believed he was animated by jealousy of the younger Berkman, either because he had dared to do what Most only talked and wrote about or, less probably, over sexual claims on Emma. Actually his shrinking from the violence of Berkman's deed had been foreshadowed by his turning from the ultraviolent doctrine of Michael Bakunin.

At an anarchist meeting in New York he attempted a public explanation of how the high priest of violence in America had come to denounce the man who had acted on his earlier preachings. At the outset he attempted to explain himself on philosophic grounds: the importance of terrorism in bringing about the desired state of anarchy had been overestimated, and furthermore it was impracticable in a country, such as the United States, with an "immature" revolutionary movement.

Then he turned to describing Berkman himself in contemptuous terms. Perhaps he had not noticed that Emma Goldman was in the audience. Gray-cloaked, she rose from her seat in the rear of the meeting hall and called him a traitor and a coward.

Advancing toward the platform, she drew a buggy whip from under her cloak. Before he could escape or defend himself, she leaped on the platform and belabored him with the whip until it broke, then flung the pieces on the floor. Several years later she regretted her act and sought a reconciliation with Most, but he refused to see her. "I often regretted having attacked the man who was my teacher," she said, "and whom I idolized for many years."[14]

Johann Most died in 1906, by which time he had been succeeded in the leadership of the American anarchist movement by Emma Goldman and Alexander Berkman. Before his death, however, he made one last gesture toward repairing what one historian had called the "stunning betrayal from which the [anarchist] movement in America never fully recovered."[15] Just after President McKinley was assassinated, he reprinted in *Freiheit* an article approving the practice of tyrannicide and was sentenced to a year in the jail on Blackwell's Island.

GERMAN ACCENT ON SOCIALISM

For many years the small and struggling American Socialist party was kept alive during periods of financial crisis by the gold watch owned by the brother of its founder. The founder, Eugene Victor Debs, would borrow his brother Theodore's watch. He would then take it to a pawnship in Chicago's Loop.

As soon as the German proprietor of the shop saw Gene Debs walking in the door, he would turn to the girl at the cash register and say:

"Giff the Socialist chentleman forty dollars."[16]

Those trips to the pawnshop occurred in the several years around the turn of the century, when the Socialist party membership was less than four thousand. Debs had founded it under the title of Social Democracy, following the style and philosophy of the German Socialist party, as opposed to the more bluntly Marxist, more radical and activist, anarchist-tinged Socialist Labor party which for some time was guided by the incantations of Johann Most and later by Daniel De Leon, who was born of Dutch parents in Curaçao but educated in Germany. The Socialist Labor party membership was drawn mostly from newly arrived immigrants. Debs's new party, on the other hand, appealed to the American-born, particularly those of German extraction, who were skilled craftsmen, fairly well paid, owned their homes, and by now (around 1900) were turning from radicalism and dynamite worship to less violent doctrines.

Debs himself was of Alsatian descent, which is to say his parents came from a French province mainly populated by Germans. Born in Terre Haute, Indiana, he was named for the French novelists Eugène Sue and Victor Hugo by his literary-minded father, who used *Les Misérables* as a means of educating his sons in the bitter realities and social injustices of life. Terre Haute was a railroad town, and Debs went to work in the shops and later as a locomotive fireman. A tall, gangling man with fiery eyes and an intense eloquence, Debs became national secretary and treasurer of the firemen's union at the age of twenty-five.

A dozen years later he decided that all railroad employees should be organized in a "vertical" union instead of by separate crafts. He then organized the American Railway Union in 1892. It was effective from the start in negotiating with what he called "the massed might of the ferocious, adament and all-conquering moguls of American railroads." Early in 1894 Debs's union struck the Great Northern, paralyzed the line and forced it to yield to his wage demands.

A short time later Debs's railroad workers, numbering about one hundred fifty thousand, decided to walk out in sympathy with the Pullman strikers. George Pullman not only refused to restore wage cuts ranging from 25 to 33⅓ percent but insisted he would not negotiate. Debs found himself confronted by the massed power of the railroads and an armed force of federal troops, state militia and ruffians deputized as United States marshals. In addition, the government obtained an injunction against the strikers. Debs, proclaiming that a war had been declared between "the producing classes and the money power of the country," refused to obey the injunction and a year later was sentenced to six months in jail. His men were being killed in clashes with the government forces, whose attitude was epitomized by a drunken regular army colonel, fraternizing with the nabobs in a Chicago club, who declared that he was ready to order his men to fire on every man who wore the "dirty white ribbon" the strikers had adopted as an emblem.[17]

In the end, Debs and his followers lost out, and the American Railway Union was destroyed. "Both sides," as Debs's counsel Clarence Darrow declared, "recognized that Debs had led a great fight to benefit the toilers and the poor. It was purely a part of the world class-struggle for which no individual can be blamed." Debs, however, was imprisoned for six months. All in all, that jail term was a bad bargain for the upper classes, for Debs spent his time reading the propaganda of the Fabian Socialists and other prophets and came out convinced that the working classes did not stand a chance for a decent life under capitalism.

He began organizing the Socialist party soon thereafter, and on January 1, 1897, published the manifesto in the *Railway Times:* "The time has come to regenerate society — we are on the eve of a universal change."

In this effort he was joined by Victor L. Berger of Milwaukee and Morris Hillquit of New York, who were to be his leading collaborators. Berger had visited him in jail and left a copy of Karl Marx's *Das Kapital* for him to read, not because he believed Marxism was necessary in the United States — society could be reformed, in the American way, through the democratic process — but because Marx was "stimulating." Debs and his collaborators were unable to interest Samuel Gompers, the head of the growingly powerful American Federation of Labor, in Social Democracy because Gompers believed that labor's fight must be waged within the confines of the capitalist system.

In the years from 1900 to the outbreak of World War I, however, they succeeded in gaining members by the hundreds of thousands. The crest of the movement was reached in 1912, when Debs made his third run for the Presidency as the Socialist candidate and polled a million votes.

In those pre-World War years the German workingmen formed the bulk of Debs's support. If their radicalism was less extreme now, they still were regarded as a dangerous element by the bourgeoisie, few of whom understood the difference between Debs's democratic socialism and the Marxist brand.

The German-American capital of Milwaukee became the citadel of American socialism. Most of the men who worked in its machine-tool factories and other industries demanding highly skilled craftsmen were members of the Socialist party. For many years, until it was torn down recently to clear the ground for a new freeway, Brisbane Hall (named for Albert Brisbane, the Socialist-minded father of Arthur Brisbane, the chief of staff and head ideologue of the Hearst newspapers, which leaned perceptibly leftward in those years) stood at Sixth and Juneau streets as the emblem of Socialist ascendancy in Milwaukee.

In Brisbane Hall, Victor Berger began publishing the socialist daily Milwaukee *Leader*, which was read by thousands and had its front page printed on a pink paper, the mere sight of which enraged the conservative section of the populace. (In New York, meanwhile, another socialist daily, the *Call*, was being published.) The paper, founded in 1901, served as the chief organ of the Socialist party, and at one time its staff included the youthful Carl Sandburg, the humorist Josh Billings, Ernest Untermann and E. Haldemann-Julius, later a pamphleteer and publisher on his own.

In Milwaukee, at least, it appeared that Debs's conviction that socialism could triumph through democratic means might be justified. Berger, a tall, moon-faced, black-haired man with scholarly interests, who often spent his evenings debating in his library with Joseph Uihlein, one of the city's leading brewers, eventually was elected to Congress from the Fifth Wisconsin District.

By 1916 socialism had attained a firm grip on the German-American electorate. Twenty-one of the twenty-five city councilmen were socialists, and so was the mayor. Milwaukee became the first — and only —

large American city taken over by the Socialist party, and it stayed socialist long after the party lost its national effectiveness.

The chief inspiration of the Milwaukee socialists was a lean, wiry, vigorous young man named Daniel Webster Hoan, half-Irish and half-German, who hung onto the mayor's office for six terms from 1916 to 1940. He bore a close physical resemblance to the playwright Eugene O'Neill, and possessed the political dexterity to hold his party and his city together during the World War I years when both socialist and German-American loyalties were subjected to the severest tests. Something of the rough-and-ready style which endeared him to the voters for so many years was indicated by his remark when it was suggested that he invite the king and queen of Belgium to visit Milwaukee. "I stand for the man who works," Mayor Hoan snorted. "To hell with the kings!"[18]

13. EVENTS LEADING TO THE

TRAGEDY

During the several decades preceding the First World War, there was a growing bumptiousness among German-American intellectuals. Germanism of the cultural, scientific, philosophic variety, if not of the crudely nationalistic sort that resulted in what came close to armed conflict with American expansion in Samoa and Manila Bay, was on the rise. It paralleled in chronology, and perhaps even exceeded in vigor, the less intellectual but more violent German-American tendencies toward political radicalism, toward a continuing if more subdued nostalgia for separateness (reflected in the hundreds of German-language newspapers, the German parochial schools, the pressure for teaching German in the public schools), toward an aggressive stance by Germans, in and out of clerical vestments, determined to assume a more important role in the Catholic Church.

The more Teutonized of the German-Americans took full advantage of Germany's prestige in pressing their claims for a more Germanic America. In those years England was still regarded by most Americans as first among the nations, next to the United States, but Germany had superseded France as the most admired of the Continental countries. The Prussian victory in 1871 was partly responsible, but Germany's achievements in science, industry and the realm of abstract thought were greatly admired and often emulated in this country.

The popularizers of scientific thought, whose work was eagerly broadcast by the American newspapers then reaching the apogee of their influence on the national life, made a cultural hero of Ernst Haeckel, the iconoclastic sage of Jena and the leading prophet of monism, the doctrine that there is only one kind of ultimate reality, as mind or matter, with no godhead as its creator and inspiration. It was the heyday of the village atheists, the crackerbarrel misanthropes, of Ambrose Bierce, Robert G. Ingersoll, Brann the Iconoclast, and all their imitators, but Haeckel's translated writings transcended them all in their impact on American thought. Haeckel denied that there was any purpose in life, said that personal freedom was meaningless, that personal immortality was a chimera, and that the conception of God as passed down by the various religions was ridiculous. He referred to God as "that gaseous invertebrate." In Germany thousands were reported leaving organized religion to join the monist societies inspired by Haeckel's doctrines. In this country, his *Riddle of the Universe* (1899) became a best-seller and was reprinted many times. Yet his form of atheism was somewhat ambiguous. He held that there was a great mysterious unity that included man and animals, all energy and matter. Man and all his earthly surroundings were mortal, but admittedly the universe seemed to be capable of self-renewal, of a form of immortality. Worlds would go on dying and being reborn through eternity — and for that Haeckel was unable to supply an explanation. "Readers of Emerson," as Professor Henry F. May has noted, "could swallow Haeckel's conclusions without much trouble."[1]

Haeckel's monism was broadcast in this country by a German immigrant named Paul Carus, with adaptations of his own. In his magazines *Open Court* and *Monist* he gathered followers, particularly among the intellectuals, with his theory that the material and spiritual realms were one, and that their mysteries could be comprehended by scientific investigation into natural law. His advocacy of the nonreligious religion of monism was financed by a wealthy Chicago manufacturer. Another propagandist of the monist nonfaith was Jacques Loeb of the

Rockefeller Institute of Medical Research, who was also a camp follower of the German philosophers of naturalism. In 1900 Loeb had succeeded in fertilizing the eggs of the sea urchin, without the participation of the male sea urchin, in his laboratory. This led him to believe that physical-chemical explanations could be found to solve all the mysteries of life and death. He had the gift of popularization, and his essays, published in *Popular Science* and *McClure's*, along with reports of his addresses to the Monist Congress exerted a wide influence. His belief that a study of the instincts was the key to human behavior, that humans were instinctively good rather than divinely inspired, naturally attracted intellectuals of a liberal and progressive cast. "We struggle for justice and truth," he held, "since we are instinctively compelled to see our fellow humans happy." The Loeb theories, of course, lent respectable support to the anarchist doctrine that government was unnecessary because humans were inherently good and didn't need laws or applied force to keep them from each others' throats.

Others in the forefront of circulating and popularizing German thought were H. L. Mencken and James Gibbons Huneker. They and other bright young men writing for *Smart Set*, a periodical which has no equivalent today but might be compared to a combination of the *New Republic* and *Ramparts* in its hostility to accepted beliefs, were vigorously promoting the works of Nietzsche as an antidote to the banalities of democracy, as a foe of puritanism and as a standard-bearer for the aristocratic principle. They were aesthetes of a rugged, virile and uncompromising school. Huneker, the son of a German father and Irish mother, had the German diligence intellectually and the Irish way with words. As music critic of *Smart Set*, he imported the best in European art and thought and made them fashionable in America. He also wrote theatrical criticism, without which, Mencken claimed, Americans would "still be sweating at the Chautauquas and applauding the plays of Bronson Howard."

Like Huneker, Mencken was vociferous in championing European — usually German — aesthetic standards. He was the declared enemy of the old Anglo-Saxon dominance in cultural matters, who tirelessly denounced the "Puritan incapacity for seeing beauty as a thing in itself, and the full peer of the true and the good." His attacks on the Anglo-Saxon majority extended, in fact, to all phases of its overlordship. The Anglo-Saxon, he asserted, was "the least civilized of white men and the least capable of true civilization. His political ideas are crude and shallow. He is almost wholly devoid of esthetic feeling. The most elementary facts about the visible universe alarm him, and incite him to put them down. Educate him, make a professor of him, teach him how to express his soul, and he still remains palpably third-rate. He fears ideas almost more cravenly than he fears men. His blood, I believe, is running thin; perhaps it was not much to boast of at the start . . ."[2] Thus he began campaigning early in his career for the American language against standard literary English; for the naturalism of Dreiser, Twain, Stephen Crane and Frank Norris against the prevailing romanticism and pseudo-elegance. Nothing in America pleased his eye — certainly not the Americanized German — and he was convinced that the "booboisie" were in the saddle for good. "One might throw a thousand bricks in any American city without striking a single man who could give an intelligible account of either Hauptmann or Cézanne, or the reasons for holding Schumann to have been a better composer than Mendelssohn."

Mencken's Germanophilia rose to crescendo during a visit to Europe and brought forth some of his most lyrical writing. The pre-World War I Munich, he believed, was greatly superior to Paris in gaiety, culture and the provision of wine, beer and food. His tour also convinced him that Anglo-Saxon optimism and boosterism, in contrast to European pessimism, was the height of vulgarity. "Search where you will, near or far, in ancient or modern times, and you will never find a first-rate race or enlightened age, in its moments of highest reflection, that ever gave more than a passing bow to optimism."

The chief enemy of any possible development of an American culture, as he described him in an admiring essay on Huneker, was "not so much the vacant and harmless fellow who belongs to the Odd Fellows and recreates himself with *Life* and *Leslie's Weekly* in the barbershop, as that more belligerent and pretentious donkey who presumes to do battle for 'honest' thought and a 'sound' ethic — the 'forward-looking' man, the university ignoramus, the conservator of orthodoxy, the rattler of ancient phrases — what Nietzsche called the 'Philistine of culture.'" His indignation was particularly aroused by the growing Prohibition movement and the cause of women's suffrage, both to be successful despite his most anguished protests. "And thus," he predicted, "we shall be quack-ridden and folly-ridden until the mobocracy comes to its inescapable debacle, and the common people are relieved of their present oppressive duty of deciding what is wrong with their tummies, and what doctor is safest for them to consult, and which of his pills is most apt to cure."

Mencken, for all his thundering against the Anglo-Saxon majority and its most sacred beliefs, did not, however, join the more extreme and unrefined German-American movements for the preservation of a Germanic influence in the United States. He held himself aristocratically aloof from such jack-booted processions as the Educational Alliance for the Preservation of German Culture in Foreign Lands, which was established in this country in 1881 with the declaration: "Not a man can we spare if we expect to hold our own against the 125 millions who already speak the English language and have pre-empted the most desirable fields for expansion." He also stood disdainfully apart from the American branch of the German-American Alliance, established here several years later with the aim of revitalizing "German national sentiment" in countries throughout the world and the proclamation, as forthright as a salvo from a battery of Krupp field guns, that "the German people is a race of rulers."

On another level, that of the German-American who had prospered in this country, yet who insulated himself from the Pan-German vulgarities and the intellectual dissidence of Mencken, Huneker and other Germanophiles, there was also a strong resistance to total Americanization. In the German upper class, of course, the resistance was polite, muted. Hermann Hagedorn has described his preparatory schooling at Bedford Academy, a New York school conducted mainly for the sons of prosperous German-Americans by Dr. George Rodemann, a stiff-backed Prussian with a cavalry moustache and a dueling scar proudly suffered at a German university. "We learned nothing from him about the American way of life, democratic processes of government or the responsibilities of freedom . . . Freedom was taken for granted and the citizen was supposed to absorb from the atmosphere any wisdom, discipline and self-control he might need to be a useful citizen. Dr. Rodemann was in his own person a particularly glaring example of what the American spirit wasn't." Instead, on visits back to Germany, Hagedorn was inculcated with the seductiveness of the German way of life, "German simplicity of living; German romanticism speaking to me in German woods and German ruins . . . I might easily have become a diluted German or, worse, a man of two countries, who did not know in which he belonged, and really belonged to neither."[3]

A BATTLE FOR THE "ROOFTOP" OF THE CHURCH

Among those "desirable fields of expansion" which caught the German eye in the latter part of the nineteenth century was the hierarchy of the Catholic Church. Almost half of all German-Americans were Roman Catholics, and in the 1880's it occurred to many of them that they did not exert an influence on its affairs in proportion to their numbers. "The Germans are a pillar of the Church in America," as Sir Shane Leslie wrote, "but the Irish have always held the rooftop."[4]

Politically, the Irish had blocked German aspirations with consummate ease by staying in the Democratic party and capturing the leadership of its big-city vote. And in the Church, Irish immigrants soon swept aside the dominant French influence which had preceded them, then proceeded to hold its highest places against the influx of German clergy. "When a hurrah is sounded for Irish ward politics," it was recently noted by two Church historians exploring its "de-Romanization," "it recalls the arrival and the impact of these rambunctious, cohesive, aggressive immigrants [that is, the Irish] . . . who fought the French clergy, fought among themselves, and have fought many others since. Their hierarchial posture in the 1960's is rooted in this pugnacious past. The siege mentality lingers . . ."[5]

In the first Catholic parish established in Philadelphia in 1733, twenty-two of the parishioners were Irish, fifteen were German. As the tide of immigration from both Ireland and Germany mounted, both nationalities tended to form themselves in "tribally organized parishes." Soon, particularly in Baltimore and Philadelphia, there was considerable friction between the Irish and the Germans, inside the parish houses and clerical circles rather than among the lay members, over the Germans' insistence on building their own churches. "The German Catholics of Baltimore had established a thriving parochial life . . ." wrote James Cardinal Gibbons's biographer. "Their parishes, mainly under the direction of the Redemptorist Fathers, had shown steady growth, and since 1859 the German-speaking Catholics of the city had their own weekly newspaper, the *Katholische Volks-Zeitung*, which kept them abreast of the activities of their fellow countrymen in other parts of the United States while giving them news of developments in the fatherland."[6]

In 1878, Archbishop Gibbons of Baltimore received a letter from the Reverend George L. Willard of St. Joseph's Church in Fon du Lac, Wisconsin, which sounded the first alarm of German-Catholic trouble-making in the Middle West, where Germans outnumbered the Irish of their faith. (One-third of all Germans were settled in rural areas, against only one-sixth of the Irish.) Father Willard warned that there was a serious conflict threatening in the Archdiocese of Milwaukee. According to Gibbons's biographer, Father Willard "explained that he was a convert of American — rather than Irish — blood and that he spoke the German language. These facts had prompted the German priests to confide in him the plans discussed in their frequent meetings, 'the principal and ulterior object' of which was, according to Willard, 'to perpetuate a young Germany here.' He told Gibbons that one of their ambitions was to secure a German successor in the See of Milwaukee to the aging Archbishop John M. Henni, and he set forth in an objective manner his reasons for believing that a German successor to Henni would have grave consequences for Catholicism in Wisconsin." Six other priests in the See of Milwaukee also petitioned Archbishop Gibbons and other eastern members of the hierarchy to put an end to the "excessive nationalism" in Wisconsin. One of those circularized, Archbishop Wood of Philadelphia, spoke out strongly against the "perpetuation of what he termed the '*germanising* process' in the Province of Milwaukee which, he believed, would be a calamity for the English-speaking Catholics of that region."[7]

That was only a premonitory rumbling of the decade of German vs. Irish controversy which was climaxed by the bitterly divisive presentation of what was called the Lucerne Memorial. By the beginning of the 1880's there were six million Catholics in the United States and the power and responsibility of acting as their spiritual shepherds was no small matter.

The effect of Irish domination in the Church in itself had been a matter of concern long before the Germans challenged the Irish leadership. Before the Civil War, Orestes Brownson, the first native Protestant intellectual to be converted to Catholicism, had expressed doubts about whether, as seemed inevitable, it would be for the best that control of American Catholicism should pass into the hands of Irish immigrants. "Thomas D'Arcy McGee and other Irish 'Forty-eighters,'" as William V. Shannon (*The American Irish*) has noted in this connection, "had in the same period tried unsuccessfully to bring the Catholic Irish immigrants into the mainstream of liberal, nationalistic, middle-class politics." The Irish, however, favored clerics of a conservative cast and the American hierarchy itself was antisocialistic, no matter what the political inclination of many of its German communicants. It was this aspect of the Irish-influenced Church that bothered the liberal-minded Orestes Brownson.

A young friend and protégé of Brownson's was Isaac Thomas Hecker, the member of a prominent German-American family in New York State, a Lutheran who made the rare reconversion to Catholicism. Before he became a Catholic, he immersed himself in the progressive thought of his time. He joined the Fruitlands colony in its sociological experiments and then the Brook Farm, where the atmosphere was dominated by the Transcendentalists and the socialist philosophy of Fourier. Among his fellow seekers at the Brook Farm were Nathaniel Hawthorne, George William Curtis and John S. Dwight, with Ralph Waldo Emerson, Margaret Fuller and W. H. Channing among the frequent visitors.

The questing liberalism he absorbed as a resident of Fruitlands and the Brook Farm stayed with him even after he was converted and subsequently joined the fiercely orthodox Redemptorists. The Redemptorist order was one of three largely German missionary groups engaged in proselytizing the United States.

Father Hecker was appalled at the outright German nationalism of his brothers-in-Christ. The Redemptorists, the Paulists and the Benedictines, all energetically establishing parishes in the United States, were "more in touch with German than American life," he protested. "Irish and native postulants had to learn German in order to say their prayers in many houses."

Father Hecker was a modernist, a progressive, a forerunner of the ecumenical-liberal-humanist movement in a day when the traditionalists held absolute sway over the Church. His one-man crusade against the narrow ambitions of his order inevitably failed. By defying his Redemptorist superiors and trying to Americanize their missionary efforts, he courted and achieved a form of clerical martyrdom. For his pains he was dismissed by the order.

Early in the 1880's, when John Cardinal McCloskey of New York was the titular head of American Catholicism, it became alarmingly apparent to the Irish that while they still held the "rooftop," the hierarchy, the Germans were burrowing away at the foundations. It was possible that the Irish might wear the red hats while in many of the parishes they would find "German Spoken Here" signs all over the place. The Roman Catholic Church had already become, in effect, the Irish Catholic Church. Would it soon become the German Catholic Church?

The Irish archbishops were being made increasingly aware of the fact that their German coreligionists were displeased at being kept out of the places of power. In the number of communicants the Irish had only a slight edge over the Germans, yet the Irish had a noticeable monopoly on the episcopal offices. Of the sixty-nine American bishops in 1886, thirty-five were Irish, only fifteen were Germanic (including the Swiss and the Austrians), eleven were French, five English, and the Dutch, Scotch and Spanish had one bishop each.

Events Leading to the Tragedy

"The Irish, of course, possessed an advantage over the Germans from the outset," John Tracy Ellis, the biographer of Cardinal Gibbons, has explained, "in that English was their mother tongue. It enabled them to become assimilated with the native population much faster than the Germans, and it probably was accountable for the fact that more Irish priests than Germans were selected for the episcopacy at a time when native-born American clergy were still few in numbers. In the years before the Civil War the intensely anti-Catholic nativist movements had a tendency to draw all Catholics in the United States together in self-defense regardless of their national origins. But in the second half of the century with nativist sentiment relatively quiet, the growing prosperity and constantly increasing numbers of the various Catholic foreign-born groups contributed to an added sense of strength with less dependence upon one another." The Irish resented the fact that the Germans clung to their mother tongue. "Wherever they settled in any numbers the familiar pattern of church, parish school, parish clubs and the German language newspaper soon appeared." Many American Catholics "became more sensitive about their German coreligionists' holding to their native language, for with good reason did they remember that the charge of 'foreignism' was one of the constant refrains against Catholics in former times." In addition, there were personality conflicts between the Germans and the Irish inevitable in peoples of their often opposed temperaments. The temperamental difference was so apparent that "for several generations American vaudeville and variety stage audiences were entertained by exaggerated versions of the contrasting characteristics of the stage Irishman and the 'Dutch' comedian. To the phlegmatic German his mercurial Irish neighbor appeared fickle and unstable, while the somewhat volatile Irishman viewed the somber and plodding German as a respectable but generally dull companion."[8]

One of the few things that drew the German and Irish Catholics together in the Eighties, cited by the authors of *The De-Romanization of the American Catholic Church*, was the mutually disturbing influx of Italian Catholic immigrants, who were treated as the French had treated the Irish newcomers earlier in the century. The Italians were

353

even more "volatile" than the Irish. As viewed by the Germans and Irish, their women were "too ostentatiously fervent" in their religious duties while their men were "notably nonconformist religiously."

But the main issue was between the Irish and the Germans, whose temperamental differences "showed up among the clergy as well as the laity and when the two groups were thrown together in the realm of church government the result frequently was friction and trouble."[9]

Early in the Eighties there were angry confrontations between the hot-tempered Irish and the stubborn Germans, not quite Christian in spirit. Many of the Irish bishops were fiery advocates of Prohibition. Drink was the curse of the Irish, and they felt that the only way their people could be saved was by closing down the saloons and leveling the distilleries. (Alcoholism continues to be an Irish problem, according to a recent study. The Reverend John L. Thomas, a Jesuit sociologist, conducted a survey of the records of the Chicago Archdiocese's Marriage Court records and has reported his findings in *The American Catholic Family*. Alcoholism and mental breakdown caused the most marital breakups among the Irish-Americans, Father Thomas's studies showed, while adultery was the chief cause of wrecked marriages among the German-Americans. His study also revealed that "mixed" marriages were more common among those of German descent than those of Irish.) The German-born or -descended clergy, on the other hand, assumed the attitude of all Germans that while drink might be the curse of the Celt, with his more impressionable makeup, it was the balm of the Teuton. They were appalled by such militant Prohibitionists as Archbishop John Ireland of St. Paul, who would come roaring down the streets of the tenement districts in his archdiocese, invading houses and throwing whiskey bottles out of windows; and they were affronted when he tossed the bottles of the Germans as well as the Irish out the windows on his forays.

The greatest friction between the Irish and the Germans in the Church government was the retention of the German language, both in church services and in the parochial schools. Beyond that, the German clerics wanted a considerable measure of autonomy even in Irish-governed archdioceses. The Irish, however, maintained their dominant position and "monopolized the right to define the Church in American terms," as William V. Shannon has observed. "The newer immigrants — the Poles, Italians, Lithuanians and others — could not look to the Germans whose ideals were the preservation of the German language and tradition in this country. These ideas were, by definition, exclusive. The Irish, no matter how parochial they might be, talked in English and bespoke an inclusive 'American' ideal. It is easy to satirize the extent to which the Irish clergy monopolized the places of power and to deplore their somewhat less than cosmopolitan intellectual outlook, but, in fact, the Catholic Church in America could not have avoided becoming an 'Irish Church.' "[10]

The battle lines were drawn in August, 1883, when a prominent German layman named Peter Paul Cahensly visited the United States. He was the secretary-general of the St. Raphael's Society for the Care of German Catholic Emigrants. A member of the Reichstag and a philanthropist, Cahensly was one of those laymen whose fervent interest in Church affairs often causes more harm than good, no matter what their intentions. This ecclesiastical buff, nominally concerned with the welfare of Catholic immigrants, spent much of his time conferring with the German priests in the Archdiocese of St. Louis, where there was considerable dissidence over Irish domination. Soon after Cahensly returned to Germany a Catholic monthly in St. Louis, the *Pastoral-Blatt*, published an article titled "Clerical Know-Nothingism in the Catholic Church of the United States," which reflected Cahensly's views that the Germans ought to have more control over the Church government. Specifically it criticized the system of "maintaining a number of German Catholic churches under the jurisdiction of English-speaking parishes."

From then until the end of the Eighties, there was constant agitation among the German clerics and a boiling sense of outrage among the Irish bishops. At one point the hotheaded Bishop John Ireland of St. Paul called a German proposal for greater autonomy "a villainous tissue of misstatements."

Fortunately for American Catholicism a wise, tactful and cool-tempered Irishman became a cardinal in 1887. James Cardinal Gibbons replaced the late John Cardinal McCloskey of New York, who had done little to ameliorate the German-Irish situation. Gibbons was born to poor parents in Baltimore in 1834. His rise in the Church was rapid. At the age of thirty-four he was the "boy bishop of North Carolina," and at fifty-three he received his red hat. Aside from an endearing trait of dribbling cigar ashes over his vestments, he was the perfect man to head the American Catholic Church in a time of heated controversy. He was a born diplomat, liberal-minded, whose great ambition was to bring all Catholics into the wider reaches of society. Unlike some of the Irish bishops, he was able to sympathize with the Germans' hopes to retain something of their overseas culture; he realized that the situation of the Irish and the Germans differed, and that time and patience would be required to prevent the difference from becoming a rupture.

At the same time he did not intend to yield authority over the contending parties. Regarding the division that threatened the Church, he remarked, "The only way to correct the evil at the beginning is to absolutely refuse to recognize any distinctions in our government of the Church, for if any one nationality is accorded special privileges, other nationalities will demand the same." He also pointed out that by a recent ruling German priests had been given "exclusive jurisdiction over children of German parents" in regard to baptism, first communion and marriage.

Despite his constantly ameliorating influence, the situation came to a head in the spring of 1891. The previous September a general European Catholic congress was held at Liège, Belgium, before which Father Alphonse Villeneuve of Albany, New York, read a paper in which he claimed that out of the twenty-five million Catholic immigrants who had entered the United States, twenty million had lost the faith. It caused great alarm. Three months later the various branches of the European St. Raphael's Society met in Lucerne, Switzerland, and the chief topic of discussion was the claims made by Father Villeneuve and how Catholics in America could be brought back to the faith. One of the moving spirits of that assemblage was the same Peter Paul Cahensly, who eight years before had stirred up trouble in St. Louis.

The society, at the end of its deliberations, issued recommendations

Cardinal Gibbons, who held the "rooftop"
of the Church

Altgeld of Illinois, hard-nosed
for justice

in the form of what became known as the Lucerne Memorial. It was an explosive document. The memorial proposed that the seventy-five territorial divisions in the United States be abolished and replaced by ethnic divisions. In the new divisions, German, Irish and Italian priests would offer a "familiar religious setting for the immigrants." There would be separate parishes for each nationality, with a priest of the same national origin to be appointed to each. Furthermore bishops would be appointed in strict proportion to the nationality they represented, which would have divided control of the Church in America almost evenly between the Germans and the Irish.

The contents of the memorial were first published in the United States, May 28, 1891, by the New York *Herald*, and a flaming controversy followed shortly thereafter. Bishop Ireland of St. Paul inquired of Cardinal Gibbons "if Cahensly was to be permitted to tell Rome how the Church of this country was to be ruled amid the silence and apparent approval of the American hierarchy. He said he knew Gibbons' 'delicacy of sentiment' which might tempt him not to act lest jealous minds should complain . . . yet there were times when delicacy must yield before stern duty." Bishop Ireland added that "we are American bishops . . . and effort is made to dethrone us and to foreignize our country in the name of religion." Another Irish bishop wrote Cardinal Gibbons that "to your Eminence we must look for salvation from the wicked wretch, Cahensly, who is striving to undo the work of the Church in our country."[11]

Cardinal Gibbons finally spoke out on June 28 when he preached at the dedication of the new St. Mary's Church, a German parish, in Washington, D.C. He pointed out that the Church was a family of many peoples, and then delivered his candid opinion of the Lucerne Memorial:

"With these facts before us we cannot view without astonishment and indignation a number of self-constituted critics and officious gentlemen in Europe complaining of the alleged inattention which is paid to the spiritual wants of the foreign population and to the means of redress which they have thought proper to submit to the Holy See."

A few days later the Washington *Post* reported under a Brussels dateline that "the political character of the [Cahensly] movement is inadvertently manifested by the statement that the European governments cannot longer regard the matter with indifference and that it is of the utmost importance to retain their influence on their people in America." By way of response to intimations from abroad that foreign governments were interfering in the controversy Cardinal Gibbons let it be known on July 11 that he had talked with President Benjamin Harrison about the Lucerne Memorial and its implications, and that the President had expressed himself as strongly in favor of the Cardinal's condemnation of Cahenslyism.

Irish-American churchmen were quick to rally their forces against the threat posed by the memorial. Shortly after Cahensly presented his memorial to Pope Leo XIII, they presented their own case to the Holy See. The Pope ruled in favor of the Irish, and proportional representation based on ethnic ratios, so far as the appointment of bishops was concerned, was turned down.

Yet it was only a partial victory for the Irish in that the idea of ethnic parishes was not ruled out by the Pope. They were to be retained, wherever necessary, for first-generation immigrants. In the Diocese of Gary, Indiana, it has been pointed out by two Church historians, twenty-five of the forty-five urban parishes catered to the various nationalities which had come to work in the steel mills from 1900 on. "The national parishes," they added, "have done at the grass roots what Cahensly wanted to do at the top." Any Catholic bishop is still required to obtain special approval from the Vatican to close or convert an ethnic parish.[12]

The controversy over Cahenslyism was damped down by Cardinal Gibbons's infinite tact and diplomacy. Cahensly himself came over on another visit in 1910, was given a "most friendly welcome" by the Cardinal and invited to dine with him. He went back to Germany reporting that he had noted a "great improvement of conditions among German Catholics and other immigrants."

As it turned out, the Catholic hierarchy has been more equally divided between bishops, archbishops and cardinals of Irish and German descent. They rule the "rooftop" together, to the notable exclusion of the Poles and the Italians. The late Cardinal Ritter of St. Louis,

Father Hesburgh, the president of Notre Dame, and others of German extraction took the lead in advancing the civil rights of Negroes and liberalizing Catholic education.

The furor over Cahenslyism, in any case, was largely confined to the clergy and had little effect on their parishioners. Thus two young Catholic politicians in New York formed a close personal alliance that was to have considerable political effect. One was Alfred Emmanuel Smith, an Irishman, and Robert F. Wagner, Sr., a young lawyer of German immigrant parentage. They went to Albany as state legislators and for several years roomed together and fought side by side for more liberal legislation. Wagner, in fact, married an Irish girl (their son, of course, was the mayor of New York City for several terms and is still a power in Democratic politics). Both were amused by rumors that Al Smith — who became majority leader in the Assembly while Wagner was Democratic leader in the Senate — was a German whose name originally was Schmidt.

THE PROLIFERATING PRESS

As a mirror of German-American attitudes, the German-language press in America encouraged its millions of readers to believe they were the keystone of American democracy. If there was a considerable element of self-esteem among them, it was tirelessly promoted by their newspapers. Looking at the state of the German-language press today, with only a handful of weeklies and monthlies surviving and many of them bilingual, it is difficult to imagine the influence they once had. Before their decline during and after the traumatic years of World War I, however, they were a chief ingredient of the atmosphere the German-Americans breathed, a leading factor in their conviction that the American future would and should be cast in a Germanic mold. By their numbers and total circulation alone, the German-language papers formed a large sector of American journalism. In 1914, of the thirteen hundred foreign-language papers published in the United States, 537, or 40 percent, were German.[13]

The number and circulation of the various *Zeitungs* and *Beobachters* and *Abend-Posts* was considerably larger than the German fraction of the population. Earlier the proportion had been even greater. In 1890, there were 727 German periodicals in the United States. By comparison in that year there were 112 Scandinavian (Danish, Swedish, Norwegian, Finnish) newspapers, 22 Bohemian, 28 Spanish, 18 Polish, 13 Italian and 40 French.

And it was as bumptious a journalistic sector as it was large and clamorous. Of all the foreign-language newspapers, the German-American were the most critical of American customs, the most arrogant in their attitude toward other minorities and the Anglo-Saxon majority. Native Americans, as one expert on the subject has noted, strongly resented the German-American editors for their "intolerant attacks on the alleged low cultural and educational standards of the United States, the ridicule of American eating and drinking habits, and the criticism of American art, architecture, literature, dirty cities, corrupt politics, and the American's absorption in business to the exclusion of all interest in intellectual and theoretical matters."[14]

Many of the editors during the post-Civil War period were Forty-eighters, who did their best to point up and exacerbate the difference between the older immigrants (the "Grays") and their self-styled intellectual and cultural superiors, the newly arrived "Greens." One of the Grays, Ludwig von Baumbach, published a book in 1856 blaming the rambunctious Greens, with their command of the burgeoning German-language press, and with their snobbish attitude toward American manners and mores, for encouraging the rise of the Know-Nothings.

For all their posturing and protesting in regard to the American political system and the spoilsmen who ran it on the lower levels — an attitude perhaps dictated in part by the German inability to shoulder aside the ubiquitous Irish ward heeler or supersede the big-city boss with his foolproof system of favors granted and favors received — the German papers were anything but impervious to corruption themselves.

Many of them, perhaps the majority, were subsidized indirectly by the huge German brewing and distilling interests, which also channeled funds into German-American societies, particularly those with a Pan-

German orientation, and into supporting the aspirations of German-American politicians.

On July 11, 1876, the Milwaukee *Germania*, which boasted the largest circulation of all the German-language dailies, began an exposé on the financial links between beer making and newspaper publishing. It showed that German brewers subsidized those papers whose editorial policies they approved of by giving them large amounts of unnecessary advertising. It also quoted a critic of this system who said the "German-American vote has floated too long on an ocean of beer."

With scant professional courtesy, the *Germania* also disclosed that the owner of the Illinois *Staats-Zeitung* and several of his closest associates were involved in the Whiskey Ring scandal which disfigured the Grant Administration, and which, the *Germania* sardonically noted, "cast a shadow on the vaunted German honesty."

Yet it would be injust to say that the whole German-language press was what it appeared to its outside critics. In general it was true enough that a German paper was inclined to sniff at American vulgarities, at Anglo-Saxon money-grubbing (though the Germans had more than their share of the exploiting class), at the day-to-day failures of democracy, at a general lack of idealism responsible in their view for the belated termination of human slavery, at the native American's lack of appreciation for Rhine wine (against whiskey), for Beethoven (against Stephen Foster), for long walks in the quiet woods (against buggy riding). Most Europeans, of course, were conscious of the same differences but were tactful enough not to harp on them. It was also true that the German paper, though edited by a man chased out of Germany for his political beliefs or his aversion to serving in a Prussian-officered army, often tended to brag about German achievements, support the old country's drive for *Lebensraum* and defend its policies.

But the German press widely differed in its attitudes on many other questions. Some papers were Republican, others Democratic. Some even favored conciliation of the South and soft-pedaled on the issue of Know-Nothingism. The one issue on which they were united, in fact, was against any laws prohibiting the sale of alcoholic beverages on Sunday; in that hearty cause they echoed the Milwaukee German-language paper which decried any tampering with the liquor laws as an "outflow of Puritan bigotry."

The oldest and most quoted of the German dailies was the New York *Staats-Zeitung*, but it was not the first German periodical to be established in the United States. That honor went to a monthly established in Germantown, Pennsylvania, in 1739, which rejoiced in the marathon title of *Der Hochdeutsch-Pennsylvanische Geschicht-Schreiber, oder Sammlung Wichtiger Nachrichten aus dem Natur und Kirchen-Reich*. It was published by Christopher Sauer, a printer who also produced the first entire Bible (in German) published in this country. Benjamin Franklin recorded that of the six printing presses in Pennsylvania two were German and another two were "half-German."

The New York *Staats-Zeitung* differed from most other German-language papers in confronting nativism and southern secession. Its editorial attitude, as a Democratic organ, was that Know-Nothingism was directed against the Irish immigrants, rather than the German. Rather pusillanimously it declared its neutrality on that issue, which it defined as a "battle between Puritanism and Jesuitism." Like many other German-language papers of the Democratic persuasion, it attacked Carl Schurz as an "ambitious demagogue." The Democratic organs mostly remained silent, too, when the XI Corps was humiliated by Chancellorsville and did not reply to English-language newspapers which referred to Schurz's troops as "flying Dutchmen" and their actions as a "Dutch Panique."

Largely to offset the apathy of the *Staats-Zeitung* toward the Civil War, Friedrich Schwedler diverted funds from his family textile business to buy up the daily *New Yorker Demokrat*. Schwedler, whose grandson described him as "a German idealist out of the storybooks," did not change the paper's logotype but did convert it into a Republican organ. In his offices in Chatham Square, Schwedler also published the weekly *Der Beobachter am Hudson*, which had a large circulation west of the Alleghenies. His grandson concedes that the two periodicals were heavy going for the reader. "A single paragraph might run three-quarters of a column; and the reader, diving into a sentence, would have had to be a strong underwater swimmer if, in Mark Twain's phrase, he were to come out at the other end 'with a verb in his mouth'; but, for a generation that took its papers seriously, there was solid substance to feed on. With sympathy and imagination the paper sought to meet the needs of the Germans in exile, reminding them of the best of their German heritage, stimulating their thinking, and holding them to their highest as American citizens. It was leadership of an exceptional quality, and in the highest tradition of nineteenth century liberalism."[15]

Many of the German papers, of course, leaned far leftward of liberalism and provided the working masses with visions of a Marxist happy hunting ground or an anarchist paradise where they would never again be hounded by tax collectors, recruiting sergeants or unsympathetic police. "The most signal effect of the German papers on America," Sir Shane Leslie believed, "has been socialism." They also encouraged German-Americans to carry trade unionism "to the anarchic extreme."[16]

A number of German-Americans gained affluence through investing in both the German- and English-language newspapers, but more through the latter than the former. The aristocratic Drexels of Philadelphia owned various Philadelphia newspapers. Adolph S. Ochs, a Cincinnati printer both of whose parents were born in Germany, founded the Chattanooga *Times*, then bought the controlling interest in the New York *Times*, which is still published by his descendants. A Chicago baker whose father migrated from Germany, Hermann Kohlstatt, at various times owned and published the Chicago *Inter-Ocean*, the Chicago *Times-Herald* and the Chicago *Record*.

Journalism in the last century was an aggressive business, and editors without strongly expressed opinions soon found their papers losing out to their competition. Undoubtedly this was partly responsible for the boisterous tone of most German-language papers. They were so unabashedly nationalistic that it was a wonder more presses weren't wrecked and type fonts scattered by indignant mobs. In 1904 the German warship *Panther* called at American ports, at a time when American relations with Germany were embittered by the narrowly averted clashes of the two navies in Manila Bay and over the Samoan intervention. Yet the German-American newspapers brashly and repeatedly published an appeal to "all Singers, Turners and Sons of Arminius — all who revere the flag of Germanism" to turn out at the various ports of call "in a welcome to the *Panther*."

Perhaps because of the narrow range of their interests, their refusal to engage their readership with the less parochial and nationalistic matters of American life, none of the hundreds of German dailies and weeklies was an outstanding newspaper. Several that came closest were the Milwaukee *Germania*, the Milwaukee *Herold* and the St. Louis *Westliche Post*, all of which published national news from the Associated Press wire and attempted to enliven their pages with something other than ponderous editorials, lengthy political and economic reports from Germany, column after column of *Klub* and *Vereine* social affairs.

The ranks of the German-language newspaper editors produced only one journalistic genius in their long, contentious history — and he wasn't even a German.

The most lustrous name in American newspaper publishing got his start in this country on a German paper: Joseph Pulitzer.* He was a German-speaking Hungarian who migrated to the United States shortly before the end of the Civil War. He was bedazzled by hopes of joining the United States Cavalry, but bad eyesight spared him the possibility of dying out West as an Indian fighter. Instead he went to work for the prestigious St. Louis *Westliche Post* and soon became its star reporter. A few years later he acquired part-ownership. At thirty-six he had saved enough money to buy the English-language St. Louis *Post-Dispatch*. His success in building up that journal enabled him to buy the New York *Morning World*. His fame and prosperity began only after he shook himself loose from the self-contained world of German journalism.

THE GERMAN-AMERICAN ESTABLISHMENT

In the years before World War I the German-Americans were undoubtedly the most solidly established of all the minorities. They

* W. A. Swanberg's magnificent *Pulitzer* was published shortly after this work was completed, unfortunately too late to be made use of.

weren't as completely assimilated as the Irish, perhaps, but they were even more a part of the machinery that ran the country, an integral and essential part of finance capitalism, of heavy industry, of education and scientific research and agriculture. It was possible to imagine that if all persons of German descent were suddenly removed from the United States, the machinery would just as suddenly break down. If they seemed backward in developing political technique, in exercising their influence as the Irish did, they nevertheless made their presence and opinions felt and heard in more subtle fashion, often through non-Germans. In 1903 Secretary of State John Hay was so troubled by German influences, in the United States Senate, which were given expression by non-German senators, that he obtained the temporary recall of the American ambassador to Germany.[17]

Statistics showed that Germans were among the most preferred nationalities — not necessarily because of their aptitude for citizenship but because of their skill and diligence. (Those qualities, of course, are still the basis of American immigration policy. The "golden door" opens to a greater variety of peoples, but priority is based on the aptitude, rather than the needs of the applicant.) A questionnaire, for instance, was sent to the governors of the various states by the Immigration Restriction League. Fourteen governors replied that they preferred more Germans; twelve favored Scandinavians; seven, English or Scotch; six, Irish, or other English-speaking people; three, French; two, Swiss; one, Dutch or Belgian.[18]

This preference was expressed in another way by a Pennsylvania steel mill superintendent who wrote: "We must be careful of what class of men we collect . . . My experience has shown that Germans and Irish, Swedes and young American country boys, judiciously mixed, make the most effective and tractable force you can find."[19]

The genius for making things work, for finding new ways to do things, the quick adaptability to the industrial age all were notable attributes of the Germans who came to America. Their rise in the industrial hierarchy, in contrast to their slow progress in that of the Catholic Church, met with little resistance. Many Anglicized their names, but the Chryslers and Studebakers were among the pioneer automobile manufacturers, the Rockefellers monopolized every phase of the petroleum industry, Henry Clay Frick and Charles Schwab were among the steel magnates, and such fields as bridge-building, brewing, musical instruments, chemicals and pharmaceuticals were almost a monopoly of the German-born or -descended.

In the careers of many there was a distinct imprint of the rags-to-riches legend so artlessly but indelibly conveyed in the works of Horatio Alger. The saga of George Westinghouse, for instance. He was a poor farm boy, born in upstate New York to German parents. He was still in his teens when he marched off with his regiment to the Civil War battlefields. Four years after the war ended, when he was only twenty-two, Westinghouse took note of all the trains colliding with large loss of life, particularly on the Erie, and decided to develop a surefire air brake. His invention saved thousands of passengers' lives and cut down the casualty rate among train crewmen.

Westinghouse was not only an inventor but a shrewd businessman. He held onto his air brake patents and formed his own company to manufacture them, as well as other railroad devices he invented and interlocking switch and signal system patents which he acquired from others. The result was a revolution in railroading, which came just at the time the rails were being extended all over the country.

Young Westinghouse tasted success early and was a full-fledged magnate by the time he was thirty, but he never became jaded by wealth and possessions. "Like a lion in the forest," his friend Nikola Tesla said of him, "he breathed deep and with delight the smoky air of his factories. Always smiling and polite, he stood in marked contrast to the rough and ready men I met. And yet no fiercer adversary than Westinghouse could have been found when he was aroused. An athlete in ordinary life, he was transformed into a giant when confronted with difficulties which seemed insurmountable. He enjoyed the struggle and never lost confidence . . . Had he been transferred to another planet with everything against him he would have worked out his salvation."[20]

It was that same special Teutonic quality of doggedness, combined with an imaginativeness rising to the surface when challenged by a mechanical, scientific or engineering problem, that distinguished the careers of many of the Germans who put their mind and muscle into building the physical-material-tangible America, the America of gigantic factories, awe-inspiring bridges and tunnels, vast fields harvested by machines. Whether it was H. J. Heinz in his pickle works or George Weyerhaeuser chewing up millions of acres of virgin timber, the German-American seemed to delight more than his non-German competitors in meeting and triumphing over challenges.

Many of these men were rather attractive as human beings, aside from their accomplishments, because they often seemed to be more interested in the work, the challenge, the opportunity to make a more comfortable world, than in keeping score with the millions their talents earned them. Often they remained simple, down-to-earth fellows with dirt under their fingernails even while their families accustomed themselves to a lordly scale of living.

One such man was Karl August Rudolf Steinmetz, better known as Charles after he came to this country, and even more widely known as the "wizard of Schenectady." It was largely owing to Steinmetz's scientific imagination, his understanding of the newly tamed and highly developed force of electricity, that the General Electric Company became a huge corporation.

He was a puckish, prankish, mischievous hunchback, so undersized that he barely came to the shoulder of his small friend Albert Einstein. Born in Breslau, in 1864, with the same deformity as his father and grandfather, he was given an excellent education at the local gymnasium and later the university. His father, a lithographer, felt guilty about bringing another deformed creature like himself into the world, but instead of letting guilt warp his affection for his only child he gave him constant encouragement and understanding. The boy early showed an astonishing grasp of mathematics and a curiosity about scientific matters, and his father was so convinced that he had nurtured a genius that he compiled and made bound volumes of the boy's classroom papers.

Both at the gymnasium (high school) and the university, his teachers agreed that Karl Steinmetz was probably a genius. His fellow students gave him the nickname Proteus — after the wizard in Greek

George Westinghouse, homespun industrialist

Frederick Weyerhaeuser, exploiter of the northern forests

mythology who lived under the sea — which followed him to the United States. He was a bookish youth, and his twisted little body made him something of an outcast, a condition he resisted by cultivating an apparent unselfconsciousness about being a hunchback, but like most Germans he loved beer, drinking songs and *Gemütlichkeit*. This yearning for fellowship led him into membership in a student socialist society. By the mid-1880's the Prussian police were busy smashing such organizations, particularly in the universities, and sending their members to jail.

Steinmetz, who was attached to socialism only to the extent that he loved to drink beer and clink steins with the members of his society (the only one that solicited his membership), had to make a run for the Swiss border when the Prussian police got on the trail of the secret organization. Thus Steinmetz became just one more inadvertent German gift to America, one it could not easily afford to make.

And America almost rejected him. He crossed in steerage, and when he arrived at Ellis Island immigration officials were dismayed at his appearance. He was not only a hunchback, but ill-kempt and sick looking from a rough passage. He also had to admit that he had no job or relatives waiting for him. The immigration officers waved him off to the detention pen, which meant he would have been returned to Germany and the waiting arms of Bismarck's secret police. A young Danish-American student whom he had met on the voyage stepped forward and announced that he would make young Steinmetz his personal responsibility.

The youth had fled Breslau just before he was to receive his doctorate, but he had no money to finish his education in the United States. Instead he went to work as a draftsman for Rudolf Eickemeyer, who produced hat-making machines in a small Yonkers factory and was trying to develop a workable electric motor. Young Steinmetz knew all about that. In a short time he promoted himself from draftsman to head of Eickemeyer's research laboratory, and began working on the problem. Until then (1890) no one had discovered how to manufacture electric motors or generators on a mass-production basis. Steinmetz

Charles Steinmetz, wizard of Schenectady

solved the problem on paper, and let others work out the details. By then word had got around that he was a genius at electrical engineering.

General Electric, then in its infancy, tried to lure Steinmetz away from the Yonkers firm. Out of loyalty to Eickemeyer, Steinmetz refused all the lures G.E. could throw out. G.E. finally acquired Steinmetz's services, but only after raising enough money to buy out Eickemeyer's firm.

During the next decade, he became the most famous young man in America, devoting eighteen hours a day to his bench in the General Electric laboratories at Schenectady, taking out scores of patents on everything from arc lamps to lightning arresters. Through his contributions to the new field of electrical engineering, American factories were able to switch over from steam to electric power. At G.E. he was referred to as "The Supreme Court," and Harvard conferred an honorary degree on him as "the foremost electrical engineer in the world."

Yet it was his human qualities — not merely the fact that people were, and still are, indebted to him every time they turn on a light switch or take a tray of ice cubes out of the refrigerator — that made him a remarkable and endearing figure. His laboratory was filled with pets as likely to meet human rejection as he himself was — a Gila monster, snakes, seven alligators, two crows who perched on his shoulders and screeched in his ears. Once an assistant found him huddled in his unheated laboratory on a winter's day, bundled up in his overcoat and fur hat. The assistant asked him why he didn't light the furnace. Steinmetz took him over to the furnace and showed him a mouse with a new litter nesting inside.

General Electric provided him with everything he asked for to the day he died in 1923. Since childhood, he had schooled himself to recognize the fact that he could never marry without the fear that the woman he chose pitied him — and he couldn't stand pity. But he still yearned to have children around him. He solved that problem in his usual direct, sensible way. He adopted his longtime laboratory assistant, Joseph Hayden, who had a wife and three children. Steinmetz, the Haydens and their children all moved into a big house, and Steinmetz delighted above everything else in his role as a foster-grandfather. He once kept Henry Ford, who had come to him with an urgent problem, waiting while he read the children their bedtime stories.

He also delighted in his role as a "wizard." He legally changed his name to Charles Proteus Steinmetz, and once made the front pages in every paper in the country by staging a demonstration of his artificial-lightning machine. Newspapermen were invited to his laboratory, in which he had built a miniature village. Steinmetz, with the flourish of a stage magician, threw the switch — there was a blinding flash — and the first man-made thunderbolt smashed the village to pieces.

Once Henry Ford asked him to work out the wrinkles in the new generator at Ford's River Rouge plant. On arrival, Steinmetz refused all assistance, walked around the generator humming to himself, asked for a piece of chalk, then climbed the ladder and drew a mark on the side of the generator. He then told Ford's men to remove the plate which he had marked and take exactly sixteen windings from the coil. The generator then worked perfectly. Steinmetz sent Ford a bill for ten thousand dollars, and in reply received Ford's request for an itemized statement. Steinmetz complied with two items: "Making chalk mark on generator, $1. Knowing where to make chalk mark, $9,999."

Another great innovator of German birth was John A. Roebling, Prussian-born and a graduate of the Royal Poly-Technicum of Berlin. He migrated to America to manufacture wire cables. His idea, after setting up a cable factory in Pennsylvania, was to convert the canal barges to the use of his product for towing purposes. Canal workers, however, were traditionalists who refused to use anything but hemp. Roebling then devised a way to use his wire cable in building bridges. Continuing as a manufacturer, he developed the suspension bridge as a means of promoting the industrial use of his cable. He built the first suspension bridge over the Allegheny, then persuaded Pittsburgh to give him the contract for construction of the 1,500-foot Monongahela Bridge. One of the great engineering feats of the mid-nineteenth century was his suspension bridge across the Niagara River, which lasted for forty-two years until the heavier trains required a bridge of different construction. He then bridged the Ohio at Cincinnati. His greatest accomplishment was of course the Brooklyn Bridge, built after years of struggle and completed after his death by his son, Washington A. Roebling, which may yet celebrate its hundredth anniversary.

Against the record of the many Germans who built the sturdy underpinnings of the modern America must also be placed that of those whose chief interest was in self-aggrandizement. One of the more rapacious monopolies before and after the turn of the century was a traction syndicate, composed of six men, which consolidated the street railways and in some cases the lighting companies of New York, Chicago, Philadelphia, Pittsburgh and a hundred other cities and towns in Pennsylvania, Connecticut, Ohio, Massachusetts, Maine, New Hampshire, Indiana and Rhode Island. It had no corporate title but was an Anglo-Irish-German syndicate formed by William C. Whitney, Thomas Fortune Ryan, Thomas Dolan, William L. Elkins, Peter A. B. Widener and Charles T. Yerkes — the names of most of whom are now socially sanctified, the money they acquired similarly deodorized by long possession and skillful public relations.

Widener and Yerkes were the Pennsylvania German members of the syndicate. The former was a jovial, blustering butcher who entered Philadelphia politics and became a ward leader and the city treasurer before going into the street railway business. He entered the traction industry just as trolley cars, loaded with singing proletarians bound for picnics and beer busts in the country, became a jolly and profitable part of American life. Once when the stockholders indicated they wanted to discuss a proposed lease, he blandly informed them, "You can vote first and discuss afterwards."

Charles T. Yerkes also rose from the lower classes and made a small fortune as a flour commission merchant early in his career. This was based on loans which were called in hastily after the Chicago fire. Yerkes was caught short, convicted of misappropriation of funds but was paroled on his promise to make restitution, which he did. Yerkes then entered the Chicago traction business and prospered by following his own prescription for success: "Buy old junk, fix it up a little, unload it on the other fellow." He also bought up the city council and the Illinois legislature, which enabled him to obtain ninety-nine-year leases on the use of Chicago streets for his trolley cars. He offered Governor

Altgeld a half-million for his official friendship, but was turned down. Eventually he monopolized the Chicago street transportation business.*

Widener in Philadelphia, Yerkes in Chicago, and their syndicate partners, Whitney and Ryan in New York, Elkins and Dolan elsewhere, made their individual fortunes by using their companies as the basis for floating gigantic stock issues. The fruition of their combined genius was the Metropolitan Traction Company, built up from a few horsecar lines in New York City and eventually capitalized most brazenly at $260,000,000. During the panic of 1907 the company went into receivership, but Widener, Yerkes and other members of the syndicate retired with multimillion-dollar fortunes quite undiminished by the disaster which impoverished thousands of their investors.[21]

During the years preceding World War I, German-Americans had every reason to be serenely confident of their place in the national life. They had made good, they considered themselves esteemed above all other peoples which had migrated to America from Europe. Hubris, the sin of pride, can afflict peoples as well as persons. It impelled the German-Americans to believe that they could decisively influence the national will; that they could prevail against the Anglo-Saxon majority and most of the other minorities in keeping America out of the war. It was almost as hopeless a fight as that which Imperial Germany itself, with only Austria, Bulgaria and Turkey at its side, undertook against France, Britain, Russia, Italy and lesser allies. It also left a scar on German-Americanism which took almost half a century to heal.

---

* Theodore Dreiser used Yerkes as the model for his dubious hero, Frank Cowperwood, in *The Titan* and *The Financier*.

14. "STARVE THE WAR AND FEED AMERICA"

Within a few days after the military and naval disaster at Pearl Harbor, federal agents began rounding up 112,000 citizens of Japanese ancestry. Many were Nisei, second-generation Japanese, who had little or no connection with, or patriotic feeling for, the islands in which their parents were born. The Japanese-Americans were herded into "relocation centers" and their property was appropriated, sometimes officially but often illegally, by neighbors jealous of their efficiency as orchardists and truck gardeners. The government began releasing them only after it developed that virtually none of them were in any way un-American or posed any threat to national security; after, also, the Japanese-American regimental combat team performed so valiantly in the Italian campaign.

Yet in the World War which preceded those events, a much more dangerous and organized minority — the German-Americans — was not interned en masse, was not in fact taken into custody individually unless and until they were charged with sedition, subversion, treason or sabotage. For several years the German-Americans had opposed American entry into the European war openly and with every weapon they could find, they had vociferously protested any step taken to aid the French and British allies, and after war was declared, many covertly worked against the war effort. Yet not even those Germans in the United States who had been born in Germany were carted off to internment camps, as they were in France and England.

Why were they spared, treated so gently in contrast to the harsh fate of the Japanese during World War II? The United States Census of 1910 indicates one good reason — there were simply too many of them. In that year there were 8,282,618 Americans who had either been born in Germany or had one or both parents born in Germany. Few of them were subversively pro-German, of course, and many obediently marched off to shoulder arms for Germany's enemies. In any case the task of interning more than eight million citizens would have been insuperable. Guarding them would have taken half the army, and besides they couldn't be spared from the war industries.

Another reason was the considerable political influence they exercised and a sizable bloc of United States senators which voiced their opinions and prejudices. Yet another, undoubtedly, was that white Caucasian America was much more willing to commit a gross injustice against the members of an Oriental race than those of European origin.

German-Americans were not, however, spared from the most violent patriotic hysteria which has ever overtaken and deranged the United States.

THE GERMAN EAGLE SCREAMS

Wilhelmine Germany regarded herself as a stern and demanding guardian of all her children overseas. Anyone with German blood was regarded as subject to the claims of the Fatherland, and was constantly reminded of that supposed bond by the incessant drum-beating of the Pan-German propagandists. In case of a Continental war the mystic unity of all Germans, no matter how long departed or how deeply rooted in America, North or South, Africa, the South Seas and the China coast, was supposed to summon them to arms for the Fatherland. One lusty chorus of "Deutschland über Alles" was supposed to send them all rushing back to the arms of the Wehrmacht's drill sergeants, from which, in fact, so many had fled rejoicing.

In 1911, the Prussian General von Bernhardi demonstrated that, among other things, Imperial Germany was still looking hopefully toward its long-lost millions overseas, particularly in North America. A military intellectual who, as a young cavalry officer, had been the first German to ride through the Arc de Triomphe when the Prussians occupied Paris in 1871, Bernhardi published a book titled *Germany and the Next War*. Its thesis was indicated by several of the chapter headings: "The Right to Make War," "The Duty to Make War" and "World Power or Downfall."

The book, which created a sensation throughout the Western world and sold millions of copies in the United States and Europe during the next several years, declared that war was a "biological necessity," that to be successful a nation must "act on the offensive and strike the first blow." Conquest, Bernhardi held, "becomes a law of necessity." The object of all that bellicosity, as the general plainly indicated, was France, which "must be so completely crushed that she can never cross our path again . . . must be annihilated once and for all as a great power."

It was a time in which many others were talking tough, including, in the United States, Admiral Mahan, who argued that European civilization might be ended if "its fighting energy" were destroyed by arbitration (the World Court at The Hague, presumably), and former President Theodore Roosevelt, who urged that his country "perform those deeds of blood, of valor, which above everything else bring national renown." Nor were French and British military commentators much more moderate than General Bernhardi in praise of bloodletting as the solution of national rivalries.

But it was Bernhardi who reaped the headlines that year, perhaps because of the forcefulness of his expression. In this country *Germany and the Next War* was regarded by those who sympathized with Germany's presumed victims as Kaiser Wilhelm's blueprint for aggression. It also made them take a long, worried look at their fellow citizens of German extraction, for Bernhardi had definitely not overlooked them in his calculations: "The German-Americans have formed a political alliance with the Irish and, thus united, constitute a power in the state with which the American government must reckon." The basis for Bernhardi's mistaken belief that the German- and Irish-Americans were as one, principally in opposing British designs, apparently was an event that had taken place several years before. The National German-American Alliance and the Ancient Order of Hibernians had combined forces in opposing an arbitration treaty, proposed by President Taft, between Britain and the United States. The proposal was defeated in Congress.

In the event of war between Germany and Britain, Bernhardi further predicted, the United States would invade and occupy Canada.

General Bernhardi's reflections and predictions were broadcast, debated and denounced in the American press, the New York *Times* giving over the front page of its Sunday magazine section to discussing the "remarkably prophetic book" which was foretelling "Germany's war plans." Owen Wister, the German-descended novelist, strongly anti-German in his sympathies, began work on a book to be titled *The Pentecost of Calamity*, using Bernhardi's work as its aiming point and denouncing Germany's plans to conquer Europe.

The trumpetings from Germany continued for the next few years and assisted in thickening the atmosphere in America. They inspired those German-Americans infected by Pan-German propaganda, alarmed those who feared the Fatherland's intentions, and created dissension with non-German-Americans who did not look forward to a kaiser-ruled Europe. In 1913 another widely circulated book titled *Germany in Arms* was published, with a foreword by the crown prince, in which that ambitious sprig announced that "The sword will remain the final and deciding factor until the world's end . . . Only with the support of our good sword we maintain that place in the sun which is due us, but not willingly accorded us."[1]

A few days later in June, 1913, the organ of the German National party attacked President Wilson as "one of the most dangerous agitators of modern times" and denounced his monetary reforms as "a new peril for the economic peace of the world . . . a frontal attack against the concentration of capital and a demagogical appeal in favor of impecunious money seekers." The German press, particularly that section controlled by its government, raged at American policy toward a Mexico then in revolution, and declared that Secretary of State William Jennings Bryan was so ignorant of foreign affairs that he had confused Budapest with Bucharest (lamentably true).

In that year before the war began, the nationalistic preachments of German artists, educators and intellectuals — whom so many Americans, as well as other Europeans, trusted to help dampen the war spirit in Germany — also echoed across the Atlantic. Hermann Sudermann, whose plays were read in most American universities, revised history in one sentence: "Prussia and Germany, since the Middle Ages, have never fought except to defend themselves." Maximilian Harden, widely read in translation for his literary criticism, asserted that "the hostility between Germany and France is being kept alive by France alone." A professor much respected in American academic circles, Adolph Wagner, announced that "we Germans are not sufficiently warlike. The military spirit came to us too late . . ." A symposium conducted by scholars from all over Germany was unanimous in declaring that France, with its constant belligerence over its "lost provinces," was forcing a reluctant Germany to arm itself in self-defense.

Meanwhile Professor Kuehnemann of the University of Breslau was embarking on a two-year lecture tour of the United States during which he spoke almost nightly to German-American organizations and other groups. "A world Germanism will evolve," was the burden of his message, "and to foster this world Germanism will be the problem of Germans in every country of the globe."[2]

Despite all the diligent preparation, the outbreak of war in August, 1914, came as a dreadful shock to all Americans, but to those of German ancestry in particular. The question immediately arose whether America could and would stay neutral, whether German-American loyalties would be given the ultimate test by American entry on the side of the Allies, whether German-Americans might be pressed into firing on their cousins, or possibly their brothers, on the other side of the battle line. Obviously the most any sensible German-American could hope for was that the United States would stay out of the war, though some were eager to believe that a British naval blockade would create so much trouble for American shipping that the United States might jump in on the side of the Central Powers.

Many, of course, were torn by the fact that part of their families were in Germany. The father and brother of Hermann Hagedorn had been living in Germany ever since his father retired as a New York cotton broker. By the time war broke out, Hagedorn's brother was a high official in the German government. Hermann Hagedorn, however, had decided to pursue a literary career in the United States; he loved many aspects of German life, but considered himself thoroughly Americanized. Thus he believed that the "kaiser and his generals were out for conquest," even while receiving letters from his father and other members of his family crying that "hostile powers have waylaid us, and want to annihilate us . . . We have been basely betrayed. Long ago everything was prepared by our foes for the assault upon us at this time." His father wrote those despairing words even as the German war machine was smashing through the Belgian forts and invading northern France. "How you must have suffered under the infamous, lying reports, dictated by hate, greed, envy, jealousy! Our enemies work against us in the press, day and night, bribe the newspapers in the neutral countries, make their lie-factories operate overtime." In his memoir, Hagedorn says that he came to realize that "I was being systematically worked upon," but it did not lessen the "grief of the family division."

For German-Americans like Hagedorn — and they probably formed the majority — the black headlines detailing the progress of the German armies, which to them signified a retrogression many had secretly feared as a sign of racial affinity for barbaric tribalism, were a "nightmare of inconceivable happenings." All they had suspected might be true of the German psyche, *their* psyche, even though physically transferred to America, had burst into reality.

Almost half a century after that nightmarish summer of 1914 Hagedorn could still write with a raw-scraped sensitivity of his remembered feelings: "Nothing in the easygoing world in which I had come to maturity had prepared me to believe in the possibility . . . of such violence and destruction, such callous inhumanity, as every day summoned me to face anew. All I had read or heard of war had dealt with armies clashing on battlefields, with civilians generally at a safe distance and protected under international codes of war . . . But here in Belgium was 'hell' — they called it 'frightfulness' — proclaimed as military policy; cities destroyed, regardless of the civilian population; cathedrals, precious libraries, whole villages wantonly given to the torch, and, picked at random, hundreds of burghers shot in reprisal for some sniper's bullet from some leaf-shrouded attic window. The stories were no product of overheated minds, no 'scurrilous lies' as my family insisted, and, I know, believed. Germany herself, through her commanding officers, proclaimed them, plastered them on the walls of public buildings, to warn and to deter."

Yet even the idealistic young Hermann Hagedorn was admittedly a divided man. "Soberly gratified though I might be at every German setback, every German victory set my Teutonic heart beating a little faster. Ambivalence is the word for it . . . it made for tension and a feeling of guilt . . ."

Then in 1914, and even more so when Hitler came to power two decades later, most German-Americans suffered not only from that inevitable ambivalence over Germany's fate but were inwardly tormented by the meaning of the German blood that coursed through them. Secretly most of them wondered at the accident of geography. Had their fathers or grandfathers not migrated to the United States, they asked themselves, "Would I now be a Uhlan helping to level a Belgian village?" or later "Would I now be a Gestapo agent torturing people in the cellar of an occupied French town?"

THE "PRUSSIANS AND THE PRUSSIANIZED"

Almost from the moment the armies of the Anglo-French Entente and the Central Powers began moving toward each other, both sides launched another kind of offensive directed at the minds and hearts of the American people. In Europe it soon developed that the opposing forces would be deadlocked in the trenches, and that the material assistance of the United States might well be, as indeed it was, the decisive factor. From both sides went up a barrage of propaganda. The Allies especially needed American help from the outset. First they would require billions to finance their war effort. Then they would need the products of American war industries, also food and other supplies in large quantities. Finally they would cry out for troops to reinforce their war-weary divisions. Imperial Germany also needed help, but essentially she could win the war if only the United States could be kept out of it. Thus the main thrust of German propaganda was toward preserving American neutrality, that of the Allies to impress Americans with the brutality of the Germans — thus the horrendous stories of crucified nuns and maimed children in Belgium — and convince them that Western civilization would be wrecked by the Hun.

In the struggle for American public opinion, the Allied cause was mightily bolstered by the skillful inventions of England's great literary men, who turned propagandists almost to a man (Shaw and a few others excepted).

But the Germans were not slow to seize the initiative, and they had the advantage of organizations, mostly self-financed, waiting for the signal to begin propagandizing. Boldly and openly, with help from Berlin, they propagated the slogans against American involvement in the European war. As Owen Wister, fighting Germanism as ruggedly as his fictional Virginian grappled with the bad men of the old West, baldly put it, the enemies of true Americanism were "the Prussians and the Prussianized . . . These latter are newcomers. Nothing that brought the South Germans brought them; they hadn't fled from horrible wars, they had run away from military service."

It was more complicated than that, the German-American attitude, and it wasn't only those of Prussian descent, or those who had been "Prussianized," who joined the broad front of organizations opposed to any American assistance to the Allies. The "cause" was substantially financed by brewing interests equally interested in preserving neutrality and keeping antiliquor laws off the statute books. As it turned out, the fears of the beer-loving German population were justified. The febrile wartime atmosphere was "exploited and directed by the activity of the propaganda experts of the time, George Creel, his notorious Committee on Public Information, and the Prohibitionists," Andrew Sinclair (*Prohibition: The Era of Excess*) has observed. Part of the patriotic idealism which swept America was diverted into the channels of the Prohibition movement, which claimed that the death of John Barleycorn would justify so many other deaths in battle. "For, in time of war," Mr. Sinclair continued, "all the specific means of conquering the Evil One are, and should be, glorified. The cult of battle requires that every common exertion (enlistment, food-saving, munition making, killing the enemy) should have the blessing of all the holy sentiments. . . . A huge majority of Americans were swept up in the fervor of patriotism, and this same fervor could be used for the dry cause if only people were convinced that prohibition spells patriotism."

H. L. Mencken, who did not conceal the fact that he considered himself one of John Barleycorn's favorite sons, demonstrated to his own satisfaction that the Volstead Act was the triumph of war hysteria. "Homo boobiens was scientifically roweled and run amok with the news that all the German brewers of the country were against the Eighteenth Amendment; he himself observed that all German sympathizers were made dreadful by dreams of German spies, he was willing to do anything to put them down, and one of the things he was willing to do was to swallow Prohibition."[3]

The propaganda war for American sympathies was fought on many fronts, but on the intellectual level it was signalized by a manifesto signed by ninety-three Germans respected throughout the world (including the aged Haeckel, the theatrical innovator Max Reinhardt, the physicist Max Planck, the playwrights Sudermann and Hauptmann, the philosopher Eucken, the psychologist Wilhelm Wundt) in which, like H. G. Wells in England and Anatole France in France, they renounced their pacifist beliefs and defended the "pure cause" of the Fatherland. The manifesto alleged that Germany was fully justified in invading France through neutral Belgium, and complained that the barbarous Allies were summoning the black and yellow races and the equally uncivilized Slavs to destroy the homeland of Goethe and Beethoven.

In the United States, at which the manifesto was mainly directed in October, 1914, there were significant echoes from American intellectuals, Oswald Garrison Villard, the New England patrician and liberal reformer, let it be known that his pacifist ideals had not been changed by events in Europe. Vachel Lindsay's poems denounced war propaganda as the ultimate sin against humanity. Ezra Pound rejected both sides in Europe as representing "atavism and the loathsome spirit of mediocrity, cloaked in graft." William Carlos Williams declared that civilization was being "deliberately murdered in the name of church and state." Willard Huntington Wright, then an aristocratic intellectual but later famous as a writer of Philo Vance detective novels, had been conducting a campaign against the *Encyclopaedia Britannica* for its neglect of modern art and literature, and allowed this anti-British aesthetic bias to widen into a bitter Anglophobia.

None of them traveled so far down the route the German propaganda bureau hoped they would follow as George Sylvester Viereck. Earlier he had gained a certain amount of notoriety as the Bohemian standard-bearer and poet of sexual freedom. A German-American, Viereck now began writing sagas in praise of Kaiser Wilhelm and hymns of the *Gott Strafe England* variety. He was editor of the vigorously pro-German *The Fatherland*, later a secret paid agent of the German propaganda bureau. That periodical proclaimed on January 27, 1915:

"We intend to organize to break the power of England upon our government, our public servants!"

By the time of that forthright announcement, the effort to propagandize German-Americans into remembering the claims of their ancestral homeland was in full swing. The German-American Press Association, in a secret meeting, formulated plans for a cable and wireless service carrying news from the German home and war fronts which was to be distributed to all German-language papers through a central bureau. An organization called The Friends of Peace was formed under the leadership of J. J. Tobias, who was quoted by the Chicago *Herald* as boasting that the five million German-American voters were "going to raise hell with any party not in our favor." Former students at German universities, whether of German origin themselves or not, were lured by nostalgia for the old days at Heidelberg into an organization called the German University League, with branches in New York, Boston, Philadelphia, Chicago, St. Louis, Richmond, Atlanta, Milwaukee, Kansas City and Dallas.

In addition to such older and more strident groups as the Pan-German Alliance and the Educational Alliance for the Preservation of German Culture in Foreign Lands, there was the much larger and more inclusive National German-American Alliance. It was a home-grown product organized in 1901 by Dr. Charles John Hexamer, whose efforts had recently been rewarded by Kaiser Wilhelm, who made Dr. Hexamer a member of the Order of the Red Eagle, Fourth Class. The group claimed a membership of two million.

In the National German-American Alliance, sympathy for the German cause, or more openly crusading for the maintenance of American neutrality, was secretly infused with a strong aroma of malt and hops. It was largely financed by the brewers and distillers. Heavy subsidies were poured into the organization in 1913 by the beer makers to combat the influence of the Anti-Saloon League. An article in the Alliance's *Bulletin* promptly declared that the Prohibition movement was directed at "German manners and customs, the joviality of the German people . . . In order to gain for the Germans of America that place in the sun which has hitherto always been denied them, it is absolutely necessary that they enjoy personal liberty, and that this shall not be whittled away by the attacks of the prohibitionists and the persecutors of the foreign born."[4] It was noted that in areas where the Alliance was strongest — Ohio, Wisconsin, New York, Pennsylvania, Indiana, Illinois and Iowa — no statewide Prohibition laws could be passed. Yet if the Alliance was correct in "considering prohibition as an attack on the more recent immigrants to America," as Andrew Sinclair has remarked, "it was foolish to place the main emphasis of its defense of the saloons on its Germanism rather than on the promise of America to all immigrants."[5]

The disastrous result of that linkup, in fact, was a Congressional investigation. The Senate passed a resolution stating that "the facts will soon appear which will conclusively show that twelve or fifteen German brewers of America, in association with the United States Brewers Association, furnished the money . . . to buy a great newspaper in one of the chief cities of the nation . . . The organized liquor traffic is a vicious interest . . . because it has been pro-German in its sympathies and its conduct. Around these great brewery organizations owned by rich men, almost all of them of German birth and sympathy, has grown up the societies, all the organizations of this country intended to keep young German immigrants from becoming real American citizens. It is around these sangerfests and sangerbunds . . . generally financed by the rich brewers, that the young Germans who come to America are taught to remember, first, the Fatherland, and second, America."

The subsequent investigation by a subcommittee of the Senate's Judiciary Committee, in hearings held in September, 1918, and included in a report titled "Brewing and Liquor Interests and German Propaganda," did not succeed in establishing any direct connection between the National German-American Alliance and the German propaganda machine. It did prove that $1,700,000 was spent to buy the New York *Daily Mail & Express*, which became a mouthpiece for the Central Powers; that the Alliance was tightly organized and exercised control over twelve hundred *Vereins* and bunds, along with such secret "inner circle" groups as the Sons of Herman.

The Alliance was forced to disband following the Senate investigation. All in all, thanks to a lack of subtlety in its methods, it served both its causes rather ineffectively. Wartime idealism among the non-German citizens was only affronted by such statements as that of John Schwaab, head of the Ohio branch of the Alliance, that "the drink question is forced upon us by the same hypocritical Puritans as over there [in England] are endeavoring to exterminate the German nation." Nor did the Alliance win any outside supporters after reports were circulated that the German flag was displayed and "Deutschland über Alles" was sung at some of its meetings. Nor by such blustering as the earnest Dr. Hexamer's assertion that a constitutional monarchy was the only decent form of government, which drew an effective reply in one of the Anti-Saloon League's pamphlets: "No loyal citizen would compare his country in this way with Germany. Who would trade freedom for slavery, or democracy for autocracy? Lives there a man in America with soul so dead, that he never said with pride, this is my native or chosen land, the best country in the world? If there be such a man let him ask for a passport at once. America is good enough for Americans." Even more recklessly, perhaps, the Alliance not only exhibited a fondness for the German monarchy, but opposed feminism — knowing how most women hated the saloons as an institution competing with the home — in all its manifestations.

It also interested itself in national politics, particularly in any bearing on the European war. Only a few days after the war broke out the Alliance was protesting that the Colt arms company was making machine guns for the Canadian army in violation of the neutrality laws. A few months later Dr. Hexamer journeyed to Washington to complain that artillery and submarines were being manufactured in the United States for shipment to Canada. He implored Congress to pass a bill prohibiting "the export of arms, ammunition and munitions from any territory or seaport of the United States."[6]

Subsequently, according to the report of the Senate subcommittee which investigated his organization, among others, the German-American Alliance bought a controlling interest in the Washington *Times* to bring journalistic influence to bear on the Congress on its home grounds, and funneled money into the campaign funds of politicians who supported its program.

The Alliance's favorite congressman, as its *Bulletin* frequently mentioned, was Representative Richard Bartholdt of Pennsylvania, whom it called "the most German of all Congressmen." It noted with approval his warning that Germany and Austria together claimed the kinship of twenty-five million Americans and that "these twenty-five million people, representing probably five million votes, are convinced that the United States is waging war against the two Germanic nations under the cover of neutrality." The *Bulletin* subsequently reported that petitions signed by two million persons favoring an embargo on all arms shipments had been sent to Congress.

Absolute neutrality, with no help of any kind given either side in Europe, was the minimum the German-American activists demanded of their country. It was also the most they could hope for. An absolutely evenly balanced neutrality would have resulted in victory for Germany and Austria. The Wilson Administration paid lip service to the idea, as in the President's famous declaration just after the war began that "we must be impartial in thought as well as in action," but Wilsonian neutrality was tilted in favor of the Allies. Even before the war started, Wilson's closest adviser on foreign affairs, Colonel E. M. House, was yearning for "a sympathetic alliance between the two countries," the United States and Britain, after conferring with an aide of the British Foreign Secretary in 1913. A fact-finding mission to Germany in the summer of 1914, just before war broke out, only confirmed the Colonel in his pro-British bias. "The situation is extraordinary," he wrote President Wilson from Berlin. "It is militarism run stark mad."

And German-Americans quickly learned that the dominant elements of American society, what would later be called the "establishment," were also pro-British, if not always outspokenly so. There was a marked difference in the way they received statements of the German case from those of the Allies, Walter Millis discovered twenty years later in his *Road to War: America 1914–1917.* "When prominent Germans, like Kuno Francke or Professor Munsterberg of Harvard leapt to perform for the German case the service which Lord Bryce and so many other prominent Britons were performing for the Allies, they were shocked and hurt by the difference with which their activities were regarded. When eminent Americans of Germany ancestry, like the Ridders in New York [the family which published the New York *Staats-Zeitung*], defended the Central Powers with the same passion which innumerable other Americans were bringing to the support of the Entente, they were dismayed to find that in their case such efforts were held to be akin to treason. Their response — as human as it was unwise — was to speak with only greater anger and violence. Since they had no news to work with, however, they were compelled to invent argument; not unnaturally, the argument was frequently mistaken or exaggerated and so easily discredited. The first German propaganda was as naïve and spontaneous as the first Allied propaganda. But where the Allied case was absorbed unconsciously through every morning paper, the German case was noisily presented by an angry and plainly ill-informed minority and so clearly stamped as mere partisanship. It did the German case little good."

German-language newspapers and German-American organizations lobbied vigorously for various embargo acts before Congress, which the Administration refused to support. As Colonel House wrote President Wilson on July 22, 1915, "our whole industrial machinery would cry out against" any embargo on munitions. In this and other measures to guarantee neutrality, the German-Americans were able to claim the sympathy of a majority of the electorate, for in 1915, as Hermann Hagedorn said, "*Safety First* became the day's popular slogan." The country as a whole devoutly hoped to stay out of involvement in the European war, and realized that shipping arms to the Allies would hardly be a neutral act.

The sinking of the *Lusitania*, the loss of American lives it involved, ironically and obliquely confirmed this fear. Beneath the uproar of indignation over the torpedoing of the liner off the Irish coast, there was the realization that the German Embassy had warned Americans not to travel on a British ship through the submarine zone. It was also true that the *Lusitania* would not have nosed to the bottom so quickly if it had not been carrying in its hold munitions consigned to the English ports.

The embargo legislation was stalled after the *Lusitania* sank May 7, 1915. Shortly thereafter the pro-British leanings of the Wilson Administration were made more apparent by the resignation of William Jennings Bryan as Secretary of State; his position was antiwar, stemming from the unsophisticated pacifism of his Populist background, but not anti-German. The Administration claimed to be antiwar but it was also pro-British. In that climate, the campaign for embargo legislation marked time until fall. It then became obvious that the British were looking for a vast increase in American aid, clothed though it was in semantic evasions.

Lord Reading came over to negotiate for a one-billion-dollar loan, even though, up to August 1, 1915, the Allies had paid only $174,000,-000 on the $450,000,000 worth of supplies they had contracted for through J. P. Morgan. Reading also arrived on this loan-arranging mission even though the United States State Department on August 15, 1914, had laid down its policy, in reply to a query from the Morgan bank, that loans to belligerents were inconsistent with the American policy of neutrality. President Wilson accommodatingly made a nice distinction between "loans" and "credits." The difference was purely semantic, but it gave a coloring of legality to the transactions with the British. Lord Reading arrived in the United States in a critical time, with the pound falling and something like a panic striking the London stock exchange and the Paris Bourse. Late in August, before the situation could get any worse, President Wilson reversed his policy and sanctioned the flotation of the Allied loan . . . and called it a loan.

The German-American organizations threw their full weight into trying to thwart the Reading mission. Dr. Hexamer signalized a campaign against the British loan on September 15 by denouncing the "Money Trust," which he claimed was the chief financier of the Allied war effort. He also urged the members of the German-American Alliance to protest to their banks and insurance companies against allowing their money to be siphoned into that cause. On September 24, the Illinois *Staats-Zeitung* published a cartoon titled "America Boards a Sinking Ship." A German-language paper in Pittsburgh editorially inquired, "Would you lend money to a gambler — especially to a gambler who has lost?" And the New York *Staats-Zeitung* on October 30 wondered "Why buy British bonds — when you can get Confederate bonds much cheaper and just as good?" Threats were also made in the German-language press and on the platforms of protest rallies to start a run on any bank or institution connected with raising the money for the British loan.

But it was all in vain, all struggling against the strong current of events. "The erection of the machinery which made us a vital part of the World War" had begun, as Walter Millis wrote. "Our neutrality was at an end."[7]

THE "HYPHENATES"

The German-American militants and their supporters, including large numbers of the Irish, pacifist groups and neo-Populists who opposed all foreign wars, began to come under a brisk counterattack in 1915 as their embargo proposals and opposition to Allied loans proved to be a considerable stumbling block to that body of opinion which believed that American participation in the war was inevitable and the sooner it came the better. In that year an Alabama-born Chicagoan named William H. Skaggs published a book titled *German Conspiracies in America*, which significantly enough was published in England but circulated mainly, and widely, in the United States.

Much of the book was ill-considered, a hastily mounted diatribe against practically all Americans of German descent and their history on this continent. Too many, he declared, were descendants of Hessian mercenaries, "the lowest and most vicious of mankind." The sainted Baron Steuben was "not a German of the present standard," and Baron de Kalb was "not a German . . . although he was born at Huttendorf, Bavaria," because he had served as a lieutenant in the French army and presumably that experience had cleansed him of all his nefarious German tendencies.

Almost to a man, Skaggs insisted, the German-Americans were "ungrateful and un-American" and could never be assimilated into a decent society. He was willing to make a last-minute exception in the case of Professor Kuno Francke of Harvard, who for years had hymned the glories of Imperial Germany in books and on lecture platforms, but who had recently refused to support the Neutrality League or the Batholdt Embargo Bill with the widely quoted statement, "It's one thing to condemn individuals carrying on this hideous [arms] traffic and another to hold our Government responsible for it."

All who opposed aid to the Allies, Mr. Skaggs emphasized, were playing into the Germans' hand, no matter how unquestioned their sincerity as humanists and idealists had previously been. He cited as the "apogee of German propaganda" a speech by Jane Addams of Hull House, the president of the Women's Peace Convention, held at Carnegie Hall in New York on July 9, 1915. Miss Addams spoke of meeting wounded German soldiers who had been sent to Switzerland for convalescence and of talking to one who said he had always fired over the enemies' heads. Five other wounded Germans, she said, told her they would commit suicide before returning to the front. Miss Addams charged that the French infantry were "doped on absinthe" before going over the top; a somewhat reckless charge which Richard Harding Davis, the noted war correspondent, refuted by simply pointing out that the manufacture of absinthe had been prohibited years before by the French government.

Mr. Skaggs's English-sponsored fulmination added little of consequence to what a later generation would call the Great Debate over the extent to which the United States should involve itself in the European war, but its tone, its barely suppressed fury, was indicative of the rising temper of the time.

Those who favored American assistance to the Allies considered themselves more truly American, somehow, than those who opposed it. The opposition, on the other hand, including many who were not of German extraction, believed they had a right to express their opinions and take appropriate action so long as America was neutral; the right, in fact, to keep her neutral.

With both sides approaching the hysterical in their discourse, President Wilson, both by ancestry and inclination an Anglophile, was strikingly ineffective in damping down the emotions of the opposing factions. He made it quite plain that he could not extend the same confidence in the patriotism of the Anglo-Saxon majority to the German and Irish minorities. The latter, but not the Anglo-Americans, were "hyphenates." Presumably, the President took the view, as most of those of like origin did, that longer residence on this continent erased the hyphen for the descendants of the English and Scottish immigrants. His attitude was made clear enough in a 1914 speech in which he attacked those Americans who "need hyphens in their names because only part of them has come over."

His leading rival for national leadership, former President Theodore Roosevelt, was considerably more effective in his appeals to the "hyphenates." Even though he was an outright and clamorous advocate of "preparedness" — the preparation inevitably leading to United States intervention on the Allied side — his frankly stated views were respectfully received by the Germans and the Irish. Instead of complaining of "hyphenism" as President Wilson did in his schoolmasterly style, Roosevelt emphasized the duties of citizenship and endlessly affirmed

393

his belief in the "loyalty" of the minorities. It helped, too, that before the war Roosevelt had openly and frequently admired Germany.

Despite President Wilson's disdain and Roosevelt's skillful cajolery, the disaffection of millions of "hyphenated" Americans only increased as the Administration's pro-Allied sympathies became more apparent. The Irish, because of their understandable grievances against the British Empire and their attitude that Britain's enemies were not necessarily Ireland's enemies, for once were drawn into a common cause with their German-American neighbors. Their anti-British prejudice, and their willingness to cooperate with supporters of the German cause, were only increased when the Easter rebellion in Dublin was crushed by British troops with no more gentleness than the Germany army suppressing an uprising behind their lines in northern France.

But the Irish-German alliance had been formed long before the Easter Rebellion. Irish-German-American Leagues were organized throughout the country. A Neutrality and Peace Convention made up of the representatives of German-American and Irish-American societies was held in San Francisco and unanimously called upon President Wilson to use all necessary force in protecting American commerce from the British blockade. The German-descended, as Gustav Ohlinger observed in his book *Their True Faith and Allegiance*, were "fraternizing ostentatiously" with their fellow citizens of Irish extraction. In 1915, for instance, the Germans united with the Irish in celebrating St. Patrick's Day, although in the past there had been frequent brawls between the two nationalities on that occasion. Subsequently joint celebrations of the birthdays of Bismarck and Robert Emmett were held.

All this was cause for genuine alarm among the Anglo-Americans. Together the Irish and the Germans formed a decisive bloc of the electorate. In the past they had generally been politically opposed, with most of the Irish fervent Democrats and most of the Germans equally devout Republicans, and each highly suspicious of the other. Together they could be offset only by the fact that the other principal minorities, the Sandinavians, the Poles and the Italians, would not join them in their more extreme positions against the Allies.

394

German propagandists in the United States accordingly devoted much attention to the Irish-Americans, pointing out that England's enemy must be their friend. According to the report of the Senate subcommittee, they enlisted the services of Jeremiah A. O'Leary, president of the American Truth Society and publisher of *The Bull*, a violently anti-English periodical which "upheld the cause of Germany as against England." The American Truth Society, the committee's investigator reported, "had a very large membership, made up principally of Germans and German-Americans and American citizens of Irish extraction."[8]

Nor was the Jewish minority neglected by the German propaganda bureau. Many Jews were descended from German immigrants, and German Jews (many of whom migrated to the United States after the war and proudly wore their Iron Crosses until Hitler came to power and converted those decorations into something less than junk jewelry) were fighting with noticeable valor in the German armed forces. To propagandize the Jewish people in the United States, Berlin dispatched Dr. Isaac Strauss to New York a few months after the war broke out. Almost immediately Dr. Strauss was reporting success in his efforts. On October 20, 1914, he wrote his superiors that "the manipulation of the Jewish Press in America, formerly casual, has now been changed by me into a regular systematic information service and organized on a firm basis."

According to the Senate subcommittee's records, Dr. Strauss obtained between four and five million dollars from the Kaiser's treasury and managed to distribute "various pro-German articles in different Jewish publications in various parts of the United States." Actually, for all the energy and money he expended, Dr. Strauss's propagandizing had little effect on the American Jewish community.[9] Few German Jews could look back upon the ghettos of the Fatherland with anything like nostalgia.

(The German propagandists neglected to focus on a much more receptive segment of the Jewish-American community, perhaps because it wasn't necessary. The Russian-Jewish immigrants were pro-German, if only because they were so violently anti-Russian. Harry Golden, who sold the *Jewish Daily Forward* on the streets of the Lower East Side of New York during the war, has recalled that "The East Side Jews were overwhelmingly pro-German. All of them had come to America to flee the pogroms. No matter what the outcome of the skirmish I shouted 'Russians retreat again!' I shouted it even if the Russians advanced. If the Russian advance was an overwhelming victory I shouted instead, 'Extra! Emperor Franz Josef dying.' Franz Josef was the old reliable. The East Side Jews adored him. And he was, fortunately for newsboys, very, very old.")[10]

Another important element in the campaign to keep the United States out of the war was supplied by the socialists, many of German descent, who opposed intervention on the grounds that the war was, as Victor L. Berger proclaimed in his Milwaukee *Leader*, a "capitalistic orgy of blood-letting."* The Socialist party called an emergency convention, with Berger and Eugene Debs urging an antiwar position, and the national membership subsequently voted three to one for the Debs-Berger resolution against intervention.

But it was the German-language press and the German-American organizations which caused the most concern in Washington as the Wilson Administration drifted slowly toward intervention. All who opposed them, particularly those of German descent, were attacked with greater vigor than that directed at non-Germans. Hermann Hagedorn, as the protégé and disciple of Theodore Roosevelt, and later the family's authorized biographer, organized writers into a group called the Vigilantes with the aim of "awakening the public, especially in the schools and colleges, to the need of education for citizenship." Put less delicately, perhaps, the task of the Vigilantes was to prepare the country to fight for whichever course the national government chose. The Vigilantes, Mr. Hagedorn has recalled, were greatly concerned by "the uncertain German-Americans, the pro-German periodicals of the prewar period converted to a poisonous pseudo patriotism; racial prejudice, class

---

* In 1918, Congress refused to seat Berger, who had recently been indicted for sedition. His Wisconsin constituents sent him back after a special election in 1919. Again Congress refused to seat him. The reelection and rejection process continued until 1922, when Berger was finally admitted to the House and served as congressman until 1926.

antagonism; all the foes of our own household . . . all the forces working against national unity." A pro-German periodical attacked Hagedorn as a renegade. "The term itself was absurd," he said. "A renegade German I could not be since I had never been a German . . . Was it possible that there were people in the United States who regarded German-Americanism as a definite entity?"

There were indeed. The German-American Alliance's organ *The Fatherland*, for instance, asserted that the German government's reply to the United States note of protest on the sinking of the *Lusitania* was "an inspiring document, on a high plane of humanity, unassailable in logic," but the American protest itself was "silly and dishonest."

Little attention was paid to such cautionaries as that of Gustav Ohlinger, who pointed out to his fellow German-Americans that their attempt to create "a state within a state" was "decidedly at variance with German character and the German's traditional sense of *Pflicht* and *Treue*. They are in essence as un-German as they are un-American."[11]

Just how vigorously the German cause was promoted in the United States between 1914 and 1917 could be determined from a study of the German-language newspapers and magazines. At times their attempts to secure German unity behind the embattled Fatherland verged on extortion. One example was an article in the Milwaukee *Germania-Herold* on September 18, 1915, retailing a warning from the Austro-Hungarian Embassy that any subjects of that empire who worked in factories filling Allied war contracts would be imprisoned for ten to twenty years if they ever returned to their native land.

One student of that section of the American press has decried the charges that it "sold its favors for German gold," simply because "there was no need for bribery."[12] But there was no doubt of the German-language papers' bias; it was definitely exposed in October, 1915, by the Milwaukee *Journal*. That newspaper, with much of its circulation among the German-descended, was then edited by Lucius W. Niemann, its founder, whose father was German and whose mother was French. Niemann suffered no divided loyalties, however, and despite the fact that Wisconsin was particularly bitter against Wilson for having helped to elect him in 1912 and that much of its population was more or less actively pro-German, he decided to show exactly what the German-language papers were telling their readers.

He assigned a reporter named F. Perry Olds to spend all his time translating articles from the German newspapers, and on October 15 began publishing a series of articles on Olds's findings. They burst like a live grenade on the *Journal*'s readership. "Day in and day out," Olds wrote, "the Milwaukee *Germania-Herold* was preached division along the lines of race and other war prejudices. Day in and day out it has endeavored to weld voters of German descent into a powerful political weapon to be used against the government of the United States at the dictation of the National German-American Alliance and other representatives of Germany here. It has virtually without exception opposed the government of the United States in every step that President Wilson has taken to protect American sovereignty and the rights of American citizens against the aggressions of Germany."

Olds not only quoted liberally from the German papers to demonstrate how violently they opposed every measure taken by Wilson to protect American interests (though never when the President acted to loosen the British blockade) against the German U-boats torpedoing ships bound for British or French ports, but also delved into the machinations of the German-American Alliance. His exposures, in part, were responsible for the cancellation, subsequently, of the Alliance's charter. He learned that the assistant superintendent of public schools in Milwaukee, who was also head of the Wisconsin branch of the German-American Alliance, pushed the teaching of German so hard, beginning in the first grade, that pupils were "German-minded instead of American-minded."[13]

In 1890 the *Journal* had campaigned for repeal of the Bennett Law, which required all Wisconsin schools to teach basic subjects in English. The statute was repealed at the urging of the *Journal*, which reversed itself because "the teaching of German in the public schools of America has not only seriously retarded the process of Americanization, but it has been used to produce worship of Germany, even of kaiserism, and to deprive America of the love of many of her native and adopted children."

"Starve the War and Feed America"

The German press had never been assailed before in such blunt terms. It was particularly outraged by the *Journal's* disclosure that thirteen of the twenty-eight editorial employees of the *Germania-Herold* were aliens. The *Journal* was denounced as a "tool of the Allies," boycotts were organized and reprisals attempted. The Milwaukee *Free Press*, a La Follette Progressive organ, snorted contemptuously over the *Journal* series: "English ruled and English led — if that were only all! But to be English bilked and English booted, and with a president to invite a repetition with 'Thanks, awfully!' is to reduce the United States to something infinitely worse than an American colony before the Revolution."[14]

Even in Milwaukee, the heart of German-Americanism, the *Journal* exposures acted as wake-up pills. Wisconsin was called a "province of Germany" in other parts of the country, but the long-term effects of the *Journal* crusade indicated the slur wasn't justified. The circulation of the socialist daily Milwaukee *Leader* began falling off despite the slogan on its masthead, "STARVE THE WAR AND FEED AMERICA," and the *Journal's* climbed to 112,000 in 1917 and 119,000 in 1918. Even the thousands of Milwaukeeans who had been leaning toward pro-Germanism were given pause by a *Journal* editorial which, in discussing the methods of the German propagandists, remarked that they did not openly call for dissension — "they simply predict it. They keep it eternally before the minds of their readers, encouraging them by repetition of their predictions to open rebellion against our authorities." Mayor Daniel W. Hoan was emboldened to break with the leadership of his Socialist party over the war issue, and was reelected even though a Berger editorial in the *Leader* harshly advised him to "get out of the party in justice to himself and the party."

The *Journal's* courage in grasping such a potentially explosive issue was rewarded in 1919, when it received the Pulitzer Prize. "In a city where the German element had long prided itself on its preponderating influence," the Pulitzer committee's citation read, "the *Journal* courageously attacked such members of that element as put Germany above America."

THE PLOTTERS

Revelation of the methods of German propagandists in Milwaukee was more than matched in sensational effect by the uncovering of more direct conspiracies elsewhere aimed at sabotaging the flow of munitions and supplies to Europe and at subverting the Wilson Administration's policies. In pleading for American neutrality, Germany meanwhile was committing decidedly un-neutral acts against the government of the United States. The names of Captain Franz von Rintelen of the Imperial Navy; Captain Carl Boy-Ed, the half-Turkish German naval attaché in Washington; Major Franz von Papen, the German military attaché in Washington, and Dr. Heinrich Albert, the commercial attaché, nominally, but also paymaster of the German espionage net in the United States, all were soon to become household words. More than that, so far as German-Americans were concerned, the disclosures of their activities on American soil served as a warning of the slippery downward path they were being encouraged to follow. Further cause for alarm, for taking second thoughts, was the disclosure that all those busily plotting emissaries of the All-Highest in Berlin were using the German-American Club at 112 Central Park South, New York City, as their meeting place.

An even larger corps of agents and propagandists, of course, was just as diligently trying to influence American policy on behalf of the Allies. The methods they used, the un-neutral acts they committed will never be fully known, because the United States Secret Service did not keep tabs on them as they did the Germans.

In any case, it seems safe to say that the Allies were not forced to resort to such extreme measures and lurid schemings as Rintelen, Boy-Ed, Papen and Albert. The exposure of their rather clumsy plotting did considerable damage to their cause if not to the security of the United States. Rintelen was engaged in trying to arrange a military coup by which General Huerta would be restored to power in Mexico, with the hope that he would declare war on the United States. He also worked on grandiose schemes to buy up the Du Pont munitions works and tie up American war industries through strikes and sabotage.

Meanwhile Major von Papen and Captain Boy-Ed were giving top priority to a project of their own involving the crews of a number of German ships which had been interned in Atlantic ports. The seamen were to be provided with high explosives and encouraged to blow up bridges, piers, canals and other installations to occupy themselves in their idle hours of internment.

But it was with the bustling Dr. Albert, about whose activities there was a certain charming inefficiency, who allowed the United States Secret Service to score one of its greatest coups. He was being shadowed night and day by a United States agent named Frank Burke. On the afternoon of July 24, 1915, Dr. Albert conferred with George Sylvester Viereck, the poet turned paid propagandist for the Germans, in his offices at 45 Broadway in New York. The two men left Albert's offices and boarded the Sixth Avenue Elevated. At Twenty-third Street, Viereck got off the train and Dr. Albert continued uptown alone. It was a hot afternoon and Dr. Albert felt drowsy, though the contents of his heavy briefcase should have kept him nervously on the alert. Instead he dozed off. Burke stole his briefcase. The papers it contained were studied with interest in Washington, since they revealed a wide variety of German undercover activity in this country. Later in the summer the government, instead of stamping "Top Secret" over the lot, handed the papers over to the New York *World* for publication. One exchange of correspondence which caused widespread embarrassment was between Arthur von Briesen, a prominent German-American businessman whom Theodore Roosevelt only a few years before had named "one of the two most useful citizens" in the United States, and William Travers Jerome, the eminent counselor, whom Briesen was offering a ten-thousand-dollar fee in return for handling a "delicate matter." Jerome was a cousin of Winston Churchill, then the First Lord of the British Admiralty. Briesen explained that he "had occasion to need the services of a criminal lawyer," which satisfied most people, but the New York *Times* published a letter from a person who signed himself only as "H.," inquiring, "If Herr von Briesen is correct in his assertion . . . how was the correspondence found in the possession of an official of the German government?" The question went unanswered.[15]

Some months later the Secret Service uncovered evidence that Captain Rintelen and other German agents were supplying arms and munitions to Pancho Villa, whose guerrilla forces attacked the American cavalry post at Columbus, New Mexico, and brought about a United States punitive expedition into Mexico that tied up a large part of the regular army during 1916.

About that time, in Berlin, Arthur Zimmermann, the undersecretary in the German Foreign Ministry, had lunch one day with United States Ambassador James W. Gerard and warned his American friend that "in case of trouble between Germany and the United States" there were "half a million trained Germans in America who will join the Irish and start a revolution."

"In that case," Gerard retorted, "there are half a million lampposts to hang them on."[16]

Ambassador Gerard's scoffing at the threat of a German-Irish-American uprising was justified, of course, but there was some substance to fears that dissident Germans and Irish would collaborate in causing trouble for the American policy of professed neutrality making aid to the Allies.

The danger of interference was focused mainly on the New York waterfront, the laboring force of which largely consisted of Irish and Germans living in the Hell's Kitchen tenement district bordering the Hudson River. Dick Butler, an Irishman who was president of the New York District Council of the International Longshoreman's Association, revealed many years later in his autobiography (*Dock Walloper*) how German agents, working through Irish sympathizers aroused by the Easter Rebellion in Dublin, tried to engineer a strike of the twenty thousand longshoremen employed in the Port of New York and thereby prevent the loading of munitions and foodstuffs bound for Allied ports.

Butler was tipped off to the plot by William T. Flynn, chief of the United States Secret Service. He was skeptical at first because it was a time when "anybody who spoke with a Teutonic accent was liable to be arrested for blowing up bridges or dropping bombs on Wall Street." But he promised to be on the alert for evidence of Flynn's claim that German agents, through intermediaries, were about to offer leaders of the longshore union a million dollars if they would promote a four-week strike on the waterfront. Shortly thereafter, Butler recalled, he was approached by the representative of a group of wealthy Boston Irish-Americans with the offer of a million for the union leaders and ten dollars a week for each longshoreman while he was on strike. Butler and his associates rejected the offer, but word of it was leaked — again — to the New York *World*, which editorially warned that "atrocious crimes might have been committed" if German schemes had not been short-circuited.[17]

Shortly after that plot was thwarted, a much more formidable figure began making his presence felt on the New York waterfront, an even more dangerous link between the Irish who hated England and the Germans who were willing to use that hatred for their own purposes. The figure was that of Jim Larkin, Irish revolutionary and socialist leader. For years Larkin, a towering man with great oratorical talent, had been the leader of the Irish Transport and General Workers Union, which constantly bedeviled the British rulers of Ireland. He was a close associate of James Connolly, "the Lenin of the Irish radicals," many of whom were strongly Marxist. Just before the Easter Rebellion, in which Connolly lost his life, he sent Larkin to the United States to obtain arms for an Irish uprising.

Larkin established his headquarters in Greenwich Village, and there, according to Benjamin Gitlow, an early American Communist leader who later turned against the party, "came smugglers who knew how to circumvent the British navy, saboteurs who cooperated with the German Imperial Government for considerations beneficial to the Irish cause, Irish-American labor leaders and longshoremen who reported on Allied munitions waiting shipment to Europe." One of Larkin's closest collaborators, according to Gitlow, was Ludwig Lore, editor of the German-language Socialist daily *Volkszeitung*, "who acted as a link between Franz von Papen, military attaché of the German Embassy, and the Irish."

One of the calamitous results of that collaboration, Gitlow believes, was the explosion which rocked New York Harbor early on the morning of July 30, 1916, blew out windows in Jersey City, killed six persons and injured thirty-five. It was known as the Black Tom Disaster. On the Black Tom peninsula, which thrust its way into the harbor, twenty-five million dollars worth of explosives being shipped to the Allies were blown up in four huge warehouses and lines of freight cars, along with barges loaded with shells and high explosives.

Lengthy investigations failed to determine exactly who, if anyone, touched off the explosion. It was a heavy blow to the Allied war effort, but Gitlow recalled that the plotters behind it were disappointed because "they counted on a large loss of human life to launch a campaign to stop the shipment of munitions to England and France. Such a campaign was actually started. The German-Americans, the Irish Republicans and the radicals united in calling for an embargo on all munitions shipments to the Allies." Included in the plot, Gitlow said, were "German agents, bankers who supplied the cash, a motley crew of American swindlers and adventurers, Irish revolutionists, conservative pro-Irish labor leaders and German-American socialists. The work of this crew was linked with revolutionary activities in Mexico and other Latin-American countries and was tied in with the antiwar peace propaganda which the radicals were conducting and which had at the time assumed large proportions. . . .

"Without the aid of the Irish revolutionists and their connections on the waterfront, without the link which the German-American social-ists established between them and Von Papen, the Black Tom catas-trophe never would have taken place. The Irish network using Lore and his aides passed on the information. The saboteurs did the rest."[18]

Despite all the desperately energetic work of the pro-German ele-ment, the United States veered sharply toward intervention in Europe in the later months of 1916 and early 1917. Much of that work, ranging from propaganda to sabotage, was canceled out by the ham-handedness of German diplomacy. Thus in January, 1917, the British Naval Intelli-gence intercepted a coded message from the German Foreign Minister, now the overly optimistic Zimmermann, to the German Minister in

Mexico City. This was the famous Zimmermann Telegram which announced that "unrestricted submarine warfare" would soon begin, and that if the United States assumed a belligerent attitude as a result Germany would propose an alliance with Mexico and Japan aimed at making so much trouble for the United States it could never send an expeditionary force to Europe. The British lost no time in passing its contents along to the American government, which in turn made them public in the newspapers of March 1. Many German-language papers claimed it was a fraud, but they were left high and dry, and frightfully embarrassed, when Zimmermann admitted at a press conference in Berlin that the contents of his telegram had been accurately reported. "The die is cast" was the theme of most newspaper editorials, some of them summoning up visions (as in the Buffalo *Express*) of "hordes of Mexicans under German officers sweeping into Texas, New Mexico and Arizona."

German-Americans were now only a few months away from the most traumatic moment in their history as a part of American life.

15. "THOSE INDISPENSABLE GIFTS"

The war can but clear both of what un-American ferment moves on their surfaces as their accepted country summons and uses those indispensable gifts which Celt and Teuton often alone can give in the service of war.
— SIR SHANE LESLIE, *Dublin Review*, August, 1918

On the night of April 2, 1917, the day that President Wilson asked Congress for a declaration of war against the Central Powers, the Cincinnati Symphony decided to go ahead with its scheduled concert in that heavily Germanic city. Orders had already gone out from Washington that "The Star-Spangled Banner" was to be played at the opening of all public events and entertainment programs.

As required, the conductor, Dr. Ernest Kunwald, led the orchestra through the strains of the national anthem. Then he turned to the audience with tears streaming down his ashen face, and defiantly announced:

"But my heart is on the other side!"[1]

There were many who wept with him that night in German-American communities throughout the nation.

Various incidents, unhistoric but humanly revealing, occurred that day to indicate the emotional stress, the rage, sorrow and frustration with which German-America received the news that American forces would be thrust into the war in Europe.

A group of pacifists led by Dr. David Starr Jordan was milling around the Capitol several hours before President Wilson made his appearance before a joint session of Congress. Heavy guards posted at the State, War and Navy Building — all three departments were housed under one antique roof only half a century ago — and the demonstrators were repulsed. Half a dozen drifted into the Senate Office Building and penetrated to the door of Senator Henry Cabot Lodge of Massachusetts, one of the war hawks. One of the demonstrators was a young man named Alexander Bannwart, of German-Swiss parentage. They button-holed Senator Lodge, then, as the senator later recounted, "the German member of their party said, 'You are a damned coward.' I walked up to hit him and said, 'You are a damned liar,' and he hit me and I hit him."[2] By nightfall, with rather exaggerated reports of the scuffle making the front pages from coast to coast, Senator Lodge was a national hero . . . and Alexander Bannwart was a pacifist jailed for assaulting a man twice his age.

In his home at Greenfield, Connecticut, Hermann Hagedorn was rejecting the appeal of an old friend of his family that he avoid any "voluntary, active espousal of the American cause." He had decided that the fact that most of his family was living in Germany "could not be allowed to interfere" with his "freedom of action." He would support his country in whatever it chose to do because "the very heart of the American experiment in free government was involved. As no other nation in the world, America depended for the unity of her people, even for her existence, on the speedy amalgamation of the aliens who came from the four corners of the earth to claim her welcome. The melting pot had done its work; and it had done it because, by and large, the men and women who had claimed the liberty and the opportunity that America offered had recognized and sought to fulfill the dream that had motivated her . . . To let sentiment, even the sentiment of family love, paralyze the capacity for action . . . would, in my eyes, be a betrayal of everything that the words 'America' and 'American' implied."[3]

Meanwhile, another young man of German parentage, and of equal but different idealism, was moving in a direction diametrically opposed to the necessity for "national unity." He was Ernest L. Meyer, who was now a student at the University of Wisconsin. His journalist father, at times a socialist and an anarchist, had inculcated young Meyer with the prior claims of humanity over nationality. The youth immediately decided that he would not serve in his country's armed forces. For that decision he was reviled on the campus, but he registered as a conscientious objector and was granted that status by the authorities. He later described his experiences in a labor battalion in a book titled *Hey, Yellowjacket*, a work which still stands as a uniquely touching documentation of what it means to stand against the majority in an atmosphere of wartime hysteria.

That night of April 2 the Metropolitan Opera was presenting Reginald De Koven's *The Canterbury Pilgrims*, with many in the company either German-Americans or German nationals. Among those attending was the United States Ambassador to Germany James W. Gerard, who fortunately was in this country when war was declared. Just before the curtain rose on the last act, Gerard stepped forward in his box, announced that he had just received news that the President had asked Congress for a declaration of war, and called upon the audience to cheer the President. They did, somewhat hesitantly. Then the curtain rose. It was apparent that Margarete Ober, singing the role of the Wife of Bath, had been unstrung by Gerard's announcement. She faltered in her recitative. A moment or two later she collapsed in a dead faint and had to be carried from the stage. The opera was continued without her.

A GERMAN HERO NAMED LA FOLLETTE

Curiously enough, not one of the millions of German-Americans had come to the surface as a national leader of their amorphous cause. Partly that may have been traceable to the fact that German-Americans, with the possible exception of Carl Schurz (who, however, appealed more to American liberals than to the conservative majority of his fellow Germans), have noticeably lacked political popularity. It was also true that the German-Americans were sharply divided. Some were all-out pro-German, others were simply antiwar or in the rural areas particularly had absorbed the isolationist sentiment of the Populists, many were Socialists or anarchists who damned both sides as furthering the aims of international capitalism, and a great many, undoubtedly the majority, were vaguely, uneasily against American involvement but unwilling to oppose themselves to the government or prevailing public opinion. Then, too, it would have been difficult for a German to voice his suspicions and resentments because his origin would have made him doubly unacceptable to the non-Germanic majority he would be trying to influence.

A political vacuum existed. Paradoxically it was filled by a man of French descent, Robert Marion La Follette, United States senator from Wisconsin. The iron-jawed La Follette, with his theatrical pompadour, bedeviled his colleagues with blunt questioning of their motives in rushing into the war as an ally of imperial Britain and autocratic Russia. His whole career was built on dissent. He had first gained statewide recognition as district attorney of Dane County, in which Madison is located, for his fight on political corruption. An outlaw as far as the regular Republican machine was concerned, he repeatedly ran for governor of Wisconsin as a Progressive Republican until he finally made it and served three terms in that office. Subsequently he was elected to the United States Senate.

Senator La Follette was already the political hero of many Wisconsin Germans for his liberalism, which was not very far to the right of socialism, but with the outbreak of war he became the ideal and possible savior of German-Americans everywhere. They were delighted that a man of his political and intellectual caliber and of his fighting spirit — and even more blessedly one with a French name — should take up their cause. Not unexpectedly with that continuing goodwill of a grateful, substantially German-descended electorate behind him, "Fighting Bob" became the founder of a political dynasty; one of his sons later served as a senator, the other as governor of Wisconsin, and a grandson is now attorney-general of the state.

From the outbreak of the war in Europe, La Follette opposed every step the United States took toward intervention. He favored the aborted Bartholdt arms embargo bill, voted against a resolution of confidence in President Wilson, pushed a Senate resolution which would have yielded to German demands for the curtailment of American trade with Europe, and introduced a resolution forbidding the arming of American ships passing through the German submarine zone.

In September, 1915, his political house organ, *La Follette's Magazine*, exposed what he considered the reasons behind the pro-Allied prejudice of the American financial and industrial establishments: "With the first clash of the great European War came President Wilson's solemn appeal . . .'The United States must be neutral in fact as well as name.' . . . But when you can boom stocks 600 percent in manufacturing munitions — to the Bottomless Pit with Neutrality! What do Morgan and Schwab care for world peace when there are big profits in world war? . . . The Stocks of the Schwab properties which stood at a market value of seven millions before they began supplying the Allies . . . are today given an 'aggregate value' of forty-nine millions. And now we are about to engage in furnishing the Allies funds . . . We have ceased to be 'neutral in fact as well as in name.' "

Intransigence was the hallmark of the La Follette style, along with what one reporter called the "peculiarly exasperating smile" imprinted on his rugged squarish face when he was standing out alone against the wishes of his colleagues in the Senate.

His qualities as a loner, who would never yield to public clamor in defense of his convictions, were never more evident than in the several days following President Wilson's request for a declaration of war. Unanimous consent was proposed for the war resolution in the name of national unity. But no, Senator La Follette rose and insisted that the resolution "go over for the day" under the rules of the Senate.

Perhaps it was meaningless, but La Follette delayed the Congressional declaration for twenty-four hours while the nation steamed with impatience and war fever. Then he rose again on the Senate floor and delivered a long dissection of the Administration and its supporters:

"I had supposed until recently that it was the duty of Senators and

Representatives in Congress to vote and act according to their convictions. Quite another doctrine has recently been promulgated . . . and that is the doctrine of 'standing back of the President' without inquiring whether the President is right or wrong. For myself, I have never subscribed to that doctrine and never shall . . .

"There is always lodged, and always will be, thank the God above us, power in the people supreme. Sometimes it sleeps, but the sovereign power of the people never dies . . . I think, Mr. President, that it is being denied expression now . . . The poor who are the ones called upon to rot in the trenches have no organized power, have no press to voice their will on this question of peace or war, but at some time they will be heard . . . there will come an awakening . . ."

Hour after hour, in what amounted to a one-man filibuster, he tore into the Administration's course in coming to see the Allied cause as a holy crusade, in blaming the Germans alone for starting the war. The Allies, as much as Germany, had violated international law and infringed upon American rights on the seas. The British, in proclaiming the North Sea a war zone, thus blockading the German ports, had brought on the German countermeasures by submarine. The United States had not held Britain to the "strict accountability" she required of Germany.

It was 11 P.M. before the Senate was able to vote on the declaration. Six senators, including La Follette, voted against it. Next day, April 6, nine Wisconsin representatives were among the fifty voting against the declaration of war in the House.

Senator La Follette continued his opposition to Americas intervention, and on September 20, 1917, when the A.E.F. had begun flooding across the Atlantic in the endless chain of troop ships, he made a bitterly antiwar speech in St. Paul, which resulted in a futile attempt to expel him from the Senate.

Dissent in the United States had now become not only "disloyal" but more dangerous to the life and liberty of the dissenter than at any other time in American history. Never was "patriotism" so feverish, so mindless, so nakedly jealous of the slightest qualification or mildest questioning. This inflammation of the war spirit occurred despite the fact that twice during his address to Congress, President Wilson insisted that the United States was not making war upon the German people, only their government, and reminded the nation that the German-Americans must be extended the same lack of hostility. "We must put excited feeling away," he insisted.

The night before his request for a declaration of war, laboring over that speech, he had told Frank I. Cobb, an editor of the New York *World*, of his fears that emotionalism would be loosed and that it would be difficult to contain. "Once lead this people into war, and they'll forget there ever was such a thing as tolerance. To fight you must be brutal and ruthless, and the spirit of ruthless brutality will enter into the very fiber of our national life, infecting Congress, the courts, the policeman on the beat, the man in the street."[4]

Overnight, or so it seemed, everything German was stigmatized, sauerkraut converted into "Liberty Cabbage," the frankfurter into the hot dog, the windows of shops bearing German names smashed by "patriotic" mobs, the bearers of German or German-sounding names hounded and often made the victim of mob violence.

The months following United States entry into the war were undoubtedly the greatest trial ever endured by a minority. For the division of loyalties which many German-Americans had to reconcile, there was no sympathy except from the similarly afflicted Irish-Americans, who resented having to fight at the side of England as much as the Germans shrank from fighting against Germany. Even an English historian, writing during the equally bitter days of 1940, could understand the situation of those who had, as "hyphenates," campaigned to keep America neutral toward Germany while favoring the Allies with money and supplies. "To retreat from their openly expressed views," he wrote, "would have been hypocritical and insincere, and to retain them would have been both technically and actually disloyal to the United States of America. The conflict within the minds of the German-Americans during the first half of 1917 must have been as devastating and as catastrophic as was the greater conflict being waged in Europe. It had split their Germanism from their Americanism, for they could no longer retain both, and it dissolved the hyphen which had for so long served to unite them."[5]

Within the hours it took to bring the United States into the war, German-Americanism disappeared forever. It could no longer exist. In those febrile times, the German-American had to make his decision to be either German or American. With startlingly few exceptions, the choice was made instantly for Americanism. Many German-Americans were among the most bloodthirsty of the *Hunnenfresser* — "Hun-eaters" — who made four-minute speeches on street corners and in factories and public meetings whipping up hatred of everything German. The most violently anti-German war propaganda films produced in Hollywood came from the studios of the German-born Carl Laemmle, Sr.

The German-Americans, it could be said, leaned over backward in their effort to prove their attachment to the American cause. "Support Wilson whatever course he may follow" was the slogan of German-Americans in Texas. The teaching of German was forbidden by statute in twenty-six states, and in Texas, with its large Germanic population, was not restored until 1929. In Cincinnati the rumors spread during the weeks following the declaration of war that German meatpackers were putting ground glass in sausages and frankfurters (that is, hot dogs).

Even Hermann Hagedorn, who devoted most of his time to writing appeals to his fellow German-Americans to know "where their heart's home really was," came under suspicion of overly watchful neighbors who wondered whether he wasn't merely an unusually devious agent of the kaiser. "A Greenfield Hill neighbor wrote the New York *Herald* that I had better be watched. I had a German name, my water tower 'commanded' the arms factories in Bridgeport — six miles away — and 'queer-looking people' — poets frequently qualify as such — were seen coming and going at my place." A short time later Theodore Roosevelt came to call upon Hagedorn and in his forthright way let it be known throughout the neighborhood that his young friend was above suspicion, with the result that "when we held war rallies in the old Congregational Church I was asked to preside."[6]

But few German-Americans had the personal protection of a Theodore Roosevelt, and many learned what it was to be persecuted, scorned, boycotted, even personally harmed. The venomous hysteria even extended to the animal world, and the lives of dachshunds, schnauzers, weimaraners and German shepherds (temporarily renamed Alsatians) were made miserable by small boys aping their super-patriot fathers. The *Saturday Evening Post* urged that "the scum of the melting pot," meaning the Germanic element, must be scoured from the national life, and declared that anyone who defended German music must be either a radical or a woolly-minded dreamer. Theodore Dreiser, by then a literary force, was attacked by the eminent critic Stuart Sherman, who charged that Dreiser's novels and characters were not only non-Anglo-Saxon but amoral and therefore tainted with Germanism. H. L. Mencken defended Dreiser, upon which Sherman assailed Mencken for his "continuous laudation of a Teutonic-Oriental pessimism and nihilism in philosophy, of anti-democratic politics, of the subjection and contempt of women, of the *Herren*-moral, and of anything but Anglo-Saxon civilization; an unsympathetic person might call it infatuated propagandism."

American tolerance was so overwhelmed by the war spirit that, as Henry F. May (*The End of American Innocence*) has observed: "Respectable people, of kindly emotions and gentle manners, repeated atrocity stories, full of detailed invention with obvious sexual overtones. Liberal ministers preached the *jehad* with the full accompaniment of promised salvation to killers of the infidel; pulpits rang with denunciations of pacifists, radicals, moderates, and, not least, those who supported the war but refused to make this a matter of religious faith."

Even the bold and outspoken H. L. Mencken waited until two years after the war ended to come out with his splenetic essay on "The Star Spangled Men"[7] in which he sardonically proposed the issuance of special decorations for those who had fought the war with their mouths, largely in hounding any who dared to disagree with American war policy.

He was certain that a gaudy medal of honor should be awarded "for the university president who prohibited the teaching of the enemy language in his learned grove, heaved the works of Goethe out of the university library, cashiered every professor unwilling to support Woodrow for the first vacancy in the Trinity, took to the stump for the National Security League, and made two hundred speeches in moving picture theaters — for this giant of loyal endeavor let no 100 percent American speak of anything less than the grand cross of the order, with a gold badge in stained glass, a baldric of the national colors, a violet plug hat with a sunburst on the side, the privilege of the floor of Congress, and a pension of $10,000 a year . . .

"For the grand cordons of the order, e.g., college professors who spied upon and reported the seditions of their associates, state presidents of the American Protective League, alien property custodians, judges whose sentences of conscientious objectors mounted to more than 50,000 years, members of George Creel's herd of 2,000 historians [Creel was head of the Committee on Public Information, the official propaganda agency and also the instrument of newspaper censorship during the war], the authors of the Sisson documents, etc. — pensions of $10 a day would be enough, with silver badges and no plug hats . . ."

Mencken would also have decorated a horde of lesser patriots but conceded there were too many of them to be individually recognized. "If the grand cordon or even the nickel-plated eagle of the third class were given to every patriot who bored a hole through the floor of his flat to get evidence against his neighbors, the Krausmeyers, and to everyone who visited the Hofbrauhaus nightly, denounced the Kaiser in searing terms, and demanded assent from Emil and Otto, the waiters, and to everyone who notified the catchpolls of the Department of Justice when the wireless plant was open in the garret of Arion Liedertafel . . . and to all who served as jurors or perjurers in cases against members and ex-members of the I.W.W. and to the German-American members of the League for German Democracy, and to all the Irish who snitched upon the Irish — if decorations were thrown about with any such lavishness, then there would be no nickel left for our bathrooms."

Nor did Mr. Mencken believe that posterity should overlook "the New York *Tribune* liar who invented the story about the German plant for converting the corpses of the slain into soap . . ." But this was an unfortunate prevision of what would happen in German concentration camps twenty-odd years in the future.

He also advocated special awards for "the patriotic chemists who discovered arsenic in dill pickles, ground glass in pumpernickel, bio-chloride tablets in Bismarck herring, pathogenic organisms in aniline dyes," and for the "Methodist pulpit pornographers who switched so facilely from vice-crusading to German atrocities." As for the sedition-hunting Attorney General A. Mitchell Palmer, he "deserves to be rolled in malleable gold from head to foot, and polished until he blinds the cosmos . . ."

As the first months after the declaration of war passed, most Americans recovered their poise and most German-Americans no longer felt themselves beleaguered. The latter supported the war effort, often reluctantly perhaps, but they "did their bit," as the contemporary saying had it. German-Americans more than fulfilled their military duty, and that was the best way of all of proving, in the eyes of their fellow citizens, that they were "loyal." Even in hard-core Milwaukee, the First Liberty Loan Drive, with the city's quota set at fourteen million dollars, ended up with eighteen million dollars subscribed; a symptom of the feeling that the German-descended had to do a little more than what was expected of them. The Milwaukee *Germania-Herold*, suddenly and rather prematurely, conceded that Germany was guilty of starting the war.

"The end of *Deutschum's* power is in sight," declared a Milwaukee *Journal* editorial. When Senator La Follette announced that he would attempt to have the conscription laws repealed, the Wisconsin Loyalty Legion was organized in response, and in March, 1918, the state legislature censured La Follette for his dissidence.

Captain Claude Manly, commanding a machine-gun company in the 32nd Division, largely composed of German-American recruits, wrote back home from a French training camp: "Our friends in Milwaukee who are worried about German propaganda and what will happen after the war need have no fear. These men will vote as they fight — for America."[8]

Much of the annealing process was accomplished among the leaders of the Catholic Church. Archbishop George Mundelein, a German-American to be elevated to cardinal in a few years, claimed that "no

416

spiritual subject of his out of over a million had been held for disloyalty" in the Chicago archdiocese. German-descended prelates were named to the Catholic War Council by James Cardinal Gibbons.

And it was also the sympathetic, understanding Cardinal Gibbons who spoke out against the campaign to end all teaching of German in the schools: "We should no more dismiss that language from our curriculum because of the danger of Prussianism that we should do away with the pagan classics, Latin and Greek, because of the fear of our children becoming contaminated with paganism."

Sir Shane Leslie, himself half-American, his mother being the sister of Winston Churchill's mother, prophesied on target when he assured those on both sides of the Atlantic who were worried about the loyalty of the Irish and the Germans, without which the American military and industrial components could hardly have been built up to war strength, that "the war can but clear both [the Irish and the German] of what un-American ferment moves on their surfaces as their accepted country summons and uses those indispensable gifts which Celt and Teuton often alone can give in the service of war."

THE DRAFT-DODGER AND THE OPERA SINGER

Much of that which was sympathetic in the attitude of non-German Americans toward the German minority, and much that they detested, were crystallized in two names now only hazily remembered, if at all, Bergdoll and Schumann-Heink.

The first, Bergdoll, typified and sensationalized all the anti-German feelings in the country, largely because that name figured on the front pages throughout the war and for several years thereafter.

Erwin R. Bergdoll and his younger brother, Grover Cleveland Bergdoll, were the sons of a prominent Philadelphia brewing family. They were eligible for the draft, but announced that they would not serve in the American army because "we do not fight our own kind."

As if those words weren't inflammatory enough, the Bergdoll brothers then became fugitives from justice and skipped from one part of the country to the other — sightings of the Bergdoll brothers were as frequently reported in the press as reports of Germans poisoning wells or plotting to blow up factories. They further inflamed public opinion by writing officials of the Justice Department taunting postcards, sneering at the inability of the federal agents to catch up with them. Eventually Erwin Bergdoll was snared and served half of a four-year sentence in a federal prison. His brother, Grover, fled to Germany after the war ended and was imprisoned here years later when he finally returned to the United States.

As an antidote to the Bergdoll brothers, the German-American community could boast of the gallant, heart-warming and self-sacrificing figure of Madame Ernestine Schumann-Heink, the great contralto, who in herself symbolized the divided heart of German America. Her sons fought on both sides of the Western front.

Stout, beaming, plump, and homely as a dumpling, Madame Schumann-Heink served as the epitome of German motherhood. Most people, because she had been a German citizen through marriage before being naturalized in this country, assumed that she was indeed German. As in the case of Victor Herbert, they were mistaken. Madame Schumann-Heink, née Roessler, was a Viennese, the daughter of an Austrian army officer and an Italian mother.

She was born with a golden contralto, and at fifteen was signed to a contract by the Royal Opera of Dresden. Three years later she married Paul Heink, the secretary of the opera. Heink abandoned her with three children, and she almost starved to death until the Hamburg Opera took her on at ten dollars a month.

Her success story was the familiar one. A prima donna quit in a burst of temperament, Ernestine Heink went on in her place and was a smashing success. Thereupon she married an actor named Paul Schumann and brought five more children into the world. In 1898 the Metropolitan Opera brought her over. She was then thirty-seven, pregnant again and nothing like the glamour girl the manager of the Met was expecting. Obviously, he said, she wouldn't be able to sing until she had given birth.

"What do you know about babies?" Madame Schumann-Heink

Grover Cleveland Bergdoll, nimblest of draft dodgers

George Sylvester Viereck, failed poet, flawed propagandist

indignantly retorted. "I have had them many a time. I shall sing regardless. You will see how I shall sing!"[9]

Eight months pregnant, she made her New York debut in *Lohengrin* and was a great success. She named the new baby George Washington Schumann as a measure of her affection for her adopted country. Her world tours were equally successful, she played baccarat with the Prince of Wales, and Queen Victoria was so pleased with her singing and her unaffected personality that she took Madame Schumann-Heink's face in her two hands and kissed her. The persona she had created for herself was further enhanced one night in Boston when, just as she was waiting in the wings to make her appearance, she was handed a telegram saying her husband had died. She went on and gave a beautiful performance.

Much that non-Germans or anti-Germans in America found to revile about those of German descent was canceled out by her maternal neutrality during the war. Her eldest son, August, joined the Austrian army and was killed during one of the early battles of the war. Her other four sons fought on the Allied side.

The singer would not disown her eldest son, though she demonstrated her own patriotic sympathies by spending most of her time appearing on programs in the training camps of the A.E.F. If Elsie Janis was the "sweetheart of the A.E.F.," as her publicists maintained, Madame Schumann-Heink, singing the Brahms "Lullaby," "The Rosary" and "Silent Night" and causing tears to stream down doughboy faces, was even more memorable.

During the postwar years, she became a radio star and was renowned as the "official Amen-maker of each Christmas Eve and every Armistice Day." Her voice, aging but still thrilling in its emotional depth, pouring "Silent Night" out of a Victrola was as much a part of Christmas in the American home of the Twenties as the lighted tree. "Many another prima donna has successfully mothered a large family," it was recorded. "But she has gone further. She has mothered audiences, mothered towns and cities, mothered the A.E.F. and now mothers the American Legion." At sixty-eight she broke both her ankles but continued trouping through farewell concert tours and vaudeville bookings, with specially braced shoes supporting her stout figure.

At the age of seventy-five she became, as she said, "Hollywood's oldest starlet," when Louis B. Mayer, who regarded motherhood as holy and Madame Schumann-Heink as the motherliest mother in the world, signed her to a movie contract. "I want to die singing," she said, "not in a manner to create a disturbance, but quietly with a song on my lips." She died before Mayer could make her a star, but millions of Americans would remember her without the help of a Hollywood soundtrack.

None of the war heroes with German names, from General of the Armies John J. Pershing to Captain Eddie Rickenbacker, did more to efface the deplorable image of German-Americans as transplanted Huns. The fact she wasn't German at all, except for a period of German citizenship through marriage, was the best-kept and the most wisely kept German-American secret of the war.

PROOF IN COMBAT

Few young German-Americans were more eager to prove their loyalty than young Joseph Wehner, and few, fortunately, had so much trouble being allowed to do so. If Wehner's case had been typical, which it wasn't, it would have seemed the ubiquitous military and naval intelligence agents spent more of their time snooping on, shadowing, badgering and leaning heavily on young German-American servicemen than on performing their more conventional function of trying to find out what the enemy was up to.

Joe Wehner was almost a textbook case in the boneheadedness and mistaken zeal of military bureaucracy. He was a tall, lean, pale-faced twenty-year-old with raven-black hair and a quiet, unassuming manner. His great misfortune was that his father, a cobbler in Everett, Massachusetts, was born in Germany.

Wehner paid his own way to enlist in the air force — the Signal Corps Air Service, as it was then officially known — at Kelly Field in Texas. His German name immediately made him the object of suspicion among the intelligence officers on the base. Perhaps some well-meaning patriot had tipped them off that he was a menace to Allied security the moment he left Everett to join up. From the moment he started training, at any rate, he was kept under surveillance.

His letters from home were opened and submitted to decoding experts, his footlocker was opened and searched almost daily, and twice he was summoned for long questioning on his motives, background and political beliefs. The intelligence officers simply refused to believe that sheer patriotism had caused him to pay his own fare from Massachusetts to join up with the Twenty-seventh Squadron.

Unfortunately, Wehner blew up finally and told his persecutors off.

"He's cracking," they assured each other. "Now he'll make a desperate move."

Instead Wehner grew more withdrawn, silent and inwardly furious at his mistreatment, at the way his comrades in the squadron avoided him or whispered among themselves that he was suspected of being a German spy.[10]

Just as the Twenty-seventh Squadron received its orders to proceed to New York for embarkation, military intelligence pounced and placed him under close arrest. He was left behind at Kelly Field. Apparently his commanding officer, prizing his native abilities as a combat pilot, then demanded a full, open and immediate investigation. It was held, Wehner was cleared and hurried to New York to catch up with his outfit.

The squadron was posted at Saintes in the old Aisne-Marne salient, just when the Germans were launching their last desperate offensives, and thrown almost immediately into combat with the veteran hunters of the Luftwaffe.

Military intelligence still hadn't loosened its hold on young Lieutenant Wehner. He was being kept under close surveillance, even though he had technically been cleared.

Shortly after his arrival at Saintes late in May, 1918, Wehner met up with another young German-American flier named Frank Luke, Jr., who had also suffered the attentions of the intelligence agents.

Lieutenant Luke was a twenty-one-year-old hardrock miner and former high school football star from Phoenix, Arizona. Towheaded, blue-eyed and quick with his fists, Luke was called the Arizona Blowhard by his squadron mates because of his frequently announced intention of decimating what he called in his letters home the "Hunfliers." Racially, Luke himself was a "Hunflier," but a thoroughly Americanized one. His paternal grandfather was an immigrant from Westphalia who had fought in the Union army, his mother was born in Berlin.

Luke was a combative, hard-nosed youth, who was disliked by his squadron mates for his readiness to fight with his fists and his large winnings at crap-shooting contests, in which he constantly bellowed, "All or nothing!" The first time he went into action, he boasted that he would bring down an enemy plane or not come back. When the combat patrol returned after being scattered in action, Luke claimed that he had shot down a German plane. The "kill" was disputed, never confirmed, but gave Luke a bad name in the squadron and made him, like Wehner, a loner.

Their commanding officer, Major Harold Hartney, later described how the young men met for the first time in his office at the Saintes air base. "Luke walked in just as I was reassuring Joe Wehner that he had nothing to worry about. Because of his name some over-anxious Intelligence operator had been hounding the boy and he was not happy about it. A funny thing, as he walked out he and Luke exchanged just a hint of a grin. I didn't know it then but in that brief encounter was born one of the greatest fighting teams the U.S. Air Service was to inscribe on its records."[11]

It was, in fact, the greatest without qualification. Within the few weeks of combat life allotted to them, Luke and Wehner compiled an amazing record. The steady, easygoing Wehner provided air cover as Luke's wingman while Luke, "cocksure, high-tempered, vociferously talkative . . . mischievous, irresponsible and absolutely impervious to any squadron regulations" as he has been described by one historian of the fledgling United States air force,[12] opened up on the enemy with the machine guns in his new Spad. On ten combat patrols, with

Wehner protecting him against enemy interference, Luke shot down four German planes and fifteen enemy observation balloons. In headlines back in the States he became famous as "The Balloon Buster." Luke was the first United States airman to be awarded the Congressional Medal of Honor. "He was the Peck's bad boy of the air," Arch Whitehouse (*The Year of the Sky Kings*), himself a World War I flier, has written, "for he deliberately broke every rule, evaded every code, disdained all laws of military discipline, and died in a savage, unreasonable scuffle in a graveyard against a platoon of German infantry, when he might have honorably surrendered and lived out the last six weeks of the war in a prison camp."

Opposite as they were in temperament, Luke and Wehner were drawn together by their status as outcasts. They decided to team up as members of the First Pursuit Group, which was flying two or three combat patrols daily with the pace of the ground war quickening as the United States army prepared to move into its first great battle in the St. Mihiel salient. With the reluctant approval of their superiors, they designated the enemy observation balloons, which cost the Germans $100,000 apiece and were protected by special formations of five German fighter planes, their objective. One day they took off with the regular patrol, then peeled off on their own mission. Two enemy "gasbags" hung on the horizon like huge sausages. While Wehner fought off the formations guarding the balloons, Luke repeatedly attacked them against machine-gun fire from the observers stationed on them. That night when they returned to their base, they had confirmed "kills" of two balloons and Wehner had shot down an enemy fighter while flying cover for Luke.

A few days later, off again on an independent mission, Wehner and Luke took on an even more dangerous target. Intelligence — by now able to divert some of its attention to the enemy — had reported a cluster of three observation balloons. Luke swore he'd get all three. As they neared their objective over the German lines, a formation of Fokkers zoomed up to intercept them.

Lieutenant Wehner alone tore into the swarming enemy fighters while Luke flew on to attack the balloons they were trying to protect. Incendiary shells known as "flaming onions" burst all around Luke as he dove on his targets, strafing them while the gunners in the observation cages of the balloons riddled his plane with machine-gun fire.

They returned from that mission with three more gasbags and two enemy planes shot down.

The next day, on a similar mission, Luke downed two more balloons and Wehner accounted for one balloon and two enemy fighters. The Wehner-Luke team had suddenly become so successful at balloon-busting that the Germans hauled down their gasbags the moment they were reported heading for the German lines. By now the First Pursuit Group had moved closer to the front, and their superiors decided to employ the team in new tactics. The Germans were keeping their balloons on a short tether during the day but just before nightfall were sending them aloft for a last look over the battlefront.

General Billy Mitchell, the commander of the American air forces, drove up from his headquarters to watch Luke and Wehner put on an exhibition of their balloon-shooting skill. The group headquarters was close enough to the enemy lines to allow General Mitchell and his staff observe the operation through field glasses. From 7:10 to 7:34 that evening the officers at the base watched Luke and Wehner destroy three enemy balloons, each busting into scarlet bloom against the night sky. Signal rockets had to be set off to guide the two pilots back to their base. General Mitchell was so impressed by the exhibition that he ordered special night-landing facilities installed at the base so that Luke and Wehner could go hunting whenever they believed they had a chance at the enemy. Their work in "blinding" the enemy was especially valuable at that moment because the American army was secretly transferring hundreds of thousands of troops from the St. Mihiel salient to a new sector in the Meuse-Argonne where the final offensive of the war would be launched.

On September 17, over St. Mihiel, they spotted two enemy balloons aloft. While Luke peeled off to attack them, Wehner dove into the middle of a formation of Fokker D-7's swarming up to protect the balloons. Luke shot down both of them, then sped back to join the dogfight. Joe Wehner was in serious trouble. Four of the Fokker fighter planes were on his tail and hammering away with their machine guns. Luke dove in and diverted two of them by going into a tight climbing turn. When he finished this maneuver, he looked around for Wehner, but his plane was no longer in the sky. One of the enemy fighters had shot him down.

In a blazing fury, Luke turned on the attacking Germans and shot three of them out of the sky. When he returned to his base that night, his now more comradely comrades swarmed over him with congratulations on one of the greatest aerial feats of the war. Inside an hour he had accounted for two balloons and three fighters, which made him the reigning ace of the Signal Corps Air Service.

"Where's Joe?" was all Luke wanted to know.

Wehner, he was told, had been killed. From then on, the exuberant Luke, his comrades said, was a changed man. He brooded over Joe Wehner's death, went up alone on unauthorized missions to "revenge Joe" and was threatened with a general court-martial by his commanding officer for disobeying direct orders not to fly without a wingman.

Late in the afternoon of September 29, 1918, Luke took off on an unauthorized flight, solo, dropping a note for his superiors which read: "Watch out for those three nearest balloons at D 1 and D 4 positions — Luke." His commanding officer swore that "if he gets back alive I'll recommend him for the Distinguished Flying Cross, then by God I'm going to have him grounded and court-martialed." That was the last anyone but the enemy and some French peasants working in the fields below ever saw of Frank Luke. He attacked and burned an enemy balloon at the Brière Farm, then was attacked by a formation of German fighters. He was shot down, but survived a crash landing near the graveyard outside the village of Murvaux. The rest of his story was told in an affidavit signed by the mayor of Murvaux and a dozen other witnesses. Luke, they said, was "apparently wounded by a shot fired from rapid-fire cannon . . . got out of his machine . . . He had gone about fifty yards when, seeing the Germans come toward him, he still had strength to draw his revolver to defend himself, and a moment after he fell dead, following a serious wound received in the chest."[13]

Frank Luke got his Medal of Honor and Distinguished Flying Cross posthumously, one citation reading: "By skill, determination and bravery, and in the face of heavy enemy fire, he successfully destroyed eight enemy observation balloons in four days." The Air Force named Luke Field in Hawaii after him, and Phoenix erected a memorial arch in his honor.

In a few blazing days of aerial action over the Western front, Lieutenants Wehner and Luke provided some indication of how many German-Americans felt about defending their country. Their story was repeated countless times, though less dramatically, by the thousands of German-Americans who served in the A.E.F. The greatest American hero of the air war was Captain Eddie Rickenbacker, whose name was Richenbacher before he became a champion auto-racing driver. No traitors were rooted out of the A.E.F. by all those diligent operatives of the intelligence corps. The army fought its way through the toughest infantry battle of the war, in the Meuse-Argonne, under a commander whose name was originally Pfoerschin.

That same commander, his name Anglicized to Pershing, studied with a special anxiety the reports of his inspector general concerning the 32nd Division. Many of his staff officers wondered whether it could be trusted in action against the Germans. The 32nd was composed largely of National Guard troops from Wisconsin and Michigan, with a high percentage of German-Americans in their ranks.

General Pershing, however, was convinced that his fellow German-Americans would fight as hard as any other nationality. The 32nd Division was sent to the Vosges Mountains early in 1918, before the bulk of the A.E.F. was committed to action in the trenches. It distinguished itself in hard fighting in the mountain snows, much of it hand-to-hand combat, and was finally marked down as "reliable." Its subsequent record on the Marne and in campaigning to the end of the war made "reliable" seem an understatement. It was one of the crack divisions of the A.E.F.[14]

The German-Americans had more than vindicated themselves in

battle against the German-Germans. They wiped out the suspicion which had been focused on their millions back home. The national reconciliation was symbolized on what was probably the greatest day in Milwaukee history, the day the 32nd Division marched down Grand (now Wisconsin) Avenue, June 6, 1919, behind its battle flags and streamers.

16. THE VOICE OF THE

GRASSHOPPERS

Because half a dozen grasshoppers under a fern make the field ring with their importunate chink, whilst thousands of great cattle . . . chew the cud and are silent, pray do not imagine that those who make the noise are the only inhabitants of the field . . .

— EDMUND BURKE

The wound in the German-American psyche was not, of course, healed overnight. The harassments to which they were subjected, the prejudice and suspicion which included even those who had not joined the National German-American Alliance or had not the slightest affection for the Germany from which their forefathers were driven, lingered in memory for years.

Nor could what Hermann Hagedorn called the tragedy of "the family that tried to live in two countries" be effaced the moment mail service was resumed between the United States and defeated Germany. Before the war ended, word of his activities reached Germany, where his father and his brother, risen to Under Secretary of State in the Food Supply Ministry in Berlin, were living with other members of the family. "The Cologne *Gazette* paid me the compliment of declaring me a *Schweinehund*, a mythical animal supposed to combine the most

429

reprehensible characteristics of bitch and swine. Another paper labeled me a *Schmutzfink*, a creature wallowing in the mire for sheer delight in filth." And his brother Fred wrote Hagedorn that "if I had any feeling at all for Father I should stop at once what I was doing." From the senior Hagedorn, after the Armistice, came a letter full of grief. "How frightful, what has befallen us!" When the French troops occupied the Rhineland, however, the Hagedorns were spared further frightfulness by hanging out an American flag, thus gaining a protection to which they had no right.[1]

The German-Americans emerged from the war, perhaps unchastened (a monograph on their attitude published a dozen years later by the German American Historical Society of Illinois declared that they were, in 1919, "as fully convinced of the superiority of their own culture as ever"),[2] but arrived at a mass conviction that they should never again be caught in such a bind. Among Germans in America there was considerable sympathy for Germany and antipathy for the Versailles Treaty, but they would never wander outside the national consensus again. The radicalism and separatism and other extremist movements, including an extreme jealousy of their rights to observe the Sabbath in their own lusty manner, were all sunk into the past. *Kaput!* As the English social historian Hawgood observed, "the German-Americans, as German-Americans, did not emerge from the war at all. The war had so enhanced the distance between the German and the American that no hyphen could stretch from the one to the other. The German-Americans, disowned and derided by the Germans of Germany, had no further reason for clinging to their *Deutschtum* at such great sacrifices to themselves. It was perceived by all, at last, that German-Americanism was obsolete."[3]

German-Americans were abashed, too, by the realization that the activities of many of their number, the fact that many imprisoned seditionists bore German names, the infamy attached to the Bergdolls and other headlined malefactors, all had contributed to a feeling in the America of the Twenties that the melting pot, hitherto one of the most sacred of totems, had been at least partially a failure. H. P. Fairchild wrote in his 1925 edition of *Immigration: A World Movement and Its*

American *Significance* that the "unique" conditions of the past century had created a hopeful atmosphere for the process of assimilating various nationalities which did not survive into the twentieth century. "The melting pot was so badly cracked," Fairchild wrote regarding the World War, "that it is hardly likely ever to be dragged into service again."

All the old nationalistic organizations, such as the disbanded National German-American Alliance, were moribund and no attempts would be made to revive them. Nor was there any sympathy between the Germans who had migrated to the United States before the war and those who came over, many sporting Iron Crosses and defensive attitudes, after the war. The latecomers often were afflicted by a nostalgia for the kaiser's Germany, a hatred for the Weimar Republic, which was in direct contrast to the hopes of the nineteenth century German immigrants who were often refugees from kaiserism, Prussianism and militarism. Thus when Hitler and Nazism rose, there was an unbridgeable gap between the two groups; the new "Greens" wanted revenge for the lost war, the new "Grays" asked nothing of the old country but that she keep the peace . . . and ask nothing more of them.

In May of 1919, partly as a result of this feeling and a revulsion from the emotionalism of 1914–1917 and the psychological effects of finding themselves widely despised, the German-Americans organized the Steuben Society. It was and is decidedly noncontroversial, unaggressive, inoffensive. The purpose of the organization, as outlined in its objectives, was to thoroughly Americanize whatever Germanism remained, without, at the same time, foreswearing any pride in the pre-World War past of the German-Americans. On their behalf it sought to "foster a patriotic American spirit among all citizens," to encourage Germans to engage in "a better participation in public affairs," to "maintain the traditions of the nation, to keep alive the memory of the achievements of the pioneers of this country, and to enlighten the public on the important part played in the Germanic element in the making of America," to "guide our citizens through the intricacies of public policies, to warn them against political intrigues and to oppose alien influenced government." Six years later the Society added another clause to its platform: "To protect citizens of German stock from insults, misrepresentations and discrimination."[4] In the latter effort, it has performed much less vigorously than like organizations formed by the Jews, the Irish, the Italians and the Poles; but perhaps that is one measure of the German-American's final success, after protracted misadventure, in achieving amalgamation.

A SMOLDERING RESENTMENT

During the postwar years the German-American community was generally cautious about expressing itself on any controversial issues. Still hungover from the wartime binge of emotionalism, it was apolitical and apathetic, mildly pleased that the old country was getting on its feet after almost being ruined by Communist uprisings, rightist reactions and a disastrous inflation. Yet it would be inaccurate to say that German-Americans did not resent the buffeting they took during the war.

They merely expressed that smoldering resentment in the privacy of the polling booth, and turned in increasing numbers to the sanctuary of isolationism, in which they were joined by hundreds of thousands, particularly in the Middle West, who were drawn from all national origins.

One vehicle of their resentment was the Nonpartisan League, originally a semi-socialist organization which had formed cooperatives among the wheat farmers of the northern plains and was linked to La Follette Progressivism in Wisconsin. The League attracted the German farmers because it was also anti-intervention. "Unable to stand in naked opposition" in the America of 1918, Samuel Lubell (*The Future of American Politics*) has observed, the German farmers of Minnesota and the Dakotas "could parade their protest in the clothes of economic grievance."

Charles Lindbergh, Sr., the father of the flier, was their candidate for governor of Minnesota in 1918. A Swedish-born lawyer of regional prominence, Lindbergh had written a book titled *Why Is Your Country at War and What Happens to You After the War*, in which he blamed everything on a conspiracy of war profiteers and international bankers. Lindbergh lost the Republican primary but got the most votes in the counties where there was a concentration of German-Americans. In the general election that year, when the Farmer-Labor party appeared on the ballot for the first time, having inherited the old populist-isolationist sentiment, five out of the eight more heavily Germanic counties in Minnesota gave their votes to its candidates.

The same slow-burning resentments made themselves visible to the watchful eye in 1924 when Robert M. La Follette, Sr., ran for President as a third-party candidate and gathered in 4,800,000 votes — close to the five million which German-American Alliance propagandists had boasted — against Calvin Coolidge and John W. Davis. Earlier the same segment of the electorate, it may be presumed, voted heavily for Warren G. Harding and helped to repudiate the visionary programs of the hated Woodrow Wilson.

A similar long-fused animosity, this one in an urban setting, was a potent factor in the picaresque political career of William Hale Thompson. The wartime mayor of Chicago endeared himself to the German electorate by refusing to receive Marshal Joffre of France during his mission to the United States on the ground that his city was the "sixth largest German city in the world," and it would be presumptuous to invite a marshal of France in the name of all the people of Chicago. Later Mayor Thompson delighted his supporters by threatening to punch the king of England in the nose if that royal personage ever ventured into fistic range. Thompson made a successful comeback in the mayoralty election of 1926 on the blunt formulation: "The Negroes, the Germans and the wide-open town." And, he might have added, a Capone brewery or distillery in every other vacant warehouse.

Then, after such high jinks were ended by the sober depression years, the spell binding figure — or more accurately voice — of Father Charles E. Coughlin, "the radio priest," whose Sunday afternoon diatribes against the international bankers, the World Court and the Versailles Treaty were heard throughout the land. He praised Mussolini and Franco (but not Hitler). He was obliquely hostile to the Jews, or so his listeners believed. Anybody raised in the Middle West during the early Thirties will recall the hold he exercised with his golden gift of radio oratory, compared to which President Franklin D. Roosevelt's soothing "fireside chats" were condescending visitations from a squire to his numbskull peasants. Radio was the "hot" medium in those years, and Father Coughlin was the master of the Gospel According to Marconi.

With his combination of invective against Wall Street leading us into another European war and his rather glib panaceas for the economic ills of the time, Father Coughlin rallied millions of supporters, mostly in the Middle West and East, mostly those of the Irish and German Catholic lower middle class. In 1936 he unwisely tested the extent of his political power by forming the Union party and offering William Lemke, an old Nonpartisan League campaigner, as a third-party candidate for the Presidency. That was the year of Alf Landon's debacle, but Lemke fared even worse. He polled about 890,000 votes, only a fifth of the number voting for La Follette a dozen years before.

The only four cities in which Lemke got more than 5 percent of the vote were heavily German and Irish Catholic — St. Paul, Dubuque, Boston and Cincinnati (where he received 12 percent). William Hale Thompson attempted another comeback in Chicago as a Union party candidate but this time got only one hundred thousand votes.

All these were manifestations of lingering resentment over the First World War, the isolationism which had given it a coating of acceptability and the suspicion that F.D.R. was heading toward another intervention in Europe, this time against Nazi Germany and Fascist Italy.

Samuel Lubell made a study of the attitudes of the German-Americans of the plains states, particularly those known as the "Russian-Germans," descendants of Germans who migrated to Russia during Catherine the Great's regime and came to this country during the 1890's. Most of them lived in North Dakota. They were (and are) racially Teutonic, pure Teutonic, because intermarriage with the Russians was forbidden during their centuries along the Volga, and they acquired few Russian habits beyond a liking for borscht and vodka. The Russian-Germans were isolationist by temperament and custom; Catherine the Great had lured them to Russia by granting them exemption from military service, and when they migrated en masse to the United States they tried to settle in closed communities. Congress refused to encourage their separatist tendency by modifying the Homestead Act on their behalf, but the Russian-Germans succeeded in shutting themselves off from the American main current. Almost half a million have clustered together in various North Dakota, Nebraska and Kansas communities to constitute what Mr. Lubell called "ethnic islands." Among those Russian-Germans the old "stockade mentality" has not lost its grip.

"The most isolationist of all Americans," Mr. Lubell wrote in 1952, "are unquestionably the 'Russian-German' farmers . . . North Dakota has the heaviest concentration of Russian-Germans and they have been a major factor in keeping it the most isolationist state in the Union. McIntosh County, for example, gave the Democrats the smallest percentage of the vote in the whole country in 1920 — only 4 percent — and showed the highest Democratic drop in the nation in 1940 — 48 percentage points. The number of Roosevelt voters fell from 1,900 in 1936 to 318 in 1940."[5]

A similar pattern emerged in Lubell's study of Stearns County, Minnesota, with a large proportion of German Catholic voters, most of them forming the base of the senior Lindbergh's political power. In 1916, Stearns County voted against a second term for President Wilson and cost him the state in that closely contested election. In 1924, it voted for La Follette, but returned to the Democratic column in 1928 to give a plurality to Alfred E. Smith; yet in 1940, after World War II began, President Roosevelt's share of the vote dropped 34 percentage points.

Throughout the country, Roosevelt lost 7 percent of his strength between 1936 and 1940. "There were twenty counties," Lubell pointed out, "where his loss exceeded 35 percent — five times the national average. Nineteen of these counties are predominantly German-speaking in background."

For many German-Americans, particularly in the Middle West, it is clear that their animosity toward the idea of participating in another

European war was strong and unqualified. It was not overt pro-Germanism as it was between 1914 and 1917, but a determination to stay out of all European conflicts, a cause which would allow them to rally around the junior Charles Lindbergh and endlessly quote that most respectable of sources, George Washington, in his warning against foreign entanglements. Never again would German-America step out of line with majority public opinion. Certainly not — except in relatively few cases — for that hideous brown blossom called the German-American Bund.

AN AMERICAN FUEHRER

". . . I make no distinction between German nationals and Germans by birth who are citizens of a foreign country. Superficially we shall have to make allowances for such citizenship. But it will be your special task to train all Germans, without distinction, unconditionally to place their loyalty to Germandom before their loyalty to the foreign state. Only in this way will you be able to fulfill the difficult tasks I shall give you . . . Whoever opposes you should know that he has nothing more to expect from the German Reich. He will be outlawed for all time. And in due course he will reap the fruits of his treacherous attitude."[6]

This was Adolf Hitler outlining his program for the millions of overseas Germans in a conversation early in the Thirties with Hermann Rauschning, then his collaborator, later a refugee from Hitlerism.

A short time later Hitler made a speech to German societies' representatives from colonies overseas: "As the front line of our German fighting movement, you will make it possible for us to complete the occupation of our positions and to open fire. You have all the functions that we older men carried out in the last war. You are the army's outposts . . . It will depend on you gentlemen whether we reach our goal with comparative ease and without bloodshed. You must prepare the ground . . . When Germany is great and victorious no one will dare give you the cold shoulder . . . You shall be my viceroys in the countries and among the people who today persecute and oppress you . . ."

A Nazi propagandist subsequently declared that the Nazis "define as German all those of German descent and of German blood who live abroad . . . German people on this side of the border, and German people on the other side of the border! These borders exist on the maps, but not in our hearts!"

Fifth columns in North and South America, as well as everywhere else Germans had settled, were integral to the Nazis' plans for world conquest. In the United States the seedbed for Nazification was rather constricted by the recent trends in immigration. Few Germans migrated to the United States during the Thirties, except, later on, the mostly Jewish refugees from Nazi terrorism. When Hitler came to power, there were approximately 1,600,000 German-born in the United States. Of this number about a million had migrated before the First World War. Only about 600,000 were recent immigrants and could be considered as possible recruits for the Nazi cause.[7]

Yet only a small minority of those 600,000 became infected by the Nazi virus, along with a few thousand of the Germans of longer residence and perhaps an equal number of Americans of non-German stock who, it may be charitably said, were psychological victims of the Depression of the Thirties. The pro-German element in the United States during those years preceding World War II were a lunatic fringe, hardly to be compared in numbers — though for a time they exceeded them in virulence — with the kaiser's adherents of 1914–1917.

The later breed, however, made up in clamor what they lacked in force of numbers. They also got off to an early start. In 1924, when Hitler and his followers were only a small group of beerhall plotters and brawlers in Munich, members were being recruited for the National Socialist party of the United States. Five years later a Nazi periodical called the *Vorposten* was founded in Chicago promising "News of the German Freedom Movement in America."

The movement was functioning with an alarming efficiency; in fact, well before Hitler consolidated his own political power over Germany.

On February 9, 1933 — twenty-four days before the Reichstag election which confirmed Hitler as chancellor — twelve hundred persons gathered at the Turnhalle in New York's Yorkville section, sang "Deutschland über Alles" and the Horst Wessel song and heiled Hitler with swastika-emblazoned banners. Richard Rollins, an undercover agent investigating the activities of the American Nazis, found their bawling of slogans, and even more the enthusiasm with which the audience responded, a frightening spectacle.[8]

Yorkville in those months just after President Roosevelt took office for his first term, with the American economy lurching almost to a full stop, banks closing and breadlines lengthening, was churning with Hitlerite activity. The Society of the Friends of the Hitler Movement was holding weekly meetings, and the Steel Helmets had been organized among World War veterans of the German army. The Nazis also attempted to gain control of the United German Societies of New York, which had a membership of seventy thousand. The move was bitterly resisted, and the organization soon broke apart, half going Nazi and the rest taking an anti-Nazi position. In violation of the 1920 Treaty of Friendship between the United States and Germany, the German government began smuggling bales of Nazi propaganda and uniforms for storm troopers and the Nazi Youth Corps into New York.

Hitler's Germany had pondered the lessons of the First World War, and one firm decision it took was not to let the Germans in America be "cowed" again into fighting against Germany.

The German-Americans, except for the recent immigrants, were on the alert this time. With very few exceptions, they strongly and forthrightly resisted the Nazi movement in the United States. The Steuben Society took the lead, and in October, 1934, the Carl Schurz Society began publishing a periodical pointedly titled the *American-German Review*. If the hyphen must reappear, it would be inverted.

German-Americans, however, were preoccupied with the struggle to make a living during the hardest days of the depression, and the haranguing of the Hitlerites was more of an embarrassment, a public nuisance, than a positive menace to their standing as part of the American community. During the rise of American Nazism, the novelist William B. Seabrook, himself of partly German extraction, undertook an investigation of its influence among American-Americans as part of his book *These Foreigners*. He concluded that of the "obviously Germanic" population, including Austrians and Hungarians, which had come over since the turn of the century, 70 percent were "totally indifferent" to the appeal of international Nazism, 20 percent were "definitely anti-Nazi," 9 percent were "pro-Nazi in a sense consistent with loyalty to the U.S.A.," and 1 percent or less, about fifty thousand, were "rabidly, militantly Nazi in a not nice way."

Being "not nice" included an open and venomous anti-Semitism which among American Nazis paralleled the persecution of the Jews in Germany. Until then, German-American-Jews and German-Americans had always been on amicable, often intimate social terms. The spread of Nazism engendered a certain amount of unavoidable suspicion among German-Jews that their old friends weren't quite wholehearted in disavowing Hitler's racial policies. The German-American organizations balked, at first, against joining the boycott against Nazi Germany organized in this country shortly after Hitler came to power. Though the Steuben Society and the Carl Schurz Society finally swung into line, the American Jewish community believed they had shown a suspicious reluctance. (Many German-Americans conceded this was true. One German-American leader told William Seabrook, "Neither the organized Germans nor their press are fulfilling in America the mission of democracy of which Americans of German descent were always so proud." Furthermore Victor Ridder, publisher of the New York Staats-Zeitung, was accused by a Congressional investigating committee of having been "intimidated" by the Friends of New Germany, which the committee labeled "for all practical purposes the American Section of the Nazi Party," into supporting Nazi Germany in his newspaper.) Jewish leaders accordingly withdrew their long-standing financial and moral support of the Carl Schurz Memorial Foundation.

In the course of his investigations, Seabrook questioned hundreds of German-Americans, particularly regarding their attitude toward anti-Semitism. One was a Bavarian-born youth named Walter, who took him around the German hangouts in Chicago and introduced him to his friends. "Three out of a dozen or so he introduced me to were Jewish or partly Jewish. Nobody seemed to care. Walter and his friends talked more freely over a cup of coffee or a glass of beer than any of my more important new German acquaintances . . . Consuls, leading intellectuals, Germans in high official positions, some few editors of German-language newspapers, had been reticent, almost stuffy, when controversial subjects had been mentioned. Walter said, 'It's simple. They are all scared your book is going to be political, attacking or defending some group, intended to help or hurt some group, and they are afraid to be quoted. Us common Americans, myself and Otto here who are Bavarian, and Joe here who was a German Jew but is an American now — we don't give a damn about those things over there. The swastika is still Hindu to us.' "

Seabrook also talked to a Prussian-born housepainter named Eric who had returned to Germany for a visit only a year before. "Look now," he told Seabrook, "I am a Catholic, and Joe here, who is a Hungarian Jew, is one of my buddies. I don't like what Hitler is doing to us Christians, to the Church, or to the Jews either, but everything has two sides. When I lived in Germany before Hitler took charge, we had confusion and starvation, unemployment. I am blond and pug-nosed, but I couldn't get a job and that's why I came away . . . I went back there last winter on a visit and everything is changed . . . It's two-sided, I tell you, and it's over there in Europe, and I'm in favor of letting them settle it over there. These bullheaded, bellyaching, German pro-Hitlerites and anti-Hitlerites over here who ought to be plain German-Americans . . . or better still plain Americans . . . give me a pain in the eye."[9]

Perhaps "Eric's" attitude was more characteristic than "Walter's." In the last volume of the German-American Historical Society of Illinois Yearbook, which was discontinued in 1932, there was the obituary notice of a man named Julius Goebel, who was something of an intellectual and a prominent member of the society. It noted that the World War had been "the major catastrophe" of his life, ending, as it did for so many of his fellows, the security they felt in American life. The obituary also quoted a favorite saying of the late Mr. Goebel's, one he used to explain the difficulties of his minority:

"The real German-American malady is *Teilnahmlosigkeit* [public inactivity]."

It applied in the middle and late Thirties as well as the earlier period to which Goebel was referring.

Middle-aged Americans will testify that it was quite possible, even probable, for a person to have lived through the Thirties without being brought face to face with the mouthings and posturings of the American Nazi movement. Most never saw a Nazi swastikaed banner flapping over the American flag, or heard a Nazi or one of their so-called Christian Front comrades ranting against the Jews, or saw hundreds of arms slanting stiffly in the "Heil Hitler" salute, or saw ranks of brown-clad youth with the hooked cross on their armbands earnestly drilling for *Der Tag*, or attended the rallies of as many as twenty-two thousand persons being whipped into frenzy by Nazi orators, bathed by searchlights and deafened by the crash of jack boots in the manner of one of those medieval convocations at Nuremburg.

One of Sinclair Lewis's lesser works of art, but a powerfully cautionary novel, was *It Can Happen Here*. Lewis had watched part of "it" happen in Germany, and fretted over the possibility that a Fascist dictatorship could force its way to power in the United States; his faith in the durability of American institutions and the astringent common sense of its people, like his friend Mencken's, was something less than overwhelming.

"It" never did happen here, or even come close to happening. Fascism, for all the disgusting and disturbing aspects of its transplantation to America, was *opéra bouffe*. Its promoters were clowns and its followers slightly demented sheep. A Nuremburg-type rally in Madison Square Garden, with all its sweating solemnity and raucous appeals to unreason, was a hilarious spectacle when looked back upon.

But only, perhaps, in retrospect. During its peak of influence and noise-making, in 1937, the Boston *Globe* assigned the star investigative reporter, Joseph F. Dinneen, to look into the coast-to-coast network of Nazi organizations. He found that their boasts of having around two hundred thousand members were probably justified. Seventy-eight different units had been organized, the largest in Los Angeles, San Francisco, Seattle, Portland (Oregon), Detroit, Toledo, Cleveland, Pittsburgh, Boston, Baltimore, Washington, Newark, Passaic and Bergen counties in New Jersey, New York City, Buffalo, Schenectady, and Sheboygan and Kenosha in Wisconsin.

In 1937, too, a group of forty Americans notorious for their Nazi sympathies were invited to Germany for an intensive course of indoctrination and to attend the Fifth Congress of Germans Abroad in Stuttgart. The United States consul general in Stuttgart, Samuel W. Honaker, attended one of their sessions in a restaurant and reported to the American chargé d'affaires in Berlin: "The gathering was presided over by Mr. G. K. Hein, of Los Angeles, Mr. Hermann Schwinn, of Los Angeles, and Mr. Wilhelm Kunze, of Philadelphia, all of whom are American citizens. They were dressed in the uniform of the Bund — black riding breeches, black boots, gray shirt, black tie and black Sam Browne belt . . . All the speeches were made in German and the tone of the gathering was distinctly Nazi-German rather than American. The greeting was 'Heil Hitler' with the Nazi salute, and the speeches were interspersed with numerous 'Sieg Heils.' The speakers indulged in the polemics so usual in Germany at the present time, praising the aims and achievements of the Third Reich, condemning the Jews and their influence in the United States, and setting forth the necessity for combating Communism. They reiterated their willingness and intention to struggle for the United States, ostensibly against Communism, the C.I.O. and Jewish influence in the press, as well as the latter's adversely prejudicial action against Germany in the matter of boycotts, etc.

". . . Further evidence of propagandistic efforts in the United States was revealed by the presence at the meeting of a young boy, who is a member of the Youth Movement of this organization, and who proudly related how he had been promoted to the rank of 'Farnrich' (term corresponds to our West Point Cadets and refers to those receiving instruction in military signs and tactics) and how he would 'carry the flag even though it cost him his life.' "[10]

From speeches he heard at the meeting Consul General Honaker reported his belief that "one of the chief purposes of the Ameriker-

Deutscher Volksbund is to develop in the United States an understanding of and a real sympathy for the actual conditions with which Germany is confronted, and at the same time to act as a balance in offsetting the forces and influences reacting adversely on Germany. It would seem that the organization is attempting to extend the theories and policies of German National Socialism to the United States and to obtain approval of the political, economic, and social measures now being carried out in the German Reich."

A Stuttgart newspaper reported that the American visitors had solemnly resolved that "we want to bring the Germans in the United States who in part have become alienated from the German fatherland and from the German nation, back to the great community of blood and fate of all Germans. To this end the spiritual regeneration of the Germans after the model of the homeland is necessary." Thus "regenerated," the millions of German-Americans would "then be used under our leadership in the coming struggle with Communism and Jewry in the reconstruction of America."[11]

That year, too, the German propagandists began stepping up their assault on American public opinion, sending over millions of books, pamphlets and broadsides and a number of lecturers who apparently didn't have too much trouble finding a platform and an audience.

George Sylvester Viereck, who had been the kaiser's man in New York during World War I, surfaced again as the chief Nazi mouthpiece in the United States. According to a report compiled by the United States Attorney General in 1946, Viereck between the fall of 1939 and the summer of 1941 "received from the Nazis for propaganda purposes approximately $350,000 . . . $240,000 of this amount went into Viereck's publishing house, Flanders Hall, and the balance of $30,000, Viereck used to pay for various 'no-war' ads."

Viereck, according to O. John Rogge, a special assistant to the attorney general in charge of wartime sedition cases, was not only a "confidential agent" of the German propaganda ministry but also "the most valuable liaison agent of the German Foreign Ministry in the United States. Through two World Wars, Viereck was one of the most notorious German propagandists in this country. Through two World

443

Wars he held a knife at our back." Captured German documents showed that Viereck was on the payrolls of the German Foreign Office, the German Library of Information in New York and *Facts in Review*, an English-language propaganda organ published in New York. He was allowed to function with a free hand even though in 1930 he had published a memoir, *Spreading Germs of Hate*, in which he boasted of his exploits, called himself "the Siamese Twins of German propaganda" and frankly explained his methods. *The Fatherland*, as the organ of the National German-American Alliance from 1901 to 1917, was "undiluted pro-Germanism. Arising spontaneously in response to a world-wide need, it became the spokesman in the English language of pro-Germans everywhere. Its influence, far exceeding its circulation, reached from North to South America. It stretched across the ocean to Asia and Africa. Its American origin enabled it to escape the English censor. . . . It has been said that patriotism is the last resort of the scoundrel. It was the first resort of the propagandist. Every propagandist draped himself in the flag . . . The cuckoo of propaganda laid its eggs in every nest."

The former exponent of free love, recalling his propaganda campaign of World War I, wrote that "it sought the old-fashioned American with Revolutionary traditions; the cotton-grower of the South, almost bankrupted by the [English] blockade; the Irish with a grudge against England; the Jew with a grudge against Russia; and last, not least, the German-American. The isolationist whose world ends with the Rocky Mountains lent a willing ear to the voice of the propagandist."

In the case of George Sylvester Viereck, technically an American citizen, this country's permissiveness toward political dissent was certainly stretched to the utmost limits of its tensile strength. In 1939 when Hitler's armies had occupied the Rhineland, Austria and Czechoslovakia, he continued to plant his "cuckoo eggs" in every available nest, including this hymn to the New Order: "The Third Reich is indeed a new Germany. Its hills and valleys are as lovely as ever. Its rivers carry their freight of romance and of commerce as of yore. But to the Rhine Adolf Hitler has added the Danube. To the cities he has added Vienna. He is now about to complete the works of the giant Bismarck."[12] His

444

whole cuckoo-egg-laying career served as a warning that the failed poet can be a dangerous prosodist, indeed.

Another effective trumpeter for the Nazi cause in this country was Colin Ross, a German spy during World War I who posed as an expert on American affairs and convinced Hitler of his capabilities in this field. Ross made lecture tours of the United States under Nazi auspices. He also published a book, *Unser Amerika*, which was widely circulated in this country and called for the emergence of a "German Thomas Paine," a German-American who would lead his people out of the wilderness of subservience to the Anglo-Saxons. "For a century and a half, men of Anglo-Saxon blood have tried to realize the tremendous idea of the equality of all men . . . Germans have helped them faithfully and unselfishly, even though they had to stand in the shadow. Today the old idea is running down and a new one is being born. For Americans of German blood arises the mission of realizing this new idea, not against, but with their compatriots of Anglo-Saxon blood."

The principal transmitter of the Nazi doctrine became, in 1936, the German-American Bund. It was the former New Friends of Germany in a new guise. The New Friends held a convention in Buffalo at which they changed the name of their organization to the *Deutschamerikanische Volksbund*, or German-American People's League, but it became notorious simply as the Bund.

It also elected a man named Fritz Lieber Kuhn as its leader. The American Nazis now had their own fuehrer.

"RIGHT IN DER FUEHRER'S FACE . . ."

For several years American Nazism was epitomized by the burly figure of Fritz Kuhn. The American fuehrer was about forty years old, German-born, decorated with the Iron Cross for his service in the German army during World War I. He was tall, broad-shouldered, square-faced, heavy-jawed, the beau ideal of Aryan supermanhood. On the platform, bawling "Vote Gentile — defeat Roosevelt" or strutting around in his booted Nazi finery, he appeared to be the prototype of the loutish, mindless storm trooper who had carried Hitler to power in the street-fighting campaigns in Germany.

But appearances were deceiving in Kuhn's case. Actually he was a well-educated man, if not an intellectual. After the war he had attended the University of Munich and received a master's degree in science. In 1927 he migrated to the United States and was employed by the Ford Motor Company in Detroit. Kuhn soon found the atmosphere of Detroit to his liking; such quasi-fascistic, night-riding organizations as the Silver Shirts, the Ku Klux Klan and the Black Legion were busy organizing the automobile workers, and there was considerable tension engendered by the countervailing activities of the Reuther brothers and the C.I.O.

Kuhn resigned from his job at the Ford plant to devote his full time to building up the Bund. He was a forceful speaker and possessed an undeniable magnetism on the platform, particularly for Germans who had recently migrated. He seemed to be motivated solely by a desire to convert the United States into a National Socialist satrapy.

But he was more racketeer than ideologue. There was money to be made from selling Nazi uniforms and collecting membership dues from his deluded following. Fritz liked the good life, and beneath the Iron Cross beat a heart quickened by the sight of a shapely blonde or champagne foaming out of a magnum, beneath the storm troop cap worked a mind corrupted by cynicism and corroded by larceny.

Unknown to his simpleminded followers, Fritz spent many of his off-duty hours, not in the honest beerhalls of Yorkville, but the nightclubs of the Broadway sector. He liked to tour the nightclubs with his girl-friends, including a former Miss America, and request the bandleaders to play "Flatfoot Floogie with the Floy-Floy," even though it was well known that the German fuehrer regarded jazz as a degraded Negroid means of corrupting Western civilization.

For a time, however, Fritz Kuhn managed to keep up appearances. He made the pilgrimage to Berlin and received an autographed photograph from the number-one fuehrer. A few days after his return from Germany he presided over a Nazi rally presuming to call itself a celebra-

The German-American Bund in pursuit of Strength Through Joy

Fritz Kuhn, self-serving Gauleiter

tion of German Day at the Madison Square Garden. (The United German Societies, representing the German-Americans of the older migrations, declined to participate.) About twenty thousand people heard Kuhn ranting about the glories of the New Germany; also Hans Luther, the German ambassador to the United States, and Avery Brundage, the chairman of the American Olympic Committee, who had won out in a fight with critics of Hitlerism over taking an American team to the Olympic Games in Berlin. Mr. Brundage was wildly cheered when he assured the crowd that the United States had much to learn from Nazi Germany if it wished to preserve its institutions.[13]

Daytimes, at least, Kuhn kept himself busy propagating Nazi ideas and forming Nazi organizations. German-Americans of the older stock, he sternly warned, would have to change their way of thinking. "When Americans of German blood become race-conscious," he proclaimed, "they will form a block which will become instinctively, automatically and forcefully a political unit . . . the Bund thereby departs completely from the way of the Germans heretofore in the country, who had nothing of race-consciousness and political influence." All German-Americans must "flatly reject the countrywide notion of the melting-pot."

Nine different camps were established at which boys and young men were drilled and taught the goose step during summer military training exercises. One such miniature Potsdam was located at Yaphank on Long Island. A witness before a Congressional investigating committee, Frank Mutschinski of Brooklyn, later testified that he drilled two hundred young men wearing German uniforms and carrying mostly wooden rifles.

Some of that diligent summer training was in evidence when Kuhn called for a massive demonstration of American Nazi "might" and obtained the reluctant permission of the New York Police Department to stage a parade. It was rather a fizzle, if it was designed to scare anyone. Only about nine hundred marchers turned out in their Bund uniforms, under American flags and swastika banners, but it took fifteen hundred police to protect them on their procession through Yorkville.

Many spectators booed and hissed, even in that heavily Germanic section, and one bystander was punched in the nose by another when he gave the stiff-armed salute to a Nazi flag.

Perhaps the most sensational display of Nazi influence came February 20, 1939, at the Madison Square Garden, an event the New York *Times* fronted-paged under the headline 22,000 NAZIS HOLD RALLY IN GARDEN; POLICE CHECK FOES. The rally was brazenly advertised as a "celebration" of George Washington's birthday. The speakers denounced President Roosevelt, Secretary of the Treasury Henry Morgenthau, Jr., and Secretary of Labor Frances Perkins, and hailed, among others, Adolf Hitler and Father Coughlin. Kuhn made a speech in his usual flame-throwing style. "If you ask what we are actively fighting for under our charter, I will here repeat the declaration I made public some time ago: A socially just, white-Gentile-ruled United States."

The *Times* was inaccurate in lumping the whole audience of twenty-two thousand together as "Nazis." Many were anti-Nazi, turning out to see just what American Nazism amounted to; others were curiosity- and sensation-seekers. Brawls broke out in the audience between Kuhn's mock storm troopers and spectators who couldn't restrain their amusement at some of the cruder remarks from the platform. The vigorously anti-Nazi newspaper columnist Dorothy Thompson and a female companion laughed out loud during the anti-Semitic diatribe delivered by Wilhelm Kunze, the Bund's national publicity director. There were angry demands that Miss Thompson be thrown out of the meeting, and a riot almost broke out until police intervened and gave the columnist and her companion a safe escort from the Garden.

A German embassy official, Johannes Borchers, reported to the German Foreign Ministry that the rally was an apparent success, judging by the size of the turnout and the enthusiasm of the audience. "All speeches were delivered in English and were extremely critical of the Jewish-Communist influence in the United States . . . The journalist Dorothy Thompson, notorious for her continual propaganda articles, was removed from the hall during the further course of the meeting on account of her obstructive behavior. . . . It is worth noting that the pro-American George Washington celebration of the Bund left a strong impression on those present at the meeting, owing to its careful preparation and disciplined execution."

Borchers coolly concluded, however, that the demonstration, "in spite of the unquestionably well-meaning intentions of its promoters, has done no service to the German cause in the United States."[14]

The blatant methods and bullyboy tactics of Kuhn and his confreres, as Borchers saw it, were simply making the American Nazis, not impressive or even menacing, but comic-strip villains. They were making German-Americans ridiculous and causing them to turn, if they had not already turned, in shuddering distaste from everything connected with the New Germany.

Worse yet, all the noisemaking had impelled Congress to pass the resolution of Representative Martin Dies of Texas calling for an investigation of all un-American activities. Dies himself headed the investigating subcommittee, which in its original manifestation was heartily welcomed for exposing pro-German activities in the United States. One particularly damaging witness before the committee was a man who had joined the Bund as an undercover investigator and was able to testify that the organization was connected with a German espionage network being set up in the United States. Other testimony clearly linked the Bund with the German consular service and other apparatus in this country. Its attempt to claim an all-American orientation thus was exposed as a lie.

The Bund, along with the revelations of the Dies committee report, also was under attack early in 1939 from the German-American establishment. The New York *Staats-Zeitung* blamed the American Nazis for "cracking-up the German-Americans in a critical period," and the chairman of the New York branch of the Steuben Society attacked the Bund's membership as "unfortunately of our blood, but of no credit to us."

An example of how the Bund was frustrated by German-Americans themselves can be found in the records of its attempts to organize in the Middle West, the heartland of German-America. The long-settled Germans in St. Louis and Milwaukee, many, of course, diluted by frequent intermarriage with other stocks, turned their backs on the movement — and without the support of those millions the Bund didn't have a chance except as a lunatic-fringe movement.

In St. Louis, the German House refused to allow the organizers of the Bund to hold meetings under its roof.

In Milwaukee, the *Journal* exposed the Bund's activities from their first fumbling beginnings in the "Munich of America." The Bund had chosen Milwaukee as the site of its Middle Western headquarters, a mistake which could have been avoided if its leaders had studied the activities of the Milwaukee *Journal* during World War I.

The Bund began holding meetings in the Milwaukee Auditorium, and the *Journal* published full accounts of the Nazi doctrines preached, the Nazi anthems sung and the home-grown storm troopers who threw out hecklers. The publicity resulted in picketing by a band of Communists from Chicago, which drew from the *Journal* the editorial reproof: "Milwaukee wants no isms, either the Nazis inside the Auditorium or the Communists and their sympathizers outside."

Shriveled by the blaze of publicity, the Bund began holding clandestine meetings in secluded areas outside the city, where military drills were conducted and schools established to indoctrinate the children of its sympathizers. But after every meeting the Bundists read a full account, gathered by three *Journal* reporters, Harvey Schwandner, Paul Ringler and Laurence C. Eklund, who had managed to infiltrate the organization.

The Nazis tried to gain control of the Wisconsin Federation of German-American Societies, but were balked by its anti-Nazi president Bernhard Hofmann and the membership itself. "Old families of German descent, remembering how they were misled by the Kaiser's propagandists in World War I, refused to be drawn into the Hitler intrigue. Even at its peak in 1938, the Milwaukee Bund had on its rolls only a few hundred families. Most of them were Germans who had arrived here after World War I."[15] In Wisconsin the Bund simply dried up in a few months and blew away like milkweed.

The leading expert on the attempted Nazi penetration of America in the late Thirties, O. John Rogge, concluded: "The Bund as such never made much headway in this country. Most Americans of German descent were not in sympathy with the Nazi regime . . . The files of the German Foreign Ministry show that . . . the Nazi regime expected considerable assistance from the German-American element in the United States. Many representatives were dispatched to the United States and German-Americans were belabored with literature, speeches and films. It soon became obvious, however, that the majority of German-Americans were utterly out of sympathy with the Nazi regime. As a result, the files of the Foreign Ministry are replete with statements berating them with having forgotten their true loyalties, pretending to be 100 percent Americans, thus 'becoming the tools of the British.' "

The Bund itself was effectively washed out when its fuehrer was indicted, convicted and imprisoned for stealing the Bund's funds. For "our Fritz" it had all been a jolly, though unsavory racket. Testimony showed that Kuhn, a married man with two children, had spent $711 of his organization's funds making long-distance calls to a woman he had met on shipboard while journeying to Germany to be received by the Fuehrer of Fuehrers, and other funds on a woman who had been married and divorced nine times — hardly an example of the vaunted Aryan morality. His defense, unimpressive in an American court, was that under the "leadership principle" he was the "absolute owner of the Bund and its properties and could do what he liked with them." A similar defense in a Nazi court, of course, would have sent him to a Gestapo basement for correction of muddled thinking, but the New York court merely packed him off to prison late in 1939.

Unlike World War I, pro-Germanism was a dead issue in the United States by the time the country went to war with the Axis. No hysteria this time, except in regard to the innocent Japanese-Americans. How could there have been with an Eisenhower leading the second American expeditionary force against Germany, a Spaatz commanding the bombers which were pulverizing Germany, a Nimitz in command of the Pacific Fleet, an Eichelberger and a Kreuger commanding the two armies under General MacArthur?

17 THE GREAT WHITE WHALE

America is the many-made-one, the children of feuding races, creeds and
nations, united by a conception that shrivels in its glow all lesser loyalties.
— HERMANN HAGEDORN, *The Hyphenated American*

The visible and physical Germanic influences on American life have
now all but disappeared or been homogenized — gone with the little
German bands that played on street corners, the German butchers in
their sawed-off straw hats and white aprons, the beer gardens, the
summer-night festivals, the May wine parades. From each national
migration American culture has taken much, adapted it to its own
purposes, and left only the faintest individual stamp to be imprinted for
more than a generation or two on the ethnic group itself. The Fourth
Rome — ours — has discovered and perfected to an almost unimagin-
able degree the process of absorption which the earlier struggled and
failed to formulate.

You can search the old German sections of American cities and find
only the faintest traces of their former way of life. The Yorkville section
of Manhattan is still the entry port for the slender stream of immigrants
from West Germany, and on its main street, East Eighty-sixth between
Lexington and First Avenues, you can actually hear German spoken
and, if you're lucky, see a Steuben Day parade or a bock beer festival.

The names emblazoned on neon signs suggest that the old country hasn't been entirely forgotten: Kleine Konditorei (with something called, significantly, Touristen-wurst in the window), Cafe Hindenburg, Lorelei Bar, Bremen House, Mozart Hall, Kreutzer Hall, 86th Street Brauhaus. But there are almost as many French and Italian restaurants on that stretch of Eighty-sixth Street; the accordion players blare out the strains of "Lili Marlene" for Ivy League college students learning to drink beer chug-a-lug, and a sign advertising a *sängerfest* is placed in the window of a Chinese restaurant. The late Fritz Lieber Kuhn would hardly recognize the place.

It's the same with other communities once heavily Germanic, only more so. Milwaukee can boast of the world-famous Mader's restaurant and the hospitable taprooms in which the breweries entertain their visitors, but its citizens are more likely to haul you off to its venturesome new repertory theater which has never echoed with the ponderous dialogue of Sudermann.

A score of miles northwest of Milwaukee is the old village of Freistadt, founded in 1839 by twenty families driven from Germany by religious persecution. The settlement's first log cabin and the old stone Lutheran church have been lovingly preserved, along with a graveyard in which the names on the stone tablets have been all but erased by a century of wind and weather, but a new house on the outskirts bears the rather irreverent name "Gesund Heights."

Not far away, on the Milwaukee River, is the almost equally old settlement of a colony of freethinkers who for eighty-odd years stoutly resisted all Christianizing influences and repelled all missionary efforts. The original settlers had their children married without religious sanction of any kind. When a nonconforming newcomer tried to raise funds for a local church, he was offered twice as much to discontinue his efforts and build his church elsewhere. The place was known as "The Godforsaken Village" and by those who attributed everything godless to the French as "Little Paris." Now Cotton Mather himself wouldn't be able to catch a whiff of heresy around Thiensville. A Catholic Church was established in 1919, but is founders were so uncertain of their reception that they brought in a portable altar on a freight car. Ten years later the Lutherans moved in, and Thiensville now is merely another quiet suburb of Milwaukee.

In the old German enclave of South St. Louis there are only a few German restaurants and taverns to remind the visitor of the times when tapping the bung out of the first barrel of bock beer caused dancing in the streets and, earlier, when its German immigrant population shouldered muskets and saved Missouri, and possibly the West, for the Union. It's the same in Cincinnati, Chicago, Baltimore, San Francisco, Cleveland. And the old communistic colony of Amana, Iowa, now admits nonmembers to work on the production lines of a highly capitalistic enterprise, the Amana Refrigerator Company, which is operated by a communal corporation; dancing is allowed in the local high school, and plain living is becoming unfashionable.

The ideas which Germans brought from their homeland — which lack nothing in diversity, ranging from Marxism and freethinking to religious colonization, separate ethnic states, the first glimmerings of a world government — have made little real impact on the commonalty. But there has been a constant fluttering in the national dovecote often caused by German-Americans, who contributed more than their share to what Professor Richard Hofstadter describes in his recent work as *The Paranoid Style in American Politics*. Certainly they have not remembered the advice of Holderlin against "making the state a school of morals" and his warning that "the state has always been made a hell by man's wanting to make it his heaven." The one point at which German-American opinion was measurably decisive, perhaps as much as that of the New England abolitionists, was in demanding an end to human slavery.

The ferment of the German-Americanism of the last century ended with the century. What had been politically volatile is now inert. No other minority stirred up so much trouble for the establishment of its time as the Germans, and no other, despite the wholesale infusion of German blood in the composite American, has subsided so gratefully, so wholeheartedly into the national consensus. If that makes them honorary Anglo-Saxons, they are more than content. An attempt to present the rough edges of any surviving Germanism would be buffed away, by

455

common consent, overnight. Of that element, all that remains is a vague feeling of best wishes for the Federal German Republic of West Germany and an equally vague but lingering sense of guilt for what happened in Germany under the Nazis.

If assimilation is the goal of all minorities, the German-Americans have succeeded beyond all others, with the Scandinavians a close second. They have all but become invisible. In their study of the leading minorities in New York City, *Beyond the Melting Pot*, Nathan Glazer and Daniel P. Moynihan have taken note of the phenomenon and called it an ethnic "disappearance." They explain that "while German influence is to be seen in virtually every aspect of the city's life, the Germans *as a group* are vanished. No appeals are made to the German vote, there are no German politicians in the sense that there are Irish or Italian politicians and, generally speaking, no German component in the structure of the ethnic interests of the city. The logical explanation of this development, in terms of the presumed course of American social evolution, is simply that the Germans have been 'assimilated' by the Anglo-Saxon center. To some extent this has happened. The German immigrants of the nineteenth century were certainly much closer to the old Americans than were the Irish who arrived in the same period. Many were Protestants, many were skilled workers or even members of the professions, and their level of education in general was high."

The Germans, Glazer and Moynihan believe, lacked the "homogeneity" of other minorities, they were "split between Catholics and Protestants, liberals and conservatives, craftsmen and businessmen and laborers. They reflected, as it were, an entire modern society, not simply an element of one."

In the sense that all traces of their origin have been rubbed away, the German-Americans can pride themselves on an exemplary success. The effect of this transference, this merging of what had been separate Anglo-Saxon and German entities into a new Anglo-Teutonic amalgamation, sealed and solidified in the years since World War II, will be of great social and political significance. No less so for having been accomplished quietly and subtly, without conscious effort or formal negotiation. Together the old breed of English, Welsh and Scotch-Irish and those of German origin are in a position of unassailable dominance; they are the lords of government, industry, business, science, agriculture, education and the military establishment. The change from an Anglo-Saxon to an Anglo-Teutonic majority will have effects ranging far into the future. It will bear on the racial situation, on the American response to the challenges of the Communist and neutralist worlds, and most particularly on whether the United States, under grinding internal and external pressure, will veer toward an authoritarian state or will attempt to solve its problems in a more liberal, flexible and permissive manner.

There is nothing more startling to a German-American than a blunt question as to what his Germanic fraction means to him, or how he might differ from a person of English origin, or an Irishman, or even a Pole or Italian. He feels no difference, and if anything resents the question. Unconsciously for the most part he has sought and found protective coloration, the good gray shade of Anglo-Saxonism, which will preserve him from the adventurism of the past.

Once alarming for his constant dissidence, the German-American indubitably is part of what has come to be known as "the great white whale," a stolid and often lethargic creature which moves in the deeps of the national subconscious and regards itself politically as "moderate," "middle of the road," expressive of middle-class attitudes.

The social and political sciences have not dissected this monster as yet, but its sluggish movements have been studied in relation to its enthusiasm for President Eisenhower, its much-qualified and tentative support of President Johnson, its wary self-defensive maneuvers when confronted by civil rights issues and the war in Vietnam. It obviously has an intense reluctance to accept or even notice change. It can obviously become aroused — perhaps violently — in defense of the status quo.

As part of the "great white whale," the Germans necessarily have had to abandon much of the pure and often feckless idealism which propelled the migration of the Forty-eighters and many others. It was German-Americans who founded the Travelers Aid Society, the Legal Aid Society, the Society for the Prevention of Cruelty to Children, the

457

Society for the Prevention of Cruelty to Animals; they have also been directly responsible for much of the social and labor legislation written into national law, but all that is in the past.[1]

They are now generally regarded as being part of the conservative element, for the most part, who leaned toward McCarthyism in the early Fifties, who are isolationist except when it comes to confronting international Communism, who are inclined to hang back on open housing and other civil rights issues. Daniel Bell, in one of his essays on the "radical right," has written that Senator Joseph R. McCarthy's most fervent supporters included "the rising middle-class strata of the ethnic groups, the Irish and the Germans, who sought to prove their Americanism, the Germans particularly because of the implied taint of disloyalty during World War II . . ."[2] In the same collection of essays, Professor Hofstadter declares that the "intense status concerns of present-day politics," in which he believes is rooted much of the blossoming conservatism, are shared not only by "some types of old-family, Anglo-Saxon Protestants" but "among many types of immigrant families, most notably among the German and Irish, who are very frequently Catholic." He adds: "The status history of the older immigrant groups like the Germans and the Irish is quite different from that of ethnic elements like the Italians, Poles and Czechs, who have more recently arrived at the point at which they are bidding for wide acceptance in the professional and white-collar classes, or at least for the middle-class standards of housing and consumption enjoyed by these classes." The Irish, he says, have "an unusually ambiguous status . . . A study of the Germans would perhaps emphasize the effects of uneasiness over national loyalties arising from the Hitler era and World War II . . ."[3]

Still, on the evidence gathered by sociologists and political analysts, there seem to be indications that German-Americans have tended to absorb conservative doctrine and be influenced by what Bell and Hofstadter stigmatize as the "radical right." Senator McCarthy was sent to Washington from the quasi-Germanic state of Wisconsin and was idolized more by the Germans and the Irish, perhaps, than any other ethnic groups. (McCarthy was born on a farm near Appleton in a section settled mostly by Germans and Scandinavians. His mother was born in Ireland, but his father was half-German and half-Irish. An Irish priest told William V. Shannon that he believed McCarthy was too timid. "It's the German in him. The Germans are sluggish and cautious. If he were pure Irish, he'd fight more.")[4]

In his *The Future of American Politics*, Samuel Lubell, who diligently employs interviewing techniques in various representative sections of the country, found that the McCarthyist tendencies of the Germans were tied in with resentment over World War II, isolationism and fear of Russian Communism. "If anything the former isolationists are more belligerent today than the country as a whole," he wrote in 1952 during the salad days of McCarthyism. "In none of the German-American counties I visited did I find a single person who believed a settlement with Russia was possible. There was much criticism of the administration for being 'too soft' with the Communists . . . None of the ethnic resistances which obstructed our getting into war with Germany would be raised against war with Russia. On the contrary, they probably would obstruct the making of peace if a settlement with the Soviets ever became possible." Mr. Lubell was also struck by the "vengeful memories of those who opposed our getting into the last war" and wondered, "But for how long can one continue to fight the war that is past? There is no Treaty of Versailles to keep alive the spirit of pro-German revenge as after World War I. In the present strategic situation American foreign policy is bound to seek to make Germany an ally."

In Stearns County, Minnesota, which Lubell used as a test case of German-American isolationism, the attitude was that American intervention in World War I wasn't necessary, that without it, "England and Germany would have come to terms. There wouldn't have been a second war and Russia wouldn't be where she is now."

In the Minnesota county and other German-American counties, Lubell reported, he "found this same tendency to see the Korean War as vindication of their earlier opposition to America's wars against Germany . . . This *memory of opposition to the last war* seems the real mainspring behind present-day isolationism." (The italics are Mr. Lubell's.)

Sociologists have also discovered an anti-Semitic attitude among

German-Americans. In a recent work, *Christian Beliefs and Anti-Semitism* (1967), Charles Y. Glock and Rodney Stark of the University of California, both raised as Lutherans, demonstrated this tendency. They based their conclusions on questionnaires answered by 2,871 church members in four California counties, matched against a national collection of 1,976 similar interviews. Sociologists and other pulse-takers insist that the range and extent of a sampling are of no greater significance than a few percentage points, and on occasion they seem to have proven their case.

The Glock-Stark statistics showed that anti-Semitic attitudes cropped up most often among "conservative" Christian sects. Anti-Semitism was displayed in 24 percent of the Southern Baptists questioned, the highest of all the denominations, but members of the Missouri Lutheran Synod were close behind with 23 percent and the American Lutheran group with 19 percent, contrasted with 11 percent among the Roman Catholics. The Lutheran Church, of course, is composed mostly of those of German and Scandinavian descent.

A similar California survey, published as *The Apathetic Majority* in 1966 by Mr. Glock, Gertrude J. Selznick and Joe L. Spaeth, delved into the social attitudes of various ethnic groups living in the Oakland and Piedmont areas. Germans, they found, gave a high rating of "social acceptability" only to other Germans, the Irish and the Anglo-Saxons. (The Irish and the Anglos, the survey indicated, were even narrower in their social attitudes. Jews and Negroes showed the widest tolerance.)

During the 1965 mayoralty election in New York City, statistics indicated that German-descended Americans topped all other groups forming the support of the Conservative Republican candidate, William F. Buckley, Jr., against the liberal Republican winner, John Lindsay, and the Democrat, Abraham Beame, and were similarly inclined toward eliminating the police review board, which was highly valued by the Negro population.

According to the Vote Profile Analysis, a computerized operation of the Columbia Broadcasting System's New York station, a little more than 50 percent of the German voters supported Lindsay while 26.3 percent voted for Buckley and 22.5 percent for Beame. The 26.3 percent portion of the German vote was the highest of the various ethnic groups which favored Buckley's candidacy, comparing with 21.9 percent of the Irish, 17.8 percent of the Italians, 26.2 percent of Catholic Central Europeans and 22.6 percent of the White Anglo-Saxon Protestants (and 1.1 percent of the Negroes). It reflected, perhaps, a growing tendency of the Germans, along with the WASP's, the Irish, the Italians and Central Europeans, to lean toward a modern conservatism, particularly if and when presented with Mr. Buckley's swinging-cutlass style.

And during the Reverend Martin Luther King's open-housing marches in Chicago during the summer of 1966, the Germans joined with the Poles, the Irish and other Caucasians in violently protesting against the invasion of white neighborhoods and against the unseemly conduct of the Negroes taking their cause to the streets — the same streets in which the lager-beer riots and the Haymarket bombing of their grandfathers' and great-grandfathers' time took place.

Obviously it is not difficult for sociological and political scientists to find evidence of reactionary, intolerant and backward-looking tendencies among the German-Americans as well as other national groups long settled in the United States. One possible test case they have ignored was the ethnic mixture of the fifty-nine liberal Democrats who were seeking reelection to Congress in 1966. Of those fifty-nine, ten bore names of obviously German origin, but that doesn't mean they represent so great a share of German-American belief in liberalism.

The same methods were used by Nathaniel Weyl in his *The Creative Elite in America* (1966), a work which takes the currently unfashionable view that there may be something to heredity after all, that environment is not necessarily the governing factor in human progress.

With the aid of a computer, using a list of the most common names on the rolls of the Social Security Administration and matching them against compilations of persons who have distinguished themselves in various creative endeavors, Mr. Weyl came up with some rather surprising conclusions. One was that the German-Americans, for all their massive contributions to American science, industrial and agricultural progress, education, music and painting, lag far behind other nationalities in the qualitative sense.[5]

In Mr. Weyl's computerized analysis, the Jews rate highest on his "creativity index," followed by the Scots, the Welsh, the Dutch, the English, the Irish, the Chinese, the Germans (eighth place) and the Scandinavians. In the various sciences, Mr. Weyl found, the Jews, the Dutch, the Germans and the Scandinavians are the most prominent. (A magazine writer who recently visited a space installation, himself of Irish extraction, expressed his surprise at coming across a fellow Irishman in the highest engineering echelon. "I can remember thinking how prejudices are programmed," John Gregory Dunne commented, "how I had never expected to find an Irish engineer; a German surely, a Scandinavian or a Jew perhaps, but not a man named McCarthy.")[6] Mr. Weyl also determined that in the higher realms of music, symphonic and operatic, Germans are the most prominent, followed by Italians.[7]

Some of Mr. Weyl's conclusions may be questioned, particularly by colleagues who believe racial background has nothing to do with a man's creative ability. It is also difficult to grasp how Mr. Weyl, or any of the computers at his command, could distinguish from his name alone a person of totally Germanic descent from, say, a man with a German name whose mother was Irish and whose paternal grandmother was French; or how it could be determined, as another instance, whether a man named Schwartz was Jewish or Protestant or Catholic. Niggling aside, however, it is probably true that the German-American has not lived up to his creative potential.

In an earlier work in the same field, Ellsworth Huntington's *After Three Centuries* (1935), the German-Americans were found to rate statistically high in science, business and invention. Mr. Huntington's survey showed that comparatively few were found to be on the public relief rolls or engaged in criminal activity. (Qualitatively, however, German-descended criminals have made their mark from time to time. Arthur Flegenheimer, alias Dutch Schultz, was a highly efficient rumrunner, distributor of bootleg liquor and gang leader in New York during Prohibition. The "crime of the century," the kidnaping of the Lindbergh baby, was committed by Bruno Richard Hauptmann, a German immigrant. Predating them was one Dutch Heinrich, an early-day Willie Sutton, who specialized in robbing banks and brokerages in

New York during the 1870's. As leader of the Hell's Kitchen Gang, he was referred to in the newspapers as "the mastermind of crime." And there were a number of other exceptions to one of the German-Americans' prouder boasts, that of being stanch upholders of law and order.)

For all the investigation of attitudes, influences, resentments and prejudices, German-Americans regard themselves, perhaps with a touch of smugness, as representative, unhyphenated, even antihyphenated citizens of the American mainstream. Their record as builders of the nation, as well as one of its most troublesome elements, is inextricably woven into the American fabric.

In moments of excessive pride, they might remember the words of William Seabrook, partly German himself, as the impressions of a perceptive literary man, which may equal in exactitude the statistical analysis of social and political scientists. With both justice and affection, he wrote in 1938 the judgment which holds true today that German-Americans "constitute the most important, and most admirable, but least lovable" of nationalities. In the past, he added, "neighbors made it difficult for them to be loving or lovable. They got into habits of being stuffy, aggressive, with chips on their shoulders. But I wish they would realize that America is a kindly land . . . The way for them to become better loved is open. It is for them to become more loving, more tolerant, sweeter, more friendly, more kind."[8]

They might also bear in mind the warning against civic lethargy, or as Julius Goebel put it, a tendency toward "public inactivity," and their inheritance of that German "mystic strain" historians have noted which encourages them, in despair of the world, to take refuge in quietism, nihilism or the search for Absolutes which has resulted in so much historic tragedy.

A people which has produced on this continent such diverse and contrasting persons of consequence as Nicholas Herkimer and Grover Cleveland Bergdoll, Eric Hoffer and Babe Ruth, Walter Lippmann and Louella O. Parsons, Rheinhold Niebuhr and H. L. Mencken, Senator Everett M. Dirksen and Walter Reuther, Wernher von Braun and Jack Parr, Dutch Schultz and John J. Pershing, Lawrence Welk and Walter

Damrosch, Theodore Dreiser and Frank L. (*The Wizard of Oz*) Baum, Carl Schurz and John Jacob Astor, yachtsman Emil Mosbacher and anarchist Johann Most, the Ringling brothers, the Flying Wallendas, Paul Tillich, Red Schoendienst, Theodore Roethke, Rod Steiger, Fritzi Scheff, and half of Grace Kelly . . . a people so rich in variety can't be all bad, or all good.

NOTES

1. A Nation of Migrants

1. Captain John Smith, *The True Travels*, Vol. I.
2. A. M. Reeves, *The Finding of Wineland the Good.*
3. John Fiske, *The Dutch and Quaker Colonies*, Vol. II.
4. Ibid.
5. Quoted in M. D. Learned, *The Life of Franz Daniel Pastorius.*
6. Albert B. Faust, *The German Element in the United States*, Vol. I.
7. Ibid.
8. The causes of German migration at the period are explored in Faust, *The German Element*, Vol. I; and George M. Stephenson, *A History of American Migration.*
9. Quoted in Faust, *The German Element*, Vol. I.
10. Gottlieb Mittelberger, *Journey to Pennsylvania.*
11. Ibid.
12. Letter by the Reverend Brunnholz, dated May 21, 1750, quoted in *Reports of the United German Evangelical Lutheran Congregations in North America*, Philadelphia, 1881.
13. William Eddis, *Letters from America.*
14. Quoted in Edith Abbott, *Historical Aspects of the Immigration Problem.*
15. *Life* magazine, August 25, 1967.
16. E. J. Pershing, *The Pershing Family in America.*
17. *Black Jack Pershing*, by the author.
18. Samuel Kercheval, *History of the Valley of Virginia.*
19. Faust, *The German Element*, Vol. I.
20. Ibid.
21. Ibid.

2. Redcoats, Bluecoats and Turncoats

1. Quoted in Faust, *The German Element*, Vol. I.
2. F. H. Reisner, "Background on the Muhlenbergs," *The Historian*, Spring, 1942.
3. George Bancroft, *History of the United States of America*, Vol. IV.

4. Quoted in *American Archives*, Series IX, Vol. VI, p. 1142.
5. Joseph Plumb Martin, *Private Yankee Doodle*.
6. Quoted in Faust, *The German Element*, Vol. I.
7. George F. Scheer and Hugh F. Rankin, *Rebels and Redcoats*.
8. Ibid.
9. John M. Palmer, *General Von Steuben*.
10. W. M. Reid, *The Mohawk Valley, Its Legends and Its History*.
11. Ibid.
12. Ibid.
13. Faust, *The German Element*, Vol. I.
14. Ibid.
15. Martin, op. cit.
16. Faust, *The German Element*, Vol. 1.
17. Baroness Friederike Riedesel, *Letters and Journals Relating to the War of the American Revolution*.
18. Quoted in Rufus W. Griswold, *The Republican Court: or American Society in the Days of Washington*.

3. Dreams of a Germania-in-America

1. Quoted in Abbott, *Historical Aspects of the Immigration Problem*.
2. Americana Germanica, Vol. I, No. 2, Philadelphia, 1897–1902.
3. Quoted in John A. Hawgood, *The Tragedy of German America*, a groundbreaking and invaluable work produced by an English social historian of great insight and compassion.
4. Ibid.
5. Davis's speech was delivered December 15, 1849, at Frankfort, Kentucky, and is quoted in Abbott, op. cit.
6. Gustav Koerner, *Memoirs*.
7. Quoted in Abbott, op. cit.
8. Quoted in Hawgood, op. cit.
9. Ibid.
10. E. D. Kargan, "Missouri's German Immigration," *Missouri Historical Collections*, Vol. II, 1900.
11. Faust, *The German Element*, Vol. I.
12. Koerner, op. cit.
13. Frederick Law Olmsted, *A Journey Through Texas*.
14. Ibid.
15. Ibid.
16. Prince Carl quoted in E. D. Adams, editor, "British Diplomatic Correspondence Concerning Texas," *Southwest Historical Quarterly*, Vols. XVI–XXI.
17. Quoted in Hawgood, op. cit.
18. Olmsted, op. cit.
19. M. Sachjen, *Immigration to Wisconsin*, a thesis deposited at the University of Wisconsin library.

4. Forty-Eighters and Know-Nothings

1. Cecil Woodham-Smith, *The Great Hunger*.
2. Quoted in *Chambers's Edinburgh Journal*, June 13, 1846.
3. Quoted in Marcus Hansen, *The Atlantic Migration*.
4. Ibid.

5. Bremen's role in the German migration to America is described by Hansen, *The Atlantic Migration;* and Mary Jane Cable, "Damned Plague Ships and Swimming Coffins," *American Heritage,* August, 1960.
6. Friederich Kapp, *Geschichte der Deutschen im Staate New York,* New York, 1867.
7. Quoted in Miss Cable's *American Heritage* article, op. cit.
8. Hansen, op. cit.
9. Ibid.
10. Quoted in Abbott, *Historical Aspects of the Immigration Problem.*
11. Ibid., quoted from Buchele's *Land und Volk der Vereinigten Staaten von Nord Amerika,* Stuttgart, 1865.
12. Ibid.
13. *The Citiaen,* an Irish-American weekly, June 14, 1856.
14. New York State Assembly Document No. 205 (1857).
15. Hawgood, *The Tragedy of German America.*
16. H. L. Mencken, "The German American" (1928), quoted by Hawgood, op. cit.
17. Quoted in Abbott, op. cit.
18. *Putnam's Magazine,* January, 1855.
19. Quoted in Hawgood, op. cit.

5. "I Fights Mit Sigel"

1. George Templeton Strong, *Diary of the Civil War.*
2. Ibid.
3. Carl Sandburg, *Abraham Lincoln: The Prairie Years.*
4. Ibid.
5. F. I. Herriott, "The Conference of German Republicans at the Deutsches Haus," *Transactions of the Illinois State Historical Society,* 1928.
6. Seward to Lieber letter in Francis Lieber Papers, Huntington Library, San Marino, California.
7. Herriott, op. cit.
8. Ibid.
9. Springfield *Daily Republican,* March 27, 1859.
10. Account of the St. Louis crisis is drawn from Bruce Catton, *This Hallowed Ground;* Robert J. Rombauer, *The Union Cause in St. Louis in 1861;* and John Fiske, *The Mississippi Valley in the Civil War.*
11. Bruce Catton, *The Glory Road.*
12. Ibid.
13. T. A. Dodge, *The Campaign of Chancellorsville.*
14. Catton, *The Glory Road.*
15. Dodge, op. cit.
16. *Official Records of the War of the Rebellion,* Vol. XXV, Pt. One, Washington, 1902.
17. Catton, *The Glory Road.*
18. Catton, *This Hallowed Ground.*
19. J. F. Rhodes, *History of the United States After the Compromise of 1850,* Vol. IV.
20. Clifford Dowdey, *The Land They Fought For.*

6. Carl Schurz, the Good, Good German

1. Carl Schurz, *Reminiscences.*
2. Quoted in Chester V. Easum, *The Americanization of Carl Schurz.*

3. Carl Schurz Papers, undated, Wisconsin Historical Society, Madison, Wisconsin.
4. Milwaukee *Sentinel*, April 1, 1900.
5. Alexander M. Thompson, *Political History of Wisconsin*.
6. Carl Schurz Papers, op. cit.
7. Quoted in Easum, op. cit.
8. Ibid.
9. Carl Schurz Papers, op. cit.
10. Ibid.
11. Quoted in Easum, op. cit.
12. New York *Evening Post*, May 14, 1906.
13. Andrew D. White, United States ambassador to Germany, quoted in the New York *Times*, May 22, 1897.
14. In Nevins's introduction to *The Autobiography of Carl Schurz*, an abridged version of the *Reminiscences*, edited by Wayne Andrews, New York, 1961.

7. The Westward Movement

1. Quoted in Faust, *The German Element*, Vol. II.
2. Evan Jones, *The Minnesota: Forgotten River*.
3. Faust, *The German Element*, Vol. II.
4. Jones, op. cit.
5. Ibid.
6. Fairfax Downey, *Indian-Fighting Army*.
7. Santa Fe *New Mexican*, July 19, 1870.
8. Las Vegas *Gazette*, February 2, 1878.
9. Quoted in Stuart Lake, *Wyatt Earp*.
10. Cleveland Amory, *Who Killed Society?*
11. Quoted in Gustavus Myers, *History of the Great American Fortunes*.
12. Ibid.
13. Henry Villard, *Memoirs*.
14. Stewart Holbrook, *The Story of American Railroads*.
15. William Martin Camp, *San Francisco: Port of Gold*.
16. Lincoln Steffens, *Autobiography*.
17. William V. Shannon, *The American Irish*.
18. Joseph Miller, *Arizona: The Last Frontier*.
19. Ibid.

8. Angel Voices in the Wilderness

1. Marguerite Young in her splendid *Angel in the Forest*, first published in 1946, happily reissued in 1966.
2. Ibid.
3. Ibid.
4. Carl Wittke, *We Who Built America*.
5. Hansen, *The Atlantic Migration*.
6. Ibid.
7. J. R. Humphreys, *The Last of the Middle West*.
8. Wittke, *We Who Built America*.
9. Quoted by Associated Press, April 16, 1966.
10. Donald A. Erickson, "The Plain People Vs the Common Schools," *Saturday Review*, November 19, 1966.
11. John Bird, "We Want to Be Left Alone," *Saturday Evening Post*, June 15, 1967.
12. Ibid.

9. The "Jewish Grand Dukes" and Others

1. Frederic Morton, The Rothschilds.
2. Amory, Who Killed Society?
3. Dixon Wecter, The Saga of American Society.
4. Eleanor Robson Belmont, The Fabric of Memory.
5. Rufus Learsi, The Jews in America.
6. Myers, History of the Great American Fortunes.
7. Cleveland Amory, The Last Resorts.
8. Rudolf Glanz, Jews in Relation to the Cultural Milieu of the Germans in America Up to the 1880's.
9. Ibid.
10. Learsi, op. cit.
11. Glanz, op. cit.
12. Morris Schappes, Documentary History of the United States.
13. Learsi, op. cit.
14. Marion K. Sanders, "The Several Worlds of American Jews," Harper's Magazine, April, 1966.
15. Quoted in Glanz, op. cit.
16. Sanders, op. cit.
17. Irving Howe, "The Lower East Side: Symbol and Fact," New York World Journal Tribune, October 2, 1966.
18. Sanders, op. cit.
19. Howe, op. cit.
20. Ibid.
21. Sanders, op. cit.
22. New York World Journal Tribune, December 9, 1966.

10. The Pursuit of Excellence

1. Charles Franklin Thwing, The American and the German University.
2. Kuno Francke, Cotton Mather and August Hermann Francke.
3. Henry Adams, The Education of Henry Adams.
4. George S. Hillard, Life, Letters and Journal of George Ticknor.
5. Quoted in M. A. De Wolfe Howe, The Life and Letters of George Bancroft.
6. Thwing, op. cit.
7. Kuno Francke, Atlantic Monthly, December, 1905.
8. Quoted in Shannon, The American Irish.
9. Faust, The German Element, Vol. II.
10. Justin Kaplan, Mr. Clemens and Mark Twain.
11. Dublin Review, August, 1918.
12. H. L. Mencken, Happy Days.

11. Down Where the Wurzburger Flowed

1. Herman Hagedorn, The Hyphenated Family.
2. Ibid.
3. Bob Considine, It's the Irish.
4. Emmett Dedmon, Fabulous Chicago.
5. Lucille Kohler, "Bock Beer Days in St. Louis," Harper's Magazine, July, 1932.

6. Alvin Harlow, *The Serene Cincinnatians*.
7. Ibid.
8. Ernest L. Meyer, *Bucket Boy; A Milwaukee Legend*.
9. Ernest L. Meyer, "Twilight of a Golden Age," *American Mercury*, August, 1933.
10. Meyer, *Bucket Boy*.
11. Felix Isman, *Weber and Fields*.
12. Quoted in Allen Churchill, *The Great White Way*.
13. Sigmund Spaeth, *Fifty Years with Music*.
14. Hammerstein's career was studied at length and in depth by Gilbert Seldes in "Hammerstein the Extravagant," *Harper's Magazine*, July, 1932.
15. Quoted in Humphreys, *The Last of the Middle West*.
16. H. L. Mencken, *A Book of Prefaces*.
17. Paul Gallico, "The Babe," a chapter in *Vanity Fair*, edited by Cleveland Amory and Frederic Bradlee, New York, 1960.
18. Lawrence S. Ritter, *The Glory of Their Times*, a superb collection of the reminiscences of old-time baseball players.
19. Ibid.

12. *The Image Darkens*

1. Wittke, *We Who Built America*.
2. Eitel W. Dobert, "The Radicals," *The Forty-Eighters*, edited by A. E. Zucker, New York, 1950.
3. Ibid.
4. Wittke, *We Who Built America*.
5. Weitling's career is studied by Carl Wittke in his *The German-Language Press in America*.
6. Quoted in James Joll, *The Anarchists*.
7. Meyer, *Bucket Boy*.
8. Dedmon, *Fabulous Chicago*.
9. Stewart Holbrook, *Dreamers of the American Dream*.
10. Harry Barnard, *Eagle Forgotten*.
11. Emma Goldman, *Living My Life*.
12. Richard Drinnon, *Rebel in Paradise*.
13. Joll, op. cit.
14. Drinnon, op. cit.
15. Barbara Tuchman, *The Proud Tower*.
16. McAlister Coleman, *Eugene V. Debs*.
17. Ray Ginger, *The Bending Cross: A Biography of Eugene V. Debs*.
18. Edward S. Kerstein, *Milwaukee's All-American Mayor*.

13. *Events Leading to the Tragedy*

1. Henry F. May, *The End of American Innocence*.
2. *Baltimore Sun*, July 5, 1923.
3. Hagedorn, *The Hyphenated Family*.
4. *Dublin Review*, August, 1918.
5. Edward Wakin and The Reverend Joseph F. Scheuer, *The De-Romanization of the American Catholic Church*.
6. John Tracy Ellis, *The Life of James Cardinal Gibbons*.
7. Ibid.
8. Ibid.

9. Ibid.
10. Shannon, *The American Irish.*
11. Ellis, op. cit.
12. Wakin and Scheuer, op. cit.
13. Faust, *The German Element,* Vol. II.
14. Wittke, *The German-Language Press in America.*
15. Hagedorn, op. cit.
16. *Dublin Review,* August, 1918.
17. Ibid.
18. Stephenson, *A History of American Immigration.*
19. Shannon, op. cit.
20. Quoted in Holbrook, *The Story of American Railroads.*
21. *Courtroom Warrior: The Combative Career of William Travers Jerome,* by the author.

14. "Starve the War and Feed America"

1. Quoted in Alen Valentine, *1913: America Between Two Worlds.*
2. Quoted in Gustavus Ohlinger, *Their True Faith and Allegiance.*
3. H. L. Mencken, *Prejudices: Fourth Series.*
4. Quoted in report of the Subcommittee of the Judiciary, U.S., Congress, Senate, *Brewing and Liquor Interests and German Propaganda,* 65th Congress, 1919.
5. Andrew Sinclair, *Prohibition: The Era of Excess.*
6. Clifton J. Child, "German-American Attempts to Prevent the Exportation of Munitions of War, 1914–1915," *Mississippi Valley Historical Review,* December, 1938.
7. Walter Millis, *The Road to War.*
8. Report of the Subcommittee of the Judiciary, 65th Congress, op. cit.
9. Ibid.
10. *Life* magazine, July 21, 1967.
11. Ohlinger, op. cit.
12. Wittke, *The German-Language Press in America.*
13. Will C. Conrad, Kathleen F. Wilson and Dale Wilson, *The Milwaukee Journal.*
14. Ibid.
15. *Courtroom Warrior,* by the author.
16. Barbara Tuchman, *The Zimmerman Telegram.*
17. Richard Butler and Joseph Driscoll, *Dock Walloper.*
18. Benjamin F. Gitlow, *The Whole of Their Lives.*

15. "Those Indispensable Gifts"

1. Harlow, *The Serene Cincinnatians.*
2. Millis, *The Road to War.*
3. Hagedorn, *The Hyphenated Family.*
4. Quoted in Millis, op. cit.
5. Hawgood, *The Tragedy of German America.*
6. Hagedorn, op. cit.
7. *New Republic,* September, 1920.
8. Quoted in Conrad, Wilson, and Wilson, *The Milwaukee Journal.*
9. Madame Schumann-Heink's career is described in *Living Biographies of Famous Women,* by Henry and Dana Lee Thomas.
10. Norman S. Hall, *The Balloon Buster.*

11. Quoted in Arch Whitehouse, *The Year of the Sky Kings.*
12. Quentin Reynolds, *They Fought for the Sky.*
13. Quoted in Hall, op. cit.
14. *Black Jack Pershing,* by the author.

16. *The Voice of the Grasshoppers*

1. Hagedorn, *The Hyphenated Family.*
2. *The Germans in Chicago,* a monograph by A. J. Townsend, Chicago, 1932.
3. Hawgood, *The Tragedy of German America.*
4. Faust, *The German Element,* Vol. II.
5. Samuel Lubell, *The Future of American Politics.*
6. Hermann Rauschning, *The Voice of Destruction.*
7. Hawgood, op. cit.
8. Richard Rollins, *I Find Treason.*
9. William B. Seabrook, *These Foreigners.*
10. Quoted in O. John Rogge, *The Official German Report.*
11. Ibid.
12. Ibid.
13. Ibid.
14. Ibid.
15. Conrad, Wilson, and Wilson, *The Milwaukee Journal.*

17. *The Great White Whale*

1. Seabrook, *These Foreigners.*
2. *The Radical Right,* a collection of essays edited by Daniel Bell.
3. Ibid.
4. Shannon, *The American Irish.*
5. Nathaniel Weyl, *The Creative Elite in America.*
6. John Gregory Dunne, "Apollo 204," *Saturday Evening Post,* June 15, 1967.
7. Weyl, op. cit.
8. Seabrook, op. cit.

BIBLIOGRAPHY

Abbott, Edith, *Historical Aspects of the Immigration Problem*, Chicago, 1926.
Adams, Henry, *The Education of Henry Adams*, Boston, 1918.
Adler, Jacob, *Claus Spreckels; The Sugar King of Hawaii*, Honolulu, 1967.
Amory, Cleveland, *The Last Resorts*, New York, 1952.
———, *Who Killed Society?*, New York, 1960.

Bancroft, George, *History of the United States of America*, Vol. IV, Boston, 1834.
Barnard, Harry, *Eagle Forgotten*, Indianapolis, 1938.
Bell, Daniel, editor, *The Radical Right*, New York, 1963.
Belmont, Eleanor Robson, *The Fabric of Memory*, New York, 1957.
Bittinger, Lucy, *The Germans in Colonial Times*, New York, 1906.
Butler, Richard J. and Joseph Driscoll, *Dock Walloper*, New York, 1933.

Camp, William Martin, *San Francisco: Port of Gold*, New York, 1947.
Catton, Bruce, *The Glory Road*, New York, 1952.
———, *This Hallowed Ground*, New York, 1956.
Churchill, Allen, *The Great White Way*, New York, 1962.
Coleman, McAlister, *Eugene V. Debs*, New York, 1931.
Conrad, Will C., Kathleen F. Wilson and Dale Wilson, *The Milwaukee Journal: The First Eighty Years*, Madison, Wis., 1964.
Considine, Bob, *It's the Irish*, New York, 1961.

Davis-Dubois, Rachel and Emma Schweppe, *The Germans in American Life*, New York, 1936.
Dedmon, Emmett, *Fabulous Chicago*, New York, 1953.
Dodge, T. A., *The Campaign of Chancellorsville*, Boston, 1881.
Dowdey, Clifford, *The Land They Fought For*, New York, 1955.
Downey, Fairfax, *Indian-Fighting Army*, New York, 1941.
Drinnon, Richard, *Rebel in Paradise*, Chicago, 1961.

Easum, Chester V., *The Americanization of Carl Schurz*, Chicago, 1929.
Eddis, William, *Letters from America*, London, 1792.
Ellis, John Tracy, *The Life of James Cardinal Gibbons*, Milwaukee, 1952.

475

Faust, Albert B., *The German Element in the United States*, two volumes, Boston, 1909.
Fiske, John, *The Dutch and Quaker Colonies*, Vol. II, Boston, 1899.
———, *The Mississippi Valley in the Civil War*, Boston, 1901.
Francke, Kuno, *Cotton Mather and August Hermann Francke*, Boston, 1896.
———, *German Ideals of Today*, New York, 1907.

Ginger, Ray, *The Bending Cross: A Biography of Eugene V. Debs*, New Brunswick, N.J., 1949.
Gitlow, Benjamin F., *The Whole of Their Lives*, New York, 1948.
Glanz, Rudolf, *Jews in Relation to the Cultural Milieu of the Germans in America Up to the 1880's*, New York, 1947.
Glazer, Nathan, and Daniel P. Moynihan, *Beyond the Melting Pot*, New York, 1963.
Goldman, Emma, *Living My Life*, New York, 1931.
Griswold, Rufus W., *The Republican Court: or American Society in the Days of Washington*, New York, 1856.

Hagedorn, Herman, *The Hyphenated Family*, New York, 1960.
Hall, Norman S., *The Balloon Buster: Frank Luke of Arizona*, New York, 1928.
Handlin, Oscar, *Immigration as a Factor in American History*, New York, 1959.
———, *The Uprooted*, Boston, 1951.
Hansen, Marcus Lee, *The Atlantic Migration*, Boston, 1949.
Hark, Ann, *Hex Marks the Spot*, Philadelphia, 1938.
Harlow, Alvin F., *The Serene Cincinnatians*, New York, 1950.
Hawgood, John A., *The Tragedy of German America*, New York, 1940.
Hillard, George S., *Life, Letters and Journal of George Ticknor*, Boston, 1876.
Holbrook, Stewart H., *Dreamers of the American Dream*, New York, 1957.
———, *The Story of American Railroads*, New York, 1947.
Holden, The Rev. Vincent F., *The Yankee Paul: Isaac Thomas Hecker*, Milwaukee, 1958.
Howe, M. A. De Wolfe, *The Life and Letters of George Bancroft*, New York, 1908.
Humphreys, J. R., *The Last of the Middle West*, New York, 1965.

Isman, Felix, *Weber and Fields*, New York, 1924.

Joll, James, *The Anarchists*, Boston, 1964.
Jones, Evan, *The Minnesota: Forgotten River*, New York, 1962.

Kaplan, Justin, *Mr. Clemens and Mark Twain*, New York, 1966.
Kennedy, John F., *A Nation of Immigrants*, New York, 1964.
Kercheval, Samuel, *History of the Valley of Virginia*, Winchester, 1833.
Kerstein, Edward S., *Milwaukee's All-American Mayor: A Portrait of Daniel Webster Hoan*, New York, 1966.
Koerner, Gustav, *Memoirs of Gustav Koerner*, Cedar Rapids, 1909.

Lake, Stuart N., *Wyatt Earp*, Boston, 1931.
Learned, M. D., *The Life of Franz Daniel Pastorius*, Philadelphia, 1908.
Learsi, Rufus, *The Jews in America*, Cleveland, 1954.
Lubell, Samuel, *The Future of American Politics*, New York, 1952.

Martin, Joseph Plumb, *Private Yankee Doodle*, Boston, 1962.
May, Henry F. *The End of American Innocence*, New York, 1959.
Mencken, H. L., *A Book of Prefaces*, New York, 1916.

Bibliography

————, Happy Days, New York, 1940.
————, Prejudices: Fourth Series, New York, 1924.
Meyer, Ernest L., Bucket Boy: A Milwaukee Legend, New York, 1947.
Miller, Joseph, Arizona: The Last Frontier, New York, 1957.
Millis, Walter, The Road to War, America 1914–1917, Boston, 1935.
Mittelberger, Gottlieb, Journey to Pennsylvania, Philadelphia, 1898.
Morton, Frederic, The Rothschilds, New York, 1962.
Myers, Gustavus, History of the Great American Fortunes, New York, 1907.

O'Connor, Richard, Black Jack Pershing, New York, 1961.
————, Courtroom Warrior: The Combative Career of William Travers Jerome, Boston, 1963.
————, Hell's Kitchen, Philadelphia, 1958.
Ohlinger, Gustavus, Their True Faith and Allegiance, New York, 1917.
Olmsted, Frederick Law, A Journey Through Texas, New York, 1857.

Palmer, John M., General Von Steuben, Port Washington, N.Y., 1937.
Pershing, E. J., The Pershing Family in America, Philadelphia, 1926.

Rankin, Hugh F. and George F. Scheer, Rebels and Redcoats, New York, 1961.
Rauschning, Herman, The Voice of Destruction, New York, 1940.
Reeves, A. M., The Finding of Wineland the Good, London, 1890.
Reid, W. M., The Mohawk Valley, Its Legends and History, New York, 1908.
Reynolds, Quentin, They Fought for the Sky, New York, 1957.
Rhodes, J. F., History of the United States After the Compromise of 1850, Vol. IV, New York, 1906.
Riedesel, Baroness Friederike, Letters and Journals Relating to the War of the American Revolution, Chapel Hill, 1965.
Ritter, Lawrence S., The Glory of Their Times, New York, 1966.
Rogge, O. John, The Official German Report: Nazi Penetration 1924–1942, New York, 1962.
Rollins, Richard, I Find Treason, New York, 1941.
Rombauer, Robert J., The Union Cause in St. Louis in 1861, St. Louis, 1909.

Sandburg, Carl, Abraham Lincoln: The Prairie Years, New York, 1954.
Schappes, Morris, Documentary History of the Jews in the United States, New York, 1950.
Schrader, Frederick F., The Germans in the Making of America, New York, 1924.
Schurz, Carl, Reminiscences, New York, 1917.
Seabrook, William B., These Foreigners, New York, 1938.
Shannon, William V., The American Irish, New York, 1963.
Sinclair, Andrew, Prohibition: The Era of Excess, Boston, 1962.
Skaggs, William H., German Conspiracies in America, London, 1915.
Smith, Captain John, The True Travels, Vol. I, London, 1744.
Spaeth, Sigmund, Fifty Years with Music, New York, 1959.
Steffens, Lincoln, Autobiography, New York, 1931.
Stephenson, George M., A History of American Immigration, Boston, 1926.
Strong, George Templeton, Diary of the Civil War, 1860–1865, edited by Allan Nevins, New York, 1962.

Thomas, Henry and Dana Lee Thomas, Living Biographies of Famous Women, New York, 1942.
Thompson, Alexander M., Political History of Wisconsin, Madison, Wis., 1924.
Thwing, Charles Franklin, The American and the German University, New York, 1928.

Tuchman, Barbara W., *The Proud Tower*, New York, 1966.
———, *The Zimmerman Telegram*, New York, 1958.

Valentine, Alan, *1913: America Between Two Worlds*, New York, 1962.

Wakin, Edward and The Rev. Joseph F. Scheuer, *The De-Romanization of the American Catholic Church*, New York, 1966.
Waters, Edward N., *Victor Herbert: A Life in Music*, New York, 1955.
Wecter, Dixon, *The Saga of American Society*, New York, 1937.
Weyl, Nathaniel, *The Creative Elite in America*, Washington, 1966.
Whitehouse, Arch, *The Year of the Sky Kings*, New York, 1959.
Wittke, Carl, *The German-Language Press in America*, Louisville, Ky., 1957.
———, *We Who Built America*, New York, 1946.
Woodham-Smith, Cecil, *The Great Hunger*, New York, 1962.

Young, Marguerite, *Angel in the Forest*, New York, 1945.

Zucker, A. E., editor, *The Forty-Eighters*, New York, 1950.

INDEX

Brauns, Ernest, 76–77
Brecht, Bertolt, 100
Bremen, Germany, 102–104, 109–110, 231
Brunckow, Frederick, 215
Brunnholz, Peter, 24–26
Bryan, William Jennings, 280, 390
Buchele, Karl, 113–117
Buckley, William F., Jr., 460–461
Bucks County, Pa., 42
Burgoyne, John, 53, 62
Busey, Samuel C., 123

Cahensly, Peter Paul, 355–360
Camden, Battle of, 51–52
Canisius, Theodore, 133
Carus, Paul, 345
Castro, Henri, 90
Catton, Bruce, 142–143, 144–147
Chambers's Edinburgh Journal, 100–101
Chancellorsville, Battle of, 129, 144–148, 170
Chautauqua movement, 280–281
Chicago *Daily News*, 326
Chicago, Ill., 291–292
Chickamauga, Battle of, 149
Choate, Joseph H., 179
Churchill, Winston, 244, 401, 417
Cincinnati, Ohio, 251–252, 256, 294–297, 406, 413
Clay, Henry, 76, 156
Cleveland, Grover, 177, 179, 253, 263, 333
Clovis I (Chlodwig), 4
Cody, William F., 203
Coggswell, Joseph Green, 270, 271, 273, 284
Committee of Safety, 39
Communia, Iowa, 319
Concord ("German Mayflower"), 16
Cooper, James Fenimore, 68
Coughlin, Charles E., 433–434, 449
Crédit Mobilier, 173
Creel, George, 383–384, 413
Crèvecoeur, St. John de, 26–28
Custer, George Armstrong, 56, 152–153, 154

Damrosch, Walter, 302
Dana, Charles A., 151
Darrow, Clarence, 341
Davis, Garrett, 75
Davis, Jefferson, 162, 253
Davis, Richard Harding, 393

Day, Doris, 6
Debs, Eugene V., 339–342, 396
Dedmon, Emmett, 330n
De Kalb, Johann, 50–52, 251
De La Motta, Jacob, 251
De Leon, Jacob, 251
De Mun, Albert, 3
Deringer, Henry, 184
De Staël, Anne Louise Germaine, 270
De Tilley, Claude, 64
Dilger, Hubert, 146, 153
Dinneen, Joseph F., 441
Dirksen, Everett, 6
Dodge, T. A., 147
Donohue, Peter, 214
Dreben, Sam, 264
Dreiser, Theodore, 308–309, 347, 375n, 414
Duden, Gottfried, 68–70, 81
Dunne, Finley Peter, 263, 275–276
Dunne, John Gregory, 462

Earp, Wyatt, 201–202
Economy, Pa., 225–229
Eddis, William, 26
Eisenhower, Dwight D., 94, 116, 452
Ellis, John Tracy, 353
Emerson, Ralph Waldo, 268
Erhard, Ludwig, 86
Erickson, Donald A., 236–238
Everett, Edward, 270, 273

Faust, Albert B., 82, 154
Fielden, Samuel, 323–329, 331
Fish, Hamilton, 106
Flandrau, Charles, 195
Follen, Carl, 72, 80–81, 284
Follen, Paul, 72, 80–81
Ford, Henry, 264, 373
Fort Christina, Del., 12
Fort Ridgely, Minn., 191
Fort Schuyler, N.Y., 53
Forty-eighters, 116, 126–128, 217, 315–317, 457
Francke, August, 270
Francke, Kuno, 274–275, 389
Frank, Leo, 263
Frankfurt, Germany, 241–242
Franklin, Benjamin, 44
Frederick the Great, 58
Fredericksburg, Tex., 86
Frederick Wilhelm IV, 125
Frémont, John C., 134, 143
Frick, Henry Clay, 331, 338, 367